Developing China: The Remarkable Impact of Foreign Direct Investment

One of the most important features of China's economic emergence has been the role of foreign investment and foreign companies. The importance goes well beyond the USD 1.6 trillion in foreign direct investment that China has received since it started opening its economy. Using the tools of economic impact analysis, the author estimates that around one-third of China's GDP in recent years has been generated by the investments, operations, and supply chains of foreign invested companies. In addition, foreign companies have developed industries, created suppliers and distributors, introduced modern technologies, improved business practices, modernized management training, improved sustainability performance, and helped shape China's legal and regulatory systems. These impacts have helped China become the world's second largest economy, its leading exporter, and one of its leading destinations for inward investment.

The book provides a powerful analysis of China's policies toward foreign investment that can inform policy makers around the world, while giving foreign companies tools to demonstrate their contributions to host countries and showing the tremendous power of foreign investment to help transform economies.

This book was commissioned by the Hinrich Foundation for sustainable global trade.

Michael J. Enright, a leading expert on competitiveness, regional economic development, and international business strategy, became the Sun Hung Kai Professor of Business at the University of Hong Kong in 1996 after six years as a professor at the Harvard Business School. He is also a director of Enright, Scott & Associates consultancy and a founder of The Competitiveness Institute. Professor Enright has consulted for companies, governments, and multilateral organizations in more than 30 countries on six continents on international business strategy, competitiveness, regional clustering, technology policy, and economic development; has appeared in 40 countries as a featured speaker; and has authored numerous books and monographs on international competitiveness and China's development.

Developing China: The Remarkable Impact of Foreign Direct Investment

Michael J. Enright

Routledge
Taylor & Francis Group

LONDON AND NEW YORK

promoting sustainable global trade

hinrich foundation

First published 2017
by Routledge
2 Park Square, Milton Park, Abingdon, Oxon OX14 4RN

and by Routledge
711 Third Avenue, New York, NY 10017

Routledge is an imprint of the Taylor & Francis Group, an informa business

British Library Cataloguing in Publication Data
A catalogue record for this book is available from the British Library

Library of Congress Cataloging-in-Publication Data
Names: Enright, Michael J., author.
Title: Developing China : the remarkable impact of foreign direct investment / by Michael J. Enright.
Description: First Edition. | New York : Routledge, 2017. | Includes bibliographical references and index.
Identifiers: LCCN 2016028224 | ISBN 9781138228153 (hardback) | ISBN 9781138228160 (pbk.) | ISBN 9781315393346 (ebook)
Subjects: LCSH: Investments, Foreign—China. | Economic development—China. | China—Foreign relations. | China—Economic policy.
Classification: LCC HG4538 .E57 2017 | DDC 338.951—dc23
LC record available at https://lccn.loc.gov/2016028224

ISBN: 978-1-138-22815-3 (hbk)
ISBN: 978-1-138-22816-0 (pbk)
ISBN: 978-1-315-39334-6 (ebk)

Typeset in Goudy
by Apex CoVantage, LLC

Contents

LIST OF FIGURES   viii
LIST OF TABLES   ix
FOREWORD   x
ACKNOWLEDGEMENTS   xiv

1   China and inward foreign investment   1

    Introduction 1
    The project 1
    Preview 2
    The book 6

2   China's approach toward foreign investment   8

    Introduction 8
    Early foreign investment in China 9
    Foreign investment in the new China 10
    China's opening and the regulation of foreign investment 11
    Foreign investment results 20
    Conclusions 27

3   The economic impact of foreign companies in China   31

    Introduction 31
    Importance of FDI in China's total investment 32
    Importance of FIEs by industry 33
    Importance of FIEs in China's trade 37
    Introduction to economic impact analysis 39
    Economic impact of FDI and FIEs in China 40
    Conclusions 52
    Appendix: economic impact analysis methodology 55

4 **Catalytic impacts and spillovers from FIEs**   59

Introduction 59
Modernizing industries and companies in China 59
Developing suppliers and distributors in China 61
Bringing R&D and technology development to China 64
Foreign R&D, local linkages, and spinoffs 66
Improving business practices and standards 68
Improving the financial system in China 70
Modernizing management training and education 72
Bringing regional and global management to China 74
Promoting legal and regulatory reform 75
Improving the environment and sustainability in China 78
Contributing through CSR initiatives 80
Policy advice 82
Counterpoints 84
Conclusions 87

5 **Foreign investment in Chinese cities**   95

Introduction 95
Shenzhen 97
Tianjin 113
Shanghai 124
Chongqing 134
Conclusions 151

6 **Corporate case studies**   156

Introduction 156
Hong Kong pioneers 157
P&G 166
Maersk 175
Samsung 182
Conclusions 193

7 **Econometric analysis of foreign investment in China**   201

Introduction 201
Background 202
Economic growth 204
Productivity 206
Innovation 212
Trade 215

Domestic investment 218
Employment and wages 222
Inequality 226
The environment 229
Conclusions 233

8   Perspectives on foreign investment in China   **245**

Introduction 245
China's approach to foreign investment 245
The impacts of foreign investment on China's economy 246
Questions 247
The future of foreign investment in China 248
Implications 250

INDEX   252

Figures

3.1   Input–output matrix schematic   56
5.1   Foreign investment versus total investment in Shenzhen   103
5.2   Trade performance of foreign invested enterprises in Shenzhen   109
5.3   Foreign investment versus total investment in Tianjin   119
5.4   Trade performance of foreign invested enterprises in Tianjin   121
5.5   Foreign investment versus total investment in Shanghai   132
5.6   Trade performance of foreign invested enterprises in Shanghai   132
5.7   Foreign investment versus total investment in Chongqing   141
5.8   Trade performance of foreign invested enterprises in Chongqing   148

Tables

2.1 FDI flows into China, 1979 to 2014   21
2.2 Top 20 sources of utilized FDI into China, 1985 to 2014   22
2.3 Utilized FDI in China, 1997 to 2014, by invested industry   24
2.4 Utilized FDI in China's provincial-level jurisdictions,
    1979 to 2013   26
3.1 Importance of FDI in investment in China   32
3.2 Importance of FIEs by industry, 2013   33
3.3 Trade performance of foreign invested enterprises   37
3.4 Economic impact of foreign direct investment (investment stage)
    in China   41
3.5 Direct revenue and value added of FIEs in the industries for
    economic impact analysis   42
3.6 Total economic impact of the operations of FIEs in Mining,
    Manufacturing, and Utilities Sectors in China   45
3.7 Total economic impact of the operations of FIEs, Mining,
    Manufacturing, and Utilities Sectors, by industry, cumulative
    1995 to 2013 and single year 2013   46
3.8 Combined total economic impact of FDI and FIEs operations
    and comparison with China national figures   53
5.1 Inward FDI into Shenzhen   102
5.2 Foreign invested industrial enterprises by industry in Shenzhen, 2013   104
5.3 Impact of the operations of FIEs, Mining, Manufacturing,
    and Utilities Sectors in Shenzhen by industry, 2013   111
5.4 Inward FDI into Tianjin   118
5.5 Foreign invested industrial enterprises by industry in Tianjin, 2011   120
5.6 Total impact of the operations of FIEs, Mining, Manufacturing, and
    Utilities Sectors in Tianjin by industry, 2011   123
5.7 Inward FDI into Shanghai   131
5.8 Inward FDI into Chongqing   140
5.9 Foreign invested industrial enterprises by industry, Chongqing, 2013   143
5.10 Impact of the operations of FIEs, Mining, Manufacturing, and
     Utilities Sectors in Chongqing by industry, 2013   149

Foreword

China's economic rise has been historically unique in a number of respects, not the least of which has been the speed and steepness of its ascent. What is less well recognized however is the profound role played by foreign direct investment, and the deliberate and carefully calibrated manner in which Chinese officials gradually permitted, and selectively encouraged, these investments.

Japan, the first East Asian economic miracle, blazed the trail for all of its neighbours, rebuilding its devastated post-war economy through an export-led development model and highly targeted industrial policies. The four Asian tigers – Singapore, Hong Kong, South Korea, and Taiwan – borrowed heavily from the Japanese approach, and likewise began their rapid economic ascent in the 1960s and 1970s.

But it was China – perhaps more so than any other country – that recognized the unique potential of FDI to catapult the country up the economic development ladder, through the absorption of capital, technology, distribution channels, and managerial know-how.

When China first embarked on its reform and opening-up process in the late 1970s, its economy was poor, isolated, and backward – and foreign direct investment was virtually zero. Little more than three decades later, China has become the second largest economy in the world, the leading exporter, and the largest recipient of foreign direct investment. Chinese companies have become highly competitive, transforming the country into the 'factory of the world', an implacable export powerhouse, and more recently an increasingly formidable presence in a variety of high technology sectors.

Adjectives such as 'remarkable', 'miraculous', and 'unprecedented' have routinely been used to describe China's trajectory, but they are hardly adequate to convey the true magnitude of the amount of ground China has covered in a handful of decades. China essentially remade its national economy 'overnight', at least in developmental terms.

The rest of the world was, for the most part, thoroughly unprepared for China's transformation. China's accession to the World Trade Organization in 2001 was a watershed, helping to accelerate the Chinese export juggernaut by providing secure access to the large consumer markets of the developed world. But previous economic models simply didn't account for – or anticipate – the impact of a country the size of China entering the world economy, nor the extraordinary leverage that foreign direct investment could provide in the process.

The impact of China's arrival on the global economic stage has been complex and multifaceted. While developed world consumers benefited from lower cost manufactured products from China, the labour force disruptions in import-sensitive industries have proven to be deeper and longer lasting than the economic textbooks would have predicted. From a corporate opportunity perspective, China has evolved from being a low-cost export platform to a substantial consumer market in its own right – a growth story in which almost every major multinational corporation feels they need to participate. By the second decade of the 21st century, China's integration into the global economy, and the influence it exerts, could hardly be more complete.

How – and why – did China take this bold gambit in opening its economy to the world? The objective from the start was to build strong Chinese companies and a strong Chinese economy – in essence, to close the massive development gap that existed between China and the West at the onset of China's reform process.

In broad strokes, the strategy was fairly straightforward: a pragmatic (rather than philosophical) acceptance of any suitably modified capitalist principles that could help China, a controlled, incremental opening-up to the global economy, and the relentless pursuit of the Western technology China desperately needed in order to leap-frog the development process. The primary means for acquiring these essential ingredients? Foreign direct investment.

The basic proposition to foreign companies was simple: China dangled the prospect of future profits from its massive domestic market, and the immediate benefit of utilizing China as a low-cost export platform, in exchange for foreign capital, technology, and managerial know-how.

The implications were clear: if you're not willing to play by our rules, your competitors will.

Foreign businesses made the calculation that they could not afford to 'miss out' on China, and willingly participated. Foreign companies in China have been willing, and – in many cases – eager participants.

Western governments were equally keen, and encouraged and facilitated China's entry into the global trade and investment system. This was done largely for geo-strategic considerations. It was argued that integration would spawn greater democratic tendencies and encourage China to become a 'responsible stakeholder' in the multilateral system.

From the start, then, both sides have been pursuing different agendas, at least in some respects.

While it is generally recognized that foreign direct investment has been a major contributor to China's economic growth and development, the full range of benefits goes far beyond anything we previously understood. In this book, for the first time, the true direct and indirect benefits of FDI for China's economy have been measured. The results are nothing short of staggering.

Over USD 1.6 trillion of foreign direct investment has poured into China in the last 35 years. This book evaluates the economic impact of this investment and concludes that investment by foreign companies and the ripple effects through their supply chains in recent years has contributed in the order of 33 percent to China's GDP and 27 percent to China's employment. The book describes the carefully controlled way in which China's leadership has directed the application of FDI to support its industrial policy of developing a stronger economy with stronger Chinese firms.

Why undertake such a rigorous examination of the Chinese experience with foreign direct investment?

To start with, a host of other developing countries, Vietnam, India, and Indonesia being notable examples, are now considering their approach to foreign direct investment. As the pages that follow will make abundantly clear, FDI can be massively impactful. But FDI, in and of itself, is neither inherently positive nor negative. The FDI experience is highly conditional. The terms, circumstances, and stipulations under which it is permitted and provided all shape the experience and outcomes. Government policy makers are confronted with a range of policy options that will collectively shape the FDI environment, and determine, at least to some extent, the volume, the structure, and ultimately, the impact of FDI in their country. These policy choices will also go a long way towards shaping the profitability foreign companies can reasonably aspire to, and that in turn will inform their decision-making on whether – and where – to invest their much-needed resources. FDI thrives when it is built on mutual understanding between the host country and the FDI-providers, and a healthy respect for the needs and perspectives of the other party.

It is hoped that with this research, China's experience with foreign direct investment can help illuminate the path forward for other countries as they seek to attract and absorb FDI. This is certainly not to imply that China's approach has been perfect, or that it is either desirable – or possible – for any other country to replicate China's policy choices. There is however much to be learned from China's experience, and many lessons – some positive and some negative – to be drawn from China's approach.

It is our hope therefore that both government policy-makers and business executives will find this book to be a useful reference point as they chart their course forward.

The China experience with FDI is relevant not just for developing countries wrestling with their approach to FDI. For large developed countries like the US, the China experience raises interesting policy questions about past assumptions – and competitiveness strategies moving forward.

While Western policy makers pursued and facilitated China's integration into the global trade and investment architecture at least to some extent for geo-strategic reasons, it's clear that they did not have a full appreciation for the magnitude of the economic shock waves they were unleashing. This is not to suggest that their decisions were incorrect. It does however raise questions about the wisdom of using trade policy as a geo-strategic instrument, without a proper accounting of – and preparation for – the full range of resulting economic impacts.

As the US and other developed countries are still struggling to understand and adjust to the full range of impacts of China's FDI-driven rise, past assumptions about a range of competitiveness issues, including tax policies, education, immigration, and infrastructure, along with broader questions about the role of the state in the economy, will have to be reconsidered. Understanding China's use of FDI, and its resulting economic rise, necessarily requires the developed world to look in the mirror and ask some tough questions about the best path forward.

The genesis of this book stretches back over several decades of observing the economic development of China and other Asian countries, and came to a formative stage with the start of discussions between Michael Enright and the Hinrich Foundation in March of 2015. It was then that we discovered our shared fascination with the transformative potential of FDI. We at the Foundation rapidly concluded that there was no one better placed than Michael to conduct the rigorous research and analysis needed to uncover the full impact of FDI in China. The book that Michael and his team have produced, and the ground-breaking analysis that underpins it, has exceeded anything we could have hoped for during those early meetings.

Merle A. Hinrich
June 2016

Acknowledgements

I would like to express my deep appreciation to the Hinrich Foundation, and in particular to its Chairman Merle A. Hinrich, CEO Kathryn Dioth, and Research Fellow Stephen Olson. Merle Hinrich initiated the year-long project on which this work is based and has contributed his passion for international trade and investment as well as his depth of knowledge and decades of hands-on experience at every stage of the process. Kathryn Dioth has managed the process in an exemplary manner and has contributed numerous insights. Stephen Olson has provided extremely valuable commentary and suggestions and has generously shared from his own extensive research on investment by multinational companies in China. In addition to providing financial support, the Foundation and its principals have been enthusiastic substantive contributors to this work throughout. I consider it an honour to have collaborated with the Foundation.

I would also like to thank my colleagues at Enright, Scott & Associates, who undertook the bulk of the research that underpins this book. In particular, I would like to thank my partner Edith Scott for her work on China's foreign investment policies and on the catalytic and spillover impacts of foreign investment in China, David Sanderson for his work on the economic impact analysis of foreign investment on China's economy at the national and local levels, Sophie Zhang for her work on the econometric literature and our own econometric analysis, Ella Dong for her work on the statistical analysis of China's inward investment flows and on the city impact case studies, and Ady Lam for managing our process flows and helping to keep us on track. Some of the types of analysis reported in this work have to our knowledge never been done before. These analyses, and this book, would not have been possible without the dedication of my ESA colleagues.

Finally, I would like to thank the hundreds of clients, managers, officials, researchers, analysts, and friends who have shared their insights on foreign investment and foreign companies in China over the years. They have contributed greatly to the foundation of knowledge that underpins much of the present work.

Michael J. Enright
Hong Kong, 2016

China and inward foreign investment

Introduction

China has been one of the world's great economic success stories since the onset of its program of economic reform and opening that started in the late 1970s. Foreign investment and foreign invested enterprises (FIEs) have been a major part of this story. While there have been numerous books, papers, and articles written on foreign companies and foreign investment in China, they tend to fall into two groups. The first group consists of scholarly works that use statistical techniques to address fairly narrow questions. However, this work can only address a limited set of questions, results are often inconclusive and difficult to interpret, and most of this work is inaccessible to all but other scholars. The second group consists largely of works that recount the trials and tribulations of foreign companies as they have tried to develop their China business. However interesting these may be, the cases tend to be idiosyncratic and hard to generalize, and only provide a partial view of foreign investment and foreign companies in China. Neither group provides a comprehensive picture of the environment for foreign investment in China or of the impact that foreign investment has had on China's economy.

Obtaining such a comprehensive picture is becoming more and more important. As China continues to develop and its indigenous companies grow stronger, it is becoming fashionable in some quarters to minimize the past and present contributions of foreign investment and foreign invested enterprises in this development. At the same time, as foreign companies appear to be coming under increasing pressure in China due to market, regulatory, and competitive shifts, it is becoming more important for foreign companies to be able to 'make their case' in terms of the contributions that they have made and are making to China's development. Many other countries in the developing world are looking to China, and how it deals with foreign investment and foreign companies, as a guide for their own policies and practices. Thus a failure to understand China's approach to foreign investment and foreign companies, and the true impact that this investment and these companies have had on China's development has implications that go well beyond China.

The project

The project upon which this volume is based had its origins in discussions between Merle Hinrich, Kathryn Dioth, and Stephen Olson of the Hinrich Foundation and Professor Michael Enright of Enright, Scott & Associates consultancy. The mission of the Hinrich

Foundation is to promote sustainable global trade by fostering research on international trade and investment policy, supporting trade related education and training, and cultivating export-led job creation. The Foundation has spent years working on a wide range of issues associated with international trade and investment. Enright, Scott & Associates (ESA) is a leading Asia-based economic and strategy consulting firm with a long history of advising governments, multilateral agencies, and major corporations on economic development, trade and investment, and international business strategy, with particular expertise in Asia in general and China in particular. ESA has a long history of advising governments on investment promotion programs, and a long history of advising multinational companies on their approaches to host countries and host governments.

The discussions soon focused on the apparent disconnect between the advantages of international trade and investment claimed by economists, multilateral agencies, and multinational companies, and the restrictive approach to trade and investment seen in many parts of the world. One reason for this disconnect appears to be the lack of a complete picture of the impact that foreign investment and foreign companies can have on host economies. A decision was taken to mount a project that would attempt to take a more comprehensive approach to the impact of foreign investment and foreign companies on a single country before moving on to others. China was the obvious choice given its importance to the global economy, the finite time frame of its economic reform program, and the fact that China is increasingly taken as a touchstone by other developing countries.

The resulting project has had several major components: a review of the academic literature on foreign investment and foreign companies in China, an investigation of the evolution of China's legal and regulatory regime governing foreign investment, a compilation of the relevant facts and figures concerning inward investment, the use of economic impact analysis techniques to estimate the impact of foreign investment and foreign invested enterprises on China's GDP and employment, a compilation of a range of catalytic impacts and spillover effects of foreign companies, a series of case studies of the impacts of foreign investment and foreign companies on particular municipalities in China, a series of case studies of the impacts of individual foreign companies on China's economy, and our own econometric analysis of some of the topics researched by academics. The goal was to go well beyond the existing literature, to combine several approaches to the analysis, to introduce some new tools and techniques while not being restricted by any particular tool, and as a result to present a fine-grained and multi-faceted picture of China's approach toward foreign investment and the impact of that investment on the nation's development. The present volume presents the highlights of our analysis and results.

Preview

There are many conclusions that have come out of the project that we will describe in this volume.

We preview several of these here.

- Most foreign observers and even foreign managers operating in China do not really understand the approach that China has taken to foreign investment and foreign companies. Openness to foreign investment and foreign companies has not been an end in and of itself, but rather a means, and in particular a means to ensure that China and Chinese companies catch up with the rest of the world as much as to increase economic growth or improve consumer welfare. Moreover, this approach has been heavily influenced by the Chinese experience with foreign powers and foreign companies from the 1840s through the 1940s.

- The history of China's approach to foreign investment over the last 35 years is a story of carefully controlled opening, always with the intention of ensuring that foreign capital, know-how, technology, and management expertise would be applied for the benefit of the Chinese economy, while preventing foreign companies from gaining too much influence. The step-by-step process was due in part to maintain control of the process, and in part because China had to develop the legal and regulatory institutions to govern a non-state economy from virtually zero.

- It took China some time to recognize that movement towards 'international standards and norms' was not something that foreign companies and governments necessarily wanted to impose on China, but rather had evolved internationally as solutions to the challenge of maintaining sovereignty and control while providing investors with the certainty and protections necessary to risk making investments.

- While foreign direct investment into China has grown to levels in excess of USD 100 billion per year, and cumulative FDI into China has reached nearly USD 1.6 trillion, inward FDI flows account for only a few percent of gross capital formation and fixed asset investment in China today. However, when one applies economic impact analysis tools to the foreign investments and the operations of foreign invested enterprises, the impact of these companies and the ripple effects through their supply chains in recent years has been on the order of 33 percent of China's GDP and 27 percent of China's employment (the figures for 2013 and the five-year average from 2009 to 2013). This does not include any impacts on downstream distribution or other catalytic and spillover effects on technology, management, business practices, and other areas.

- Foreign invested enterprises have been instrumental to China's emergence as the world's largest trading nation. Although their share has declined in recent years, foreign invested enterprises still account for nearly half of all of China's trade. Foreign companies have also facilitated China's trade by leveraging productive resources in China into world markets and by providing the physical and financial infrastructure associated with trade.

- Foreign invested enterprises have also been crucial to the development of many of China's leading industries, including industries with substantial spillovers into the local economy, export-oriented industries, and industries that provide needed inputs for the rest of China's economy. Sino-foreign joint ventures modernized the Chinese auto industry and allowed China to become not only the world's largest producer of automobiles, but a significant exporter of autos and auto parts. Without foreign invested enterprises, China would not have much of a computer industry, and would not have developed nearly as extensive modern activities in chemicals, clothing, accounting, consulting, and numerous other industries.

- In addition to the impacts listed above are a whole range of catalytic impacts and spillover effects of foreign investment in China that are difficult or impossible to quantify. These include the modernization of Chinese industries (some of which were decades behind at the beginning of the reform program), the creation of suppliers and distributors in China, bringing improved technologies and R&D to China, fostering spin-offs, improving business practices and standards (including accounting, engineering, and quality control standards), improving the financial system in China, modernizing management training and education, bringing regional and global management to China, promoting legal and institutional reform, improving environmental and sustainability practices in China, contributing through corporate social responsibility (CSR) initiatives, and providing advice on economic and business-related policies. The impact of foreign companies in these areas is hard to overestimate.

- The results indicate that while one can argue that China would have benefitted more if it had opened its economy earlier or more completely, the introduction of foreign investment and foreign enterprises into China has been an enormous success with large impacts across the national economy.

- Case studies of Shenzhen, Tianjin, Shanghai, and Chongqing show how China's approach to foreign investment, and to economic reform overall, evolved over time, and how China's rapid development has changed the economic landscape. Shenzhen, just north of Hong Kong, was the initial experiment in economic opening. Its success as an exporter of light manufactured goods gave impetus to further the reform process. Shenzhen itself has become a leading high-technology hub and a modern service centre for South China. Tianjin, near Beijing in Northern China, became a focal point for large-scale manufacturing investments to serve the Chinese domestic market as well as exports, and is presently diversifying and upgrading its service economy. Shanghai was able to re-establish its position as China's leading business city with the help of foreign investment and foreign enterprises, and has become a headquarters, financial, service, transportation, and manufacturing location of international importance. Chongqing, which was opened later than the other cities, shows how China's program of western development has also featured the attraction of foreign investment to build up the city as well as its economy, and how foreign investment has helped turn what was once a relatively backward city into a modern metropolis linked to the global economy.

- Also of interest is the fact that most of the major initiatives that led to the development of these four cities, Shenzhen, Tianjin, Shanghai, and Chongqing, as leading economic cities in China have involved attracting foreign investment. Even today, the most important initiatives to further develop these cities also involve attracting more and different types of foreign investment. In all four cases, the path to the next level of development will involve further opening to foreign invested enterprises.

- Corporate case studies on foreign companies in China, including Hong Kong pioneers in China, Procter and Gamble, Maersk, and Samsung, show the wide range of influences of foreign investment on China's development. Hong Kong companies were early investors in light manufacturing, ports, roads, utilities, hotels, property, and services, not just in China as a whole, but in virtually all of China's major provinces and cities. In many instances, Hong Kong companies provided the examples and the basic business infrastructure that allowed other foreign companies to follow.

- P&G helped in creating entire product categories in China, developed local suppliers and distributors that now serve the country as a whole, brought modern advertising and marketing practices to a country that had little expertise in these areas previously, invested in public health and education initiatives, developed its Chinese staff so it is now a net exporter of management talent from China, and brought world-class environmental and CSR practices to China. Maersk invested in helping establish Chinese shipyards (now world leaders) as viable producers of ships for the international market, in connecting China to the rest of the world, thus helping China become the world's leading trading nation, in improving port efficiency and environmental performance in China, and in tackling logistics difficulties that have held the Chinese economy back. Samsung became one of China's largest foreign investors, created complete production chains, including advanced components in China, and set up several cutting-edge R&D centres in China. However, as costs increased in China and Samsung became more concerned about its position in China, it shifted some of its focus to Vietnam, where its investment rivals that which it has made in China.

- The academic literature on foreign investment in China focuses on the influence of foreign investment on China's GDP and GDP growth, productivity, technological capacity, domestic investment, employment and wages, trade, environment, and a number of other parameters. Many of the results of this literature are expected, such as a positive influence of foreign investment on economic development, trade, wages, and environmental performance. The results also indicate that the impact of foreign investment depends on the industry, source country, and location within China of the investment. There are also some counterintuitive results that might be due in part to questions of variable use, statistical methods, and time period.

- One interesting feature of this academic literature, particularly the Chinese literature, is the focus on the impact of foreign investment on Chinese firms, rather than China's economy as a whole, and the focus on issues that the Chinese Government has flagged as important, such as industrial and trade upgrading. The results of this literature, particularly the Chinese literature, provide grounds for some scepticism about the benefits of foreign investment. It is crucial for companies, analysts, and foreign governments to understand this because this literature influences China's policy stance toward foreign investment.

- ESA's own econometric work focused on several of the major issues addressed in the academic literature, only using expanded time frames, clearer variable definitions, and more modern statistical techniques than some of the existing literature. The bulk of the results support a positive impact of foreign investment on GDP growth, productivity, innovation, domestic investment, incomes, trade, and environmental performance (foreign firms perform better than domestic firms). The results include some reversals of negative results found in prior literature, particularly on domestic investments. The results also show regional differences and time period differences in the impact of foreign investment on China's economy. Overall, our results show a more positive picture of the impact of FDI on China's development than some of the existing literature.

- The story of foreign companies and their influence on China's economy is by no means over. Slowing growth, rising costs, a difficult economic transition, and perceptions that China is becoming in some ways less welcoming to foreign companies are causing many companies to reassess their China positions. China is moving away from a regime that required *ex ante* approvals for foreign investment to one in which foreign companies will be subject to *ex post* regulation of behaviour. While this should be a positive for foreign investment, it all depends on how China uses its legal and regulatory tools, and the role that China's leaders wish foreign investment to play.

The book

The main goal for this volume is to provide a more comprehensive and nuanced view of China's approach toward foreign investment and the impact of this investment on China's economy than is generally available. In extracting results from the larger project, we have done so with three main audiences in mind.

One audience for this work is policy makers inside China and outside China who can use the descriptions, impacts, and tools reported to get a fuller picture of the impact of foreign investment on China's development for use as input into their own policy making. Another audience is managers of foreign invested enterprises in China and elsewhere, as well as chambers of commerce and governments that represent foreign invested enterprises, who can use the results and tools reported here to 'make their case' when it comes to justifying their presence in host countries. Finally, another audience is analysts and researchers who perhaps can add to their own knowledge and analytical toolkit when it comes to assessing the impact of foreign investment and foreign invested enterprises in China and elsewhere.

The structure of the remaining parts of this volume is as follows. Chapter 2 traces China's approach toward foreign investment since the onset of the reform program, with special attention focused on the legal and regulatory frameworks used to govern inward investment, as well as the basic statistics of foreign investment since China's economic opening. Chapter 3 looks at the importance of inward investment to total investment in China and applies the tools of economic impact analysis to assess the impact of the investment, operations, and supply chains of foreign invested companies in China. The latter is the first analysis of this type across an entire national economy of which we are aware.

Chapter 4 highlights the wide range of catalytic impacts and spillover benefits of foreign investment in China that go beyond those estimated in the previous chapter and has helped to shape China's development. Chapter 5 focuses on case studies of the impact of foreign investment on four major cities in China, Shenzhen, Tianjin, Shanghai, and Chongqing, that differ in terms of state of economic development, geography, timing of opening to foreign investment, development goals associated with foreign investment, and the mix of types of investment. Each shows how foreign investment has been crucial to municipal development. Chapter 6 consists of summaries of three corporate case studies of Hong Kong pioneers in China, Procter and Gamble, Maersk, and Samsung, that highlight the range of impacts that different types of foreign companies have had on China's development and perhaps provide some cautions for the future. Chapter 7 provides a brief summary of existing academic literature as well as summary results from our own econometric work on impacts of foreign investment on China's economy. Chapter 8 provides a summary of some of the lessons from the work as well as views on the future of foreign investment in China.

We hope the multifaceted approach represented in this volume will give a more complete and nuanced view of China's approach to foreign investment and the impact of foreign investment on China's development than has been available to date. We hope that officials, business people, analysts, and others can learn from the China experience and put these lessons to work in their own undertakings in China and elsewhere.

2

China's approach toward foreign investment[1]

Introduction

China's economic rise has been one of the most important features of the global economy for the last several decades. One of the most important components in China's economic opening and reforms that began at the end of the 1970s has been the successive opening of China's economy to inward foreign direct investment. This opening, it was hoped, would bring not just capital, but also know-how, technology, and management expertise. It was hoped that foreign firms would provide linkages to support China's exports and outward investments, examples of how world-class businesses operated, and controlled competition that would stimulate improvement on the part of Chinese firms. Over time, these motivations remained and new ones emerged. For example, when China acceded to the World Trade Organization (WTO), it traded greater openness to foreign companies in a wide range of industries for access to international markets.

While China has become more and more open to foreign investment over the years, it is still nowhere near completely open. The number of industries in which foreign investment is either encouraged or permitted has expanded, but substantial lists of industries in which foreign investment is restricted or prohibited remain. This is consistent with a view that China has always viewed openness to foreign investment as a means to an end, rather than an end in and of itself. And a significant part of that end is a strong Chinese economy with stronger Chinese firms succeeding domestically and internationally, rather than a local economy dominated by foreign firms.

China's policies toward foreign investment have evolved substantially since the onset of the reform period. This has been reflected in the policy and legal regime, the industries in which investment has been encouraged and discouraged, the geographies within China that have been opened for investment, and the administration of rules and regulations regarding foreign investment. The consistent goal of China's leaders since the onset of China's reform and opening program has been to gain the advantages of inward foreign investment, while ensuring the Chinese Government remains in control, that the potential for foreign companies to dominate China's economy is limited, and that foreign investment results in a positive impact on Chinese companies. After all, much of China's historical experience with foreign investment has been one that has generated scepticism and concern about foreign investment. The trade-offs inherent in this approach have changed over time, creating a dynamic environment in which foreign enterprises attempt to profit from their presence in China, while China tries to maximize the benefits and limit the potential downsides associated with foreign investment.

The result of this step-by-step approach to opening has been a dramatic rise in inward foreign direct investment, which went from virtually zero in 1980 to exceed USD 100 billion per year by 2008 and to reach nearly USD 1.6 trillion in cumulative inward foreign direct investment (FDI) by 2014. China's approach can be seen not just in the growth of inward FDI, but its distribution by industry and by province, which has followed China's policies, along with economic opportunities. Through its careful approach, China has tried to manage one of the greatest economic transformations in history, while attempting to limit social disruption and avoid the pitfalls associated with foreign investment in China in the past.

Early foreign investment in China

In the 19th century, openness to foreign investment was imposed on China by force. The Treaty of Nanking of 1842, which ended the Opium Wars, opened five treaty ports to trade between China and the West. To carry out this trade, foreign shipping companies, trading companies, and banks set up in foreign-controlled enclaves at the ports. In addition to trade-related activities, foreign merchants began to produce a range of goods in workshops and factories within the enclaves, even though this was not allowed by the original treaties. One of the concessions extracted by Japan in the Treaty of Shimonoseki of 1895, which ended the Sino-Japanese War, gave Japanese companies the right to manufacture in the open ports (ports opened by treaty or by decree of the Chinese Government, usually under foreign pressure).[2] Companies from other treaty countries obtained the same rights as the Japanese through 'most favored nation' clauses in the relevant treaties.[3]

From the initial base in the treaty ports, foreign direct investment spread to other parts of China. Foreign capital soon funded many of the major infrastructure projects in China. By 1911, for example, there was more foreign capital invested in railroads than in any other industry in China. The total amount of assets owned by foreign entities through direct investments in China was estimated at USD 503 million in 1902, USD 1,067 million in 1914, USD 2,493 million in 1931, and USD 2,682 million in 1936 (Hou, 1964, p. 13). The last figure would be on the order of USD 46 billion in 2016 dollars.[4] Though the United Kingdom had been by far the largest foreign investor and foreign trader in China from the mid-19th century through the early 1930s, by 1936, Japan was the largest foreign investor (accounting for 40.0 percent of total inward investment including loans), followed by Britain (35.0 percent), the United States (8.6 percent), France (6.7 percent), and Germany (4.3 percent) (Hou, 1964, pp. 16–7).

By the mid-1930s, foreign investment had financed railroad construction, linked China to the world economy through ships and shipping, developed the mining and metals sector, and accounted for around 35 percent of the output of manufacturing in China, and 50 percent or more in 'modern' manufacturing. The influence of foreign investment was so extensive one analyst stated that foreign capital was 'largely responsible for the development of whatever economic modernization took place in China before 1937' (Hou, 1964, p. 130). On the other hand, extraterritoriality, economic spheres of influence, dominance of foreign enterprises in some key industries, difficulty in collecting tax from foreign companies, and huge differences between the incomes and lifestyles of foreign executives and local workers were causes of resentment. The fact that many of these features had been imposed meant many in China associated foreign investment with exploitation.

Foreign investment in the new China

The position of foreign companies in China changed with the end of the Second World War and then again with the founding of the People's Republic of China in 1949. Under the Treaty of San Francisco, which ended the war in the Pacific, China was granted rights to all previously Japanese-owned assets in the country (Levi, 1953; U.K. Secretary of State for Foreign Affairs, 1952). Foreign firms from other nations continued to operate in China even after the establishment of the People's Republic of China in October 1949. While they faced difficult conditions in a war-ravaged country, foreign invested enterprises were initially told that they would be protected by the new regime (*Liberation Daily*, 6 August 1950, quoted in Thompson, 1979, p. 21).

However, the new government issued orders that prevented firms from shutting down or reducing employment without permission, and others that set wage rates. Foreign firms were required to stay open, pay taxes, and continue to employ and pay workers at government determined levels even as their businesses declined. Top executives of foreign companies were not allowed to leave the country. With the onset of the Korean War and the resulting embargo of China, and with shifts in sentiment within the Chinese Communist Party against private enterprises, pressure mounted against the foreign firms. While many had decided to exit China by 1952, getting exit applications considered and negotiating the terms of exit proved difficult. The Korean Armistice of July 1953, the Geneva Conference of April 1954, and the movement by the Chinese Government to completely socialize the economy brought matters to a head. The result was protracted negotiations and the eventual transfer of the assets and operations of foreign companies to Chinese control. By 1957, essentially all Western companies had exited China (Thompson, 1979; Shai, 1993).

In the meanwhile, China had turned to the Soviet Union and the Eastern Bloc for partnership, creating joint ventures, such as the Sino-Soviet Zhongchang Railway, the Sino-Soviet Xinjiang Non-ferrous Metal Company, the Dalian Sino-Soviet Shipbuilding Company, and shipping joint ventures with Poland and Czechoslovakia. However, the cooling of Sino-Soviet relations resulted in the Soviet Union suspending economic cooperation and asking for loan repayments in 1960. The Sino-Soviet joint ventures as well as the Sino-Czech ventures were shut down, though the Sino-Polish shipping venture continued. In the 1960s, China formed only two other Sino-foreign joint ventures, the Sino-Albanian Joint Stock Shipping Company in 1962 (which closed in 1978) and the Sino-Tanzanian Joint Stock Marine Transportation Company in 1967 (Wei and Liu, 2001, p. 9).

Given its historic experience with foreign investment, the socialization of its economy, and difficult international relations, it is not surprising that foreign direct investment in China through the 1960s and into the 1970s was minimal. The initial groundwork for this to change was laid by the rapprochement between the People's Republic of China and the United States signaled by United States President Richard Nixon's meetings in China with Chairman of the Chinese Communist Party Mao Zedong and the release of the joint Shanghai Communiqué in 1972. However, it was not until further rounds of international diplomacy, the end of the Cultural Revolution in China in 1976, and Deng Xiaoping's rise to leadership that China began to reassess its stance toward foreign investment.

China's opening and the regulation of foreign investment

The Third Plenary Session of the Eleventh Central Committee of the Chinese Communist Party in 1978 marked the beginning of China's opening and reform process. The Plenum called for the so-called 'Four Modernizations' (of agriculture, industry, science and technology, and national defense) in order to improve the economy, improve the people's standard of living, and to enhance national security (Wei and Liu, 2001). One of the ways to achieve modernization was to open more to foreign capital. China's leaders wished to industrialize China and modernize industrial sectors that often lagged best practice by two or three decades. Opening to FDI appealed to China's leaders as a 'package deal' that would provide technology, management skills, and access to foreign markets (Chen, 2011, p. 34). Over the next ten years, China's leadership built an initial framework of FDI laws and regulations one step at a time.

The legal and regulatory regime

Three major laws, the *Law of the People's Republic of China on Joint Ventures Using Chinese and Foreign Investment* ('Equity JV Law', 1979), the *Law of the People's Republic of China on Enterprises Operated Exclusively with Foreign Capital* ('WFOE Law', 1986), and the *Law of the People's Republic of China on Contractual Joint Ventures Using Chinese and Foreign Investment* ('Contractual JV Law', 1988), would form the legal basis for foreign investment in China. Implementing regulations for the three laws were issued in 1983, 1990, and 1995, respectively. Other major initiatives in the early reform period included the *Regulations on Special Economic Zones in Guangdong Province* ('SEZ Regulations', 1980), and the *Provisions of the State Council of the People's Republic of China for the Encouragement of Foreign Investment* ('Encouragement Provisions', 1986).

The Equity JV Law provided the first legal basis for FDI in China and set forth principles for setting up, operating, and winding down foreign equity joint ventures in

China. It was followed by additional laws governing the operation and taxation of foreign invested enterprises. At this time, foreign invested joint ventures were required to earn foreign exchange and access to the Chinese domestic market was strictly limited. In addition, joint ventures had a finite lifetime, with control reverting to the Chinese party at the end of the venture, and the chairman of each venture had to be Chinese. Approvals for foreign investments were given on a case-by-case basis after review by multiple agencies at the national level (U.S. State Department, 2015, p. 4). The 1983 implementing regulations filled gaps in the Equity JV Law with specifics, reducing confusion over what could and could not be done and improving the investment climate substantially (Wang, 1997, p. 3).

One problem for foreign investment at the time was the lack of a legal status for privately held companies in China's socialist economy. Another was the unwillingness of many foreign companies to invest in joint ventures. In 1984, the Chinese Government officially recognized the private economy and began discussions about the establishment of wholly foreign-owned enterprises (WFOEs) in China. The first multinational firm to set up a WFOE following this decision was 3M, which set up in Shanghai in 1984. The ability to create WFOEs was subsequently enshrined in the 1986 WFOE Law. This law, and the Encouragement Provisions of the same year, showed a shift in approach from extremely tight control, which had resulted in limited investment, to a more welcoming approach. The Encouragement Provisions granted incentives, such as reduced land-use fees, labour subsidies, preferential tax treatment, and preferential access to water and electricity to export-oriented and technologically advanced firms (Kundra, 2009, pp. 187–8).

On his landmark 'Southern Tour' of January 1992, Deng Xiaoping encouraged further reform and opening domestically, and greater economic interaction internationally, signaling a more open environment for foreign companies. In 1990, requirements that joint ventures had to be chaired by a Chinese person and had to have a finite time limit were lifted. It was also declared that under normal conditions that the state would not expropriate foreign investments. China enacted statutory regimes for foreign enterprise income tax, copyright, software protection, patent and trademark protection, banking, securities, and foreign exchange control. The *Company Law* of 1994 introduced to China the limited liability company and company limited by shares. It also stated that foreign invested enterprises were subject to the Law except for provisions overridden by the special foreign investment laws. Foreign-invested holding companies were allowed, subject to certain conditions, as of 1995. The decade of the 1990s saw the structuring of an overarching legal and regulatory framework for foreign investment, as well as the framework for developing the private sector in general in China.

China's entry into the World Trade Organization in 2001 caused substantial change in the regulation of FIEs in China. While the WTO governs international trade among members, its rules require unanimous approval among existing members for a new member to join. Each existing member has the right to negotiate concessions with a newcomer, which are combined into an accession agreement.

Thus, while nominally an agreement about trade, China's WTO accession agreement included a wide range of concessions regarding foreign investment. In order to comply with the agreement, China amended all of its laws related to foreign investment. Many additional industries were opened to foreign investment. Requirements on foreign exchange balances, local content, and export performance previously imposed on FIEs were removed. For the first time, foreign companies in China were allowed to purchase foreign currency from banks rather than draw down their internal foreign currency accounts. In addition, multinational firms in China were no longer required to file production and business plans with government authorities (Chen, 2011, pp. 55–6).

In 2005, China amended its Company Law, bolstering shareholders' rights by allowing shareholder actions and petitions for dissolution, protecting minority shareholders in limited liability companies, introducing independent directors, requiring independence of auditors, and providing for piercing the corporate veil. These provisions applied to domestic and foreign firms in China where not over-ridden by other statutes. China introduced its first comprehensive regulations on cross-border mergers and acquisitions, the *Provisions on Mergers and Acquisitions of Domestic Enterprises by Foreign Investors*, in 2006. Benchmarked on international practice, the Provisions allowed equity interests in Chinese companies to be purchased with shares of an overseas company (Ministry of Commerce, People's Republic of China, 2006). The Provisions also included measures to further transparency in acquisitions involving affiliated companies and to make it more difficult for Chinese companies to 'round trip' capital from China to offshore and back into China. The Provisions also introduced screening requirements on cross-border M&As in which a foreign investor acquires controlling rights in a Chinese company involving a 'major industry', national economic security, 'famous' trademarks, or 'traditional' Chinese brands (Chen, 2011, p. 58; Cheng and Ma, 2009).

China's first *Anti-Monopoly Law* ('AML'), which was enacted in 2007, aims to prevent monopolistic practices, promote fair market competition, foster the efficient operation of the economy, and protect legitimate consumer rights and interests. Its adoption was in line with international practice and its commitments upon joining the WTO, and many provisions of the AML are modeled upon practice in the US, EU, and Japan. While on its face it is applicable to foreign and domestic firms without distinction, it specifically exempts state-owned monopolies and oligopolies, aims to 'promote the healthy development of the socialist market economy', requires enforcement agencies to 'take into account industrial policy considerations' (Shek, 2015), and includes provisions for a national security review of foreign investors. A 2011 State Circular called for a national security review in the cases of foreign companies acquiring domestic companies involving military industries and supporting firms, enterprises in the vicinity of sensitive military facilities, and other entities related to national defense and security. A separate list calls for a national security review of acquisitions involving major agricultural products, major energy and other resources, infrastructure, transport, key technologies, and major equipment (Davies, 2013, pp. 26–7).

In January 2015, the Chinese Ministry of Commerce released the draft of the proposed *New Foreign Investment Law* (FIL) for public consultation. The Draft FIL would replace the previous laws concerning foreign investment with a single statute. WFOEs, foreign invested equity JVs, and contractual JVs would no longer have separate legal regimes. Instead, FIEs would come under China's Companies Law (Betts et al., 2015). Foreign investments would be made on the same terms as domestic investments, without approvals or sector restrictions unless otherwise required by law. Once the New Law is enacted, most foreign investment, except those into industries on the 'negative list' or involving investment amounts exceeding the level set by the State Council, would no longer need pre-approval, but instead would be required to submit an information report at the time of investment and annual follow-up reports to local authorities. In theory, this will substantially reduce the administrative burden associated with foreign investment. The proposed law also provides a statutory basis for the national security review of foreign investments that harm or may harm the national security of China. In March 2016, MOFCOM announced its commitment to finalizing the draft Foreign Investment Law for submission to the National People's Congress in 2016.

Sector-based investment policies

Since 1978, China's overall industrial development policy has involved the targeting of favored or high-priority industries, sectors, and activities for FDI, and the restriction or prohibition of FDI into sensitive industries. Its policies toward FDI have been intended from the start to guide investment into targeted industries while protecting strategic interests and their evolution since then has taken shape in tandem with China's changing industrial policy priorities. National industrial policy, in turn, serves higher ends, including political stability, often summed up in the phrase 'economic and social development'. As a result, sector-specific industrial policies toward FDI, despite the opening of the economy pre- and post-WTO entry, can be very sensitive to the political direction of the top Chinese leadership, as evidenced in the national Five-Year Programs.

The first regulations to 'guide' FDI into China by industry, issued in 1995, were the *Interim Provisions on Guiding Foreign Investment and the Catalogue for the Guidance of Foreign Investment Industries* ('the Catalogue'). The Catalogue, which has been amended many times, is a first-stop for foreign investors considering investment in China. Since 2002, FDI into China has been classified by sector into 'encouraged', 'permitted', 'restricted', and 'prohibited' categories, pursuant to the *Provisions on Guiding the Orientation of Foreign Investment*, a separate set of provisions adopted in connection with China's WTO accession.[5] In 'encouraged' industries, wholly foreign-owned enterprises, equity joint ventures, and cooperative joint ventures are permitted. Industries not listed, unless forbidden by other laws and regulations, are 'permitted' and generally open to FDI via the same vehicles. In 'restricted' industries, FDI is subject to strict examination and approval on a case-by-case basis, with potential limitations on company vehicles and foreign control. In 'prohibited' industries, FDI is not permitted at all. There are also specific catalogues for specific sectors and for some geographic regions. The catalogues' restrictions are not comprehensive – additional restrictions often exist for investments within the 'encouraged' and 'permitted' categories, and regulators can restrict investment for unspecified reasons (U.S. State Department, 2015, p. 7). In addition, the catalogues also include requirements that certain investments take specific forms (for example, as a domestic-foreign equity joint venture) and/or equity caps on the foreign shareholder's proportion of investment.

The 2007 Catalogue marked several turning points concerning foreign investment in China. Concern that China's trade surplus was expanding through low value-added export-processing resulted in the omission of investments exporting 100 percent of production from the encouraged category. Efforts to increase FDI in high-technology industries resulted in over 500 high-technology industries being added to the encouraged category. Concern about the environment resulted in several industries associated with high consumption of resources or pollution being placed in the restricted and prohibited categories. On the other hand, resource saving and alternative energy investments were placed in the encouraged category. Efforts to build the service sector also resulted in services outsourcing and modern logistics being placed in the encouraged category. Publishing and media remained prohibited, and a variety of Internet-based businesses were added to the prohibited category.

The 2011 Catalogue had minor changes, involving the encouragement of environmentally friendly investments along with several sub-sectoral adjustments that dovetailed with the latest industrial policy. The 2015 Catalogue removed restrictions on foreign investment in several sectors, including manufacturing, with more limited revisions in services, agriculture, and infrastructure (Kaja et al., 2015). According to the National Reform and Development Commission (NDRC), the 2015 Catalogue lowered the number of 'restricted' industries from 79 to 38; the number of sectors in which Chinese-controlled joint ventures are required from 44 to 35; and the number of industries requiring joint ventures with Chinese partners, but allowing foreign control, from 43 to 15. It exempted the e-commerce sector from the foreign equity cap of 50 percent applicable to value-added telecom services. Restrictions on foreign investment remained in traditionally restricted areas including banking, telecommunications, and cultural industries (U.S. State Department, 2015, pp. 8–9).

The sector-specific approach toward FDI has also been reflected in the foreign capital adjuncts to the *Five-Year Programs for Economic and Social Development*. In the *11th Program for Foreign Capital Utilization*, issued in 2006, for example, China changed its emphasis from the quantity to quality of FDI, with a focus on upgrading its industrial structure. FDI in traditional manufacturing industries in which Chinese firms had mastered the technologies and built up strong production capacity was no longer to be encouraged. The target shifted to high-technology manufacturing of high-end equipment, new materials, infrastructure, and modern agriculture. The *12th Five-Year Program for Utilization of Overseas Capital and Investment Abroad* issued in 2011 called for FDI into a specified set of 'strategic' and 'newly emerging' industries: energy efficient and environmental technologies, next-generation information technology, bio-technology, advanced equipment manufacturing, new energy, new materials, and new-energy vehicles. The Program also undertook to encourage foreign multinationals to set up regional headquarters and R&D centers in China and to encourage foreign investment into 'production services' including modern logistics, software development, engineering design, vocational skills training, information consulting, technology, and intellectual property services. Banking, securities, insurance, telecom, fuel, and logistics industries were to be steadily opened up, while education and sports were to be opened up 'gradually'.

Geography-based investment policies

Since allowing foreign investment was an experiment for China, its leaders took a cautious approach in terms of geographic opening, allowing investment into specially-designated geographic zones which, if successful, could serve as a laboratory for overall economic reform. Based on earlier experiments by South Korea, Taiwan, and other developing Asian economies, China's first Special Economic Zones ('SEZs') combined free-trade and export processing zone functions. The first SEZs, Shenzhen, Zhuhai, Xiamen, and Shantou, were strategically located along the coast of Guangdong and Fujian Provinces. The intent was to link into the international trading networks of overseas Chinese from these areas and minimize political and military risk by locating away from major cities and military installations in the Mainland. The SEZs operated under special regulatory regimes designed to offer foreign companies preferred terms and a favorable environment, including income tax reductions of various kinds, duty exemptions on imports used in the production of exports, export duty exemptions, and facilitated entry and exit formalities. The four SEZs and their respective provincial governments also were granted fiscal and foreign exchange privileges that generated funds that helped develop their localities (Wang, 1997, pp. 28–9).

In 1984, the Chinese government announced the opening up of an additional 14 coastal cities and Hainan Island. The newly opened areas were encouraged to set up Economic and Technological Development Zones ('ETDZs') offering terms as generous as in the SEZs. The coastal development strategy expanded in the mid-1980s. The Yangtze River Delta (including Shanghai), Pearl River Delta (near Hong Kong), and Min Nan Delta (including Xiamen in Fujian Province) regions were designated as coastal economic open areas in 1985 and received most of the same preferential policies as the open coastal cities. In 1988, the Liaodong and Shandong peninsulas also became coastal economic open areas. That year, the Chinese Government decided to extend the open policies for FDI to coastal areas in general, with the result that China had 'opened' basically all its coastal cities and counties with a total population of 280 million people. Hainan Island became an SEZ in 1988.

In 1992, under Deng Xiaoping's leadership, China decided to pursue a more market-oriented economy, resulting in a revamp of its FDI policy. FDI incentives were expanded and the government started dovetailing FDI policies with national and local industrial development priorities. Regardless of its location, any FDI project that fulfilled state or local industrial policy objectives and promised sufficient technology content would receive the same preferential treatment as in the ETDZs. Fifty-two cities across China were opened to foreign investors and 15 'open border cities' were created, under a variety of FDI preferential schemes. There was also geography-specific partial opening of certain service sectors. By the end of September 1992, there were nearly 2,000 ETDZs across the country, most of them in inland areas (Chen, 2011, p. 42). In the wake of this expansion, the Government brought approval of all new ETDZs under central control in 1993.

In 2000, the State Council issued its *Policies and Measures for the Western Development Strategy* to promote economic growth across Western and Central China. Key focal points included infrastructure, science and education, industrial restructuring, economic reform, and openness to FDI. The Central Government issued a series of preferential policies to attract FDI into the West, including tariff-free treatment and VAT exemptions on imported technology and equipment. Foreign firms already present in China's coastal areas were offered preferential treatment for investments in the central and western regions. Since then, China has continued to encourage foreign firms to set up operations in Western, Central, and Northeastern China, via the *Catalogue of Priority Industries for Foreign Investment in the Central-Western Regions*, which outlines incentives to attract investment in targeted sectors to those parts of China, and follow-on initiatives (Huang et al., 2010).

The most recent geographically based foreign investment policies have involved the creation of new Free Trade Zones and New Areas. In September 2013, the Shanghai Pilot Free-Trade Zone was launched as a testing ground for foreign investment and market access reforms, including the 'negative list'. The principal aim was to help grow the economy in directions set by targeted industrial policy. A second aim was to use the Shanghai Pilot FTZ as a test bed for regulatory innovation that if successful could be rolled out across a wider geographic area. The Shanghai Pilot FTZ was joined in April 2015 by additional Pilot FTZs in Tianjin, Fujian, and Guangdong.

The experimental reforms launched in the Shanghai Pilot FTZ focused on facilitating flows in trade, investment, capital, talent, and innovation. While the Shanghai Pilot FTZ supports the functions of a typical FTZ – the import, processing, and export of goods free of Customs duties – its Bonded Area offers streamlined procedures for its logistics and shipping center; the Jinqiao Export Processing Zone offers facilitated export processing arrangements focused on advanced manufacturing and production services; and the Lujiazui Financial Area has policies to support its roles as a financial, shipping, and trade center. Financial sector reforms have included interest rate liberalization, free convertibility of the renminbi, and relaxed limits on foreign participation in financial services and offshore banking. The 'negative list' approach to FDI approvals introduced in the Shanghai FTZ in 2013 effectively superseded the prohibited, restricted, and encouraged categories for the first time in China (Deloitte Touche Tohmatsu Limited, 2015, p. 3).

The reforms in the Tianjin Pilot FTZ have targeted the development of high-value services and manufacturing, and related value chain activities, consistent with the roles assigned to Tianjin as a major Northern China hub for finance, shipping and logistics, R&D, and advanced industries. Overall, the Tianjin Special FTZ aims to realize the full potential for economic growth in Northern China by promoting coordinated development in the area encompassing Beijing, Tianjin, and Hebei. Encouraged industries reflect the industrial make-up of the region and include high-technology manufacturing, aviation and spacecraft, equipment manufacturing, financial services and financial leasing, shipping and logistics services, electronic information, and pharmaceuticals (Dezan Shira & Associates, 2015).

The Guangdong and Fujian Special FTZs serve broadly as test beds for policies to promote economic integration with Hong Kong, Macau, and Taiwan in order to grow their own economies. In the Fujian Special FTZ, reforms in the Xiamen subzone are focused on financial services for China and Taiwan as a 'region'. In the Guangdong Special FTZ, reforms in the Nansha area focus on Nansha as a center of shipping, logistics, trade, and high-end manufacturing, while reforms in Qinhai and Shekou focus on fostering synergies with Hong Kong in the sorts of financial and other high-end services required to support growth at home. Hengqin, in turn, received reform initiatives geared to its own positioning in service sectors such as tourism, leisure, health, and education (Dezan Shira & Associates, 2016).

Building on the 'negative list' approach to foreign investment approval introduced in the Shanghai FTZ, a revised 'negative list' was introduced in all four Special FTZs in 2015. While the list remained long and detailed, the trend was toward greater openness. The Special FTZs have also eased incorporation requirements and speeded up administrative procedures, as foreign investment not subject to the Negative List no longer faces the traditional approval process and instead proceeds via a less onerous filing system.

Taxation of foreign invested enterprises

Another area that shows the evolution of China's approach toward foreign investment has been its approach toward taxation. Since its economic opening, China has used tax incentives to direct FDI into regions, sectors, and industries. The approach has evolved from across-the-board tax concessions to foreign firms operating in the SEZs, coastal cities, and other preferred locations, to a more unified, national approach that combines a level playing field for domestic and foreign investment with more narrowly defined tax preferences to encourage specific regions and sectors.

The 1980s witnessed the sequential roll-out of a wide variety of tax incentives aimed at attracting foreign investment. The principal laws governing these tax concessions were the *Equity Joint Venture Income Tax Law*, the *Foreign Enterprise Income Tax Law*, and the *Industrial and Commercial Tax Provisions* (Zhang, 2008). *The Equity Joint Venture Income Tax Law*, applicable within the SEZs, introduced tax holidays for new joint ventures planning to operate for at least ten years, including total tax exemptions for two years starting from the first profit-making year, 50 percent reductions for the following three years, loss carry-forward provisions, tax incentives to continue operating for an additional ten years in remote and low-income areas, and incentives to encourage the reinvestment of profits. It also authorized local governments to grant their own tax exemptions and reductions. The *Foreign Enterprise Income Tax Law* offered a similar range of incentives including tax exemptions for enterprises engaged in agriculture, forestry, and other low-profit operations such as deep-pit mining. *The Industrial and Commercial Tax Provisions* dealt primarily with exemptions on machinery and equipment imports used in offshore oil exploration and extraction joint ventures (Chen, 2011, p. 69).

From 1986 through 1990, tax policies for FIEs focused on offering tax incentives to attract FDI, targeting preferred industries and activities, encouraging technology inflows, and boosting exports. Tax incentives proliferated at the national, provincial, and local levels, and local governments vied with each other in offering incentives to foreign investments. The Central Government eventually put an end to this 'tax concession war', and ordered local governments to eliminate tax provisions outside the mandates of national legislation (Chen, 2011, p. 70). In 1991, China took steps to rationalize the tax incentive system through the *Foreign Investment Enterprise and Foreign Enterprise Income Tax Law*. This law offered incentives to broadly defined sectors, such as manufacturing, infrastructure, and agriculture, and to all types of foreign invested firms in selected industries and areas. It took steps to control tax evasion with new transfer pricing standards. It also made business income tax exemptions available to foreign firms located throughout China, a major change from the prior regime under which they were restricted to firms located within the SEZs and ETDZs (Yin and An, 1998, pp. 211–5).

In 1994, China introduced a comprehensive taxation system including business and individual income, value-added, and consumption taxes. A unified business income tax rate of 33 percent was announced for both domestic and foreign firms, as well as a value-added tax rate of 17 percent. The intention was to place domestic and multinational firms on a level playing field through a gradual reduction of tax concessions to foreign firms. In the wake of the Asian Crisis, however, preferential tax treatments for foreign investment were maintained (Yin and An, 1998, pp. 211–5). In addition, tax incentives continued to be used to target foreign investment in line with industrial policy and local priorities.

On January 1, 2008, *China's Enterprise Income Tax Law* unified tax rates for domestic and foreign firms at 25 percent (KPMG 2013, pp. 46–7; State Council, 2007). It rolled back many tax incentives and holidays for foreign investors that existed under the previous tax regime. This was implemented gradually, so that the tax rate for FIEs was raised to 18 percent in 2008, 20 percent in 2009, 22 percent in 2010, 24 percent in 2011, and 25 percent in 2012. In addition, as of December 2010, China took the additional step of imposing the city maintenance and construction tax and the educational surcharge on foreign-invested firms, which previously had been exempted. This step was heralded by *People's Daily* as the end of the 'super national treatment' of foreign invested firms in China and the start of a 'fully unified national tax system for domestic and foreign firms' (People's Daily, 2010).

The Enterprise Income Tax Law reflected the view that China no longer had to provide incentives as it had previously for foreign investors. In addition, the objectives of national industrial policy had shifted toward high-value adding services, technologies, and the development of domestic firms. These new directions were reflected in the preferential provisions of the Law, which focused on projects for environmental protection, modern agriculture, water conservation, energy efficiency, production safety, high technology, and the public welfare. Certain tax preferences were still available to favored locations including SEZs and China's western areas. Chinese policy makers also now understood that tax incentives tended to have the greatest attraction for low-value adding activities and the least attraction for high-value activities of foreign firms.

The tax incentives available in China as of 2016, both inside and outside FTZs were targeted to specific industrial and regional development goals. The main tax incentives for foreign-invested firms included a preferential tax rate of 15 percent for new high-technology enterprises and a deduction of 50 percent for certain R&D spending. An additional two-year tax holiday for such firms was available on a geography-specific basis. The 15 percent preferential tax rate also was available to qualifying 'high-tech' service businesses in 21 specified cities as well as 'encouraged business' in specified regions including Western China. Tax exemptions also applied to sectors including agriculture, forestry, animal husbandry and fishery, software and integrated circuits, certain infrastructure and environmental projects, and technology transfer (Deloitte Touche Tohmatsu Limited, 2015, p. 4).

Foreign investment results

The results of China's step-by-step approach to foreign investment can be seen in the rapid growth of inward FDI in the reform period, as well as its sectoral and geographic breakdown. The results indicate the success that China has had in attracting foreign investment, and how this success is being spread to new industries and new geographies.

Number and value of FDI projects

As indicated earlier, uncertainty over the legal and regulatory regime, as well as China's relatively backward infrastructure and economy limited foreign investment in the early years after the economic opening. As the situation for foreign investment became clearer, incentives were put in place, and more areas opened, and investment began to take off. As a result, utilized foreign investment increased from USD 4,104 million in the 1979 to 1984 period, to USD 3,487 million in 1990, to USD 40,715 million in 2000, to USD 114,734 million in 2010, to USD 119,562 million in 2014 (see Table 2.1).[6] While the growth rate of FDI into China has slowed in recent years, it has done so at a

Table 2.1 FDI flows into China, 1979 to 2014

Year	Annual Flows			Cumulative Flows		
	Number of Projects	Contracted Value (USD mn)	Utilized Value (USD mn)	Number of Projects	Contracted Value (USD mn)	Utilized Value (USD mn)
1979–1984				3,724	9,750	4,104
1985	3,073	6,330	1,960	6,797	16,080	6,064
1986	1,498	3,330	2,240	8,295	19,410	8,304
1987	2,233	3,709	2,314	10,528	23,119	10,618
1988	5,945	5,297	3,194	16,473	28,416	13,812
1989	5,779	5,600	3,392	22,252	34,016	17,204
1990	7,273	6,596	3,487	29,525	40,612	20,691
1991	12,978	11,977	4,366	42,503	52,589	25,057
1992	48,764	58,124	11,007	91,267	110,713	36,064
1993	83,437	111,436	27,515	174,704	222,149	63,579
1994	47,549	82,680	33,767	222,253	304,829	97,346
1995	37,223	91,282	37,521	259,476	396,111	134,867
1996	24,556	73,276	41,726	284,032	469,387	176,593
1997	21,046	51,004	45,257	305,078	520,391	221,850
1998	19,799	52,102	45,463	324,877	572,493	267,313
1999	16,918	41,223	40,319	341,795	613,716	307,632
2000	22,347	62,380	40,715	364,142	676,096	348,347
2001	26,140	69,195	46,878	390,282	745,291	395,225
2002	34,171	82,768	52,743	424,453	828,059	447,968
2003	41,081	115,070	53,505	465,534	943,129	501,473
2004	43,664	153,479	60,630	509,198	1,096,608	562,103
2005	44,019	189,065	72,406	553,217	1,285,673	634,509
2006	41,485	200,174	72,715	594,702	1,485,847	707,224
2007	37,888	N/A	83,521	632,590	N/A	790,745
2008	27,537	N/A	108,312	660,127	N/A	899,057
2009	23,442	N/A	94,065	683,569	N/A	993,122
2010	27,406	N/A	114,734	710,975	N/A	1,107,856
2011	27,712	N/A	123,985	738,687	N/A	1,231,841
2012	24,925	N/A	121,073	763,612	N/A	1,352,914
2013	22,773	N/A	117,586	786,385	N/A	1,470,500
2014	23,778	N/A	119,562	810,163	N/A	1,590,062

Note: The Chinese Government ceased reporting Contracted Value of inward FDI after 2006. The annual flows represent the projects and investments in a particular year. The cumulative figures are the sums of the relevant flows from 1979 up to the year in question. All values are recorded in the relevant dollars for the year of inflow i.e. the values have not been adjusted for inflation.

Sources: CEIC; *China Statistical Yearbook 2014*.

level that made China the single largest destination for FDI in 2014. What makes this even more extraordinary, is that most of the FDI into China is greenfield FDI. Greenfield FDI is defined as FDI that involves the creation of new capital facilities in the host countries, as distinct from merger or acquisition activity that involves the sale of existing assets. In China, most FDI has been greenfield FDI (90 percent or more), while most FDI into developed economies represents merger and acquisition activity rather than greenfield FDI (Long, 2005; Naudé et al., 2015).

In 2014, China was the world's top destination for FDI, reporting 23,778 FDI projects and utilized FDI of USD 119,562 million. From 1979 to 2014, China recorded a total of 810,163 projects with a cumulative utilized FDI value of USD 1,590,062 million.[7] China had gone from receiving virtually no FDI to the world's leading destination for FDI in 30 years.

Sources of investment

According to Chinese statistics, Hong Kong has been the top source of foreign direct investment into China (Table 2.2). From 1985 to 2014, investment into the Chinese Mainland from Hong Kong was USD 744,827 million, equal to 47 percent of investment from all sources. The Virgin Islands was second, followed by Japan, the United States, Singapore, Taiwan, and Korea. Eight of the top 30 sources of FDI into China have been tax havens (the Virgin Islands, West Samoa, the Cayman Islands, Mauritius, Bermuda, Luxembourg, Barbados, and Brunei), which usually pass through investment from elsewhere, rather than being sources of investment themselves. Together they accounted for over 13 percent of FDI from all sources to China over the period. Combined with Hong Kong, the figure was 60 percent.

Table 2.2 Top 20 sources of utilized FDI into China, 1985 to 2014

Source	Cumulative 1985–2014 (USD mn)	Percentage of all Sources (%)
Hong Kong	744,827	47.0
Virgin Islands	*132,104*	*8.3*
Japan	98,049	6.2
United States	74,809	4.7
Singapore	72,106	4.5
Taiwan	60,690	3.8
Korea	59,825	3.8
Cayman Islands	*28,684*	*1.8*
Germany	23,877	1.5
West Samoa	*23,106*	*1.5*
United Kingdom	19,055	1.2
Netherland	14,712	0.9
France	13,359	0.8
Mauritius	*12,304*	*0.8*
Macau	11,716	0.7
Canada	9,668	0.6
Australia	7,725	0.5
Malaysia	6,707	0.4
Bermuda	*6,466*	*0.4*
Italy	6,398	0.4

Note: Economies in italics are regarded as tax havens, through which investment is often routed to take advantage of favorable tax treatment or favorable treatment of other kinds.

Sources: *China Statistical Yearbooks* (various years); Enright, Scott & Associates analysis.

According to official Chinese statistics, Hong Kong has been the dominant investor into the Chinese Mainland during all of the sub-periods from 1985 to 2014. Its share went from 60 percent from 1985 to 1990, to 31 percent from 2001 to 2005, and back to 60 percent from 2011 to 2014. Japan, the United States, Korea, Taiwan, and Singapore have also been among the top six investors (excluding tax havens) in each period since 1991, though with different orders in different periods, notably the United States moving down and Singapore moving up in recent periods.

Hong Kong statistics do not allow one to trace how much of the foreign investment that has come into Hong Kong has been redeployed into the Chinese Mainland. However, we note that from 1998 to 2013 the British Virgin Islands (a tax haven in which many Hong Kong-based companies have incorporated) and the Chinese Mainland each accounted for approximately 34 percent of FDI into Hong Kong. Bermuda (another favorite place for the incorporation of Hong Kong firms) accounted for another 8 percent (HKCSD, various years). The inability to trace investments that come from Hong Kong and various tax havens means that the ultimate source of a significant portion of China's inward FDI is unclear. In the 1990s and early 2000s, there was speculation that a significant portion of the inward FDI was 'round-tripped' from the Chinese Mainland in order to obtain favorable treatment granted foreign investors, to achieve better protection of property rights, and to access better financial services.[8] As the playing field between foreign and local companies was leveled in the 2000s and 2010s, at least for tax purposes, the incentive for round-tripping should have been reduced. On the other hand, many more companies from the Chinese Mainland have listed on the Hong Kong stock exchange and then deployed the capital raised back in the Chinese Mainland. In addition, companies from elsewhere may choose to route investments through Hong Kong vehicles because companies based in Hong Kong can receive favorable tax and other policies under the Closer Economic Partnership Arrangement – CEPA.

While Hong Kong companies have been major investors in China in light manufacturing, real estate, infrastructure, and other industries, again Hong Kong is unlikely to be the ultimate source of all of the investment registered as having coming into China from Hong Kong.

Investment by industry

In the early years of China's opening, the vast majority of inward FDI was in manufacturing. This was not surprising since China initially opened the country to foreign investment as a way to build up export-oriented manufacturing, and then to improve the rest of the manufacturing economy. Services, which were viewed as more sensitive, were opened later and not to the same extent. According to data covering even a relatively recent period, 1997 to 2014, manufacturing accounted for just under 50 percent of utilized FDI in China (Table 2.3), with the leading recipient sectors within manufacturing being Communication, Computer, & Other Electronic Equipment (8.2 percent of total investment), followed by Chemical Material & Products, Universal Machinery,

Table 2.3 Utilized FDI in China, 1997 to 2014, by invested industry

Industry	Utilized FDI 1997–2014 (USD mn)	% of All Industries
Manufacturing	705,922	49.9
Communication, Computer, & Other Electronic Equip	115,531	8.2
Chemical Materials & Products	51,666	3.7
Universal Machinery	41,059	2.9
Textile	33,408	2.4
Special Purpose Equipment	33,164	2.3
Medical & Pharmaceutical Products	13,483	1.0
Other Manufacturing	417,611	29.4
Services	676,403	47.9
Real Estate	248,350	17.6
Banking & Insurance	90,974	6.4
Leasing and Commercial Services	72,519	5.1
Wholesale and Retail Trade	69,147	4.9
Transport, Storage, & Postal Service	38,590	2.7
Electricity, Gas, & Water Production & Supply	35,270	2.5
Information Transmission, Computer Service, & Software	23,688	1.7
Scientific Research, Polytechnic Service, & Geological	18,759	1.3
Construction	17,638	1.2
Residential and Other Service	10,276	0.7
Accommodation & Catering Trade	8,954	0.6
Water Conservancy, Environment, & Public Utility Mgt	5,965	0.4
Culture, Sport, & Recreation	5,273	0.4
Health Care, Social Security, & Welfare	589	0.0
Education	254	0.0
Public Management & Social Organization	23	0.0
Other Services	30,134	2.1
Primary	31,144	2.2
Agricultural	20,846	1.5
Mining	10,298	0.7
Total	1,413,469	100.0

Notes: Only the top six manufacturing industries are shown in the table. Some industries were not reported separately before 2004. 'Other services' represents the investment that could not be apportioned to the other categories due to changes in reporting.

Sources: CEIC; Enright, Scott & Associates analysis.

Textiles, Special Purpose Equipment, and Medical & Pharmaceutical Products. The large share held by Other Manufacturing (29.4 percent) shows how widely diversified FDI into the manufacturing sector has been. Over the same period, the service sector accounted for nearly 48 percent of inward FDI, with the leading recipients being Real Estate (17.6 percent of total investment), Banking and Insurance, Leasing and Commercial Services, and Wholesale and Retail Trade.

These overall figures, however, mask a substantial shift over time. Manufacturing's share of inward FDI went from just under 60 percent during the years 1997 to 2000, to over 66 percent from 2001 to 2005, to 48 percent from 2006 to 2010, to 39 percent from 2011 to 2014. The rise in the percentage of investment in the Communication, Computer, & Other Electronic Equipment sector was due to the global expansion of the industry, the massive shift of production from Taiwan to China in the early 2000s, and the subsequent establishment of China as the leading assembly platform for consumer electronics globally. FDI in the chemical sector brought large-scale investments from world class companies to enhance and in some cases replace inefficient facilities. Investment in the textile sector ramped up to take advantage of low-cost labour in China and the end of the Multi-Fiber Agreement's garment quota regime in 2005. Subsequently, the share of the sector in inward FDI diminished as investment in other sectors grew, Chinese production increased, and costs in China made the sector somewhat less competitive than it had been.

Meanwhile, the service sector's share went from 38 percent during the years 1997 to 2000, to over 31 percent from 2001 to 2005, to 50 percent from 2006 to 2010, to 59 percent from 2011 to 2014. The biggest movers among the service sectors have been the Real Estate industry (which accounted for 24 percent of inward FDI from 2011 to 2014), Leasing and Commercial Services, Wholesale and Retail Trade, and Banking and Insurance. Growth in service sector FDI has been linked to the growth of China's economy, a shift from manufacturing to services across the economy, China's drive to improve the service sector, the opening of particular sectors, and global economic trends. The Banking and Insurance sector, for example, went from zero percent of China's FDI during the years 1997 to 2000 when the sector was closed to foreign investment, to nearly 11 percent from 2006 to 2010 as the sector was opened and many foreign financial institutions entered or obtained stakes in Chinese institutions or both.[9]

The industrial pattern of FDI has followed global economic forces, China's economic development, China's sector-specific approach to FDI, the relative competitiveness of indigenous and foreign companies, and the sectors in which footloose investment (investment not tied to the market in the host country) was made in the period. The pattern shows a rapidly developing economy, moving from a pattern of inward investment similar to lesser developed countries to one similar to more advanced economies.

Foreign investment in China's provinces

Just as China's inward investment has varied by industry, it has varied by geography, with investment into particular provinces linked to the size and sophistication of the local economies, the presence of infrastructure, and policies that opened some provinces before others. Table 2.4 shows the utilized FDI into China's 27 provinces and autonomous regions, and the four municipalities with provincial-level status (Beijing, Chongqing, Shanghai, and Tianjin) from 1979 to 2013. For the whole reported period, Jiangsu (USD 316,070 million in FDI, or 15.3 percent of the total) and Guangdong

Table 2.4 Utilized FDI in China's provincial-level jurisdictions, 1979 to 2013, USD mn

Province/City	1979–2013	%	1979–1990	%	1991–2000	%	2001–2010	%	2011–2013	%
Jiangsu	316,070	15.3	429	3.0	43,237	13.2	171,254	17.0	101,151	14.1
Guangdong	311,679	15.1	6,574	45.5	90,743	27.6	144,064	14.3	70,299	9.8
Liaoning	175,693	8.5	568	3.9	13,981	4.3	81,044	8.1	80,100	11.1
Shanghai	148,912	7.2	1,381	9.6	28,772	8.8	74,193	7.4	44,566	6.2
Shandong	136,927	6.6	371	2.6	20,655	6.3	78,335	7.8	37,566	5.2
Zhejiang	125,033	6.0	192	1.3	11,008	3.3	74,939	7.5	38,894	5.4
Tianjin	105,964	5.1	352	2.4	12,963	3.9	47,748	4.7	44,901	6.2
Fujian	95,094	4.6	1,050	7.3	32,623	9.9	42,204	4.2	19,218	2.7
Beijing	78,700	3.8	1,520	10.5	13,082	4.0	40,478	4.0	23,620	3.3
Henan	63,594	3.1	137	0.9	4,311	1.3	23,489	2.3	35,657	5.0
Hunan	53,226	2.6	58	0.4	5,168	1.6	25,870	2.6	22,130	3.1
Sichuan	52,281	2.5	97	0.7	2,896	0.9	18,641	1.9	30,647	4.3
Jiangxi	49,332	2.4	32	0.2	2,665	0.8	26,200	2.6	20,434	2.8
Hubei	48,246	2.3	111	0.8	6,319	1.9	24,608	2.4	17,209	2.4
Anhui	48,066	2.3	33	0.2	2,968	0.9	19,105	1.9	25,960	3.6
Hebei	45,672	2.2	104	0.7	7,404	2.3	21,228	2.1	16,936	2.4
Chongqing	44,495	2.2	63	0.4	2,720	0.8	16,505	1.6	25,206	3.5
Heilongjiang	30,531	1.5	136	0.9	3,568	1.1	15,067	1.5	11,760	1.6
Inner Mongolia	28,227	1.4	7	0.0	699	0.2	15,095	1.5	12,426	1.7
Shaanxi	21,043	1.0	393	2.7	2,663	0.8	9,019	0.9	8,969	1.2
Hainan	20,435	1.0	398	2.8	6,733	2.0	8,330	0.8	4,975	0.7
Jilin	14,867	0.7	32	0.2	2,940	0.9	6,946	0.7	4,949	0.7
Guangxi	14,831	0.7	256	1.8	6,168	1.9	5,944	0.6	2,463	0.3
Shanxi	14,492	0.7	19	0.1	1,488	0.5	5,601	0.6	7,383	1.0
Yunnan	12,073	0.6	23	0.2	1,324	0.4	4,288	0.4	6,437	0.9
Guizhou	4,731	0.2	20	0.1	383	0.1	1,083	0.1	3,245	0.5
Xinjiang	2,631	0.1	50	0.3	338	0.1	1,019	0.1	1,224	0.2
Qinghai	2,466	0.1	6	0.0	152	0.0	1,839	0.2	469	0.1
Gansu	1,465	0.1	26	0.2	469	0.1	759	0.1	211	0.0
Ningxia	1,357	0.1	4	0.0	220	0.1	565	0.1	568	0.1
Tibet	569	0.0	1	0.0	36	0.0	192	0.0	340	0.0

Note: The sum of the reported provincial figures is greater than the national total.

Sources: *China Data Online*; *Statistical Materials for China Commercial and Foreign Economy 1952–1988*; *China Foreign Economic and Trade Statistical Yearbooks*; Provincial *Statistical Yearbooks*.

(USD 311,679 million in FDI, or 15.1 percent of the total) have been by far the leaders in attracting FDI. The top two were followed by Liaoning, Shanghai, Shandong, Zhejiang, Tianjin, Fujian, Beijing, and Henan. Nine of the top ten destinations for FDI in China were coastal provinces/municipalities, covering most of China's eastern coastline. The only inland province in the top ten, Henan Province, which is just inland from Zhejiang and Jiangsu, was in tenth position.

The dominance of coastal provinces and municipalities is not surprising. China's coastal provinces have long been the leaders in China's economy. As China opened its economy to foreign investment, it was the coastal provinces that were opened first: in part because they were more advanced, in part because they were near the sea and therefore easier to reach, and in part because they were considered to be better able to absorb the lessons from foreign investors to improve the competitiveness of indigenous industries.

The table also shows the shift in geographical distribution over time. Guangdong, just north of Hong Kong and the first of China's provinces to open to foreign investment, received the lion's share of the early investment into China, with Fujian, the other early opening province, and Beijing and Shanghai, China's two leading economic cities, also prominent. These were followed by other coastal provinces, such as Jiangsu, Liaoning, Zhejiang, Shandong, and the municipality of Tianjin, as these were opened in the 1980s and early 1990s. The later emphasis on western development can be seen in the later development of foreign investment in places like Henan, Sichuan, Anhui, and Chongqing.

Conclusions

The above discussion illustrates the step-by-step nature of China's approach towards its reform process in general and its approach toward foreign investment in particular. The gradual approach was necessitated by the fact that international investment and even the private sector were literally 'foreign' concepts to China at the onset of its reform program. It was not a matter of China having pre-existing legal, regulatory, tax, and administrative systems for a market economy that could be readily extended to cover foreign investors. Instead, such systems had to be created, in some cases from scratch. The gradual approach allowed China to build these systems one step at a time, rather than trying to create these systems in a single stroke.

The gradual approach also allowed China's leaders to ensure that foreign companies did not wield too much influence in the country. While this notion may seem farfetched to many non-Chinese, it has been a very real concern in China. In addition, one has to remember that the idea of enterprises outside the direct control of the state was a new feature for the New China and its leadership. It is not surprising that the institution of systems to govern the economy without directly controlling all major decisions has been extremely sensitive in China. The step-by-step approach has allowed for a relatively smooth transition from a controlled economy without foreign investors to a more market-oriented economy that includes foreign investors as well as the domestic private economy.

Geographic and sector-specific opening have given Chinese authorities the ability to experiment, to scrutinize and monitor the experiments, and then use the results to promulgate laws and regulations that were eventually spread to the nation. It allowed China's leadership to direct investments first to geographic areas most likely to be able to absorb and govern investment, and then to areas that were relatively disadvantaged. It also allowed China's leadership to direct investment initially toward sectors that would allow China to ramp up exports and foreign exchange earnings, and then to sectors that would contribute to China's further industrial development.

The gradual approach also reflects the dynamic interaction of China's desire to control and direct investments with the desire for foreign companies to make profits and to have an environment with sufficient certainty as to the rules of the game to allow them to invest. As China became more comfortable with foreign investment, more experienced in dealing with foreign investors, and more knowledgeable about the impacts of foreign investment, it was able to open to a wider and wider range of investments. As the legal, regulatory, and tax regimes within China became clearer, and more and more foreign companies became knowledgeable about China, more companies were willing to invest. The step-by-step approach resulted in a dramatic rise in foreign investment from virtually zero in the 1970s to a world leading position by the 2010s. The evolution of inward investment shows the impact of China's gradual geographic and sectoral approach, with flows of investment shifting over time.

In subsequent chapters, we will look beyond the headline numbers to explore the wide-ranging impact that foreign investment and foreign invested enterprises have had on China.

Notes

1 Supporting work for this chapter was carried out by Edith Scott of Enright, Scott & Associates.
2 There were a total of 105 open ports established in China from 1842 to 1930 (Hou, 1964, p. 106).
3 'Most favoured nation' clauses meant concessions given to one foreign country signatory must be given to all other foreign country signatories.
4 Estimated by Enright, Scott & Associates based on US Government historical inflation charts.
5 The WTO agreement also extended the industries open to foreign investors. For example, a wide range of service sectors including financial services, distribution, business services, communications, travel and tourism, healthcare, environmental services, and education were progressively opened to foreign investors, with geographic, business scope, and ownership restrictions generally being phased out.
6 In China, foreign direct investment is defined as investment from other countries or jurisdictions into the Chinese Mainland into an entity that has at least 25 percent of its capital

provided by foreign entities. Foreign invested enterprises are enterprises in which foreign entities have at least 25 percent ownership. For purposes of foreign investment, entities from Hong Kong, Macau, and Taiwan are counted as foreign.

7 The cumulative values in the Chinese statistics are the simple sums of the number of projects and investment flows from 1979 up to the year in question. The official statistics do not estimate a capital stock for foreign investment in China, nor do they adjust for inflation.

8 According to UNCTAD (2007), in the late 1990s and early 2000s, round-tripping might have accounted for as much as 25 percent of China's inward FDI. We note, however, that this appears to be a repetition of earlier estimates that could have been obsolete well before 2007.

9 FDI into financial services was influenced by China's World Trade Organization accession agreement, which helped open both the insurance and banking sectors. The agreement opened the insurance sector on a limited basis. Foreign banks were allowed to take stakes in Chinese banks starting in 2002. From 2002 to 2005, 16 Chinese banks received foreign investment. In late 2006, China opened its banking sector to foreign banks, reducing geographic or client restrictions. The influx of investment in the years 2006 to 2010 represented investments to establish or expand China operations during that period. Subsequent lower investment levels indicate that some of the 2006 to 2010 investments represented one-time opportunities to enter or to invest in Chinese financial institutions.

References

Betts, C.W., W.H. Cai, Z.J. Gao, and G.G.H. Miao, 2015, 'China's MOFCOM Aims to Fundamentally Change the Legal Landscape on Foreign Investments', *Skadden Insights*, February 2015.

Chen, C., 2011, *Foreign Direct Investment in China, Location Determinants, Investor Differences and Economic Impacts*, Cheltenham, Edward Elgar.

Cheng, C.B. and M. Ma, 2009, 'China', in Global Legal Group, *Mergers & Acquisitions 2009*, London.

Davies, K., 2013, 'China Investment Policy: An Update', *OECD Working Papers on International Investment 2013/01*, Paris, OECD Publishing.

Deloitte Touche Tohmatsu Limited, 2015, *Taxation and Investment in China 2015*.

Dezan Shira & Associates, 2015, 'The New Free Trade Zones Explained, Part III: Tianjin', *China Briefing News*, 39(486).

Dezan Shira & Associates, 2016, 'A Guide to China's Free Trade Zones', *China Briefing*, 162.

HKCSD, various years, Hong Kong Census and Statistics Department, *Inward Investment Statistics*.

Hou, C.M., 1964, *Foreign Investment in China 1840–1937*, Cambridge, Harvard University Press.

Huang, N., J. Ma, and K. Sullivan, 2010, 'Economic Development Policies for Central and Western China', *China Business Review*, 37(6), pp. 24–28.

Kaja, A., N. Lu, and T.P. Stratford, 2015, 'The Chinese Government Issues 2015 Foreign Investment Catalogue – Effective April 10, 2015', *Global Policy Watch*, Covington & Burling, 24 March 2015.

KPMG, 2013, *Investment in the People's Republic of China*, KPMG Advisory (China) Limited.

Kundra, A., 2009, *India-China, a Comparative Analysis of FDI Policy and Performance*, New Delhi, Academic Foundation.

Levi, W., 1953, *Modern China's Foreign Policy*, St. Paul, University of Minnesota Press.

Long, G., 2005, 'China's Policies on FDI: Review and Evaluation', in T.H. Moran, E.M. Graham, and M. Blomström, eds, *Does FDI Promote Development?* Washington, DC, Institute for International Economics, pp. 315–36.

Ministry of Commerce, People's Republic of China, 2006, *Regulations for Merger with and Acquisition of Domestic Enterprises by Foreign Investors*, 17 October 2006.

Naudé, W., A. Szirmai, and A. Lavapa, 2015, 'Industrialization and Technological Change in the BRICS: The Role of Foreign and Domestic Investment', in W. Naudé, A. Szirmai, and N. Haraguchi, eds, *Structural Change and Industrial Development in the BRICs*, Oxford, Oxford University Press, pp. 324–51.

People's Daily, 2010, 'China Ends Foreign Firms' "Super-national Treatment"', *People's Daily*, 1 December.

Shai, A., 1993, 'Hostage Capitalism and French Companies in China: A Hidden Element in Sino-French Relations', *Études chinoises*, XII(1).

Shek, C., 2015, 'Understanding China's Anti-Monopoly Law', *CKGSB Knowledge*, 18, pp. 36–40.

State Council, 2007, *Regulations of the People's Republic of China on the Implementation of the Enterprise Income Tax Law*, Decree of the State Council of the People's Republic of China No. 512.

Thompson, T.M., 1979, *China's Nationalization of Foreign Firms: The Politics of Hostage Capitalism, 1949–57*, Baltimore, School of Law University of Maryland.

UNCTAD, 2007, 'Rising FDI into China: The Facts Behind the Numbers', *UNCTAD Investment Brief*, No.2, Geneva, UNCTAD.

U.K. Secretary of State for Foreign Affairs, 1952, *Treaty of Peace with Japan, San Francisco, 8th September, 1951*, London, H.M. Stationary Office.

U.S. State Department, 2015, *China Investment Climate Statement*, Washington, DC.

Wang, Y., 1997, *Investment in China: A Question and Answer Guide on How to Do Business*, New York, American Management Association.

Wei, Y., and X. Liu, 2001, *Foreign Investment in China: Determinants and Impact*, Cheltenham, UK, Edward Elgar.

Yin, J.S. and Y. An, 1998, 'Strategic Response to the Income Tax Reform for Enterprises in China', in T. Fulton, J. Li, and D. Xu, eds, *China's Tax Reform Options*, Singapore, World Scientific, pp. 211–5.

Zhang, X., 2008, *Study on Tax System Reform in China*, February 2008, www.econ.hit-c.ac.jp/~Koky/sympo-feb08/PDF/tax%20reform%20in%20china.pdf.

3

The economic impact of foreign companies in China[1]

Introduction

Foreign direct investment (FDI) and foreign invested enterprises (FIEs) have had a major influence on China's economy. In this chapter, we first highlight the role that foreign investment has played in total investment, specific industries, and trade in China. We see that except for trade, the relative importance of FDI appears to be low and falling as a portion of China's economic aggregates.

We then apply the tools of economic impact analysis to estimate the economic impact of FDI and FIEs on output, value added (GDP), and employment in China. Economic impact analysis is a way to estimate the impact that an investment has had or will have on the surrounding economy. It is quite common to perform such analyses for large infrastructure investments, such as ports and airports, or for tourism-related investments, such as theme parks and exhibition centres. In such analyses, it is common to estimate the impact associated with the physical construction or initial capital investment and then to estimate the impact associated with the subsequent operation of the business facilitated by the investment. The idea is that the investment and its operations have ripple effects through supply chains, through distribution channels, and through spillovers that would not be recognized otherwise.

The economic impact analysis shows that when we include the direct impacts of the investments and the operations of FIEs, their supply chains, and the consumer spending of their employees, that the FDI and FIEs were associated with between 16 percent and 34 percent of China's GDP and between 11 percent and 29 percent of China's employment in the years 1995 and 2013. Furthermore, this influence has not been diminishing significantly, as the FDI and FIEs accounted for 33 percent of China's GDP and 27 percent of China's total employment in the year 2013, the latest year for which we have data, and similar levels for the five-year averages from 2009 to 2013.

While these numbers seem large, we must remember that they do not include any impact on the downstream distribution and retailing of the goods of FIEs, nor do they include any technological, managerial, or other spillovers from FIEs into the Chinese economy (which are described in the next chapter). As such, these estimates should be viewed as substantial underestimates of the impact of FDI and FIEs on China's economy.

Importance of FDI in China's total investment

While China has been a leading destination for foreign investment, it is useful to assess how important foreign investment has been to investment in China as a whole. As can be seen in Table 3.1, foreign investment's share in gross capital formation and fixed asset investment in China grew significantly in the early years of China's economic opening, peaked at 14.3 percent in terms of gross capital formation and 11.8 percent in terms of fixed asset investment in the early to mid-1990s, and declined through the 2000s and

Table 3.1 Importance of FDI in investment in China

Year	Utilized FDI Flow (USD mn)	Gross Capital Formation (USD mn)	FDI/Gross Capital Formation	Total Investment in Fixed Assets (RMB bn)	Foreign Investment in Fixed Assets (RMB bn)	Foreign Investment/ Total Fixed Asset Investment
1981				96.1	3.6	3.8%
1982				123.0	6.1	4.9%
1983	920	103,205	0.9%	143.0	6.7	4.7%
1984	1,420	108,408	1.3%	183.3	7.1	3.9%
1985	1,960	117,736	1.7%	254.3	9.2	3.6%
1986	2,240	114,166	2.0%	312.1	13.7	4.4%
1987	2,314	119,879	1.9%	379.2	18.2	4.8%
1988	3,194	153,145	2.1%	465.4	27.5	5.9%
1989	3,392	168,194	2.0%	441.0	29.1	6.6%
1990	3,487	141,056	2.5%	451.8	28.5	6.3%
1991	4,366	147,801	3.0%	559.4	31.9	5.7%
1992	11,007	182,902	6.0%	808.0	46.9	5.8%
1993	27,515	272,784	10.1%	1,307.2	95.4	7.3%
1994	33,767	236,010	14.3%	1,782.7	176.9	9.9%
1995	37,521	304,979	12.3%	2,052.5	229.6	11.2%
1996	41,726	346,215	12.1%	2,335.9	274.7	11.8%
1997	45,257	361,504	12.5%	2,526.0	268.4	10.6%
1998	45,463	378,238	12.0%	2,871.7	261.7	9.1%
1999	40,319	398,049	10.1%	2,975.5	200.7	6.7%
2000	40,715	420,883	9.7%	3,311.0	169.6	5.1%
2001	46,878	480,477	9.8%	3,798.7	173.1	4.6%
2002	52,743	550,504	9.6%	4,504.7	208.5	4.6%
2003	53,505	676,124	7.9%	5,861.6	259.9	4.4%
2004	60,630	835,690	7.3%	7,456.5	328.6	4.4%
2005	72,406	950,132	7.6%	9,459.1	397.9	4.2%
2006	72,715	1,165,797	6.2%	11,895.7	433.4	3.6%
2007	83,521	1,458,334	5.7%	15,080.4	513.3	3.4%
2008	108,312	1,990,677	5.4%	18,291.5	531.2	2.9%
2009	94,065	2,407,454	3.9%	25,023.0	462.4	1.8%
2010	114,734	2,859,619	4.0%	28,577.9	470.4	1.6%
2011	123,985	3,533,942	3.5%	34,598.4	506.2	1.5%
2012	121,073	4,004,435	3.0%	40,967.6	446.9	1.1%
2013	117,586	4,524,968	2.6%	49,161.3	431.9	0.9%

Sources: CEIC; *China Statistical Yearbook 2014*; World Bank, *World Development Indicators*.

2010s to under 3 percent or under 1 percent depending on the measure. This is consistent with three periods in China's development: China's initial opening, a China that had difficulty in deploying domestic capital in the 1990s, and a China that developed domestic sources of capital that made the annual amount of inward foreign investment very small in terms of the economy as a whole.

These figures indicate that foreign investment was particularly important during parts of the reform period, but is becoming less so in recent years, at least in terms of the absolute amount of capital invested. While some have taken this to mean that China no longer needs foreign investment, at least not as much as it once did, we will argue later in this volume that the raw investment percentages substantially understate the ongoing importance of foreign investment to China's economy.

Importance of FIEs by industry

While foreign investment as a whole accounted for only a small portion of gross capital formation and fixed asset investment in China by 2013, the importance of foreign invested enterprises (FIEs) in some industries in China was much higher. As can be seen in Table 3.2, there are several industries in which FIEs accounted for 20 percent,

Table 3.2 Importance of FIEs by industry, 2013

Industry	FIE Assets (RMB bn)	FIE Assets % of Ind Ent	FIE Revenue (RMB bn)	FIE Revenue % of Ind Ent	FIE Profits (RMB bn)	FIE Profits % of Ind Ent
Manufacture of Computers, Communication, and Other Electronic Equipment	2,992.91	59	5,553.95	72	189.27	57
Manufacture of Leather, Fur, Feather, and Related Products and Footwear	267.61	44	457.24	37	26.63	33
Manufacture of Paper and Paper Products	536.08	41	356.61	26	21.86	29
Production and Supply of Gas	213.35	41	159.02	38	19.28	50
Manufacture of Automobiles	1,879.86	40	2,805.79	46	279.48	55
Manufacture of Textile, Wearing Apparel, and Accessories	415.87	38	622.63	32	32.51	28

(*Continued*)

Table 3.2 (Continued)

Industry	FIE Assets (RMB bn)	FIE Assets % of Ind Ent	FIE Revenue (RMB bn)	FIE Revenue % of Ind Ent	FIE Profits (RMB bn)	FIE Profits % of Ind Ent
Manufacture of Articles for Culture, Education, Arts/ Crafts, Sport, Entertainment Activities	218.26	37	411.99	34	17.70	28
Manufacture of Foods	402.90	36	547.24	30	52.36	34
Manufacture of Rubber and Plastic Products	618.42	35	701.16	26	38.52	22
Manufacture of Furniture	132.51	33	170.28	26	9.07	22
Manufacture of Chemical Fibers	194.84	31	203.44	28	9.79	38
Manufacture of Measuring Instruments and Machinery	192.20	30	233.37	30	19.81	31
Repair Service of Metal Products, Machinery, and Equipment	36.80	30	26.09	28	0.64	14
Manufacture of General Purpose Machinery	984.00	28	1,077.29	25	78.99	28
Printing and Reproduction of Recording Media	114.99	27	112.11	21	10.78	26
Manufacture of Electrical Machinery and Apparatus	1,215.20	26	1,616.31	26	83.62	24
Manufacture of Liquor, Beverages, and Refined Tea	333.58	26	393.25	26	33.83	20
Manufacture of Raw Chemical Materials and Chemical Products	1,471.57	25	1,747.80	23	104.35	25
Manufacture of Medicines	444.56	24	455.17	22	50.16	24
Manufacture of Special Purpose Machinery	697.33	24	635.19	20	44.25	21

Industry	FIE Assets (RMB bn)	FIE Assets % of Ind Ent	FIE Revenue (RMB bn)	FIE Revenue % of Ind Ent	FIE Profits (RMB bn)	FIE Profits % of Ind Ent
Manufacture of Metal Products	486.20	23	631.88	19	33.89	18
Processing of Food from Agricultural Products	613.56	23	1,108.36	19	49.10	16
Manufacture of Textile	478.27	22	607.63	17	33.42	17
Utilization of Waste Resources	34.35	22	52.92	16	0.08	1
Other Manufacture	39.70	20	51.86	22	2.63	21
Manufacture of Railway, Ship, Aerospace, and Other Transport Equipment	371.46	19	305.64	18	23.48	25
Manufacture of Non-metallic Mineral Products	622.08	15	549.93	11	40.50	11
Production and Supply of Water	108.37	15	23.44	16	4.41	38
Smelting and Pressing of Non-ferrous Metals	460.90	14	515.11	11	14.69	10
Processing of Timber, Manufacture of Wood, Bamboo, Rattan, Palm, Straw Products	66.94	13	103.01	9	5.68	7
Processing of Petroleum, Coking and Processing of Nuclear Fuel	277.55	12	456.26	11	10.13	21
Smelting and Pressing of Ferrous Metals	634.17	10	820.73	11	14.77	9
Production and Supply of Electric Power and Heat Power	663.30	7	306.96	6	53.40	15
Mining and Processing of Non-ferrous Metal Ores	22.62	5	13.82	2	2.57	4

(Continued)

Table 3.2 (Continued)

Industry	FIE Assets (RMB bn)	FIE Assets % of Ind Ent	FIE Revenue (RMB bn)	FIE Revenue % of Ind Ent	FIE Profits (RMB bn)	FIE Profits % of Ind Ent
Support Activities for Mining	13.35	5	13.07	7	1.46	223
Extraction of Petroleum and Natural Gas	75.73	4	69.07	6	21.73	6
Mining and Washing of Coal	196.19	4	183.76	6	22.36	9
Mining and Processing of Non-metal Ores	9.99	3	11.72	2	0.78	2
Mining and Processing of Ferrous Metal Ores	23.35	2	27.46	3	1.86	2
Manufacture of Tobacco	–	0	–	0	–	0
Mining of Other Ores	–	0	–	0	–	0
All Industries	18,561.11	22	24,138.78	23	1,459.92	23

Notes: 'Ind Ent' = industrial enterprises. 'Industrial Enterprises' includes industrial enterprises of all types of ownership with revenue over RMB 20 million in 2013. Information for foreign enterprises in the Manufacture of Tobacco was not reported in 2013. Some enterprises had losses, so the profit of foreign invested enterprises could be larger than total profit of enterprises of all types of ownership.

Sources: *China Statistical Yearbook 2014*; Enright, Scott & Associates analysis.

30 percent, 40 percent, or more of the assets, revenues, and/or profits in individual industries in China. Overall, foreign invested industrial enterprises accounted for 22 percent of total assets, 23 percent of total revenue, and 23 percent of total profit of all industrial enterprises (above scale) in China.[2]

Foreign invested enterprises are clearly major players in some industries in China. In Computers, Communication, and Other Electronic Equipment, foreign invested enterprises accounted for 59 percent of total assets, 72 percent of total revenue, and 57 percent of total profits in 2013. In Automobiles, foreign invested enterprises accounted for 40 percent of total assets, 46 percent of total revenue, and 55 percent of total profits. In some other manufacturing industries, such as Leather, Fur, Feather, and Related Products and Footwear, Paper and Paper Products, and the Production and Supply of Gas, foreign invested enterprises also take up a significant portion (over 40 percent of assets, revenue, or profits).

In any case, it is clear that foreign investment is far more important in some critical industries in China than the economy-wide aggregates would suggest. Several of these industries are important in terms of exports, in terms of spillovers into the domestic economy, or in terms of their technology levels. Of course, the importance of FDI in particular industries is also influenced by whether the industries are in the encouraged, restricted, prohibited, or permitted categories for foreign investment in China.

Importance of FIEs in China's trade

Before China's opening started in 1979, the country was largely separated from world markets with the exception of some commodities and trade that resulted from the Canton Fair and that trickled in and out through Hong Kong. Two-way trade equalled only 11.3 percent of GDP in 1979. By 1990, the figure was 26.8 percent (OECD, 2003). By 2014, it was 41.6 percent (World Bank, 2015). By the latter year, China had become the world's leading trading nation, as well as its leading exporter (accounting for 12.3 percent of global merchandise exports) and second leading importer (accounting for 10.3 percent of global merchandise imports) (World Trade Organization, 2015).

By the early 1990s, FIEs accounted for 40 percent of China's imports and 28 percent of its exports (Table 3.3). In those days, FIE imports exceeded FIE exports due

Table 3.3 Trade performance of foreign invested enterprises

Year	FIE Exports (USD mn)	FIE Imports (USD mn)	FIE Exports/ FIE Imports (%)	China's Exports by FIEs (%)	China's Imports by FIEs (%)	FIE Net Exports (USD mn)	FIE Net Exports as % of China GDP	FIE Domestic Revenue (USD mn)	Domestic Rev/ Exports (%)
1993	25,237	41,833	60	28	40	−16,596	−2.7		
1994	34,713	52,934	66	29	46	−18,221	−3.3		
1995	46,876	62,943	74	32	48	−16,067	−2.2	74,257	158
1996	61,506	75,604	81	41	54	−14,098	−1.6	68,639	112
1997	74,900	77,721	96	41	55	−2,821	−0.3	82,155	110
1998	80,962	76,717	106	44	55	4,245	0.4	N/A	N/A
1999	88,628	85,884	103	45	52	2,744	0.3	128,405	145
2000	119,441	117,273	102	48	52	2,168	0.2	152,899	128
2001	133,235	125,863	106	50	52	7,372	0.6	181,153	136
2002	169,985	160,254	106	52	54	9,731	0.7	206,836	122
2003	240,306	231,864	104	55	56	8,442	0.5	286,544	119
2004	338,592	324,448	104	57	58	14,144	0.7	360,126	106
2005	444,183	387,456	115	58	59	56,727	2.5	514,586	116
2006	563,779	472,490	119	58	60	91,289	3.4	677,042	120
2007	695,371	559,793	124	57	59	135,578	3.9	954,284	137
2008	790,493	619,428	128	55	55	171,065	3.8	1,319,464	167
2009	672,074	545,404	123	56	54	126,670	2.5	1,527,515	227
2010	862,229	738,386	117	55	53	123,843	2.1	1,925,392	223
2011	995,227	864,672	115	52	50	130,555	1.8	2,352,379	236
2012	1,022,620	871,500	117	50	48	151,120	1.8	2,493,494	244
2013	1,043,724	874,590	119	47	45	169,134	1.8	2,852,293	273

Sources: *China Statistical Yearbooks* (various years); Enright, Scott & Associates analysis.

to imports of capital equipment and inputs (much of which were destined for China's export-oriented industries), as well as sales in the Chinese domestic market. By 1996, FIEs accounted for 41 percent of China's exports and 54 percent of China's imports. The FIE contribution to trade peaked at 58 percent of exports and 60 percent of imports in 2006. By 2013, FIEs accounted for 47 of China's exports and 45 of China's imports. Given the growth in China's trade, however, these represented greater export and import values than had been registered previously. It is quite clear that China would never have become the trading powerhouse it is today without the presence of foreign invested enterprises.

In terms of the contribution of FIE trade to GDP, it is net exports (exports minus imports) that adds to or subtracts from GDP. Thus the trade performance of FIEs in the early to mid-1990s actually made a negative contribution to China's GDP. Of course, this was a temporary phenomenon. As FIEs ramped up production in China, the net export contribution turned around and by 2007 FIE net exports exceeded USD 100,000 million per year and by 2013 exceeded USD 169,000 million per year. As a portion of GDP, the FIE net export contribution peaked at 3.9 percent of GDP in 2007 before falling below 2 percent by 2011.

Foreign invested enterprises (FIEs) have had a major role in China's emergence as a trading nation. One of China's goals in opening to foreign investors was to ramp up its exports and net exports. Many investments, particularly in the early days of China's opening, were approved under the condition that a certain portion of the output had to be exported. In addition, many FIEs engaged in export processing. Export processing is a mode of production in which an enterprise (usually a foreign invested enterprise) is allowed to import inputs and capital goods duty free as long as the production is subsequently exported. Export processing accounted for at least 40 percent (and as much as 55 percent) of China's total exports in the 1990 to 2012 period.

As mentioned above, even though FIEs have been instrumental in China's rise as a trading (and in particular export) powerhouse, FIE sales in the China domestic market have exceeded FIE exports from China in every year from 1995 to 2013 (the latest year for which data was available at the time of writing). Thus, while the typical stereotype outside of China is the foreign enterprise that produces in China for export, the reality is that FIEs have had substantially greater domestic sales in China than exports since at least the mid-1990s. By 2013, FIE sales in the China domestic market were equal to 2.73 times their exports from China. While export-oriented production was the purpose of many of the initial investments into China, over time, the primary purpose of FDI into China has been to sell into the Chinese market rather than to use China as a base for exports.

The figures in this section are consistent with a China that opened to foreign investors in part to ramp up exports and net exports to help China's economy develop, and that provided access to the China domestic market for foreign companies in return for the trade and other benefits that foreign invested enterprises have brought to the country.

Introduction to economic impact analysis

While the comparisons of FDI and FIEs to total investment, portion of individual industries, and trade are interesting, they do not nearly tell the complete story of the impact of FDI and FIEs on China's economy. Here we will use the tools of economic impact analysis to provide a more complete picture of this impact.

Economic impact analyses of investments tend to focus on three or four types of impacts. **Direct** impacts are generated by the construction of facilities and the daily operations of the invested enterprises. **Indirect** impacts are generated by the supply chain for the 'direct' activities and the direct industry's suppliers. **Induced** impacts are generated from the spending of the employees of the enterprises involved in the direct and indirect activities. Some analyses add a fourth category, **Catalytic** impacts, which are impacts on downstream industries and other spillovers into the local economy. We note that relatively few studies cover catalytic impacts due to the substantial amounts of data required.

In a standard economic impact analysis, there are three main variables estimated. **Output** represents the value of the goods or services produced, equivalent to the investment spending for a capital investment or the revenue or sales from operations subsequent to the investment. **Value Added** represents the sum of worker compensation, taxes on production, fixed asset depreciation, and operating surplus (this is equivalent to the GDP contribution). **Employment** represents the number of jobs generated by the investments.

Due to data limitations, the analysis in this chapter will focus on the direct, indirect, and induced impacts of FDI and of FIEs in China. This means the impact of the foreign investments and the subsequent operations of the FIEs, their upstream domestic supply chains, and the consumer spending of the employees in the FIEs and their upstream domestic supply chains. Downstream and any other spillover impacts of FIEs, such as impacts on increasing competition, forcing domestic firms to be more productive, opening new markets, technology transfer, transfer of management expertise, etc. are not taken into account in the analysis. Thus the estimates in this chapter will significantly underestimate the total impact of FDI and FIEs on China's economy.

There are two main methods for carrying out economic impact analyses. One uses multiplier models based on input–output tables (tables that describe the inputs required for a unit of output in an industry) and the other uses general equilibrium models based on detailed macroeconomic models of the economies in question. Multiplier models have the advantage of simplicity and availability, as far more economies have publicly available input–output tables than publicly available detailed macroeconomic models. The disadvantage of multiplier models is that they are most useful for marginal analysis, i.e. for investments that are not too large compared to the economy in question.

General equilibrium models have the advantage that they take into account the potential for new investments to bid up prices of labour and other resources and take into account shifts in resources from one part of the economy to another. The disadvantage of general equilibrium models is the lack of availability of models or sufficient data to generate the models in many cases. Given model and data availability, we have used multiplier models in the following analysis. The underlying assumption is that foreign investment has been incremental to China's economy. That is, foreign investment supplemented domestic investment, or if it displaced domestic investment in a particular sector or location that the capital and resources displaced were applied in other parts of China's economy. This seems reasonable given the limited portion of FDI in total investment in China.

To use the multiplier models, we first compile data for the cash flows associated with FDI and the operations of the FIEs, and then apply the relevant multipliers to estimate the direct, indirect, and induced output, value added, and employment associated with the cash flows.

Economic impact of FDI and FIEs in China

We estimate the impact of FDI and FIEs on China's economy in two stages. The first stage involves estimating the impact of the foreign investment itself, including injected capital, construction costs, and other start-up costs. The second stage involves estimating the impact of the subsequent operations and sales of the foreign invested enterprises.

Economic impact of the capital investment associated with FDI

Table 3.4 shows the economic impact of the investment phase associated with foreign direct investment in China over time. The investments generate economic impacts within the Chinese economy mainly through the construction of production facilities such as factories and office blocks; the purchase of machinery and equipment; and the various services required to setup a new business such as business management, law, accounting, human resources, and government services among others. In the absence of specific data on individual investments, a reasonable working approximation would be to assume that one-third of the investment value would flow through the 'building industry', that a third would be spent on the 'machinery and equipment manufacturing' industry, and one-third would flow through the 'business services' industry. We further assume that half of the machinery and equipment used by FIEs is imported and one-half is purchased from Chinese sources.

The Chinese Government publishes sets of input–output (I–O) tables from which economic impact multipliers can be estimated. Input–output tables that divide China's economy into approximately 41 sectors are available for 1990, 1992, 1995, 1997, 2000, 2002, 2005, 2007, and 2010. For the years 1997, 2002, and 2007, expanded tables covering 135 sectors are available. Multipliers for the various industries were generated

Table 3.4 Economic impact of foreign direct investment (investment stage) in China

	1995–2000	2001–2005	2006–2010	2011–2013	Cumulative 1995–2013	2013
Output (USD bn)						
Direct	209	238	394	302	1,144	98
Indirect	299	365	716	559	1,938	181
Induced	76	84	180	159	500	51
Total Output	584	687	1,291	1,020	3,582	331
Value Added (USD bn)						
Direct	82	72	114	92	360	30
Indirect	102	121	210	160	594	52
Induced	32	35	68	59	195	19
Total Value Added	216	228	392	312	1,148	101
Employment (persons)						
Direct	7,260,658	3,776,401	2,900,717	2,605,375		2,223,114
Indirect	9,064,561	6,871,610	4,672,893	3,721,636		3,205,120
Induced	4,510,134	2,857,926	2,356,371	1,959,059		1,680,941
Total Employment	20,835,353	13,505,937	9,929,982	8,286,070		7,109,175

Note: The output and value added estimates are cumulative over the relevant period. The employment estimates are the averages over the relevant periods, except for 2013.

Source: Enright, Scott & Associates.

from these input–output tables as described in the Appendix to this chapter. Multipliers for intervening years were estimated through interpolation. Since earlier I–O tables do not separate out exports and imports, for 1995 and 1996 we have used the multipliers generated for 1997. For years later than the most recent input–output tables, output and value added multipliers were set to the value estimated from the latest available input–output tables, while employment multipliers were adjusted to take wage inflation into account.

Using the corresponding multipliers for the relevant industries, we estimated the total (direct + indirect + induced) cumulative impact of the capital investment associated with FDI from 1995 to 2013 to be USD 3,582 billion in output and USD 1,148 billion in value added. The cumulative output and value added for different periods is also included, as are annual average employment estimates for each period. We note that the average employment estimates go down over time even as the investment value goes up. This is due to changes in the structure of employment in the construction and related sectors whereby these sectors became much less labour-intensive in China over time. We note that the results for 2013 alone were USD 331 billion in output, USD 101 billion in value added, and 7,109,175 in employment. The value added estimate was equivalent to 1.1 percent of China's GDP and the employment estimate was equivalent to 0.9 percent of China's total employment in 2013, indicating a small, but significant impact.

Economic impact of the operations of industrial FIEs

A range of statistics (assets, revenue, profit, value added, and employment) for FIE operations in China is available for industries in the mining, manufacturing, and utility sectors in China (no such statistics have been published on the service sectors). The industries and the cumulative revenues and value added from FIE operations in the industries are shown in Table 3.5. The Computers, Communication, and Other Electronic Equipment industry has had by far the largest cumulative revenues by FIEs in China from 1995 to 2013, followed by Transport Equipment industry (mostly automobiles), Electrical Machinery and Apparatus, and Raw Chemical Materials and Chemical Products industries, all of which had cumulative FIE revenues in excess of RMB 10,000 billion. The cumulative value added by FIEs across industries shows a basically similar pattern. We note that these industries received approximately 53 percent of the inward FDI in China in the years 1997 to 2014.

Table 3.5 Direct revenue and value added of FIEs in the industries for economic impact analysis

Industry	Cumulative FIE 1995–2013 (RMB bn)	
	Revenue	Direct Value Added
Manufacture of Computers, Communication, and Other Electronic Equipment	41,174	7,885
Manufacture of Transport Equipment	19,370	5,259
Manufacture of Electrical Machinery and Apparatus	11,640	2,956
Manufacture of Raw Chemical Materials and Chemical Products	10,845	3,141
Processing of Food from Agricultural Products	7,397	1,819
Manufacture of General Purpose Machinery	6,943	1,898
Smelting and Pressing of Ferrous Metals	5,899	1,324
Manufacture of Textile	5,613	1,523
Manufacture of Metal Products	4,942	1,260
Manufacture of Textile, Wearing Apparel, and Accessories	4,793	1,495

Industry	Cumulative FIE 1995–2013 (RMB bn)	
	Revenue	Direct Value Added
Manufacture of Special Purpose Machinery	4,199	1,214
Manufacture of Plastics Products	4,101	1,111
Manufacture of Non-metallic Mineral Products	4,002	1,285
Manufacture of Foods	3,580	1,103
Manufacture of Leather, Fur, Feather, and Related Products and Footwear	3,545	1,032
Smelting and Pressing of Non-ferrous Metals	3,378	787
Processing of Petroleum, Coking, and Processing of Nuclear Fuel	3,193	590
Production and Supply of Electric Power and Heat Power	3,044	1,260
Manufacture of Measuring Instruments and Machinery	2,881	700
Manufacture of Liquor, Beverages, and Refined Tea	2,834	1,001
Manufacture of Paper and Paper Products	2,831	762
Manufacture of Medicines	2,705	1,119
Manufacture of Rubber Products	2,673	753
Manufacture of Articles for Culture, Education, Arts and Crafts, Sport and Entertainment Activities	2,044	550
Manufacture of Chemical Fibers	1,505	330
Other Manufacture	1,499	447
Manufacture of Furniture	1,311	335
Printing and Reproduction of Recording Media	886	301
Processing of Timber, Manufacture of Wood, Bamboo, Rattan, Palm, and Straw Products	855	242
Production and Supply of Gas	776	188
Mining and Washing of Coal	671	279
Extraction of Petroleum and Natural Gas	613	942
Utilization of Waste Resources	287	51
Production and Supply of Water	156	82

(Continued)

Table 3.5 (Continued)

Industry	Cumulative FIE 1995–2013 (RMB bn)	
	Revenue	*Direct Value Added*
Mining and Processing of Non-ferrous Metal Ores	132	84
Mining and Processing of Ferrous Metal Ores	119	53
Mining and Processing of Non-metal Ores	115	44
Support Activities for Mining	25.9	10.7
Manufacture of Tobacco	15.5	7.3
Mining of Other Ores	0.58	0.16
Timber and Bamboo Harvesting	0.03	0.01

Note: Data for revenue and value added was missing for 1998 and for value added was missing from 2008 to 2013. These were estimated from existing data and ratios.

Source: *China Statistical Yearbook* (various years).

Direct output, value added, and employment were taken from these figures with data gaps filled through interpolation. Since data for the service sectors was not available the following economic impact estimates are only for the mining, manufacturing, and utility sectors. Industry-specific economic multipliers were generated from China's input–output tables following the method given in the Appendix with three amendments. The first was to use input–output table industry categories that are the closest match to the FIE data industry categories if there was not an exact match. The second was to adjust for the greater propensity of FIEs to use imported inputs in their production process. The third was to remove estimates of the inputs sourced from other FIE suppliers. Adjusting for the propensity to import among FIEs is important because imported inputs will result in a lower impact on China's economy than domestically sourced inputs. Adjusting for inputs sourced from FIE suppliers eliminates double counting of FIE impacts in the supply chains. The latter two adjustments are described in the Appendix to this chapter.

Table 3.6 shows the total economic impact of the operations of the FIEs in the Mining, Manufacturing, and Utilities sectors in China based on the annual revenues of the enterprises. For the period 1995 to 2013, the cumulative economic impact was USD 43,345 billion in total output and USD 12,407 billion in total value added. In 2013, FIEs in these sectors had a combined total (direct + indirect + induced) impact on China's economy of USD 6,967 billion in total output, USD 1,957 billion in value added, and 125,333,060 persons in employment. The value added estimate is equivalent to 21 percent of China's GDP and the employment estimate to 16 percent of China's total employment from all sources in 2013. Again, we note that these impacts are just for the Mining, Manufacturing, and Utilities industries for which the sales data

Table 3.6 Total economic impact of the operations of FIEs in Mining, Manufacturing, and Utilities Sectors in China

	1995–2000	2001–2005	2006–2010	2011–2013	Cumulative	2013
Output (USD bn)						
Direct	1,085	2,875	9,988	10,905	24,853	3,971
Indirect	618	1,658	5,762	6,418	14,456	2,330
Induced	145	376	1,688	1,828	4,037	666
Total Output	1,848	4,909	17,438	19,150	43,345	6,967
Value Added (USD bn)						
Direct	290	763	2,604	2,854	6,510	1,039
Indirect	254	546	1,514	1,636	3,950	593
Induced	70	183	801	892	1,946	325
Total Value Added	615	1,492	4,919	5,381	12,407	1,957
Employment (ave. man-years)						
Direct	5,119,125	12,513,063	24,293,500	27,990,328		30,268,629
Indirect	28,778,356	42,046,056	67,308,325	72,957,797		68,020,954
Induced	9,785,798	15,031,953	28,069,840	29,057,046		27,043,476
Total Employment	43,683,279	69,591,072	119,671,665	130,005,171		125,333,060

Note: The output and value added estimates are cumulative over the relevant period. The employment estimates are the average man-years over the relevant periods, except for 2013.

Source: Enright, Scott & Associates.

for FIEs is available. The impacts do not include the impact of foreign investment in the service sector.

Table 3.7 shows economic impact from operations of FIEs in Manufacturing, Mining, and Utilities on an industry-by-industry basis. The leading sectors in terms of value added impact have been Computers, Communication, and Other Electronic Equipment; Transport Equipment; Food from Agricultural Products; Raw Chemical Materials and Chemical Products; and Electrical Machinery and Apparatus. These have been the leaders in cumulative value added impact for the 1995 to 2013 period as well as the leaders in 2013, the latest year for which we are able to carry out the estimates. These five industries accounted for USD 5,747 billion in cumulative value added impact (46.3 percent of the cumulative value added impact of industrial FIEs) over the period and USD 939 billion in value added impact (47.9 percent of the value added impact of industrial FIEs) in 2013 alone, showing the large investments of FIEs and the high multipliers in these industries.

The leading sectors in terms of employment impact have been Food from Agricultural Products; Computers, Communication, and Other Electronic Equipment; Textile; Foods; and Transport Equipment. These five sectors accounted for 46.8 percent of the cumulative employment impact of industrial FIEs for the 1995 to 2013 period, and 49.5 percent of the impact for the year 2013. The differences in the value added and

Table 3.7 Total economic impact of the operations of FIEs, Mining, Manufacturing, and Utilities Sectors, by industry, cumulative 1995 to 2013 and single year 2013

Industrial Sectors	Cumulative 1995–2013					2013				
	Output (USD bil)	Value Added (USD bil)	% of Value Added	Employment (FTEs, job-years)	% of Emp	Output (USD bil)	Value Added (USD bil)	% of Value Added	Employment	% of Emp
Manufacture of Computers, Communication, and Other Electronic Equipment	8,900.8	2,096.7	16.9	185,915,564	11.6	1,398.8	329.0	16.8	17,958,376	14.3
Manufacture of Transport Equipment	4,560.3	1,170.1	9.4	84,455,539	5.3	806.3	202.1	10.3	8,288,974	6.6
Processing of Food from Agricultural Products	2,564.1	961.9	7.8	283,936,471	17.8	427.4	159.3	8.1	22,518,401	18.0
Manufacture of Raw Chemical Materials and Chemical Products	2,761.6	769.2	6.2	66,483,232	4.2	488.3	132.5	6.8	5,154,185	4.1
Manufacture of Electrical Machinery and Apparatus	3,101.6	749.5	6.0	78,849,976	4.9	491.8	115.6	5.9	6,657,920	5.3
Manufacture of General Purpose Machinery	1,780.6	508.2	4.1	43,388,338	2.7	304.3	84.5	4.3	3,387,662	2.7

Manufacture of Textile	1,607.3	497.1	4.0	108,146,278	6.8	204.5	62.9	3.2	6,271,133	5.0
Smelting and Pressing of Ferrous Metals	1,598.7	480.5	3.9	33,825,948	2.1	243.1	72.0	3.7	2,151,226	1.7
Manufacture of Textile Wearing Apparel and Accessories	1,245.6	380.7	3.1	75,405,675	4.7	186.3	55.1	2.8	5,066,672	4.0
Manufacture of Metal Products	1,384.8	361.4	2.9	40,154,260	2.5	203.7	51.3	2.6	2,829,112	2.3
Manufacture of Foods	1,055.6	359.8	2.9	86,123,290	5.4	180.3	60.2	3.1	6,978,452	5.6
Manufacture of Non-metallic Mineral Products	1,161.5	358.9	2.9	36,767,791	2.3	182.9	53.8	2.7	2,723,043	2.2
Manufacture of Special Purpose Machinery	1,086.9	312.0	2.5	26,644,698	1.7	180.1	50.8	2.6	2,138,356	1.7
Production and Supply of Electric Power and Heat Power	844.4	293.2	2.4	26,027,667	1.6	101.1	32.4	1.7	1,130,768	0.9
Manufacture of Liquor, Beverages, and Refined Tea	762.0	289.6	2.3	54,652,176	3.4	118.7	44.4	2.3	3,714,390	3.0
Manufacture of Medicines	747.8	275.0	2.2	39,797,838	2.5	139.9	50.6	2.6	3,907,700	3.1

(Continued)

Table 3.7 (Continued)

Industrial Sectors	Cumulative 1995–2013					2013				
	Output (USD bil)	Value Added (USD bil)	% of Value Added	Employment (FTEs, job-years)	% of Emp	Output (USD bil)	Value Added (USD bil)	% of Value Added	Employment	% of Emp
Manufacture of Leather, Fur, Feather, and Related Products and Footwear	886.0	263.3	2.1	73,530,705	4.6	126.7	37.1	1.9	4,645,750	3.7
Smelting and Pressing of Non-ferrous Metals	909.5	243.5	2.0	18,860,230	1.2	151.2	39.9	2.0	1,308,423	1.0
Manufacture of Plastics Products	891.2	224.5	1.8	29,066,493	1.8	121.1	29.2	1.5	1,844,885	1.5
Manufacture of Paper and Paper Products	683.4	213.7	1.7	29,763,434	1.9	96.2	29.1	1.5	1,788,843	1.4
Processing of Petroleum, Coking, and Processing of Nuclear Fuel	725.8	206.9	1.7	11,794,285	0.7	108.7	29.9	1.5	792,628	0.6
Manufacture of Rubber Products	673.8	189.5	1.5	28,567,474	1.8	188.3	50.6	2.6	3,536,374	2.8
Manufacture of Articles for Culture, Education, Arts and Crafts, Sport and Entertainment Activities	556.4	178.9	1.4	35,938,513	2.2	125.8	40.4	2.1	4,481,445	3.6

Manufacture of Measuring Instruments and Machinery	639.4	171.9	1.4	19,262,147	1.2	61.2	16.4	0.8	935,304	0.7
Extraction of Petroleum and Natural Gas	135.9	154.9	1.2	2,274,754	0.1	17.4	20.6	1.1	152,522	0.1
Manufacture of Furniture	348.7	110.0	0.9	16,689,277	1.0	51.2	16.0	0.8	1,192,631	1.0
Other Manufacture	365.7	107.9	0.9	18,337,155	1.1	14.6	4.1	0.2	217,747	0.2
Mining and Washing of Coal	196.3	86.2	0.7	3,893,198	0.2	56.4	24.8	1.3	801,439	0.6
Manufacture of Chemical Fibers	346.7	85.5	0.7	8,183,102	0.5	52.6	12.5	0.6	482,081	0.4
Processing of Timber, Manufacture of Wood, Bamboo, Rattan, Palm, and Straw Products	229.3	74.5	0.6	14,805,938	0.9	31.8	10.1	0.5	860,065	0.7
Printing and Reproduction of Recording Media	198.6	69.9	0.6	8,317,968	0.5	28.5	9.5	0.5	512,460	0.4
Production and Supply of Gas	193.8	59.1	0.5	4,115,977	0.3	41.8	12.6	0.6	474,639	0.4
Utilization of Waste Resources	48.3	37.8	0.3	290,955	0.02	9.6	7.5	0.4	39,317	0.03
Production and Supply of Water	43.9	18.8	0.2	1,161,969	0.07	7.2	3.1	0.2	119,595	0.10

(Continued)

Table 3.7 (Continued)

Industrial Sectors	Cumulative 1995–2013					2013					
	Output (USD bil)	Value Added (USD bil)	% of Value Added	Employment (FTEs, job-years)	% of Emp	Output (USD bil)	Value Added (USD bil)	% of Value Added	Employment	% of Emp
Mining and Processing of Non-ferrous Metal Ores	35.2	18.7	0.2	846,760	0.05	4.0	2.2	0.11	51,560	0.04
Mining and Processing of Ferrous Metal Ores	32.4	11.5	0.09	562,077	0.04	7.9	2.8	0.14	85,793	0.07
Mining and Processing of Non-metal Ores	30.4	11.2	0.09	1,043,103	0.07	3.6	1.3	0.07	62,274	0.05
Support Activities for Mining	7.8	2.7	0.02	214,695	0.01	4.0	1.4	0.07	69,451	0.06
Manufacture of Tobacco	2.9	1.8	0.01	327,829	0.02	0.0	0.0	0.00	1,461	0.00
Mining of Other Ores	0.1	0.0	0.00	4,776	0.00	–	–	–	–	–
Timber and Bamboo Harvesting	0.007	0.004	0.00	1,326	0.00	–	–	–	–	–

Source: Enright, Scott & Associates.

employment rankings are due to the difference in labour intensities across the relevant sectors and their supply chains.

Although not shown in the tables,[3] the mix of FIE value added and total employment impact among the industrial sectors has changed over time. The FIE-related value added in the Computers, Communication, and Other Electronic Equipment industry went from 10 percent of all industrial FIE-related value added in 1995 to 17 percent in 2013. The figure for Transport Equipment went from 7 percent in 1995 to 10 percent in 2013. That for Textiles went from 8 percent in 1995 to 3 percent in 2013 and that for Textile Wearing Apparel and Accessories went from 7 percent 1995 to 3 percent in 2013. The employment impact also shifted, with FIE-related employment in Computers, Communication, and Other Electronic Equipment going from 6 percent of all industrial FIE-related employment in 1995 to 14 percent in 2013. The figure for Transport Equipment went from 4 percent in 1995 to 7 percent in 2013. That for Textiles went from 10 percent in 1995 to 5 percent in 2013 and that for Wearing Apparel and Accessories went from 6 percent in 1995 to 4 percent in 2013. The results show a dynamic pattern, with foreign invested enterprises gradually shifting to higher value added activities in the industrial sector, consistent with China's goals.

Estimates of the impact of the operations of service sector FIEs

As indicated above, the data is not available to do a similar analysis of the impact of service sector FIEs directly. However, if we make some assumptions about the nature of FIEs in the service sector in China, it is possible to come up with coarse estimates that can be used to start discussions about the potential impact of FDI and FIEs across the entire Chinese economy.

In order to make the service sector value added impact estimates, we assume that the ratio of the value added (and employment) impacts of FIE investment in the service sector versus that in the industrial sector is similar to the ratio of value added (and employment) per unit of investment in China's service sector versus that in the industrial sector. With this assumption, estimates of China's GDP and capital stock in the industrial and service sectors,[4] data on cumulative FDI in the industrial and service sectors in China, and our previous estimates of the value added and employment impacts from operations of FIEs in the industrial sectors, we are able to develop a rough estimate of the annual value added and employment impact of the operations of FIEs in China's service sector.

From 1995 to 2013, we estimate that the cumulative impact of the operations of service sector FIEs in China was USD 4,907 billion in value added and 809,730,688 in job-years (for an average of 42,617,405 employees per year). The impacts have ranged from 3 percent to 10 percent of China's GDP and from 3 to 10 percent of China's total employment. In 2013, the most recent year available, we estimate that the impact of the operations of FIEs accounted for USD 931 billion in value added (10 percent of China's GDP) and 77,573,984 in employment (10 percent of China's employment).

Combined impact of inward FDI and the operations of FIEs

Table 3.8 shows the combined value added and employment impact of the investment phase associated with all foreign direct investment in China and the operations of FIEs in China from 1995 to 2013. The estimates for 2013 alone are USD 2,989 billion in value added and 210,016,218 in employment. The table shows that the estimated impacts have accounted for between 16 percent and 34 percent of China's GDP and 11 percent to 29 percent of China's employment each year from 1995 to 2013. What is more, these impacts have not been diminishing significantly, as the estimates for 2013 place the impact of the FDI and FIEs at 33 percent of GDP and 27 percent of employment.

These results show that FDI and FIEs have been, and continue to be, enormously important to China's economy. The results are all the more impressive when we recognize that they do not include any catalytic benefits such as spillovers into the local economy, the impact on productivity in indigenous firms, the impact on technological and managerial capabilities in China, the social contributions by FIEs, or other impacts. The results suggest that China has benefitted tremendously from foreign investment and that these benefits continue to be extremely important today.

Conclusions

The analysis in this chapter shows that foreign direct investment has declined from a peak of low double-digit percentages of China's gross capital formation and fixed asset investment in the mid-1990s to the low single digits by the mid-2010s. FIEs play a much larger role in China's trade, accounting for 45 percent of China's imports and 47 percent of China's exports in 2013. However, these figures give only a partial picture of the impact of FDI and FIEs on China. Using the tools of economic impact analysis, it is possible to estimate the effect of the investments, operations, and supply chains of the foreign invested enterprises.

Economic impact analysis is often used to estimate or project the impact of a major investment on a local economy. Economic impact analysis often uses multipliers generated through the manipulation of input–output tables (tables that capture the relationships between different industries in an economy) to estimate the impact of the investment itself (in terms of construction, equipment, and services required to set up or expand the business) as well as the impact of the subsequent sales from operation of the invested business. The typical approach estimates the impact on the local economy in terms of output, value added (or GDP contribution), and employment by estimating the direct impacts (the impact of the actual investment and operation of the invested entity), the indirect impacts (the positive impact through the supply chain), and the induced impacts (the impacts of the consumer spending of the employees in the direct and indirect industries).

Table 3.8 Combined total economic impact of FDI and FIEs operations and comparison with China national figures

Year	Value Added Impact (USD billion)					Employment Impact (persons)				
	Annual Investment	Secondary Industry	Tertiary Industry	Total	% China GDP	Annual Investment	Secondary Industry	Tertiary Industry	Total	% China Total Employment
1995	33	70	21	124	17	20,955,392	35,003,000	16,488,198	72,446,590	11
1996	36	75	22	134	16	23,199,955	37,145,472	17,620,337	77,965,764	11
1997	40	90	27	157	16	25,089,495	43,999,735	20,590,080	89,679,310	13
1998	39	106	36	181	18	22,558,111	46,154,073	22,577,522	91,289,706	13
1999	34	122	43	199	18	17,687,248	47,499,028	23,524,449	88,710,725	12
2000	34	152	52	238	20	15,521,918	52,298,365	26,006,041	93,826,324	13
2001	39	175	61	274	21	15,175,087	53,520,566	25,638,860	94,334,514	13
2002	43	209	72	324	22	14,043,252	55,392,383	27,360,607	96,796,242	13
2003	43	278	90	410	25	12,713,903	68,484,648	33,379,751	114,578,302	16
2004	48	353	103	504	26	12,670,158	77,598,904	35,311,031	125,580,093	17
2005	56	476	138	670	30	12,927,285	92,947,943	41,470,297	147,345,526	20
2006	57	608	180	845	31	10,654,172	102,959,937	45,591,095	159,205,205	21
2007	68	799	259	1,126	32	9,507,822	114,770,660	50,902,111	175,180,592	23
2008	89	1,045	360	1,494	33	10,742,880	126,689,548	60,384,262	197,816,690	26
2009	79	1,090	422	1,590	32	8,729,079	121,154,548	61,219,748	191,103,375	25
2010	99	1,377	566	2,042	34	10,015,955	132,783,633	71,012,872	213,812,460	28
2011	106	1,654	718	2,479	34	9,492,409	134,554,419	75,971,728	220,018,557	29
2012	104	1,770	806	2,680	33	8,256,626	130,056,468	77,107,715	215,420,810	28
2013	101	1,957	931	2,989	33	7,109,175	125,333,060	77,573,984	210,016,218	27
Total	1,148	12,406	4,907	18,460		267,049,922	1,598,346,390	809,730,688	2,675,127,003	

Note: China total employment includes both public and private sectors in both urban and rural areas. Employment figures are FTEs in job-years.

Sources: Enright, Scott & Associates; China Statistical Yearbook 2014; World Bank, World Development Indicators.

In this chapter, we report what we believe is a first of its kind economic impact analysis across foreign investment and FIEs in China. The economic impact of the investment phase associated with foreign direct investment in China across all sectors was estimated by assuming that one-third of the investment goes into the domestic construction industry, one-third into the domestic leasing and business service industry, and the remaining one-third into equipment and machinery (half assumed to be bought locally and half imported). Using these assumptions and the corresponding multipliers, we estimated the impact of the investment associated with FDI from 1995 to 2013 as USD 3,582 billion in output and USD 1,148 billion in value added. The employment associated with the foreign direct capital investment was estimated at 7,109,175 persons in 2013. The total impact of the capital investment associated with FDI in 2013 accounted for 1.1 percent of China's GDP and 0.9 percent of China total employment.

Data for foreign invested enterprises in the Mining, Manufacturing, and Utilities sectors and multipliers derived from China's input–output tables were used to estimate the impact of the operations of these FIEs on China's economy from 1995 to 2013. In 2013, FIEs in these sectors had a combined direct, indirect, and induced economic impact on China's economy of USD 6,967 billion in total output, USD 1,957 billion in value added, and 125,333,060 persons in employment. The latter two figures were equivalent to 21 percent of China's GDP and 16 percent of China's total employment from all sources in 2013. For the period 1995 to 2013, the cumulative economic impact was USD 43,345 billion in total output and USD 12,407 billion in total value added. FIE operations in the Manufacture of Computers, Communication, and Other Electronic Equipment and Manufacture of Transport Equipment industries generated the largest impacts.

Rough estimates of the impact of the operations of FIEs in the service sector, which accounted for 47 percent of cumulative FDI over the period, ranged from 3 to 10 percent of both GDP and employment in China. In 2013, the latest year for which estimates could be made, the impacts were USD 931 billion in value added and 77,573,984 in employment, or 10 percent of GDP and 10 percent of employment. The cumulative impact on value added for the 1995 to 2013 period was estimated at USD 4,907 billion.

When we include the direct impacts of the investments and operations, their supply chains, and the consumer spending of their employees, the combined economic impact of the investment phase associated with all foreign direct investment in China and the operations of FIEs in China from 1995 to 2013 was estimated at USD 18,460 billion in value added and 2,675,127,003 in cumulative employment (FTEs in job-years), or an average of 140,796,158 per year over the 19-year period. The figures for 2013 were USD 2,989 billion in value added and 210,016,218 in employment, or 33 percent of China's GDP and 27 percent of its employment in that year.

The results suggest that China has benefitted tremendously from foreign investment and that these benefits will continue to be extremely important well into the future. The results are all the more impressive when we recognize that they do not include any catalytic benefits such as spillovers into the local economy, the impact on productivity in indigenous firms, the impact on technological and managerial capabilities in China, the social contributions by FIEs, or other impacts. These will be the subject of the next chapter.

Appendix: economic impact analysis methodology

Economic impact analysis (EIA) estimates the impact of a new investment on a host economy. The most common impacts that are estimated are the direct, indirect, and induced impacts. For an industry or company, direct impacts are those that come from the expenditures on new facilities and the incremental sales revenues generated by those facilities. Indirect impacts are those that come from the ripple effect on the supply chains associated with the operation of the facilities. Induced impacts are those that come from the consumer expenditures of the people employed in the operation of facilities, and their suppliers. The typical impacts estimated are on output (total sales in the economy), value added (which approximates the contribution to local GDP), and employment.

There are two main ways of doing the economic impact analysis of any major investment. The most common is the 'input–output' or 'multiplier' method. This involves taking the relevant cash flows and multiplying them by multipliers that have either been pre-determined by governments (like in the US or in Japan, for example) or can be calculated from input–output tables. The advantage of this method is its simplicity. The disadvantage is that it is designed for 'marginal analysis' (i.e. for small changes from the status quo) and will tend to overestimate for very large impacts because the method cannot take into account the potential to bid up prices and wages as a result of the investment (general equilibrium or 'diminishing returns' effects). The input requirements are the relevant input cash flows and either pre-determined multipliers or publicly available input–output tables from which multipliers can be calculated.

The second method involves using sophisticated macroeconomic models that allow what economists call 'general equilibrium' effects (the bidding up of prices and wages described above) to be taken into account. The advantage is that the estimates are likely to be better, particularly when the revenue streams and economic impacts are large. The disadvantage is that there are far fewer economies for which the relevant information is available than for the multiplier method. The input requirements are the relevant input cash flows (revenue streams and related inputs just like the multiplier model) and an available sophisticated macroeconomic model. The general equilibrium macroeconomic model approach essentially takes the new revenue streams as perturbations to the existing economy and estimates what new state the economy will settle into after the perturbation. For a large investment with a large impact, this might mean a bidding up of prices and wages in the local economy and a reshuffling of resources from one set of economic activities to another. As a result, macro model estimates are usually lower than simple multiplier model estimates for a given investment. While multipliers can be derived from macro models, they are derived from the results of the analysis rather than as inputs to the analysis.

In the present case, China has input–output tables from which multipliers can be derived, but not a publicly available macro-model from which a macro-model approach could be derived. Thus the simple multiplier approach was used.

Deriving economic multipliers from input–output tables

As indicated, the most common form of economic impact analysis uses multipliers derived from input–output tables to generate the indirect and induced output, value added, and employment estimates from the direct revenue streams. The input–output tables reflect transactions and relationships between industries in an economy. In particular, the most basic form has the shipments of each row industry being consumed by each column industry. Final demand items such as imports, exports, government purchases, and others are outside the core matrix, as are value added items, such as wages, profits, and taxes. The form of the input–output tables is often given as follows, where Z is the cross-industry transaction matrix, final demand represents final demand features in the economy, and value added represents value added elements in the economy.

To obtain the total requirements matrix A (the requirements from input industries for each output industry), Z is divided by the matrix made from the inverses of the diagonal elements of the production vectors X, or:

$$A = ZX^{-1}$$

This in turn can be rearranged to give:

$$Z = AX$$

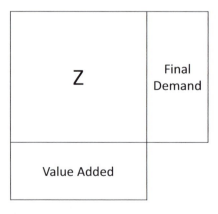

Figure 3.1 Input–output matrix schematic
Source: Enright, Scott & Associates.

So that

$$X = (I - A)^{-1}Y$$

Where X are the production vectors and Y are the final demand vectors. The matrix $(I\text{-}A)^{-1}$ is called the total requirements matrix, because it provides information on the total requirements necessary from the whole range of input industries to produce a unit of output in a production industry. Summing up all the direct requirements for an industry allows for an estimation of the impact that an industry has on other upstream industries, and therefore its economic impact.

Input–output table adjustments

Given the large share of FIEs in China's imports and exports, there is a presumption that FIEs might import more of their inputs than Chinese companies. This would tend to reduce their economic impact on China. In order to adjust for this potential effect, we modified the input–output tables by scaling up the import component by the ratio of (FIE Imports/FIE Revenues) to (Total Imports/Total Revenues) for the economy as a whole, since there is no industry-specific data for FIE imports. The estimated FIE imports for each output industry (column industry z) is given by:

$$Import\ Scale\ Factor = \left(\frac{FIE\ Imports \big/ FIE\ Revenue}{Total\ Imports \big/ Total\ Revenue} \right)$$

$$FIE\ Imports_z = Imports_z \times Import\ Scale\ Factor$$

$Imports_z$ = Total Imports utilized in production of output in industry$_z$
$FIE\ Imports_z$ = Total Imports utilized in production of output in FIE industry$_z$

If FIE imports increase then the amount of domestically sourced inputs for production will naturally have to be less given the same value added and total output.

FIEs source intermediate inputs from both domestic and FIE companies, thus intermediate inputs originating from FIE companies have to be removed to ensure that we do not double count FIE activities. Therefore for each output industry (column Industry z) in the input-output table, intermediate inputs for each input industry (row Industry y) were adjusted as follows:

$$FIE\ I \times I_{z,y} = I \times I_{z,y}\left(1 - PTS \frac{FIE\ Revenue_{Industry\,y}}{Total\ Revenue_{Industry\,y}} \right)$$

$$FIE\,Consumption_{y} = Consumption_{y}\left(1 - PTS\frac{FIE\,Revenue_{Industry\,y}}{Total\,Revenue_{Industry\,y}}\right)$$

PTS = Propensity of an FIE firm to source from other FIEs

$I \times I_{z,y}$ = Industry$_y$ Intermediate input utilized in production of industry$_z$ output

$FIE\,I \times I_{z,y}$ = Estimated domestic only (non FIE) intermediate inputs

$FIE\,Consumption_{y}$ = Estimated domestic only (non FIE) consumption in industry$_y$

Since there is no data on the propensity to source from the China operations of other FIEs, a scale factor similar to the 'import preference' scale factor described above was used.

Notes

1 Supporting work for this chapter was carried out by David Sanderson and Ella Dong of Enright, Scott & Associates.
2 'Industrial Enterprises' (above scale) includes industrial enterprises of all types of ownership with revenue over RMB 20 million in 2013.
3 Further information may be found in the project reports available from the Hinrich Foundation or Enright, Scott & Associates.
4 Yanrui Wu, private communication.

References

OECD, 2003, *OECD Investment Policy Review: China*, Paris, OECD.
World Bank, 2015, *World Development Indicators 2015*, Washington, DC, World Bank.
World Trade Organization, 2015, *International Trade Statistics 2015*, Geneva, WTO.

Catalytic impacts and spillovers from FIEs[1]

Introduction

Foreign firms and foreign investment have made a wide range of contributions to China and its development. Although the economic impact analysis of the previous chapter concludes that the investments, operations, and supply chains of foreign invested enterprises may account for as much as a third of China's economy, this is only part of the story. Foreign companies have had numerous additional catalytic impacts and spillovers into China's economy. They have developed supply and distribution chains that sell broadly within China and internationally. They have brought world-class R&D and technology development to China, resulting in numerous spillovers. They have brought modern management education and training to China, which has improved management capabilities right across the board. They have brought regional and global management activities to China, which has enhanced management development in China and has made it easier for Chinese companies to access international networks. They have worked to improve the financial sector in China, among others.

Foreign invested enterprises (FIEs) have worked to improve the environment and to enhance sustainability in China. They have contributed through CSR initiatives and have provided examples for Chinese firms in terms of CSR and CSR reporting. They have also provided advice to Chinese policy makers and have advocated for China in international trade and economic relations. However, there are also examples of negative impacts, such as foreign companies or their suppliers engaging in inappropriate worker relations, foreign companies engaging in corrupt practices, and foreign companies engaging in anti-competitive behaviour.

This chapter provides examples of these additional impacts. While it is not possible to cover the full range of the impacts of foreign firms in China, the chapter shows that there is a wide range of catalytic impacts and spillovers that goes well beyond the investment and employment of the individual firms, or the impacts that can be estimated or quantified.

Modernizing industries and companies in China

After decades of a command economy cut off from international markets, international technology and know-how, and international competition, China's economy had become moribund and unproductive. It was hoped that the introduction of foreign investment and foreign companies would help China regain lost ground. One Chinese report cited a 1985 survey of major Chinese companies that showed that only 13 percent had production equipment that even came close to international levels and that by 1991 about 40 percent of the technologies introduced by foreign companies were obviously much more advanced than what had been available in China previously, another 7 percent filled domestic gaps, and that many of the products produced by foreign companies in China had become important exports, import substitutes, and foreign exchange earners (Deng, 1991).

The modernization started in traditional industries, such as garments, footwear, toys, and plastic products. Even though these sectors had been represented in China, it was Hong Kong and Taiwanese companies that made them into export successes. The Hong Kong and Taiwan firms were familiar with modern technologies, international quality standards, market demands, and managing production and logistics to serve international buyers. Their reputations and reliability also meant that many buyers preferred to purchase from Hong Kong and Taiwan companies rather than direct from Chinese suppliers (Liu, 2009a). Thus it was the presence of the Hong Kong and Taiwanese firms that allowed China to become a major exporter in traditional industries. How did a China cut off from world markets for so long understand the technologies, supply chains, logistics, international tastes, and global marketing necessary to become an export powerhouse within a few years of its economic opening? The answer is that 'China' did not; those functions were carried out by foreign invested enterprises.

The auto industry has been a major target of China's upgrading efforts. Before the opening, the focus of China's vehicle industry had been trucks, and the companies used systems and designs based on Soviet models from decades earlier. In 1984, Premier Zhao Ziyang announced that China wanted to produce autos up to world standards by 1990, and in 1986, the auto sector was designated as a 'pillar' industry for China. Foreign companies were allowed to enter, but only in joint ventures with Chinese partners and only if they met increasing local content requirements. Access to the local market was granted in return for modernizing the auto sector (Thun, 2006). As we have seen, the quantifiable impact of foreign invested enterprises in the transport equipment sector in China has been huge, but the impact has gone much further.

According to the 1991 report:

> In the course of making Santana sedans a domestic product, the Dazhong Automobile Company has not only raised the level of Shanghai's auto industry by 30 years but also given a great impetus to the technological transformation and renovation of many supporting and pertinent enterprises such as machine building, electrical, chemical, metallurgical, and meter and instrument enterprises. Its technological effect has been spread to 126 enterprises and units across the country.
>
> (Deng, 1991, p. 64)

By 2015, China was the world's largest auto producer, with the majority of the vehicles produced by Sino-foreign joint ventures. The auto sector did become a pillar industry for China and an especially important industry for several of the cities that hosted Sino-foreign joint venture auto companies. According to analysts, although Chinese companies had made huge strides over the years, the industry in China was still reliant on foreign companies, with the Chinese companies themselves not competitive enough to succeed in world markets on their own (Kassab, 2015). Thus the ongoing presence of the foreign auto companies is crucial to keep China's industry at the cutting edge.

There are numerous other examples. Thailand's CP Group, one of the first foreign companies to enter China after the onset of the economic reforms, has been credited with helping to bring modern agribusiness to China. The CP Group's large investments in poultry in China helped change the country's diet, as per capita consumption of poultry in China doubled in a decade after its entry (St James Press, 2004). When US soft drink companies re-entered China in the 1980s, they found themselves competing against local firms that were using the same equipment that they had left behind more than 30 years earlier. Coca-Cola was particularly important in modernizing the industry. In 1994, the Chinese Government adopted Coke's factory and production standards for the entire industry (Liu, 2009a). SGS, the Swiss inspection company, was allowed to enter China in 1991 in a joint venture that broke the prior state monopoly on inspection services in an effort to improve the quality of goods produced in the country (author's interviews). By 2015, SGS had 40 offices and laboratories in China. In 1994, Kodak was allowed to take over three loss-making Chinese state enterprises in an effort to modernize the photographic film industry. In 1999, the Chinese Government gave Kodak an award as a 'successful model of a foreign investment and restructuring of an SOE' (Zinzius, 2004, p. 142). By 2015, more than 300 foreign retailers had set up in China (Wang, 2009), bringing modern retail formats, merchandizing, advertising, and sourcing to the nation. Many practices were adopted by Chinese retailers, with the foreign presence transforming the sector in China through example, competition, as well as the foreign company operations. In each case, the presence of foreign companies helped modernize complete sectors of China's economy.

Developing suppliers and distributors in China

One of the important contributions that foreign companies have made in China is the development of upstream and downstream capabilities. In many instances, leading multinational firms have made large investments in developing supplier and distribution networks in China that have helped build the overall economy and spur the development of Chinese companies. In many cases, suppliers have been introduced to international standards by the foreign companies, have been taken into their international supply chains, and have learned to sell internationally beyond the multinationals' networks. The creation of modern distribution systems in China has not only helped develop Chinese firms, it has also dramatically improved the quality of life for Chinese residents.

Coca-Cola essentially created an entire partner, supplier, and distribution base in China. When Coke re-entered China in the 1980s, all of these were lacking. Coca-Cola began to build a national base of local bottler partners to whom it transferred its world-class expertise in all aspects of the bottling operations. Since the company could not find glass bottles of acceptable standard from Chinese suppliers, it selected five of the better performing, state-owned Chinese glass factories and gave them free advice on how to improve bottle quality. Coca-Cola made similar efforts to develop Chinese suppliers for plastic bottles, aluminium cans, sugar, and packaging equipment. Many Chinese suppliers were able to expand geographically, following Coca-Cola's own expansion across China, and benefitted from the reputation of being a Coca-Cola supplier, and in several cases started exporting. A study carried out by researchers at Peking University and in the United States estimated that by 1998, Coca-Cola had created around 14,000 jobs in China directly, and another 350,000 through its bottling system and supply network (Peking University et al., 2000). The same study concluded that Coca-Cola transmitted 'competitive business practices' to 'a new generation of Chinese entrepreneurs' across its nationwide distribution network, supporting another 50,000 jobs in wholesale and retail. Beneficiaries included entrepreneurial distribution partners selling to retailers and small wholesalers, as well as independent small and large wholesalers.

Foreign auto companies also made major investments to improve supplier networks in China. When companies like Volkswagen, General Motors, Nissan, and others entered China, they found local components and parts of poor quality. VW, for one, set up engine, powertrain, transmission, and automotive seating operations in China, helping to drive the region's auto components cluster in the process (Vahland, 2010). Nissan's strategy of common global platforms, and the fact that its Huadu, Guangdong, facility is its largest manufacturing base in the world has resulted in global scale economies for its chosen Chinese suppliers (Guangzhou Government, 2013). Companies like VW, GM, Nissan, and others also encouraged foreign parts and component suppliers to invest in China, in cases of foreign investors encouraging others to invest in the country. They also brought international quality standards and rigorous testing and qualification practices to China, working with Chinese suppliers to bring them into global supply chains, forcing them to meet international quality standards, and helping Chinese suppliers build the capabilities to export themselves (Nissan, 2015; Thun, 2006, p. 105; van Winden et al., 2006, pp. 104–5).

The foreign auto companies also brought their expertise in auto distribution and service to China. VW provides continuous support to set up new dealers and to improve sales performance, marketing plans, and customer satisfaction across a dealer network approaching 3,000 members (Volkswagen, 2015). VW Finance China, which helped pioneer automotive financial services in China, engages in automotive finance, leasing, branded insurance, and after-sales services, and operates an internal communication platform for its cooperating dealers, an important contribution to the maturation of this sector (Volkswagen, 2013). Nissan has instituted an array of dealer training measures to upgrade dealer operations, dealership design standards, risk management, and service quality, by introducing case sharing, experience exchange, and after-sales technical and nontechnical training (Nissan, 2015). SAIC General Motors Sales Co. has set up a network of state-of-the-art dealerships across China that will be further expanded in China's Central and Western regions. In auto sales finance, GMAC-SAIC Automotive Finance was the first financing company to operate in China when it opened in August 2004. By year-end 2013, it had more than 1.2 million customers spread over 7,000 dealers in more than 300 Chinese cities (General Motors, 2015).

It is not just foreign manufacturing companies that have set up supply networks in China. Trading companies and retailers have done so as well. Li & Fung, which operates one of the world's largest consumer product and distribution platforms, requires its suppliers of light manufactures to meet stringent cost, quality, and reliability standards. In the 1980s and 1990s, it taught thousands of factories in the Pearl River Delta, the Yangtze River Delta, and elsewhere in China to meet world-class specifications, abide by commitments, and upgrade production and process management. In addition, it has provided knowledge of international markets and in some cases finance, and supplied the sales network and distribution channels for the exports of Chinese companies. This has made it much easier for Chinese companies, in particular small and medium-sized firms producing light manufactured goods, to supply both Chinese and international markets, often with their own branded goods, and to keep pace with rapidly changing demand. Major retailers had also built extensive supply chains in China as well. As of 2011, Wal-Mart reportedly sourced 70 percent of the goods that it sold globally from 20,000 suppliers in China (Schell, 2011).

Across many industries, managers report a pattern in which foreign companies invest into China, identify potential local suppliers and partners, and then work extensively with these suppliers and partners to bring them to international standards. The benefits for the foreign firm are clear in terms of higher quality, lower cost, and more readily available inputs. The benefits for the suppliers are that they get help in improving their operations and a leg up in their own competition with other domestic and international firms (author's interviews). Sometimes working with a foreign firm can place a Chinese firm on an extraordinary growth path. Wanda's first commercial property development was a project for Wal-Mart in which the American company provided detailed specifications and engineering support, as well as information on the needs for retail properties (Liu, 2009a). Wanda went on to become the largest developer of commercial properties in China, with some 95 shopping malls developed by August 2014, making Wanda's chairman one of China's richest men.

Foreign company investments can also generate additional foreign investment in the supply chains. In 2013, Korea's LG Group launched in Guangzhou Science City a USD 4 billion investment in 8.5th generation LDC panel production, generating an additional 1,500 jobs and making it the largest foreign investor in Guangzhou. LG was an attractive player to the Guangzhou Government because it was the world leader in this segment at the time and would bring the world's most advanced technology to Guangzhou. The Guangzhou Science City investment is also an example of how LG's state-of-the-art, world-scale investments have fostered the geographic clustering of upstream and downstream producers. To be near to the LG project, upstream producers have invested nearby, including Nippon Electric Glass, Korean Daesung, Korean Comet, LG Chem, and LG Innotek (Invest Guangzhou, 2013).

These are just a few examples of foreign companies developing suppliers and distributors in China. The result has been the emergence or expansion of thousands if not tens of thousands of Chinese companies, and employment for millions of workers. At the same time, many of these new or expanded companies have developed the capabilities to sell to others inside and outside of China at world cost and quality standards.

Bringing R&D and technology development to China

Foreign companies have been instrumental in expanding research and development capabilities in China. Foreign-invested R&D is an important driver of innovation in China (Schwaag-Serger, 2008). Research and development by foreign companies in China has the potential to enhance China's scientific and technological capabilities through their own research, by training researchers, by providing examples to local companies, by boosting the capabilities of local universities and research institutes, and through the impact of competition. World-class companies doing R&D in China bring in science and technology from their international networks and create the potential for substantial spillovers into the domestic economy. They also act as a training ground for future entrepreneurs and researchers who then start up or go into Chinese companies. Foreign-invested R&D can spur innovation in Chinese firms, as well as domestic entrepreneurship. Modalities include sponsoring research programs, laboratories, faculty and student scholarships, introducing education curricula for academic, technical and vocational training, and setting up strategic alliances in specific areas of science and technology.

According to a PwC study, China was the second-largest location for R&D worldwide in 2015 with total R&D spending by all firms (foreign and domestic) of USD 55 billion, surpassed only by the United States' USD 145 billion. Foreign invested enterprises accounted for USD 44.2 billion (81 percent) of this investment in China, with US companies accounting for USD 18.2 billion and Japanese firms USD 9.2 billion. According to the study, as late as 2007, virtually all of the private sector R&D carried out in China was by foreign firms (Jaruzelski et al., 2015). Thus foreign firms have been the dominant drivers of private sector R&D in China.

The number of foreign-invested R&D centres in China has grown from fewer than 30 in 1999, to 600 in 2004, to more than 1,300 in 2013, to more than 1,500 in 2015, with a 20 percent increase expected by 2020 (Abrami et al., 2014; Jolly et al., 2015; Yip and McKern, 2014). Over this period, the focus of multinational R&D efforts in China has changed from low-cost support to local operations, to adopting technologies to serve local demand, to fundamental research. In a 2014 survey of foreign R&D centres in China, 18 percent of respondents were focused on low-cost R&D, 54 percent market driven R&D, but 18 percent were developing 'significant science and technology know-how' in China (Jolly et al., 2015; Yip and McKern, 2014). These firms are interested in R&D across the full spectrum: development, applied research, and, increasingly, fundamental research. Many of the multinational firms in this third phase of R&D are from the pharmaceuticals sector, while others are from chemicals and electronics, all priority sectors in the Chinese government's five-year programs.

Foreign-invested, China-based R&D generates direct social benefits for the Chinese population. Two fields that are high priority in China, and in which foreign R&D has been prominent, are healthcare and alternative energy. In 2010, GE announced it would invest USD 500 million in R&D in China over three years to 'expand R&D and innovation capabilities in China to create new technologies in healthcare' in areas such as ultrasound, CT-scan, and patient monitoring systems (Chen, 2010). Astra-Zeneca's Innovation Center China has focused on diseases prevalent in Asia, such as gastric and liver cancers, and aims to raise the standard of cancer care in China and elsewhere in the region (Teo, 2012). Roche Pharma China has received approval to export an anti-cancer drug made in China to the United States and expects such exports to upgrade China's pharmaceutical industry (Wang, 2011). The Merck-Serono biopharmaceutical R&D hub in Beijing is focusing on early detection and development of personalized medicines for cancer and neurodegenerative diseases in China and is liaising with Chinese regulatory officials, academic institutions, and other research-oriented organizations (Merck-Serono, 2011). Reduction in fossil fuel utilization has been a major priority of the Chinese Government. Companies like Siemens and GE have been working to promote sustainable power generation in China through research on wind turbines, wind power plants, and grid management in China (Bullis, 2010).

The international standing of China-based foreign R&D is also on the rise. In the 2015 *European Business in China Confidence Survey*, 25 percent of responding firms reported having at least one R&D centre in the Chinese Mainland. Seventy-one percent of the companies with an R&D centre in China claimed that to 'tailor products or services to Chinese market needs' was a 'primary goal' of having an R&D centre in China, 62 percent to 'improve R&D cost competitiveness', and 59 percent 'to tap into local pool of talent' (multiple responses were allowed). Twenty-five percent of firms with a China R&D centre reported a level of innovation at their China R&D centre(s) comparable to their global/regional R&D centres and 15 percent expected these levels of innovation to be comparable in the near future. The sectors with firms most likely to report that the level of innovation in their R&D centres in China is on par with that of their global or regional centres were professional services (60 percent), energy and utilities (50 percent), IT and communications (44 percent), and medical/pharmaceuticals (44 percent) (Wang et al., 2015).

Foreign companies are increasingly setting up China-based R&D centres that operate at a regional or global level. A study sponsored by the Swedish Institute for Growth Policy Studies (ITPS) estimated that by 2006, between 30 and 40 foreign companies had set up global R&D centres in China (Schwaag-Serger, 2008). Sanofi-Aventis upgraded its China R&D Centre in Shanghai into its Asia-Pacific Research Centre in 2014. This centre coordinates the activities of R&D centres in 12 countries in the Asia Pacific (Ding, 2014). BASF's Innovation Campus Asia-Pacific in Pudong, Shanghai (opened in 2004 and expanded in 2014) is its most important R&D site in Asia and one of its most important outside of Germany (BASF, 2014). In 2008, IBM set up its China Development Lab in Shanghai as a research platform serving BRIC countries and other fast-growing regions. As of 2015, CDL was developing software products for world markets (Shih et al., 2012; IBM, 2015). In 2009, Novartis announced the USD 1 billion transformation of its R&D facility in Shanghai into a global centre (China Economic Review, 2009). The mission of Microsoft Research Center, set up in Beijing in 1998, has become 'innovation in China, innovation for the world' (McKinsey and Company, 2015). By 2010, Microsoft had made Beijing its centre for global research outside the United States. Bayer & Schering Pharma opened its R&D Center in Beijing in 2009, with the status of global research centre from its inception (Tselichtchev, 2011).

Foreign companies are inserting China into global R&D networks in a way that no Chinese company could do. GM's Advanced Technical Center in Shanghai carries out R&D for both China and GM's operations worldwide (Leibowitz and Roth, 2012). In July 2015, GM announced that it will work with state-owned SAIC to overhaul how it designs and builds cars for developing markets. This move is reported to represent 'the auto maker's first major development project in China to address global markets' (Stoll, 2015). PepsiCo's Shanghai Innovation Center, opened in 2012, is its largest R&D centre outside North America. The facility serves as a hub for innovation in products, packaging, and equipment for China and throughout Asia (Bloomberg News, 2012). The Shanghai centre was designed to work collaboratively with other PepsiCo R&D centres worldwide, to help R&D locations outside Asia achieve breakthroughs. As of 2014, Siemens employed more than 4,500 R&D researchers and engineers, had 20 R&D hubs, and had over 10,000 active patents and patent applications in China. In China, Siemens designs and develops products and solutions for the Chinese market and develops technologies for global application (Siemens, 2015).

Foreign R&D, local linkages, and spinoffs

Foreign companies have created numerous linkages with universities and research institutes in China and have been responsible for numerous spinoffs. Literally hundreds of foreign companies have set up research linkages with Chinese universities and research institutes. In one example, Siemens has set up relationships with more than two hundred universities and colleges in China, helping them set up laboratory centres and also providing scholarships for scientific and technical exchanges. Through cooperation agreements with Tsinghua University, Siemens has helped set up the Center of Knowledge Interchange (CKI), which facilitates exchanges in talent development and science information (Tsinghua University, 2015). In 2011, Siemens signed a memorandum of cooperation with China's Ministry of Education to collaborate in promoting the development of engineering education in China. Siemens is helping train engineering professionals for Chinese universities and vocational institutes, contributing its industrial technologies, training programs, and systems (Siemens, 2011).

Auto companies also have numerous research linkages. Ford Motors began cooperation with educational and research institutes in China in the early 1980s and set up the Ford China Research and Development Fund in 1994. In 2007, Ford Motor formed strategic alliances with Nanjing University of Aeronautics and Astronautics (NUAA) and Shanghai Jiaotong University (SJTU) and set up the Ford Professor Chair for Materials Science at NUAA. In 2008, it entered into a strategic alliance with Chongqing University in the area of automotive technologies. By 2008, Ford Motor had worked on more than one hundred projects involving research and educational institutes in more than 20 cities across China (Ford, 2008). Toyota Motor Corporation started holding joint technology courses with Tsinghua University in 1997 and expanded into joint research in the university's labs in 2003. In 2011, Toyota signed the second phase of its five-year cooperation agreement for the Tsinghua University–Toyota Research Center, which carries out joint research in environmental science, energy, auto safety techniques, and materials science (Toyota, 2011).

Foreign firm R&D investments have also led to numerous spin-offs of local companies in China. A leading example is provided by firms in the Zhongguancun Science Park (Z-Park), China's pre-eminent science park. By year-end 2005, it was the site of more than 50 universities, more than one hundred research institutions, one-third of China's national laboratories, and one-fifth of China's total R&D expenditures. Multinational firms, like IBM, Microsoft, Bell Labs, Fujitsu, Intel, Motorola, and Oracle started setting up R&D centres in the Z-Park in 1995. A study published by the National Bureau of Economic Research found that the 'spike in the entry of domestic firms since the late 1990s coincided with the significant presence of MNEs in the Z-Park and their decision to build R&D centres.' Field interviews suggested that this was not a coincidence: multinational firms have been 'a critical part of the high growth of the Z-Park'. The presence of multinationals and especially their R&D centres 'has profoundly changed the landscape of the Chinese IT industry as well as business opportunities' (Cai et al., 2007, p. 7).

The R&D activities of multinational enterprises were found to promote local entrepreneurship by stimulating the entry of domestic firms into the same industry and by enhancing the R&D activities of Chinese start-ups. The specific mechanisms of knowledge diffusion were found to include 'learning by doing' inside foreign research centres, R&D inter-firm cooperation between foreign firms and domestic institutions, and technical assistance in outsourcing provided by foreign firms to domestic firms (Cai et al., p. 25). TechFaith, a Z-Park based domestic cell phone software firm, was formed by a former Motorola sales manager and a dozen designers and engineers who left Motorola to join the new company, bringing skills, capabilities, and customer contacts from their years at Motorola. Smartdot, a Z-Park based domestic provider of solutions and services for enterprise office automation, e-government work, and information management, chose to build its solutions and services on IBM software platforms, and benefitted from strategic cooperation with IBM. Ultrapower Software, another domestic firm that got its start in the Z-Park, derived a 'unique advantage' from its 'sustained strong partnership in R&D and outsourcing relationships with multinational industrial leaders, such as BMC Software, Hewlett Packard, and IBM' (Cai et al., 2007, pp. 8–9).

Improving business practices and standards

Foreign companies have been instrumental in improving business practices and standards in the Chinese Mainland. Two examples of this have been the emergence of the accounting and management consulting sectors in China.

The founding of the People's Republic of China marked the end of the accountancy and auditing sector that had existed up until that time, as they were viewed as unnecessary in a system in which the state controlled the means of production. In contrast, after the PRC opened up to foreign investment, an accountancy and auditing sector was needed to enable inflows of investment, the formation of Sino-foreign joint ventures, and the growth of domestic stock markets. In the 1980s, the world's leading accountancy and audit firms – then the Big Six – set up representative offices in China. By the early 1990s, the Central Government permitted them to set up joint ventures with domestic, state-owned 'entities', frequently no more than a university professor appointed by the government. The firms started up from scratch in China at that time, importing senior talent, training people, and writing practice manuals. They sent promising Chinese professionals to the United States and United Kingdom for experience. These professionals would include the future chairman of China's regulatory body, the Chinese Institute of Certified Public Accountants (CICPA), and the future chairman of the Chinese Ernst & Young joint venture (Deng and Macve, 2015, p. 33). In addition, they brought in Hong Kong CPAs to manage their Chinese Mainland operations, and the Hong Kong influence is still strong to this day.

Together with international and professional bodies, the big foreign firms contributed to structuring China's accounting standards, including conceptual frameworks, detailed accounting and audit practices, and key elements of financial statements. Deloitte, for example, served as consultants in 1993 to China's Ministry of Finance in developing the Chinese Accounting Standards (CAS). Partners at the large firms continue to serve in leadership roles in the professional bodies driving development of accounting professional and industry standards in China, including the Ministry of Finance's Accounting Standards Committee. As domestic accounting firms have grown and improved, the Chinese Government has taken steps to ensure that they dominate the market, encouraging Chinese firms to join forces with smaller international firms and for Chinese companies to appoint domestic auditors and accountants.

In the early years after China's opening, the Big Six were essential to foreign investment as their management directly performed the audits required by foreign firms seeking to establish subsidiaries in China. They also have been essential to the process whereby China's state-owned enterprises have been partially privatized and have enabled Chinese firms to adopt internationally recognized forms of corporate governance (such as non-executive directors, a two-tier board, and an audit committee) as well as professionally conducted audits. The Big Four firms also have been a driving force in the rise of China's domestic accounting and audit firms, many of whom were founded by professionals trained in the Big Four's China operations.

The management consulting services sector virtually did not exist in China before the 1990s. Before that, most consulting projects were in the fields of engineering, construction, and science and technology, and projects were assigned by the government. Foreign management consulting firms began to enter the Chinese Mainland informally in the 1980s and started setting up branches in the early 1990s.[2] Foreign consulting firms introduced the concept and business of management consulting into China, injecting business models for local enterprises to emulate, and creating a customer base. The earliest clients for management consultancy services in China were foreign multinational corporations and their joint ventures. In the late 1990s, state-owned enterprises awakened to the need to increase efficiency in the face of foreign competition and privately owned domestic firms that were emerging in large numbers. As the demand for consulting services from Chinese clients grew, the client base of the foreign firms shifted to be dominated by local clients (author's interviews).

The contribution of the foreign management consulting firms has taken on a variety of forms. Their presence and advice facilitated the entry and expansion of foreign firms in China. Their presence also allowed for a much quicker transfer of international best practice in terms of business strategy and operations to Chinese firms than would have been the case otherwise. Many leading-edge management tools and processes, such as ISO certifications, Six Sigma, and modern human resource practices were introduced to China by foreign firms. In addition, foreign management consulting firms also played a key role in training up the first generation of Chinese management consultants. Within the branch offices of foreign firms, the Mainland professionals learned the world-class professional skill sets and the business aspects of succeeding as management consultants. The founding partners of many of China's leading management consulting companies learned their trade as employees of leading international firms.

However important the accounting and management consulting professions have been to raising business practices and standards in China, managers from both those industries interviewed for this project indicated that the example of leading foreign companies in their day-to-day operations were far more important. Having world-class companies bring their management systems, human resource management systems, training systems, quality control systems, and other practices provided an impetus to

China by increasing productivity, training people who went on to other countries, and introducing these practices to Chinese companies who emulated many of the practices and in some cases are becoming leaders in their own right. According to interviewees, the notion that if foreign companies could operate efficiently in China, then Chinese companies could do so as well, has had an impact that should not be underestimated (author's interviews).

Improving the financial system in China

The activities of foreign multinational firms have resulted in significant improvements in China's financial sector with a cascade of benefits for the entire Chinese economy.

The 'Big Six' (later 'Big Four') accounting firms have been instrumental in the development of capital markets within China, by providing technical expertise that has improved the Chinese environment for investors, which in turn has allowed the Shanghai and Shenzhen stock exchanges to become the world's seventh and ninth by capitalization (Deng and Macve, 2015, pp. 4, 34). Foreign accounting firms continue to contribute on an ongoing basis to developing and regulating China's capital markets. Public service appointments of partners with the 'Big Four' firms include the China Securities Regulatory Commission (CSRC), China Banking Regulatory Commission (CBRC), the Shanghai Stock Exchange Listing Committee (SSELC), and the China Mergers and Acquisitions Association (CMAA) (Deloitte Touche Tohmatsu, 2012). In addition, it is the 'seal of approval' of the major international accounting firms that has allowed Chinese companies to access international capital markets, further facilitating the development of indigenous Chinese companies.

The Chinese banking sector has also benefited from the entry of foreign firms. Several econometric studies have found that foreign bank entry has introduced more competition into the sector and has improved the performance of Chinese banks (Chen and Chen, 2012; Li and Han, 2008; Zhang and Pei, 2015). Foreign competition has been credited with raising the efficiency of Chinese banks, improving the availability of local bank credit, and having a positive impact on domestic risk management (Lv, 2006; Mao et al., 2010; Zhang and Wu, 2010). Although the activities of foreign banks were highly circumscribed in the years just after China's initial economic opening, competition from the foreign banks stimulated their local competitors to engage in financial innovation. China's accession to the WTO in 2001 resulted in foreign banks being able to own up to 25 percent in domestic banks. Foreign financial houses poured money into the sector in the form of minority investments, and Chinese banks raised billions of dollars via IPOs. Beginning in late 2001, the bank branches and representative offices of foreign banks entered a phase of rapid growth, and foreign bank participation came to be seen as integral to reforming China's banking sector (Hope et al., 2008, p. 5).

The foreign banks injected management expertise into their new Chinese partners. Citibank sent in a high-level manager and introduced a matrix management structure that created incentives for product and service innovation into the Shanghai

Development Bank, which also benefited from Citibank's expertise in personal financing, as it became the first bank to issue a local currency credit card in China. Goldman Sachs proposed measures to bolster risk management as well as expansion into derivatives, money market funds, and offshore capital management to the Industrial Bank of China (ICBC). The Bank of America (BOA) worked to upgrade China Construction Bank's systems and operations, seconding numerous professionals to help improve international operations, customer service, retail operations, and electronic banking, as well as management of information, human resources, and assets and liabilities. Some foreign–Chinese partnerships encountered difficulties due to culture clashes, adherence to past practices, and resulting disputes among the parties. These episodes, and the eventual divestment by some foreign banks of holdings during the Global Financial Crisis, highlight the difficulty in bringing about meaningful management change with only a minority position (Hope et al., 2008, p. 20). In any case, the Chinese banks learned a great deal from their overseas investors.

Venture capital (VC) was literally a foreign concept in China until the 1980s. The first domestic VC firms were government and university backed firms focused more on supporting policy than on building profit-making enterprises (White et al., 2002). A few foreign VC companies, including IDG Capital Partners, entered in the early 1990s. Most of the foreign firms that entered in the early 1990s did so through joint ventures with Chinese SOEs due to restrictions on fund raising in China, though by the end of the 1990s many entered on their own. By 2001, IDG, Softbank, Goldman Sachs, Walden International, H&Q, Intel Capital, ASIMCO, and dozens of other foreign venture capital firms were active in China. According to the AVCJ (2001), venture capital investments in China equalled USD 16 million in 1991, USD 583 million in 1992, and USD 678 million in 1995. Foreign venture capital firms accounted for 97 percent of the VC funds raised for China from 1991 to 1997, as private fund raising by individuals and non-SOEs was not allowed in China at the time. Growing markets and the first foreign IPOs of Chinese companies, which provided exit possibilities, spurred the activities of foreign VCs (author's interviews). Many foreign VCs managed risks in China by forming joint ventures with state-owned enterprises, which presumably had the connections necessary to smooth the way and to help find deals.

Further economic reforms helped usher in another wave of venture capital investment in China in the late 1990s. The growth of NASDAQ and mechanisms that allowed foreign-incorporated shell companies to control Chinese entities also contributed. Foreign VC firms increasingly operated on their own without local partners, and their focus shifted from low-tech SOE investments to investments in new, private, high-tech Chinese enterprises, many of which were eventually listed on NASDAQ (Zeng, 2004). In this period, foreign venture capital in many cases substituted for the capital not provided to private sector companies in China due to policy preferences for funding state-owned companies through the domestic banking sector and domestic stock markets (author's interviews). By 2005, an estimated USD 1.2 billion was raised by venture capital firms for China investment funds. In that year, there were approximately 250 foreign and 250 local venture capital firms active in China, but foreign firms accounted for eight of the top ten investors (Liu et al., 2006).

In 2014, 258 new venture capital funds focused on China were set up, with plans to raise a total of USD 19 billion in new funds. Exits through IPOs or mergers and acquisitions of venture capital funded Chinese companies reached USD 13.6 billion (Ernst & Young, 2015; Zero2IPO Research Center, 2015). The Chinese venture capital market had become the world's second largest, behind only the United States. The venture capital industry in China was providing the funds for Chinese start-ups (particularly technology-based start-ups) that other sources simply were not providing, thus fuelling China's technology boom. By the mid-2010s, there were hundreds of domestic venture capital companies operating in China, and the Chinese environment for venture capital continued to be very different from that in other countries. Nevertheless, foreign-owned venture capital companies still played an extremely important role in identifying and funding Chinese companies. In addition, many Chinese who once worked for the big US VC companies have started their own funds backed by Chinese investors (author's interviews).

Modernizing management training and education

Foreign entities, both educational institutions and companies, have been instrumental in bringing modern management training and education to China. As early as 1980, a group of Chinese officials and academics visited several business schools in the United States to assess the contribution that Western-style business education could make to China. Before then, business education in China was rudimentary, and focused more on plant operation and engineering issues. The group recommended that Western-style management education be set up in China and agreements were signed with the United States Department of Commerce and the European Community Commission to set up exploratory programs. These resulted in the creation of the China–European Management Institute (CEMI) in Beijing and a US-sponsored training program in Dalian. By 1984, these two efforts began offering Western-style MBA programs. CEMI eventually moved to Shanghai and was reconstituted as the China–European International Business School (CEIBS) in 1994. By 2015, CEIBS claimed 75 percent of its faculty was foreign, and that it had more than 17,000 alumni and more than 100,000 managers trained (CEIBS, 2015). The number of Chinese institutions offering MBA programs, on their own or in partnership with foreign institutions went from nine in 1990, to 26 in 1993, to 35 in 1994, to 56 in 1997, and to 90 in 2004 (Goodall and Warner, 2009).

Eventually hundreds of such programs would develop, in many cases with the participation of foreign institutions. Several European schools are involved in CEIBS (along with Shanghai Jiaotong University). The Guanghua School of Management at Peking University was named after the Hong Kong-based foundation that funded it. As of 2015, Guanghua had joint programs with 11 foreign universities, while the Fudan University (Shanghai) School of Business had joint programs with 12 foreign universities and academic collaboration with 83 foreign universities (author's interviews). In most joint programs, the foreign partner provided substantial portions of the curriculum and teaching staff. Chinese schools also began to seek international accreditation. As of 2015, 12 Chinese business schools had been accredited by the Association to Advance Collegiate Schools of Business, the US-based accreditation body, and 15 had been accredited by EQUIS, the Europe-based accreditation body (AACSB, 2016; EQUIS, 2016).

Foreign companies were also pioneers in setting up corporate universities in China. Motorola University was set up in 1993 to provide management and technical training for its own personnel, clients, suppliers, partners, and some Chinese officials as well. By 2005, it had arrangements with 21 universities in China and offered EMBA and DBA programs. The Ericsson China Institute, established in 1997, developed training programs in Beijing, Chongqing, Guangzhou, and Hong Kong in collaboration with Chinese institutions as well as Western institutions, industrial experts, and training companies. It also began to confer MBA degrees. Siemens created the Siemens Management Institute in China also in 1997. Other foreign companies that set up corporate universities in China include Novartis, Procter & Gamble, GE, IBM, Amway, McDonald's, New World, and HP (Liu, 2009b). Chinese companies eventually followed suit. By 2011, it was estimated that there were 80 corporate universities founded by foreign companies and 320 by Chinese companies in China (Qianzhan Business Information Co., 2015). Most of these corporate universities provided Western-style management training and education.

Several foreign companies have provided business-specific training in China. Boeing has worked extensively in China to improve standards and training in the aviation sector, including work on aviation safety, aviation quality practices, business and executive training, and technical support. Since 1993, in cooperation with local Chinese customers, regulators, and government agencies, Boeing has provided enhanced professional training to almost 50,000 Chinese aviation professionals at no charge. The training has covered areas such as piloting techniques, flight operations, maintenance engineering, regulation, air traffic management, executive management, airline management and marketing, manufacturing, quality assurance, finance, and industrial engineering. Boeing launched its 'Boeing Academy' in China in 2012 to provide a central platform for its training initiatives in China (Boeing Company, 2015; Cliff et al., 2011; Liu, 2009a).

Finally, the corporate training and management market in China has become extremely large. Though there are no authoritative sources, the number of companies engaged in these businesses and related consulting activities must be in the tens of thousands. Again, many provide Western-style management development and education.

Foreign companies and entities have had an enormous influence on management training and development in China. Foreign universities and companies have been pioneers in bringing modern management education and training systems to China. Foreign companies have also been major customers for the foreign, Chinese, and joint institutions that have been set up and have therefore been influential in the development of curriculums and programs. Finally, it has been competition with foreign firms (or the example of business practices provided by foreign firms) that has pushed many Chinese firms to invest in management development and training, with outside providers or through their own activities.

Bringing regional and global management to China

Many foreign multinational companies are integrating China into regional and global management through the location of regional headquarters, business unit headquarters, and other high-level corporate functions in China. The benefits of headquarters operations to their host economy go far beyond the management and coordination activities for which they are best known. Regional and business unit headquarters link the host economy to international networks in several ways. They bring top corporate decision makers and highly qualified personnel into China, attract world-class suppliers, and build up the surrounding services support structure (Enright, 2005). Regional and business unit headquarters of multinationals in China enhance China's position as a regional and global management centre. As a result, employees in China get more exposure to international networks and Chinese companies have an easier time accessing the multinational companies' international networks.

Multinational regional headquarters in China – those responsible for an Asian or Asia-Pacific geography – grew strongly in the wake of China's WTO entry and then again during and after the Global Financial Crisis. Alcatel was the first foreign multinational to set up an Asia-Pacific regional headquarters in the Chinese Mainland (in Shanghai) and by September 2012, there were nearly 60 regional headquarters in Shanghai responsible for Asia or the Asia-Pacific, according to the Shanghai Commerce Commission, and Shanghai ranked first among Chinese Mainland cities (He, 2013). In 2014, 39 new regional headquarters of foreign multinationals were set up in Shanghai, of which 'more than 30 percent' were responsible for the Asia-Pacific region (author's interviews). From this data set, a reasonable estimate of the number of Asia-Pacific regional headquarters in Shanghai alone in mid-2015 would be over 100. We note that Shanghai has a very expansive definition of regional headquarters and claims that there were 484 such operations in Shanghai as of December 2014 (Wang, 2014).

In some cases, foreign companies have upgraded their China national headquarters to a regional headquarters for Asia or the Asia-Pacific. In others, foreign companies have moved regional headquarters from other locations. The main driver is often the importance of the China market and the perceived benefits of locating closer to customers. Ford Motors moved its regional headquarters for Asia-Pacific and Africa, including manufacturing, product development, purchasing, and public relations responsibility, from Bangkok to Shanghai in 2009 (Hille and Jacob, 2011). In 2012, Astra Zeneca moved its Asia-Pacific regional headquarters from Singapore to Shanghai and Nokia moved its regional headquarters from Singapore to Beijing. In 2015, Ashland designated its China office in Shanghai as regional headquarters for the Asia-Pacific, recognizing the role that the office has played 'in providing shared services – including finance, legal, human resources, communications, and information technology' – to the firm's other entities in Asia (Ashland, 2015).

In some cases, foreign firms have placed headquarters for global business units, or global operations, in China, injecting world-class skills and capabilities into China in the process. In 2006, ABB opened a global headquarters for its Robotics Business (a USD 1.7 billion business) in Shanghai. One goal was to help both foreign and indigenous companies in China increase their levels of automation and improve their competitiveness (ABB, 2006). After moving its Asia headquarters from Tokyo to Shanghai, IBM established a 'Growth Markets' headquarters in Shanghai in 2008, responsible for the Asia-Pacific (excluding Japan), Latin America, Russia, Eastern Europe, the Middle East, and Africa, embedding in China global management and coordination skills as well as on-the-ground knowledge of emerging markets from Latin America to Asia in China (IBM, 2013; Shanghai Daily, 2008). In 2011, Bayer Materials Sciences transferred the global headquarters of its polycarbonates business from Leverkusen, Germany, to Shanghai. With this move, Bayer Materials Sciences contributed 'cost leadership and creative thinking' skills in China (Bayer, 2012, pp. 5, 32). Also in 2011, Roche China announced Shanghai would become its third strategic operations centre in the world, after Basel and San Francisco (Wang, 2011). Also in 2011, GE moved its global headquarters for its Healthcare Global X-Ray business from the United States to Beijing (Burkitt, 2011). Again, these moves have brought management and coordination skills in running world-class global operations to China, which can provide spillovers for local companies as well as demand for high-end services.

The placing of regional or global headquarters in China shows that foreign companies are increasingly viewing China not just as a market and source of supply, but a key management centre. The result is enhanced management development, demand for advanced support services, and better access to international networks for Chinese employees and companies.

Promoting legal and regulatory reform

Foreign investors and organizations have played a significant role in the evolution of China's legal, regulatory, and institutional regimes. China's leaders have made the critical decisions, but foreign investors and organizations have provided context, information, technical assistance, and examples of international practices. The need to establish a legal framework governing foreign investment was clear to many in China. A 1991 article in *Beijing Guojimaoyi Wenti* [*International Trade Journal*] indicated:

> We should improve and perfect the legal system concerning foreign nationals. Whether or not the legal system is sound is usually the most important parameter in addition to the political situation that is used internationally to measure the degree of investment risk in a country. Foreign-funded enterprises are a special part of China's enterprise community for their operational and management

methods are very different from domestic enterprises. An environment of sound legal system concerning foreign nationals is a key to ensuring that foreign-funded enterprises can 'come in, stay, and stand steadily'.

(Deng, 1991, p. 67)

The evolution of the legal regimes governing foreign investment in China can be seen in terms of trade-offs for China's leaders and foreign investors (Fu, 2000; Wilson, 2009). For China's leaders, the trade-offs have been between the potential gains to China of foreign investment and a perceived risk of loss of national sovereignty. For the foreign investors, the trade-offs have been between the potential gains from operating in Chinese markets and the risks associated with uncertain legal and regulatory regimes. The act of opening China's economy to foreign investment, and therefore to entities not strictly controlled by the Chinese state, required the development of a legal system and regulatory regime to govern their activities. Organizations like the US–China Business Council, with technical assistance through its 'Rule of Law' program, and foreign law firms helped communicate and educate Chinese officials as to the international norms in commercial law. The importance of this was not that they were international *per se*, but rather the norms had evolved around the world to meet the requirements of providing governments with adequate governance powers and companies with adequate safeguards for them to make investments.

In the early years of China's opening, the nation's leaders tried to mitigate their risks by limiting the geographic scope, industry scope, and organizational form of foreign investment. This allowed China to attract investment in low-wage labour-intensive activities largely from Hong Kong and Taiwan (who could better navigate the uncertainty and ambiguity involved in investing in China at the time) and using contract joint ventures that minimized the foreign firm commitments. It did not, however, allow China to attract committed investments involving larger amounts of capital or higher levels of technology from more advanced countries. In order for that to occur, changes had to be made that would provide greater opportunities and fewer risks for the sorts of companies and investments that China wished to attract. The desire to obtain more advanced technology investments was an important factor in legal changes to allow wholly foreign-owned enterprises (WFOEs). In return, the WFOEs were supposed to benefit China through transferring advanced technology, helping China meet environmental or other goals, or exporting more than 50 percent of their final products (State Council, 1990).

China's entry into the World Trade Organization involved foreign governments negotiating from positions heavily influenced by their firms. In order to comply with the accession agreement, China would have to rewrite virtually all of its commercial laws. It should be noted that China's leaders did not do this for the sake of foreign firms, but rather to achieve a desired goal for its own industries (better trade access) and to push a reform agenda that was considered necessary in order to develop and strengthen the country. Thus, while foreign firms have been influential in the evolution of China's legal and regulatory regimes, they have influenced through providing alternative models that had been developed over time, through competition that forced greater efficiency over time, by communicating what companies needed in order to make the investments that China desired, and by providing technical assistance and information to allow China to make the transitions.

Another example of the interaction of foreign companies and China's regulatory and legal regime has been the evolution of commercial arbitration in China. In the early days of China's opening, many foreign companies insisted that commercial disputes be resolved through arbitration outside of the Chinese Mainland. China's accession in 1987 to the New York Convention on International Economic Arbitration, which bound Chinese courts to enforce international arbitration awards of other signatory countries, was a landmark in China's legal development. China went on to develop rules for the China International Economic Trade and Arbitration Commission (CIETAC) which gradually approached the norms suggested by the UNCITRAL Model Law on International Commercial Arbitration. Through CIETAC, China created an alternative system of contract dispute resolution for foreign firms in China closer to international standards than its judicial system, avoiding a sudden overhaul of the latter. CIETAC has become one of the busiest arbitration centres in the world. Criticisms of CIETAC bias against foreign parties led to significant changes, including an increase in the number of foreign nationals on the CIETAC list of arbiters and other moves towards international standards over time (Wilson, 2009).

Another area of foreign firms' influence is employment regulation. Before China's reforms, Chinese SOEs followed the 'iron rice bowl' policy of permanent employment, which involved overstaffing and limited productivity incentives. China's leaders realized that this was not sustainable from a development perspective. In addition, as foreign companies entered China, a mechanism had to be set up to govern labour relations when the state itself was not the employer. The contract labour system was developed through a back and forth process in which foreign firms indicated which conditions would allow them to be viable and which would not. The early success of Hong Kong and Taiwanese companies in Shenzhen, which had allowed more flexible labour policies than the rest of China, caused many to focus on the highly market-oriented policies of these firms as a model for China. As time went on, this view changed: China's leaders looked increasingly to pay-for-performance policies, like those put in place by a number of American companies, as a model for SOE labour reform (Wilson, 2009).

The influence of foreign companies and organizations on China's legal and regulatory regime had had far wider implications than its impact on foreign companies, since many of the provisions of Chinese law that govern indigenous companies, and the domestic economy as a whole, have been developed first in the context of dealing with foreign firms.

Improving the environment and sustainability in China

Environmental sustainability has become a critical goal of China's leadership. The Twelfth Five-Year Program made the promotion of sustainable development a responsibility of for-profit and state entities in cooperation with non-profits, with a focus on injecting sustainability with innovation into business models, processes, and products (Zadek et al., 2012). Public concern over environmental degradation, environmental watch groups, and increasingly government standards have made sustainable development a top priority for firms across all industries and sectors. Multilateral agencies and foreign companies have been important contributors to these efforts in China (Gucovsky, 2004, p. 354). Contributors to environmental standards and technology among multinational firms often have international corporate policies for sustainability and are active in associations such as the World Business Council for Sustainable Development (WBCSD). Examples include BP, Corning, Rio Tinto, and Shell, as well as the environmental services firms such as ERM and CH2MHill.

The nature of a firm's sustainable development efforts often reflects how it impacts the environment, for example, as a producer of chemicals, heavy industrial products or consumer goods, or a provider of services. At BASF, one of the world's largest chemical companies, the fostering of sustainable development through innovation is central to its strategies for China and the Asia-Pacific. BASF, one of the first companies worldwide to set up an internal sustainability council, created the Sustainability Council of BASF Greater China, and is a co-founder of the China Business Council for Sustainable Development (CBCSD). Shell contributed world-class technologies to the CNOOC Shell Petrochemicals joint venture for the environmentally friendly and efficient production of petrochemicals, and used its expertise to develop fuels and lubricants for the Chinese market that boost fuel efficiency and reduce emissions (Shell, 2015). BP has introduced several new technologies at its petrochemicals plant in Zhuhai that recycle water, recapture heat, and generate electricity. As a result, BP estimates that the Zhuhai PTA facility generates around 75 percent less water discharge, 65 percent less greenhouse gases, and 95 percent less solid waste than a similar plant using conventional technology. Its Stage 3 development, completed in 2015, will generate additional efficiency gains (BP, 2015).

In the automotive sector, GM's sustainability campaigns in China are focused on developing green products and green systems and fostering environment protection and awareness. GM China is working to create 'greener, safer and healthier communities' by 'building a green supply chain'. It is sponsoring the GM Restoring Nature's Habitat Project to help save wetlands in Eastern China (General Motors China, 2013). In energy, Siemens is working to promote sustainable power generation in China through wind power plants and innovation. It has teamed up with the Central Government to support Beijing's development as a sustainable city, through cooperation in infrastructure construction and urban development. It also is assisting business formation in China through its new China investment vehicle for RMB venture capital investment, Siemens Venture Capital Co., Ltd.

Since 2003, Sony as a worldwide policy procures components only from suppliers designated as its 'Green Partners' (Sony, 2015). Sony China has put in place a portfolio of programs spanning the value chain to promote the sharing of environmentally responsible practices with and among its suppliers (Lee et al., 2014, p. 28). Panasonic China is working in support of implementation of the Clean Development Mechanism of the Kyoto Protocol and sponsors recycling programs. As part of its drive to be a Green Innovation Company, it has opened the Panasonic Center in Beijing to provide an interface with customers where their interests and needs can be expressed. Unilever stands out for its progress in developing environmentally friendly products such as concentrated cold-water detergents and smaller aerosols for consumers, pursuant to its Sustainable Living Plan (2010–2020) that has the stated aim of doubling revenue in China and cutting by half 'the environmental footprint of the making and use of our products' (Rees, 2014).

In banking, the HSBC Group has developed 'sustainability lending policies' that govern lending to certain sectors, derived from leading international standards. In China, HSBC China enforces policies for 'sustainability lending' through its credit and risk management departments. Lending proposals are assessed for environmental risks, particularly in sectors singled out by Chinese government policy as being most at risk for high energy consumption and pollution (HSBC China, 2015). In accountancy and audit, Deloitte sponsors the Deloitte China Sustainability Awards, launched in 2013 and supported by the United Nations Development Program (UNDP), to encourage and recognize best practice in sustainability among multinational firms in China (Deloitte Touche Tohmatsu, 2013). Following from the 12th Five-Year Program, the Shanghai and Shenzhen Stock Exchanges have taken actions to promote disclosure on sustainability by listed companies (Deloitte Touche Tohmatsu, 2014).

Foreign environmental engineering firms have been instrumental in improving environmental standards and practices in China. CH2MHill, for example, is active in many sectors in China including pharmaceuticals, automotive, transportation, government facilities, infrastructure, electronics, and advanced technology. It works with multinational clients to ensure compliance with ISO standards. It also provides expertise to large Chinese firms directly or via their joint ventures. For example, it has worked on multiple flat panel display manufacturing facilities for Tian Ma, a Chinese flat panel display producer. The Xiamen Tian Ma project is the 'largest and most advanced single FAB of its kind in the world' (CH2MHILL, 2015). Granted a General Constructor's license in 2006, which broadened the range of services it offers in China, CH2MHill has helped grow the environmental engineering consulting sector in China.

Foreign firms have played a major role in introducing sustainable design and construction standards to China. Rob Watson, known as the 'father of LEED', has worked since 1997 with the Ministry of Construction in Beijing to develop green building standards and energy codes. By 2009, there were 14 buildings in China with Leadership in Energy and Environmental Design (LEED) certification, of which foreign firms had built eight for their own use and tenant-occupied another two (Lewis, 2009). In 2006,

US-based Plantronics was the first foreign multinational to apply for LEED certification (for its Suzhou facility) in China. Next came Nokia, GM, Coca-Cola, and ExxonMobil. Other subsequent LEED certified facilities have been created for US medical technology firm Stryker, Nike's largest distribution facility in China, Johnson & Johnson's Suzhou facility, four PepsiCo plants, and numerous others. Foreign property developers such as Tishman Speyer (US) and Parkview Group (Hong Kong) have also been driving LEED standards in China. With foreign firms at the forefront, LEED building standards have spread rapidly in China. In 2014, China ranked third worldwide among countries outside the US with LEED projects, with 1,156 registered and certified projects and 66.5 million gross square meters of total building area (Tan et al., 2014).

The influence of foreign firms has contributed to the environment and sustainability in several ways. In addition to the initiatives described above, foreign firms have helped set the standard for sustainability practices and reporting in China.

Contributing through CSR initiatives

Foreign companies have profoundly shaped the corporate social responsibility (CSR) landscape in China. Foreign companies brought the concept of CSR to China in the 1990s and have introduced CSR practices, oversight boards, and reports to China. Early leaders included Intel China, which put forward the CSR3.0 standards, and Canon China, which issued one of the country's first CSR reports. Foreign firms also contributed indirectly, as Chinese suppliers to foreign companies were the first Chinese companies to adopt CSR programs (CSR Asia and the Embassy of Sweden in Beijing, 2008, p. 105). Today, it is the norm for leading Chinese firms to issue their own CSR reports, a practice brought to China initially by foreign firms. The PRC Government has turned into a major driver as well, with national legislation starting to mandate CSR standards and responsibilities.

Many early CSR activities by foreign firms in China focused on poverty alleviation and disaster relief. In the 1980s and 1990s, the standard of living in many areas was so low that the jobs and income that would follow a foreign-invested facility's arrival were viewed by many Chinese as social goods in themselves. Since then, environmental practices, honest company practices, and workers' rights have risen quickly to the fore. In some cases, CSR activities may be separate from or loosely related to the company's business operations, while in other cases they may be closely intertwined. Examples of the former would include many of the traditional areas of CSR in China, such as building primary schools and clinics in poor areas; providing outreach programs to poor children, the elderly, and the disabled; and disaster relief. More recently, many CSR programs have been developed that are closely linked to the firms' lines of business.

In education, widespread modes of CSR in China include building schools, volunteering teacher hours, and funding scholarships for rural students and the children of migrant workers. The Hope Schools project has won the participation of Coca-Cola, LG, P&G, and many others in building schools for poor students across China, and the

Library Project's efforts to build libraries across China has been supported by Pratt & Whitney and others. Top-down efforts targeted at tertiary education tend to win support from firms in knowledge-intensive industries that value and benefit from high standards of tertiary education in the domestic workforce. Siemens cooperates with more than 200 universities in China and provides scholarships in many. LG Electronics sponsors scholarships at more than 60 universities in China, providing RMB 7 million to pay university fees for deserving students. Boeing has engaged in support for education at the primary, secondary, and tertiary levels. By 2015, it had reached more than 75,000 primary school students with its 'Soaring with Your Dream' project; had launched robotics contests at the secondary level; and had supported scholarships, faculty training, student technology projects, course development, and student aviation clubs at several local partner universities (Boeing Company, 2015).

In the health area, CSR activities have included building rural clinics and hospitals; and providing surgical, psychiatric, and therapeutic services to the rural poor and disadvantaged. Many if not all of the large Western, Japanese, and Korean multinational firms launched programs of this sort upon first entering China, and have continued them over time. More specific programs include Coke's 'Balanced Diet, Healthy Lifestyle' public health campaign. Launched in 2010, it has mobilized students at more than 50 colleges in 20 cities into activities designed to bring about healthy lifestyle changes, and has mounted a Weibo micro-blog to build engagement and promote healthy habits (R3, 2012, pp. 7–8). In a similar vein, Nestlé has set up a Free Health Check program for the elderly across China that provides a free basic heart check, and blood pressure and electrocardiogram tests. Nestlé also partners with the Chinese Society of Cardiology and other groups to provide free elderly health services. As of 2012, Nestlé had reached some 1.5 million elderly in around 100 Chinese cities (Nestlé, 2012).

From the earliest days of corporate CSR in China, disaster relief has been seen as an important corporate responsibility, and the size and speed of disaster relief has been viewed by the public on social media as indicators of a firm's commitment to the public good in China. While other types of CSR have risen to the fore since the 1990s, disaster relief is still a potent litmus test for foreign firms' CSR in China (Fang, 2010, pp. 23–5). Leading multinationals such as Samsung and Panasonic China reliably donate to locations stricken by natural disasters. In 2008, in the aftermath of the Sichuan Wenchuan earthquake, Chinese bloggers posted lists of corporate disaster relief contributions. Foxconn's rapid pledge of more than USD 8.6 million met with wide-spread approval (Business and Human Rights Resource Center, 2008). In 2008, Maersk won 'Best CSR Initiator' Award for its earthquake relief and rebuilding efforts after the Sichuan earthquake, including the innovative reconstruction of Mianyang No. 6 Middle School using shipping containers (Shipping Online, 2009).

Foreign companies are also leveraging their ecosystems to encourage CSR in China. BASF's '1 + 3' Project model, recognized as a best practice case by the United Nations Global Compact, focuses on mobilizing its customers, suppliers, and logistics services providers. The aim is to give guidance to business partners in the form of best practices, expertise, and customized solutions. Each partner company then provides guidance to three companies in its respective supply chain, creating a snowball effect (BASF, 2015). Foreign chambers of commerce in China have specifically called on their members to improve CSR throughout their business ecosystems (American Chamber of Commerce in Shanghai, 2012).

The social issues chosen by a firm for its China CSR efforts often relate to its areas of expertise. For example, empowering social entrepreneurship and NGOs in China is one of the main priorities of KPMG, a firm with expertise in accountancy, auditing, and management consulting. Under the oversight of the KPMG Foundation, KPMG develops social entrepreneurship among university students and fosters business expertise for local NGOs and social enterprises (KPMG, 2014, p. 41). Sometimes, CSR outreach efforts are intended to alleviate by-products of a sector's development. Traffic safety is an area where foreign automotive firms have taken the lead in introducing standards, programs, and awareness. BMW introduced its Children's Traffic Safety Education into China in 2005. VW's flagship CSR programs include its Volkswagen Road Safety TV Education Program. GM China runs a Safe Road Project. In traffic safety, Toyota works with the Traffic Management Bureau of the Beijing Police Department via the Toyota Safe Driving Training Program, among others, and also works to promote traffic safety in Chengdu.

Worker governance has come to the fore as a CSR topic closely watched by the media, governments, NGOs, and consumers, particularly for firms reliant on skilled and unskilled labour. Foxconn, faced with the challenge of managing its massive workforce of 1.06 million employees, is undertaking worker governance efforts on an unprecedented scale. The company is in the process of creating a system of worker governance that will set up 25,000 workers councils across China. Through these councils, Foxconn's employees will become familiarized with China's labour laws, worker rights, and council electoral processes (Voyles, 2013). As of year-end 2014, Foxconn had set up 23,882 labour union units including 5,732 units on its Shenzhen Campus alone, and had implemented a pilot program for union leadership elections, as well as a committee for labour dispute resolution and a rights protection hotline (Foxconn, 2014, p. 28).

Foreign companies have made extensive contributions to China through their CSR programs over and above the benefits generated by their investments and employment. At the same time, they have set the standards for CSR programs and reporting that are being picked up by many Chinese companies, resulting in an even greater overall impact.

Policy advice

Since China's opening, its central and local governments have frequently turned to leading multinational firms for advice related to economics and business. The process received a jump start from the famous exhortation from Deng Xiaoping in 1983, to 'beef up reform and opening-up with more help from foreign brains' (Zhang, 2011).

Since then, high-level advisory groups of foreign executives have been set up by leading municipalities and provinces across China including Shanghai, Beijing, Guangdong Province, and Chongqing.

The first meeting of the International Business Leaders' Advisory Council (IBLAC) for the Mayor of Shanghai was held in 1989. The twenty-fifth IBLAC meeting, held in November 2013, attended by executives from FIAT, Bekaert, Luksic Group, Bain & Company, and others, was intended to solicit advice on Shanghai's competitiveness in soft power, as well as strengthening the China (Shanghai) Free Trade Zone (Office of the Mayor of Shanghai, 2013; Wang, 2013). The twenty-sixth IBLAC meeting, held in November 2014, followed up on the prior year's efforts by focusing on how to accelerate development of the FTZ. The Shanghai press reported that significant progress had been made on several fronts thanks to efforts by the likes of HSBC, Ernst & Young, and PWC (Shanghai Daily 2014; Ye, 2014). Beijing's IBLAC, set up in 1999, includes top executives from 30 multinational firms, representing around 18 industries and 11 countries and regions (ING, 2014). The theme of Beijing's 2014 IBLAC Conference was how to cure the city's 'urban diseases' including overcrowding, traffic congestion, and pollution. The multinational firms represented included ABB Group, Nokia Corp., Carrefour Group, Deutsche Bank, HSBC Holding plc Group, Panasonic Corporation, and Veolia (Liao, 2014). In 2015, the tenth Annual Meeting of the Chongqing Mayor's International Economic Advisory Council brought in top executives from multinational firms to address how to foster Chongqing's role in China's 'One Belt, One Road' initiative. Participating firms included Ford Motor, ANZ Bank, HSBC, ABB, BASF, SK Hynix, United Technologies, HP, Ericsson, Mitsui, BP, and AT&S (AT&S, 2015). The prior year's meeting had focused on promoting the competitiveness of Chongqing. Multinational executives participating in the debate included CEOs and chairmen of firms including Lafarge, Suzuki, POSCO, and Shui On Land.

At the provincial level, the 2013 Guangdong International Consultative Conference brought in 18 executives from Fortune 500 and other leading foreign firms, to share proposals and suggestions for upgrading the business environment and supporting and promoting international cooperation, with emphasis on industrial technology. Guangdong Governor Zhu Xiaodan stated that most of the opinions expressed in the previous conference had been taken into account in Guangdong's development policy, and had given rise to 'several major projects', including the SYSU-CMU Joint Institute of Engineering and the Foshan Sino-German Industrial Services Zone. The input by foreign MNC executive advisers had lifted 'the level of industry, technology, education, training and social development' as well as enhancing cooperation and exchange (NEWSGD.com, 2013).

Executives of foreign companies and foreign experts have provided advice in numerous other forums in China. Foreign executives and experts participate in a wide range of industry advisory and standards groups. Shanghai has an annual conference at which it solicits input from foreign think tanks. Foreign economists are regularly invited to discuss economic policy with Mainland officials. So too are heads of international banks, accounting companies, stock exchanges, and other business-related entities. China is one of the major clients of multilateral agencies, such as the World Bank and the Asian Development Bank. In recent years, China has solicited input on a wide range of other issues, including sustainability, the environment, improving China's competitiveness, developing smart cities, and financial reform. In each case, China's leaders seek to learn from international best practice in order to apply relevant lessons to China.

Counterpoints

Despite the contributions foreign companies have made to China's economy, foreign companies are not always seen in a positive light by Chinese and foreign critics. Foreign firms have been criticized for labour practices in China factories, lapses in food safety and labelling, environmental impacts, monopolistic behaviour, engaging in corrupt activities, and a series of other transgressions including tax shifting, overcharging, providing poor customer service, and even for being a threat to national security. While in some cases, the criticisms are clearly valid, in others there are questions about whether foreign companies are being scrutinized more carefully than local companies. In any case, one must understand that some foreign companies have not acted up to standard in China and from the Chinese perspective that the presence of foreign investment and foreign companies is not all beneficial.

Labour is one area in which foreign NGOs have criticized foreign companies operating or sourcing in China. Many allegations of labour violations involving well-known foreign companies in China involve suppliers that are owned by Mainland Chinese, Hong Kong, or Taiwanese companies manufacturing under contract rather than the foreign firms that own the brands or retail outlets for which they produce (Hong Kong Confederation of Trade Unions, 2015; Moore, 2012). Companies like Nike, Wal-Mart, Uniqlo, Apple, Samsung, Dell, Hasbro, Mattel, and others have been cited over the years as having suppliers that did not meet labour standards (Arthur, 2014; Bora, 2015; Gallagher, 2015; Hern, 2013; Nisen, 2013; Teather, 2005; Townsend, 2012). Taiwanese company Foxconn had several suicides among employees before instituting wideranging programs for the workforce (Heffernan, 2013; Tam, 2010). Critics of the brand holders and retailers allege that the large overseas firms put enormous cost pressures on their suppliers and then look the other way when it comes to their suppliers meeting labour standards. A variety of NGOs and labour organizations outside the Chinese Mainland have investigated labour practices of foreign companies and their suppliers in China and have brought pressure on the foreign companies to make improvements over and above what Mainland authorities have required. In addition, Chinese authorities have begun to step up enforcement of worker rights. Faced with mounting public awareness at home and abroad, and greater enforcement in China, many companies have taken steps to monitor, audit, and improve worker conditions, though independent observers claim problems persist.

Food safety is a very sensitive topic in China. In 2008, six babies died in China and an estimated 300,000 took sick after drinking adulterated milk from China's Sanlu Group and some 20 other Chinese dairy companies. Confidence in local dairy products fell, foreign brands soon accounted for 80 percent of the milk powder market in China, and shelves around the world were emptied by Chinese consumers wishing to avoid locally branded and manufactured products (BBC News, 2010; Huang, 2014). Foreign firms have not been immune from food safety charges. Husi Food Co. Ltd., a Shanghai-based subsidiary of US-based OSI Group was found to have committed numerous violations, including reprocessing and selling expired meat, adulterating and mislabelling meat products, and selling substandard products. McDonald's, KFC, Burger King, Starbucks, Papa John's, Ikea, and several other foreign and domestic restaurant chains were affected (Boehler, 2014; Bottemiller, 2012; *The Economist*, 2014; SCMP, 2014). The scandal hit the bottom lines of several chains (SCMP, 2015; Trefis, 2014). In separate incidents, Wal-Mart stores were found to have sold adulterated meat and a store was alleged to have sold pork from diseased pigs (Burkitt, 2012; Sullivan, 2014; Lee and Kwok, 2011). While foreign producers and brands are still generally considered far safer and more reliable than their domestic counterparts, it has become clear that foreign firms also have not always performed up to par when it comes to food safety and accuracy in food labelling.

China's rapid economic development has resulted in significant environmental problems. There is a question to what extent foreign companies have contributed to this degradation. The general consensus in the research that has been conducted to date is that foreign companies on the whole have had better environmental performance than indigenous Chinese companies. A 2005 study in Jiangsu Province found that foreign-controlled companies had environmental performance superior to locally controlled joint ventures and far superior to local firms (Stalley, 2010). The same study found the best environmental performance among Japanese and European companies, followed by US companies, with companies from elsewhere in Asia performing similarly to local firms. Academic studies have found little or no evidence that foreign firms from OECD countries have engaged in 'pollution haven-seeking' behaviour in China, but that firms in polluting industries from Hong Kong, Macau, and Taiwan in the 1990s sought locations in Chinese provinces with less stringent environmental regulations and enforcement for their activities (Dean et al., 2005). In addition, while foreign firms may have had better environmental performance than local firms, examples like the leakage from a ConocoPhillips invested oil platform in 2011 indicate that foreign invested firms can have environmental lapses as well.

Foreign companies have been involved in some high-profile corruption cases in China. In March 2010, four Rio Tinto employees were found guilty in a Chinese court of accepting millions of dollars in bribes and stealing commercial secrets. Rio Tinto dismissed the employees, stating its belief that 'they acted wholly outside our systems' (Barboza, 2010). In June 2013, GSK was accused of routing of improper payments on the order of RMB 3 billion to doctors via a travel agency in Shanghai. The criminal probe of GSK and subsequent guilty plea resulted in nearly USD 500 million in fines and five

GSK managers received suspended prison sentences. According to a GSK spokesperson, 'The illegal activities of GSKCI are a clear breach of GSK's governance and compliance procedures; and are wholly contrary to the values and standards expected from GSK employees' (Plumridge and Burkitt, 2014). GSK sacked 110 of its China staff for misconduct after detailed internal investigations into the activities of GSK's Chinese operations (Hirschler, 2015). In August 2013, Eli Lilly was alleged to have paid USD 4.9 million in kick-backs to doctors in China (Jack and Waldmeir, 2013; Mitchell, 2013). Lilly had previously been cited by the US Securities and Exchange Commission for falsifying expense reports and buying gifts for government officials in China in violation of the US Foreign Corrupt Practices Act. These high-profile cases have indicated that foreign companies have not been immune to corrupt activities in China.

Foreign firms have also fallen afoul of Chinese anti-monopoly legislation. In August 2013, six foreign milk powder producers were fined USD 110 million by the National Development and Reform Commission (NDRC) in an antitrust review that did not include any domestic firms (Reuters, 2014). Mead Johnson, Danone, and Nestlé, among others, cut their infant formula prices by as much as 20 percent (DW, 2013). Investigations of price-fixing and monopolistic behaviour in the automotive and automotive components sector resulted in fines against Mercedes-Benz, Chrysler, Volkswagen, and 12 Japanese auto component suppliers (Mathew, 2015; DW, 2014). In February 2015, the NDRC found US cellular chip-maker Qualcomm in violation of the Chinese Anti-Monopoly Law. Qualcomm reached a settlement agreement that included a fine of USD 975 million and discounted royalties on high-speed wireless communications systems (Clover, 2015; Zhang, 2015). The Qualcomm case hinged on pricing policies that had passed muster with US and EU competition authorities (Jenny, 2014; Mozur and Hardy, 2015).

Criticism of foreign companies has also emerged in the Chinese press. In 2013, a Chinese magazine identified US tech firms Cisco, IBM, Google, Qualcomm, Intel, Apple, Oracle, and Microsoft, as 'eight guardian warriors' that 'have seamlessly infiltrated China' (Tejada, 2014), dominating critical technologies and potentially compromising China's national security or extracting too large profits from Chinese companies and consumers. In March 2013, CCTV accused Apple of not giving its customers in China the same post-sales service as it gave users in other markets. In October 2013, CCTV reported that Starbucks' coffee and mugs were more expensive in China than in other countries. In January 2014, Wal-Mart was accused of bypassing quality, trade, and food-manufacturing permit procedures and working with unlicensed vendors. In July 2014, CCTV pronounced iPhone's location-tracking function a 'national security concern' (Dou, 2014). In May 2014, China banned Windows 8 from government official use for security reasons, and in a separate move, ordered state-owned enterprises to cut ties with US consulting firms such as McKinsey and Boston Consulting Group, because of fears they are spying on behalf of the US government. These actions show concern about the activities of foreign companies in China.

Conclusions

One of China's goals in opening its economy to foreign companies has been to strengthen the economy through the direct impact of the foreign firms in areas such as investment and employment. Another, larger goal has been to improve the entire economy and its support structures through the presence, influence, and operations of foreign companies. This impact has been felt through the modernization of Chinese industries and companies, the development of suppliers and distributors, investments in R&D and technology development, linkages and spinoffs, improved business practices and standards, a deeper financial system, the modernization of management training and education, the establishment of regional and global management in China, the promotion of legal and institutional reform, improved environmental and sustainability practices, CSR initiatives, and policy advice. The impact of foreign invested enterprises in these areas is hard to overestimate, and even though most of these contributions are difficult to impossible to quantify, this does not diminish their importance.

What is striking is the range of the activities of foreign invested enterprises in China, and the equally wide range of impacts that foreign companies have had on China's development. What is also striking is the way these contributions have been encouraged and accepted by Chinese officials at all levels. Managers from foreign companies have not only brought business capabilities to China, they are often sought out as advisors to provide input on how China, as well as Chinese provinces and municipalities, should proceed. It is clear that China's economy would not have developed at nearly the speed it has without the input and contribution of foreign enterprises.

However, there have been issues associated with the foreign company presence in China, particularly in the areas of worker treatment in foreign companies or their suppliers, food safety, environmental performance, anti-competitive behaviour, corrupt activities, and acting in ways that some Chinese believe are not in the best interests of the country. Even so it is hard to imagine that China's economy would have progressed at the rate and to the extent it has without the contributions of foreign companies.

We should note that the contributions of the foreign firms in China in part represent the desire of many companies to be good corporate citizens in the countries in which they operate. The contributions also represent business decisions. Some contributions have served to make China an easier place in which to operate. Some have helped develop the supply chains, distribution networks, and workforces that the companies need. Some have served to generate demand for future business. In addition, some have created relationships that facilitate approvals, licenses, and other governmental decisions the companies need in order to succeed in China. Thus there is a substantial self-interest in many of these contributions. In fact, it is the mutual benefit and mutual self-interest that has been vital to the foreign enterprise contributions in China.

Notes

1 The work supporting this chapter was carried out in conjunction with Edith Scott of Enright, Scott & Associates.
2 Firms like McKinsey, BCG, Bain, Roland Berger, A.T. Kearney, Accenture, and others entered in the 1990s.

References

AACSB, 2016, website, http://www.aacsb.edu/, accessed June 2016.

ABB, 2006, 'ABB Global Robotics Business Headquarters Opens in Shanghai', *ABB Press Release*, 4 April.

Abrami, R.M., W.C. Kirby, and F.W. McFarlan, 2014, 'Why China Can't Innovate', *Harvard Business Review*, 92(3), pp. 107–11.

American Chamber of Commerce in Shanghai, 2012, *The China CSR Imperative: Integrating Social Responsibility into the China Supply Chain*, Shanghai, American Chamber of Commerce.

Arthur, C., 2014, 'Samsung Finds Labour Violations at Dozens of Its Chinese Suppliers', *The Guardian*, 1 July.

Ashland, 2015, 'Ashland Formally Designates Shanghai Office as AP Regional Headquarters', *Ashland Press Release*, 11 June.

AT&S, 2015, 'AT&S Participates in Chongqing Mayor's International Economic Advisory Council', *iconnect007*, 30 September.

AVCJ, 2001, *The Guide to Venture Capital in Asia*, Hong Kong, Asian Venture Capital Journal.

Barboza, D., 2010, 'China Sentences Rio Tinto Employees in Bribe Case', *The New York Times*, 29 March.

BASF, 2014, 'BASF Expands Innovation Campus Asia Pacific in Shanghai', *BASF Press Release*, 28 July.

BASF, 2015, 'China Corporate Social Responsibility Monitoring and Evaluation System', *BASF Case*, 8 April.

Bayer, 2012, *Annual Report 2011*.

BBC News, 2010, 'Timeline: China Milk Scandal', *BBC News*, 25 January.

Bloomberg News, 2012, 'PepsiCo Opens China R&D Center as Competition Heats Up With Coke', *Bloomberg News*, 13 November.

Boehler, P. 2014, 'Starbucks, Dicos Withdraw Sandwiches as China Launches Nationwide Probe into "Rotten Meat" Firm', *South China Morning Post*, 21 July.

Boeing Company, 2015, *Boeing in China*.

Bora, K., 2015, 'Labor Law Violations at Chinese Supplier to Hasbro, Mattel, Takara Tomy', *International Business Times*, 21 July.

Bottemiller, H., 2012, 'McDonald's Apologizes to Chinese Consumers for Food Safety Violations', *Food Safety News*, 19 March.

BP, 2015, 'Building a More Efficient PTA Plant', *BP Case Studies*.

Bullis, K., 2010, 'GE to Boost Research in China', *MIT Technology Review*, 8 April.

Burkitt, L., 2011, 'GE Bases X-Ray Unit in China', *The Wall Street Journal*, 26 July.

Burkitt, L., 2012, 'Wal-Mart Faces New Food-Safety Complaints in China', *The Wall Street Journal*, 14 June.

Business and Human Rights Resource Center, 2008, *Company Contributions to Sichuan, China.*

Cai, H., Y. Todo, and L.A. Zhou, 2007, 'Do Multinationals' R&D Activities Stimulate Indigenous Entrepreneurship? Evidence from China's "Silicon Valley"', *National Bureau of Economic Research, Working Paper 13618*, November.

CEIBS, 2015, *Introduction.*

CH2MHILL, 2015, *CH2M HILL's Presence in China.*

Chen, Q., 2010, 'GE Setting up 6 Healthcare R&D Centers in China', *China Daily*, 30 November.

Chen, X. and Z. Chen, 2012, '[Whether the Entry of Foreign Banks Increased the Competition Intensity in the Banking Industry – Empirical Research from China]', *Inquiry into Economic Issues*, no. 5, (in Chinese).

China Economic Review, 2009, 'Novartis to Spend $1b on Shanghai R&D Center', *China Economic Review*, 5 November.

Cliff, R., C.J.R. Ohlandt, and D. Yang, 2011, *Ready for Takeoff: China's Advancing Aerospace Industry*, Los Angeles, The Rand Corporation.

Clover, C., 2015, 'China: Monopoly Position', *Financial Times*, 25 January.

CSR Asia and Embassy of Sweden in Beijing, 2008, *A Study on Corporate Social Responsibility Development and Trends in China.*

Dean, J.M., M.E. Lovely, and H. Wang, 2005, 'Are Foreign Investors Attracted to Weak Environmental Regulations?', *World Bank Policy Research Working Paper.*

Deloitte Touche Tohmatsu, 2012, *Deloitte China Responsibility Report 2012.*

Deloitte Touche Tohmatsu, 2013, 'Inaugural Deloitte China Sustainability Awards Open for Nomination', *Deloitte Press Release*, 1 November.

Deloitte Touche Tohmatsu, 2014, '2014 Deloitte China Sustainability Awards Winners Announced', *Deloitte Press Release*, 28 February.

Deng, J., 1991, '[Foreign Capital Infusion Should Emphasize Direct Foreign Investment – On the Strategic Readjustment of China's Foreign Capital Structure]', *Beijing International Trade Journal*, 2, 28 February, pp. 2–7, (in Chinese). Published in English as, 'Shifting Emphasis to Direct Foreign Investment', *JPRS-CAR-91-032*, 13 June 1991, p. 63–8.

Deng, S. and R.H. Macve, 2015, *The Development of China's Auditing Profession: Globalizing Translation Meets Self-Determination in Identity Construction*, 6 January, http://dx.doi.org/10.2139/ssrn.2562226.

Ding, Y., 2014, 'Sanofi Sets Up Asia Pacific R&D Center in Shanghai', *Shanghai Daily*, 26 September.

Dou, E., 2014, 'China Labels iPhone a Security Threat', *The Wall Street Journal*, 13 July.

DW, 2013, 'Nestle to Cut Baby Formula Prices in China in Response to Probe', *DW*, 4 July.

DW, 2014, 'China Fines Volkswagen, Chrysler for Price-fixing', *DW*, 11 September.

The Economist, 2014, 'Not Yum!', *The Economist*, 23 July.

Enright, M.J., 2005, 'Regional Management Centers in the Asia-Pacific', *Management International Review*, 2005, 45 (Special Issue 1), pp. 59–82.

EQUIS, 2016, website, https://www.efmd.org/accreditation-main/equis, accessed June 2016.

Ernst and Young, 2015, *2014 Venture Capital Review.*

Fang, Y., 2010, *Corporate Social Responsibility in China: A Study on Corporate Social Responsibility for Multinational Corporations in China*, School of Communications, American University.

Ford, 2008, 'Ford to Collaborate with Chongqing University on Automotive Research, Development and Education Program', *Ford Press Release*, 29 October.

Foxconn, 2014, 'Communications and Employee Rights Protection', *2014 Social and Environmental Responsibility Report*.

Fu, J., 2000, *Institutions and Investments: Foreign Direct Investment in China during an Era of Reforms*, Ann Arbor, University of Michigan Press.

Gallagher, C., 2015, 'Uniqlo Tells China Suppliers to Improve Work Conditions after Report', *Reuters*, 15 January.

General Motors, 2015, *General Motors in China*.

General Motors China, 2013, *2013 Corporate Social Responsibility Report*.

Goodall, K. and M. Warner, 2009, 'Management Training and Development in China: Laying the Foundation', in M. Warner and K. Goodall, eds, *Management Training and Development in China: Educating Managers in a Globalized Economy*, London, Routledge, pp. 15–26.

Guangzhou Government, 2013, *Fumiaki Matsumoto: Guangzhou is the Center of All Functions*, 30 July.

Gucovsky, M.M., 2004, 'Drivers of Environmental Industry in Asia: Bilateral and Multilateral Cooperation and Multinational Corporations', in R. Hirono, ed, *Environmental Industry Development in Selected Asian Developing Countries: China, India, Indonesia and Republic of Korea*, Environmental Industry Project, Institute for Global Environmental Strategies (IGES), p. 341–80.

He, X. 2013, 'How Do Transnational Corporations Glocalize: A Case Study of Transnational Corporations' Regional Headquarters in Shanghai', *Working Paper, School of Economics, Fudan University*.

Heffernan, M., 2013, 'What Happened After the Foxconn Suicides', *CBS News*, 7 August.

Hern, A., 2013, 'Dell Suppliers Accused of Human Rights Violations in China', *The Guardian*, 6 November.

Hille, K. and R. Jacob, 2011, 'Intel Joins Beijing Push with Executive Move', *Financial Times*, 24 May.

Hirschler, B., 2015, 'GSK Sacks 110 China Staff in Wake of Drug Bribery Case-Sources', *Reuters*, 6 March.

Hong Kong Confederation of Trade Unions, 2015, *Growing Labour Conflicts: More Strikes due to Hong Kong Enterprises' Labour Violations*.

Hope, N.C., J. Laurenceson, and F. Qin, 2008, 'The Impact of Direct Investment by Foreign Banks of China's Banking Industry', *Stanford Center for International Development, Working Paper No. 362*.

HSBC China, 2015, *Ethical Banking, Responsible Lending*.

Huang, Y., 2014, 'The 2008 Milk Scandal Revisited', *Forbes*, 16 July.

IBM, 2013, 'IBM in the Growth Markets', *IBM Press Release*, 7 November.

IBM, 2015, *China Development Lab (CDL) Overview*.

ING, 2014, 'Jan Hommen Attends the 11th Beijing Mayor Advisory Council Meeting', *ING Press Release*, May.

Invest Guangzhou, 2013, *Exclusive Interview of General Manager of LG Display: The 8.5th Generation of LCD Display: Making the Best LCD Panel*, 9 December.

Jack, A. and P. Waldmeir, 2013, 'Eli Lilly Drawn into Pharmaceutical Corruption Claims in China', *Financial Times*, 22 August.

Jaruzelski, B., K. Schwartz, and V. Staack, 2015, 'Innovation's New World Order', *Strategy-Business*, Winter.

Jenny, N., 2014, 'The Politics of China's Anti-Monopoly Investigations', *International Policy Digest*, 17 September.

Jolly, D., B. McKern, and G. Yip, 2015, 'The Next Innovation Opportunity in China', *strategy+business*, 80, Autumn.

Kassab, C.R., 2015, 'Competitiveness of Auto Industry Presents Challenges to Ford Motor Company', *Ford Online*, 21 January.

KPMG, 2014, *Embedding CSR in Our China Business*.

Lee, M. and D. Kwok, 2011, 'Wal-Mart China CEO Quits after Pork Scandal', *Reuters*, 17 October.

Lee, S.Y., A. Ramasamy, and J.H. Rhee, 2014, *Green Leadership in China: Management Strategies from China's Most Responsible Companies*, New York, Springer.

Leibowitz, G. and E. Roth, 2012, 'Innovating in China's Automotive Market: An Interview with GM China's President', *McKinsey.com*, February.

Lewis, G., 2009, 'Building the Future', *China International Business*, February.

Li, W. and L. Han, 2008, '[On the Market Competition of Foreign Bank in the Banking Industry in China: An Empirical Analysis Based on the Panzar-Rosse Model]', *Journal of Financial Research*, no. 5, (in Chinese).

Liao, W., 2014, 'Top Business Leaders Share Advice on Beijing's Sustainable Development', *China Daily*, 29 May.

Liu, C., 2009a, *Multinationals, Globalisation and Indigenous Firms in China*, London, Routledge.

Liu, J., 2009b, 'Novartis Opens Corporate Campuses', *China Daily*, 3 August.

Liu, M., J.A. Zhang, and B. Hu, 2006, 'Domestic VCs versus Foreign VCs: A Close Look at the Chinese Venture Capital Industry', *International Journal of Technology Management*, 34(1/2), pp. 161–84.

Lv, J., 2006, '[The Influence of Foreign Banks' Entry into China's Banking – Based on Panel Data Analysis]', *International Business*, no. 5, (in Chinese).

Mao, Z., J. Wu, and M. Liu, 2010, '[An Empirical Study of Foreign Banks' Effect on Chinese Credit Supply]', *Journal of Financial Research*, no. 1, (in Chinese).

Mathew, J., 2015, 'Mercedes-Benz fined $57m in China Over Price Fixing', *International Business Times*, 23 April.

McKinsey and Company, 2015, 'The China Effect on Global Innovation', *McKinsey Global Institute Research Bulletin*, July.

Merck-Serono, 2011, *Beijing Hub*.

Mitchell, T., 2013, 'China Begins Probe into Sanofi Whistleblower's Bribery Claim', *Financial Times*, 11 August.

Moore, M., 2012, '"Mass Suicide" Protest at Apple Manufacturer Foxconn Factory', *The Telegraph*, 11 January.

Mozur, P. and Q. Hardy, 2015, 'China Hits Qualcomm with Fine', *The New York Times*, 9 February.

Nestlé, 2012, *Nestlé in China, Creating Shared Value*.

NEWSGD.com, 2013, '2013 Guangdong International Consultative Conference Opens', *NEWSGD.com*, 21 November.

Nisen, M., 2013, 'How Nike Solved Its Sweatshop Problem', *Business Insider*, 9 May.

Nissan, 2015, *2015 Social Responsibility Report of Nissan's Subsidiaries in China*.

Office of the Mayor of Shanghai, 2013, 'Yang Meets IBLAC Chairman', *Office of the Mayor of Shanghai Press Release*, 22 November.

Peking University, Tsinghua University, and University of South Carolina, 2000, *Economic Impact of the Coca-Cola System on China*.

Plumridge, H. and L. Burkitt, 2014, 'GlaxoSmithKline Found Guilty of Bribery in China', *The Wall Street Journal*, 19 September.

Qianzhan Business Information Co, 2015, *China Corporate University Report, 2013–2017*, Qianzhan Business Information Co.

R3, 2012, *Benchmarking CSR in China*.

Rees, E., 2014, 'Unilever and the Case for Sustainable Business', *Chinadialogue*, 16 April.

Reuters, 2014, 'China Fines Milk Powder makers US$110m for Price-fixing', *Reuters*, 24 November.

Schell, O., 2011, 'How Walmart Is Changing China', *The Atlantic*, December.

Schwaag-Serger, S., 2008, *Foreign R&D Centers in China: Development, Drivers, Spillovers*, Swedish Institute for Growth Policy Studies (ITPS) and Research Policy Institute, University of Lund.

SCMP, 2014, 'China's "Rotten Meat" Scandal Firm Sacks 340 People at Shanghai Plant', *South China Morning Post*, 22 September.

SCMP, 2015, 'China Sales Slide Pushes Yum into the Red', *South China Morning Post*, 5 February.

Shanghai Daily, 2008, 'IBM Locates New Unit HQ in Shanghai', *Shanghai Daily*, 25 April.

Shanghai Daily, 2014, 'IBLAC Conference to Focus on FTZ', *Shanghai Daily*, 10 September.

Shell, 2015, *Our Business in China*.

Shih, W., K. Bliznashki, and F. Zhao, 2012, 'IBM China Development Lab Shanghai: Capability by Design', *HBS Case*, Harvard Business School Publishing, Boston.

Shipping Online, 2009, 'Maersk Social Responsibility Award for Sichuan Quake Role', *Shipping Online*, 27 August.

Siemens, 2011, 'Siemens Signs Memorandum with Ministry of Education of China to Jointly Promote Engineering Education', *Siemens China Press Release*, 16 February.

Siemens, 2015, *Siemens R&D in China*.

Sony, 2015, *Corporate Information: Basic Philosophy of Supply Chain Management*.

St James Press, 2004, 'Charoen Pokphand Group History', *International Directory of Company Histories Vol 62*, London, St James Press.

Stalley, P., 2010, *Foreign Firms, Investment, and Environmental Regulation in the People's Republic of China*, Stanford, Stanford University Press.

State Council, 1990, *Detailed Rules for Implementing the Law of the People's Republic of China on Enterprises Operated Exclusively with Foreign Capital*, State Council of the People's Republic of China.

Stoll, J.D., 2015, 'GM, SAIV Plan to Jointly Design New Cars', *The Wall Street Journal*, 28 July.

Sullivan, G., 2014, 'Wal-Mart to Triple Food Safety Spending in China After Donkey Meat Disaster', *The Washington Post*, 17 June.

Tam, F., 2010, 'Foxconn Factories are Labour Camps', *South China Morning Post*, 11 October.

Tan, Z., Y. Wang, and E. Ng, 2014, *"LEED-Oriented" Projects in Mainland China and the Indication to Sustainable Practice in Developing Countries*, Presented at the 30th International PLEA Conference, CEPT University, Ahmedabad.

Teather, D., 2005, 'Nike Lists Abuses at Asian Factories', *The Guardian*, 14 April.

Tejada, C., 2014, 'Microsoft, the "Guardian Warriors" and China's Cybersecurity Fears', *The Wall Street Journal*, 29 July.

Teo, J., 2012, 'Innovating in China's Pharma Market: An Interview with AstraZeneca's Head of R&D in Asia and Emerging Markets', *Insights and Publications*, McKinsey & Company, February.

Thun, E., 2006, *Changing Lanes: Foreign Direct Investment, Local Governments, and Auto Sector Development*, New York, Cambridge University Press.

Townsend, M., 2012, 'Nike Raises Factory Labor and Sustainability Standards', *Bloomberg Business*, 4 May.

Toyota, 2011, 'TMC and Tsinghua University to Continue Joint Research', *Toyota Global News-Room*, 30 March.

Trefis, 2014, 'McDonald's Faces Declining Sales in Asia after China Food Scandal', *Trefis*, 11 September.

Tselichtchev, I., 2011, *China versus the West: The Global Power Shift of the 21st Century*, Singapore, Wiley.

Tsinghua University, 2015, *Enterprise Cooperation*.

Vahland, W., 2010, *Volkswagen Strategy to 2018*, Beijing, Volkswagen Group China – Investor Conference.

van Winden, W., L. van den Berg, L. Carvalho, and E. van Tuijl, 2006, *Manufacturing in the New Urban Economy*, New York, Cambridge University Press.

Volkswagen, 2013, *Volkswagen Finance: Company History*.

Volkswagen, 2015, *Volkswagen (China) Investment Co., Ltd, Corporate Information*.

Voyles, B., 2013, 'Foxconn Faces Its Future', *CKGSB Knowledge*, 29 August.

Wang, H. 2011, 'Roche Sees New Shanghai Center One of its Hubs', *China Daily*, 15 April.

Wang, J., Z. Liang, and L. Yue, 2013, 'Multinational R&D in China: Differentiation and Integration of Global R&D Networks', in *The Selected Works of Jian Wang*, Leuven, KU Leuven.

Wang, S., 2009, 'Foreign Retailers in Post-WTO China: Stories of Success and Setbacks', *Asia Pacific Business Review*, 15(1), pp. 59–77.

Wang, Y., 2013, 'IBLAC 2013 Closes as Top Business Figures Share Views on City's Soft Power', *Shanghai Daily*, 27 October.

Wang, Y., 2014, 'More MNCs open HQ in Shanghai', *Shanghai Daily*, 11 December.

White, S., J. Gao, and W. Zhang, 2002, 'China's Venture Capital Industry: Institutional Trajectories and System Structure', *Working Paper-INSEAD*.

Wilson, S., 2009, *Remade in China: Foreign Investors and Institutional Change in China*, Oxford, Oxford University Press.

Ye, Z., 2014, 'Executives Laud Reform, Point to Unfinished Agenda', *Shanghai Daily*, 3 November.

Yip, G. and B. McKern, 2014, 'Can Multinationals Innovate in China?' *Forbes Asia*, 17 December.

Zadek, S., K. Yu, and M. Forstater, 2012, *Corporate Responsibility and Sustainable Economic Development in China: Implications for Business*, Washington, DC, Asia U.S. Chamber of Commerce.

Zeng, F., 2004, *Venture Capital Investments in China*, Los Angeles, Rand.

Zero2IPO Research Center, 2015, [*China Private Equity Market 2014 Annual Review*], (in Chinese).

Zhang, J., 2011, 'Fortune Favour 500 as China Courts Foreign Advisors', *China.org.cn*, 21 December.

Zhang, J., 2015, 'China's Antitrust Crackdown Hits Qualcomm with US$975 Million Fine: What Can Other Host States Learn from the Story?' *Investment Treaty News*, International Institute for Sustainable Development (IISD), 21 May.

Zhang, J. and Y. Wu, 2010, '[A study for threshold effects of foreign bank entry's influence on the efficiency of domestic commercial bank: Evidence from commercial banks in China]', *Journal of Financial Research*, no. 6, (in Chinese).

Zhang, X. and Z. Pei, 2015, '[The Competition Effect of Foreign Banks on Domestic Banks – Empirical Tests Based on China's Bank Industry During 2000 and 2013]', *China Price*, no.1, (in Chinese).

Zinzius, B., 2004, *Doing Business in the New China*, Westport, CT, Praeger.

5

Foreign investment in Chinese cities[1]

Introduction

In this chapter, we will drill down into the impact of foreign investment on individual municipalities in China. We will focus on four municipalities, Shenzhen, Tianjin, Shanghai, and Chongqing. Geographically, these cities represent the South, North, East, and West in China. Temporally, they represent different periods of economic opening. Shenzhen started to receive significant foreign investment in the 1980s, Tianjin and Shanghai in the 1990s, and Chongqing in the 2000s. Sectorally, they also represent different mixes with Shenzhen initially focused on light manufacturing and then high technology development mostly for export; Shanghai on a widely diversified mix of industrial, service, and headquarters activities linking to global markets; Tianjin on manufacturing industries geared for the domestic market, then services; and Chongqing with a mix of resource-based industries, transportation equipment, computers, and real estate. In each case, foreign investment and foreign invested enterprises have been instrumental to the municipality's economic development and remain highly relevant today.

Shenzhen was the first Chinese city opened to trade and investment in the reform period. Shenzhen's special status and its proximity to Hong Kong helped turn what was a backwater into one of China's most successful and dynamic cities. In the process, it has evolved from a low labour cost location to one of China's leading technology and innovation centres. Foreign investment and foreign enterprises have been critical to this development.

Tianjin historically was China's second leading industrial city. It was among the second set of cities to be opened to foreign investment. While much of the output of FIEs in Tianjin has historically focused on the domestic market, FIEs dominate Tianjin's trade as well. The creation of TEDA, a government economic development agency, and the development of several industrial parks put Tianjin on the path to attracting multinational companies. While continuing its industrial tradition, Tianjin has increasingly focused on attracting FDI into the service sector, including finance. Its main development thrusts involve the attraction of foreign investment into the Binhai New Area.

Shanghai is China's leading economic city and its leading destination for foreign investment. It was not until the opening of the Pudong New Area and the push for investment in the 1990s that Shanghai emerged as the leading destination for foreign investors in China. Given the size and diversification of its economy, Shanghai has attracted investment in a wide range of sectors. It has also emerged as the leading centre for the China headquarters of foreign multinationals and is increasing in importance as a location for a variety of headquarters activities. Foreign investment and foreign firms have played a critical role in Shanghai's development, and even though Shanghai is probably China's most advanced city when it comes to economic development, further openness and further attraction of the activities of foreign companies remains a cornerstone of its development program.

While called a 'municipality', Chongqing extends over 82,400 square kilometres, with rural area accounting for 80 percent of the total area. This makes Chongqing larger than Hainan (35,400 sq. km.) and Ningxia (66,000 sq. km.) among China's provinces. Located in Western China, Chongqing is far from the coastal provinces that were the focal points of the first waves of China's economic opening. Chongqing is therefore an example of a 'late mover' as a recipient of foreign investment. It started receiving significant quantities of investment only after China's Government started heavily promoting its 'Go West' program in 2000. Even so, foreign investment has been instrumental to developing Chongqing's major industries, and Chongqing is a good example of the crucial role that foreign investment is playing in developing several of China's newly emerging cities.

In each case, the impact of FDI and FIEs on the municipal economies has been large, even when the impact estimates are based on only a modest portion of the total inward investment in the cities. For the most recent year available, in Shenzhen we estimated that foreign investment and the operations of foreign invested enterprises in industries that account for 66 percent of cumulative investment accounted for 41 percent of GDP and 43 percent of employment. For Tianjin when the operations in industries that account for 51 percent of cumulative FDI are taken into account, the impact of FDI and FIEs was 22 percent of GDP and 21 percent of employment. In Chongqing, when the operations in industries that account for 34 percent of FDI are taken into account, the impact of FDI and FIEs was 16 percent of GDP and 7 percent of employment. If FDI and FIEs in other industries where the impacts cannot be traced at present have anything like the impacts in the other sectors, then the total impact of FDI and FIEs in these cities could range from 35 to 60 plus percent of GDP. And in Shanghai, where data was not available to carry out this type of analysis, official sources have indicated that FIEs directly account for two-thirds of exports, imports, and industrial output; one-third of tax and employment; and 90 percent of high technology output.

The case studies show that these leading Chinese cities have relied heavily on foreign investment and foreign invested enterprises to develop their economies during the reform period. In many cases, foreign enterprises dominate industries that have been critical to development. In some cases, foreign enterprises have literally built the foundations upon which the municipal economies have been developed. In many cases, FDI and FIEs have provided technology, managerial capabilities, and resources that were not available in the local market. The studies also show that Chinese officials have learned from each of the cities and have used the lessons to refine their own policies and programs.

Shenzhen

Shenzhen was the first municipality in China to be opened to foreign investment and has been a leader in receiving inward investment ever since. From 1996 to 2013, Shenzhen received USD 58.55 billion in FDI, which ranked it sixth among Chinese cities during that period (CEIC, various years). By the end of 2014, Shenzhen had attracted a total of 50,453 foreign invested projects, with a cumulative contracted value of USD 100 billion, and a utilized value of USD 65 billion (Shenzhen, various years). In 2013, 52 percent of gross industrial output in Shenzhen was from foreign invested enterprises, and 48 percent of Shenzhen's exports came from foreign invested enterprises (Shenzhen, 2014). Shenzhen had grown from a small fishing village, with only around 30,000 residents, to a thriving metropolis with a population in excess of 10 million, the fourth largest GDP in the Chinese Mainland, and the largest exports among Mainland cities. This development had been based largely on foreign investment.

The evolution of foreign investment in Shenzhen

In the 1960s and early 1970s, Shenzhen had few people, no industrial base, and no modern infrastructure. In 1979, the Chinese Central Government decided to set up Special Economic Zones (SEZs) in Shenzhen, Zhuhai, Shantou, and Xiamen. In 1980, the Standing Committee of the National People's Congress approved the *Regulations on Special Economic Zones in Guangdong Province*, which marked the official launch of the Shenzhen SEZ. The strategy was for the SEZs to become export-oriented industrial complexes that would serve as catalysts for the transformation of the economy and society. Shenzhen was selected due to its proximity to Hong Kong, so that Hong Kong would connect Shenzhen, and China, to the rest of the world.

Shenzhen's opening

From the onset of the economic opening, Shenzhen's development strategy relied on foreign investment. The 1982 Shenzhen Master Plan was based on the assumption that 58 percent of the investment costs through the year 2000 would come from foreign sources (Leong and Pratap, 2011). The first area in Shenzhen to be opened was the Shekou Industrial Zone in Nanshan District, which was developed by China Merchants Group, a state-owned company headquartered in Hong Kong, which constructed the infrastructure including roads, utilities, and ports in Shekou, and then attracted foreign investors to set up in the Zone. Shekou was transformed into an energetic industrial town with hundreds of foreign-invested (mostly Hong Kong) enterprises. The 'Shekou model' was soon copied in other areas of Shenzhen, and massive infrastructure projects were started in Luohu and Futian.

In order to attract foreign investment, the Shenzhen SEZ was given flexibility in the application of foreign funds, the introduction of foreign technologies, and the undertaking of foreign economic collaboration. Preferential policies were granted in areas such as taxation, customs, staffing, land use, and labour rules. Shenzhen was exempted from submitting tax revenues to the central and provincial governments for ten years, allowing it to reinvest locally. At the time, Hong Kong's light manufacturing industries began moving facilities to Shekou to take advantage of land, incentives, and labour costs one-tenth of those in Hong Kong. In 1981, the four SEZs accounted for 59.8 percent of total foreign direct investment in China, with Shenzhen accounting for 50.6 percent and the other three roughly 3 percent each (Leong and Pratap, 2011). By the mid-1980s, Shenzhen was home to nearly 40 percent of all Sino-foreign joint ventures in China. Millions of migrant workers had come to Shenzhen, and Shenzhen also attracted thousands of managers from elsewhere in the Chinese Mainland, Hong Kong, and the rest of Asia. Foreign enterprises and Sino-foreign joint ventures accounted for 53 percent of total output value in Shenzhen in 1983.

Hong Kong firms were by far the main investors in Shenzhen in those years, accounting for over 96 percent of joint ventures in textiles and dyeing in the Shenzhen SEZ, 78 percent in metal products, 86 percent in rubber and plastics, 95 percent in garments, and 85 percent in electrical machinery from 1979 to 1990 (Wu, 1997). According to one source:

> Shenzhen's first-mover advantages got a big early lift from its heralded neighbor Hong Kong. Given Hong Kong's historical economic relationships with international markets, it was well prepared to provide Shenzhen with an entry point to markets outside of China. This allowed low-cost production in Shenzhen, where land and labor were relatively cheap; low-cost and convenient shipping of raw materials and products to international markets; easy supervision of the production process and excellent quality control; and streamlined coordination with headquarters in Hong Kong. The end result was the efficient, expeditious export of quality, inexpensive finished goods to international markets through Hong Kong.
> (Chen and de'Medici, 2009, p. 13)

Shenzhen was the first place in China to experiment with different labour regimes. The wage system that developed in Shenzhen was modelled on the laissez-faire approach of Hong Kong, with base wages, position wages, and floating wages, the last of which varied by performance (JPRD, 1983, p. 114; Wilson, 2009). Inspired by the Shenzhen experience, short-term labour contracts started replacing lifetime employment in China, and this system was included in later laws governing the entire economy. Shenzhen was also the first place in China to tender openly for infrastructure contracts, to loosen price controls, to introduce foreign exchange swaps, to have Sino-foreign joint ventures in the real estate sector, to sell land use rights to joint ventures, and to use auctions for land use rights. It has also been the first to reduce levels of government, provide legal status to non-governmental organizations, and implement other political reforms. Based on the early results, Deng Xiaoping during his tour of the SEZs in early 1984 called upon the nation to 'learn from Shenzhen', firmly establishing Shenzhen as a trend setter within China. In many cases, experiments introduced in Shenzhen were later spread to the rest of the country.

Development and diversification

Shenzhen received a further push in 1992 when Deng Xiaoping visited the Pearl River Delta and called for further reforms. FDI into Shenzhen jumped to USD 4.97 billion in contracted value on 3,255 new contracts in 1993. By the end of 1999, there were over 12,000 foreign enterprises from 66 countries/regions invested in Shenzhen, among which 76 were Fortune 500 companies. By 1999, there were 52 foreign financial institutions operating in Shenzhen (Shenzhen, 2000). By 2006, 113 of the Global 500 had set up operations in Shenzhen. By 2012, this figure was 189 (Shenzhen ETO, 2013). Over that period, there was extensive diversification in Shenzhen's economy.

In the early years, most foreign invested joint ventures in Shenzhen were export processing ventures in which the foreign company provided materials (including parts and components) and designs, and the local company did the processing or assembly work. Since the 1990s, Shenzhen has placed more emphasis on the technological development of the economy. Policies frequently included explicit provisions for technology transfers in the form of local content requirements, and/or collaboration in production, research, or training. Many FDI contracts included explicit conditions for technology sharing. Output in Shenzhen's new and high-tech products increased from RMB 2.3 billion in 1991 to RMB 180 billion in 2003. Shenzhen's exports of new and high-tech products in 2003 accounted for 23.2 percent of the national total (China Briefing Media, 2004). The Shenzhen High-Tech Industrial Park, one of the five state-level high-tech parks in China, was established in 1996. International companies attracted to Shenzhen included Intel, IBM, Toshiba, Sanyo, Seagate, ISTC, Phillips, Compaq, Samsung, Emerson, Olympus, Epson, Alcatel-Lucent, Thomson, and many others. Shenzhen also attracted highly educated people from the rest of China. In 2007, it was claimed that Shenzhen was home to 20 percent of all of China's PhDs (author's interviews with Shenzhen officials).

Foreign investment, mainly from Hong Kong, also helped develop housing and infrastructure in Shenzhen. From 1980 to 1990, the Central Government invested only 1.4 percent of the funds used for the physical development of Shenzhen, and the local government 13.1 percent (World Bank, 2013, p. 84). Housing and infrastructure construction joint ventures with private developers (mainly from Hong Kong) financed much of the physical infrastructure. The Bamboo Garden Hotel, a joint venture between a Shenzhen catering company and a Hong Kong investor started in 1979 was the first case of land commercialization in China. By 1981, five Hong Kong developers were working on housing estates in Shenzhen in conjunction with Shenzhen partners (Zhu, 1999). The introduction of a land market and the sale of land use rights through auctions in 1987 led to a boom in property development and increased the capital available to the local government to improve infrastructure and implement development plans.

Hong Kong entities were also directly investing in infrastructure. Chiwan Port, co-owned by Chiwan Port Company and two Hong Kong-based companies (Kerry Properties and Modern Terminals Limited), started construction in 1982. It was the first port in China jointly constructed by domestic and foreign partners. Hong Kong-based Hutchison-Whampoa and the Shenzhen Government started construction on Yantian Port, in May 1988. Construction of the Daya Bay Nuclear Power Plant, 25 percent owned by Hong Kong-based CLP, started in 1987.

In 1982, the first foreign-invested bank in China, Nanyang Commercial Bank, opened its branch in Shenzhen. Eventually, numerous foreign banks would start operations in Shenzhen including HSBC, Citibank, UBS, Dah Sing, Bank of East Asia, and others. By 1999, there were 52 foreign financial institutions operating in Shenzhen (Shenzhen, 2000). Shenzhen's growing income levels attracted Hong Kong investment in consumer services such as retail, catering, real estate, and tourism, and Hong Kong firms became the dominant foreign investors in Shenzhen's real estate and hotel sectors. Other foreign companies also entered Shenzhen's service sector. Wal-Mart, for example, placed a global sourcing hub in Shenzhen, and established stores in Shenzhen along with many other international retailers.

Recent years have also seen substantial growth in foreign investment into service sectors in Shenzhen. Utilized FDI in service industries has risen to nearly half of total FDI since the mid-2000s from less than 30 percent before. In 2014, contracted FDI into secondary industries in Shenzhen was USD 1.01 billion, 18.2 percent lower than the prior year, and only 9.22 percent of total contracted FDI value in Shenzhen in that year. Contracted FDI value into tertiary industries in Shenzhen was USD 9.89 billion or 90.7 percent of the total, with finance (USD 5.06 billion), wholesale and retail (USD 1.86 billion), and leasing and business services (USD 1.57 billion) the three leaders (Shenzhen, 2014).

Hong Kong continues to be the dominant source of foreign investment into China. In 2013, Hong Kong and Macau accounted for 77 percent of total FDI into Shenzhen, the vast majority of which came from Hong Kong (Shenzhen, 2014).[2] The 2003 Closer Economic Partnership Arrangement (CEPA) between the Chinese Mainland and Hong Kong, and a series of supplements signed in following years, have brought Hong Kong and Shenzhen closer together. Hong Kong-Shenzhen linkages were further expanded by 2008 calls by China's National Development and Reform Commission for Shenzhen and Hong Kong to further integrate their economies and the designation of Qianhai as a Shenzhen-Hong Kong Modern Service Industry Cooperation Zone in 2010.

New challenges and directions

Shenzhen has also faced challenges. It lost its leadership position as a location for FIEs to Shanghai, and as costs increased in Shenzhen, many companies shifted to neighbouring Dongguan or other parts of China. In 2005, Mayor Xu Zongheng noted the city faced issues of limited land, shortages of energy and water, demographic pressures, and environmental degradation. Policy responses included restrictions on land approvals, increases in minimum wages to the highest levels in the nation, banning several polluting industries, and the creation of new industrial parks to facilitate the relocation of facilities to cheaper locations (Chen and de'Medici, 2009).

After the global financial crisis in 2008, the Shenzhen Government shifted focus to the industrial upgrading of the city economy, and began urging companies in lower value added industries to move elsewhere. Rising costs also became a major concern, as it was estimated that the average monthly salary of migrant workers in Shenzhen reached 3,300 yuan (roughly USD 533) in 2011, 32 times greater than the 100 yuan (roughly USD 16) in 1980 when the Shenzhen SEZ was set up (Xie et al., 2013). The policy environment and rising costs for labour and land forced many manufacturers to move to other parts of China, or East Asia. Foxconn, the Taiwanese electronics manufacturer that once employed approximately 500,000 in Shenzhen, started moving capacity to Zhengzhou, Taiyuan, Wuhan, Chongqing, and Chengdu in 2007. Eventually, it plans to use Shenzhen mostly for R&D (author's interviews).

Shenzhen plans to base its next stage of development on high-technology, innovation, and the service sector. Foreign investment is viewed as critical to this undertaking. One of the key focal points is the Qianhai Shenzhen-Hong Kong Modern Service Cooperation Zone. This area is to focus on finance, modern logistics, information, professional services, and high-technology business. Qianhai has been given special policies for financial services, preferential tax treatment, Hong Kong-based legal frameworks, professional services, education, and telecommunications. Many of these policies involve opening to Hong Kong-based partners and professionals. In 2014, Qianhai accounted for 63.13 percent of contracted FDI into Shenzhen (MOFCOM, 2015).

Overview of FDI and FIEs in Shenzhen

FDI into Shenzhen started slowly after its initial opening. Cumulative utilized FDI did not exceed USD 1 billion until 1986, six years after the establishment of the Shenzhen SEZ (Table 5.1). Investment only started to take off after Deng Xiaoping's Southern Tour and a second wave of reform in the early 1990s. The annual flow of utilized investment was USD 489 million in 1992, passed the USD 2,000 million mark in 1996, the USD 3,000 million mark in 2002, the USD 4,000 million mark in 2008, and the USD 5,000 million mark in 2012. By 2013, the cumulative value of contracted FDI was USD 99,578 million and the cumulative utilized value was USD 65,215 million, indicating that there should continue to be substantial FDI inflows well into the future.

Table 5.1 Inward FDI into Shenzhen

Year	Number of Contracts		Contracted Value (USD mn)		Actual Utilized Value (USD mn)	
	Annual	Cumulative	Annual	Cumulative	Annual	Cumulative
1979	37	37	18	18	5	5
1980	33	70	240	258	28	33
1981	70	140	864	1,121	86	119
1982	66	206	175	1,297	58	177
1983	253	459	294	1,590	113	290
1984	334	793	533	2,124	186	476
1985	282	1,075	793	2,917	180	656
1986	224	1,299	244	3,161	365	1,021
1987	310	1,609	567	3,728	274	1,295
1988	591	2,200	430	4,158	287	1,582
1989	647	2,847	469	4,627	293	1,874
1990	757	3,604	679	5,306	390	2,264
1991	951	4,555	1,086	6,392	399	2,663
1992	1,553	6,108	2,495	8,887	449	3,112
1993	3,255	9,363	4,969	13,857	989	4,101
1994	2,221	11,584	2,831	16,688	1,250	5,351
1995	1,633	13,217	3,463	20,151	1,310	6,661
1996	999	14,216	1,680	21,831	2,051	8,712
1997	957	15,173	1,354	23,185	1,661	10,373
1998	1,391	16,564	2,035	25,220	1,664	12,037
1999	797	17,361	1,210	26,430	1,778	13,815
2000	1,130	18,491	1,738	28,168	1,961	15,776
2001	1,501	19,992	2,723	30,891	2,591	18,367
2002	1,917	21,909	3,544	34,435	3,191	21,558
2003	2,254	24,163	4,847	39,282	3,623	25,182
2004	2,718	26,881	4,121	43,403	2,350	27,532
2005	2,797	29,678	5,251	48,654	2,969	30,500
2006	3,105	32,783	5,264	53,918	3,269	33,769
2007	4,200	36,983	8,572	62,490	3,662	37,431
2008	3,046	40,029	7,283	69,773	4,030	41,461
2009	1,498	41,527	3,558	73,331	4,160	45,621
2010	1,929	43,456	5,652	78,983	4,297	49,918
2011	2,513	45,969	7,633	86,616	4,599	54,518
2012	2,428	48,397	6,262	92,878	5,229	59,747
2013	2,056	50,453	6,700	99,578	5,468	65,215

Source: *Shenzhen Statistical Yearbooks* (various years).

According to Chinese statistics, Hong Kong and Macau have been the dominant investors in Shenzhen, accounting for 63 percent of total FDI into Shenzhen from 1991 to 2013. Japan and the United States were next, each accounting for 4 percent of total inward FDI from 1991 to 2013. From 2011 to 2013, the Hong Kong and Macau share actually increased to 74 percent of the total FDI into Shenzhen, reflecting in part the favourable conditions for Hong Kong companies to invest in Qianhai (Shenzhen, various years). Industrial sectors (i.e. mining, manufacturing, and utilities) have been the major recipients of FDI into Shenzhen, accounting for 66 percent of total inward FDI from 1991 to 2013. The Real Estate and Wholesale, Retail Trade, and Catering industries each accounted for 13 percent of total FDI into Shenzhen from 1991 to 2013. Over the years, especially after 2005, the balance of FDI started shifting from the industrial sector to services. For example, from 2011 to 2013, industrial sectors received 50 percent of inward FDI into Shenzhen, while the Wholesale, Retail Trade, and Catering industry received 26 percent, and the Real Estate sector received 16 percent.

The importance of FDI and FIEs

Figure 5.1 shows that FDI has equalled at least 10 percent of gross capital formation in Shenzhen every year since 1992, with a peak of 24 percent in 1994 and a slight uptick to 12 percent in 2012. Foreign investment in fixed assets has exceeded 10 percent of the total every year since 1995, with a peak of 21 percent in 1998, and fairly steady levels in the mid-teens since 2007. On these measures, foreign investment is ten or more times as important to the Shenzhen economy as to the economy of China as a whole.

Overall, foreign invested industrial enterprises accounted for 53 percent of total revenue, 48 percent of total assets, and 47 percent of total profits of all the industrial enterprises in Shenzhen in 2013 (Table 5.2). Manufacture of Computers, Communication, and Other Electronic Equipment industry (2013 revenue RMB 603,366 million), Manufacture of Electrical Machinery and Apparatus industry (2013 revenue RMB 123,190 million), and Manufacture of Articles for Culture, Education, Arts and Crafts, Sport and Entertainment Activities (2013 revenue RMB 58,170 million) were the three largest industries in terms of revenue of FIEs in Shenzhen.

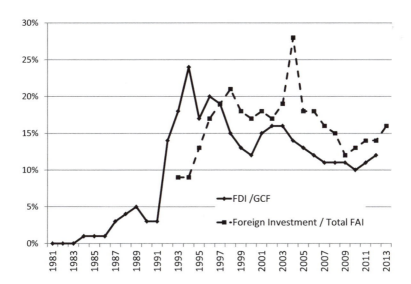

Figure 5.1 Foreign investment versus total investment in Shenzhen

Source: *Shenzhen Statistical Yearbooks* (various years).

Table 5.2 Foreign invested industrial enterprises by industry in Shenzhen, 2013

Industry	Revenue (RMB mm)	% of Shenzhen Total	Assets (RMB mm)	% of Shenzhen Total	Profits (RMB mm)	% of Shenzhen Total	FIE Revenue/ Assets (%)	FIE Profits/ Revenue (%)	FIE Profits/ Assets (%)
All Industrial Sectors	1,186,760	53	962,420	48	60,066	47	123	5.1	6.2
Manufacture of Computers, Communication, and Other Electronic Equipment	603,366	50	395,338	42	16,320	28	153	2.7	4.1
Manufacture of Electrical Machinery and Apparatus	123,190	62	95,349	55	3,002	48	129	2.4	3.1
Manufacture of Articles for Culture, Education, Arts and Crafts, Sport and Entertainment Activities	58,170	38	43,736	44	1,740	69	133	3.0	4.0
Manufacture of General Purpose Machinery	49,902	78	30,214	61	1,679	64	165	3.4	5.6
Manufacture of Rubber Products Plastics Products	45,906	67	34,208	58	843	46	134	1.8	2.5
Extraction of Petroleum and Natural Gas	43,259	100	36,756	100	15,439	100	118	35.7	42.0

Manufacture of Metal Products	31,197	67	31,051	65	1,903	79	100	6.1	6.1
Manufacture of Special Purpose Machinery	25,931	50	33,317	46	985	21	78	3.8	3.0
Manufacture of Automobiles	22,895	81	41,443	83	-895	N/A	55	-3.9	-2.2
Manufacture of Measuring Instruments and Machinery	15,574	52	14,576	44	1,477	57	107	9.5	10.1
Manufacture of Non-metallic Mineral Products	14,830	55	16,451	46	1,321	58	90	8.9	8.0
Manufacture of Textile, Wearing Apparel, and Accessories	13,048	57	9,983	54	934	60	131	7.2	9.4
Manufacture of Raw Chemical Materials and Chemical Products	12,701	54	12,235	41	691	40	104	5.4	5.6
Processing of Food from Agricultural Products	12,589	77	8,936	80	719	91	141	5.7	8.0
Smelting and Pressing of Non-ferrous Metals	11,440	39	12,904	62	113	49	89	1.0	0.9

(Continued)

Table 5.2 (Continued)

Industry	Revenue (RMB mn)	% of Shenzhen Total	Assets (RMB mn)	% of Shenzhen Total	Profits (RMB mn)	% of Shenzhen Total	FIE Revenue/ Assets (%)	FIE Profits/ Revenue (%)	FIE Profits/ Assets (%)
Production and Supply of Electric Power and Heat Power	11,222	15	24,313	19	3,520	36	46	31.4	14.5
Manufacture of Leather, Fur, Feather and Related Prods, Footwear	10,660	78	14,469	91	1,472	95	74	13.8	10.2
Manufacture of Liquor, Beverages, and Refined Tea	9,612	93	6,070	89	319	98	158	3.3	5.3
Manufacture of Medicines	9,608	56	12,432	33	2,165	57	77	22.5	17.4
Printing and Reproduction of Recording Media	8,363	46	9,542	40	463	26	88	5.5	4.9
Manufacture of Rail, ships, and other transport Equipment	7,950	76	8,831	81	268	71	90	3.4	3.0
Manufacture of Furniture	7,510	50	8,034	50	299	76	93	4.0	3.7
Manufacture of Paper and Paper Products	6,813	51	6,827	51	189	49	100	2.8	2.8
Production and Supply of Water	6,211	62	30,347	74	1,635	75	20	26.3	5.4

Production and Supply of Gas	6,093	100	8,211	100	1,624	100	74	26.7	19.8
Processing of Petroleum, Coking, and Processing of Nuclear Fuel	5,147	97	4,275	96	1,160	98	120	22.5	27.1
Manufacture of Textile	3,916	61	3,745	54	76	23	105	1.9	2.0
Manufacture of Foods	3,906	69	4,135	67	252	108	94	6.5	6.1
Smelting and Pressing of Ferrous Metals	2,177	36	1,625	41	35	150	134	1.6	2.2
Other Manufacture	1,789	39	1,319	37	35	15	136	2.0	2.7
Repair Service of Metal Products, Machinery, and Equipment	849	79	1,081	89	124	91	79	14.6	11.5
Support Activities for Mining	388	13	375	15	165	27	103	42.5	44.0
Processing of Timber, Manufacture of Wood, Bamboo, Rattan, Palm, and Straw Products	319	23	221	11	-2	Na	144	-0.6	-0.9
Manufacture of Chemical Fibers	203	40	47	23	2	18	432	1.0	4.3
Utilization of Waste Resources	26	31	25	37	-7	N/A	104	-26.9	-28.0

(Continued)

Table 5.2 (Continued)

Industry	Revenue (RMB mn)	% of Shenzhen Total	Assets (RMB mn)	% of Shenzhen Total	Profits (RMB mn)	% of Shenzhen Total	FIE Revenue/ Assets (%)	FIE Profits/ Revenue (%)	FIE Profits/ Assets (%)
Manufacture of Tobacco	–	–	–	–	–	–	–	–	–
Mining and Processing of Ferrous Metal Ores	–	–	–	–	–	–	–	–	–
Mining and Processing of Non-ferrous Metal Ores	–	–	–	–	–	–	–	–	–
Mining and Processing of Non-metal Ores	–	–	–	–	–	–	–	–	–
Mining and Washing of Coal	–	–	–	–	–	–	–	–	–
Mining of Other Ores	–	–	–	–	–	–	–	–	–

Sources: *Shenzhen Statistical Yearbook 2014*; Enright, Scott & Associates analysis.

In many industries in Shenzhen, FIEs played a dominant role, such as Production and Supply of Gas (100 percent of total revenue of the industry in Shenzhen); Processing of Petroleum, Coking and Processing of Nuclear Fuel (97 percent); Manufacture of Liquor, Beverages, and Refined Tea (93 percent); Manufacture of Automobiles (81 percent); Manufacture of General Purpose Machinery (78 percent); and Manufacture of Leather, Fur, Feather, and Related Products and Footwear (78 percent). In other important industries like Manufacture of Computers, Communication, and Other Electronic Equipment; Manufacture of Electrical Machinery and Apparatus; and Manufacture of Measuring Instruments and Machinery; and Manufacture of Rubber Products Plastics Products, the FIE revenue share is 50 percent or higher. Clearly FIEs play an important if not dominant role in several leading industries in Shenzhen.

FIEs are also critical to Shenzhen's trade (Figure 5.2). FIEs accounted for more than 50 percent of Shenzhen's exports and imports from 1995 through 2013. FIE net exports have been positive in every year during that period. FIE net exports accounted for over 20 percent of Shenzhen's GDP as early as 1997, and accounted for 22 percent in 2013. This means just the trade performance of Shenzhen's FIEs accounted for over one-fifth of GDP, showing the huge contribution that FIE trade makes to Shenzhen's economy.

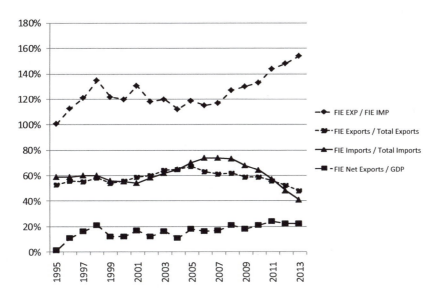

Figure 5.2 Trade performance of foreign invested enterprises in Shenzhen

Note: The FIE trade figures are extracted from *Guangdong Statistical Yearbooks* while the Shenzhen trade figures are extracted from *Shenzhen Statistical Yearbooks*, which might have some discrepancy in statistical scope.

Sources: *Shenzhen Statistical Yearbooks* (various years); *Guangdong Statistical Yearbooks* (various years).

Economic impact of FDI and FIEs on Shenzhen

In this section, we apply the tools of economic impact analysis to estimate the economic impact that FIEs have had on output, value added (GDP), and employment in Shenzhen. The methodology employed was similar to that described in Chapter 3. Statistics were available for FIE sales, value added, and employment in Shenzhen in 33 industry categories (Shenzhen, various years) and the Guangdong Provincial input–output tables were used to generate multipliers specific to Guangdong, and by extension Shenzhen. The industries covered in the analysis accounted for approximately 66 percent of the inward FDI in Shenzhen in the years 1991 to 2013.

The estimated impact for the investment phase for investments made in 2013 was USD 10,963 million in output, USD 3,878 million in value added, and 144,766 in employment. The impact of the capital investment associated with FDI equalled 1.7 percent of Shenzhen's GDP and 1.6 percent of Shenzhen's total employment in 2013. The economic impact of the operations of FIEs in Mining, Manufacturing, and Utilities in Shenzhen in 2013 was USD 343,198 million in total output, USD 91,126 million in value added, and 3,604,925 persons in employment. This equalled 39 percent of Shenzhen's GDP and 40 percent of Shenzhen's total employment from all sources in 2013. Again, these impacts are the result of operations of FIEs in industries that accounted for 66 percent of the total FDI into Shenzhen over the period 1991 to 2013. If the service sectors could be included, the estimated impacts would be even higher. The estimated combined economic impact of the investment phase associated with all foreign direct investment in Shenzhen and the sales of FIEs in the Mining, Manufacturing, and Utilities sectors in Shenzhen in 2013 was USD 354,161 million in output, USD 95,004 million in value added, and 3,749,691 in employment. The estimates were equivalent to 41 percent of Shenzhen's GDP and 42 percent of Shenzhen's total employment from all sources in 2013.

Again, we note that the impacts from operations are just for the Mining, Manufacturing, and Utilities industries for which the sales data for FIEs is available. The impacts do not include the impact of the operation of FIEs in the service sector. We note that since the multipliers are derived from Guangdong input–output tables, the estimates include the upstream spillovers to the rest of Guangdong Province as well, but do not include wider spillovers into China's economy beyond Guangdong. Thus they understate the economic contribution of FDI and FIEs in Shenzhen to China's total economy.

Table 5.3 shows the economic impact of FIEs for the leading Mining, Manufacturing, and Utilities sectors for the year 2013. The operations of FIEs in Computers, Communication, and Other Electronic Equipment industry (direct revenue RMB 603,366 million) generated the largest impact, with a total impact of USD 177,586 million in output, USD 39,531 million in value added, and 1,605,606 jobs. FIEs in Electrical Machinery and Apparatus (direct revenue RMB 123,190 million) generated a total impact of USD 35,293 million in output, USD 8,782 million in value added, and 357,464 jobs. FIEs in Paper and Paper Products; Printing, Reproduction of Recording Media; and Manufacture of Articles For Culture, Education and Sport Activities industries (direct revenue RMB 73,346 million) generated a total impact of USD 22,483 million in output, USD 6,836 million in value added, and 318,769 jobs in 2013.

Table 5.3 Impact of the operations of FIEs, Mining, Manufacturing, and Utilities Sectors in Shenzhen by industry, 2013

Industry	Output (USD mn)	Value Added (USD mn)	Employment
Manufacture of Computers, Communication, and Other Electronic Equipment	177,586	39,531	1,605,606
Manufacture of Electrical Machinery and Apparatus	35,293	8,782	357,464
Manufacture of Paper and Paper Products; Printing, Reproduction of Recording Media; Manufacture of Articles For Culture, Education, and Sport Activities	22,483	6,836	318,769
Manufacture of General Purpose Machinery	14,188	4,021	170,701
Manufacture of Rubber and Plastic Products and Chemical Fibers	13,180	4,059	161,877
Manufacture of Metal Products	9,159	2,556	105,664
Extraction of Petroleum and Natural Gas	8,185	5,490	15,603
Manufacture of Transport Equipment	8,182	2,160	85,408
Manufacture of Special Purpose Machinery	7,373	2,090	88,704
Manufacture of Textile, Wearing Apparel and Accessories, Leather and Fur	7,300	2,828	171,770
Production and Supply of Electric Power, Gas, and Water	6,472	2,344	40,830
Manufacture of Non-metallic Mineral Products	4,577	1,434	56,418
Processing of Food from Agricultural Products	4,403	1,679	96,923

(*Continued*)

Table 5.3 (Continued)

Industry	Output (USD mn)	Value Added (USD mn)	Employment
Manufacture of Measuring Instrument and Machinery for Cultural Activity and Office Work	4,327	1,048	44,452
Smelting and Pressing of Ferrous and Non-ferrous Metals	3,689	772	18,434
Manufacture of Raw Chemical Materials and Chemical Products	3,631	1,118	44,591
Manufacture of Liquor, Beverages, and Refined Tea	3,362	1,282	74,003
Manufacture of Medicines	2,746	846	33,730
Manufacture of Furniture	2,627	856	47,833
Manufacture of Food	1,366	521	30,073
Manufacture of Textile	1,187	401	20,549
Processing of Petroleum, Coking, and Processing of Nuclear Fuel	1,073	223	2,868
Manufacture of Artwork and Other Manufacturing	811	251	12,655

Source: Enright, Scott & Associates analysis.

Shenzhen conclusions

Shenzhen was the pioneer of foreign investment in China. Shenzhen's position as the leader in terms of attracting foreign investment in China has been eclipsed by Shanghai and a few other Chinese cities. However, Shenzhen remains one of the leading destinations in China for foreign investment. It is also fourth among China's cities in GDP, first among China's cities in exports, and in recent years has had the world's third busiest container port. One analysis has described Shenzhen's success as being due to openness, proximity to Hong Kong, huge outside investments, the attraction of talent from China and elsewhere, and entrepreneurship (Gu, 2006).

Analysis of the FDI figures show that FDI and FIEs still account for substantial percentages of Shenzhen's gross capital formation and fixed asset investment. Foreign companies are dominant in several of Shenzhen's leading industries. FIE net exports alone have been contributing over 20 percent of Shenzhen's GDP. And in our economic impact assessment, which covers the investment phase for all investment, but only the operations of investment comprising 66 percent of total FDI in Shenzhen, the estimates were that FDI and FIEs accounted for roughly 41 percent of Shenzhen's GDP and 42 percent of Shenzhen's total employment from all sources in 2013. Again, these results do not include the service sector or any catalytic benefits such as spillovers into the local economy, the impact on productivity in indigenous firms, the impact on technological and managerial capabilities in Shenzhen, the social contributions by FIEs, or other impacts.

The results suggest that Shenzhen has benefitted tremendously from foreign investment and that these benefits continue to be extremely important today. To the extent that Shenzhen remains a leading economy in China, both in terms of its size and its importance as a laboratory for economic development, the benefits to China as a whole go far beyond those estimated for Shenzhen alone. Shenzhen's ability to maintain or extend its position will very much depend on foreign investment and the combination of local and foreign companies in Shenzhen. What may be more important is that some 35 years after the Shenzhen SEZ was founded Shenzhen is still a city on the leading edge of China's reform and opening, and that foreign companies continue to play an extremely important role in the city's economy.

Tianjin

Tianjin was also an early pioneer in terms of economic opening in China. Although it did not receive one of the first Special Economic Zones in China, some of the early examples of foreign investments, such as the first Sino-foreign joint venture, were started in Tianjin. Tianjin has been known over the years for its success in attracting foreign investment and the important role that foreign investment has played in Tianjin's development. Despite the fact that Tianjin was not one of the first of China's cities to be opened to foreign investment, it eventually became an important destination for foreign companies. In the years 1996 to 2013, Tianjin received USD 108.19 billion in foreign investment in 13,920 projects, placing Tianjin second only to Shanghai in the Chinese Mainland as a recipient of foreign investment (CEIC, 2015). By 2014, a total of 674 projects had resulted in USD 22.82 billion in contracted foreign investment flowing into Tianjin (Tianjin, 2015).

The evolution of foreign investment in Tianjin

Tianjin has historically been known as an important industrial and port city. Tianjin was one of the open ports in China from the 1860s, serving as the commercial and logistics centre for north coastal China while Beijing, about 100 kilometres inland, served as the political centre. By the 1930s, Tianjin had become a business and financial centre second only to Shanghai within China (Hendrischke, 1999). It was the birth place of the first domestically produced television set, bicycle, and fax machine in China.

Tianjin was one of the 14 coastal cities declared eligible to receive foreign investment in 1984.

Development Zones

The Tianjin Economic and Technology Development Zone (TEDA) was founded as one of the first state-level economic development zones in 1984. Additional areas were added to TEDA in 1993, 1996, 2003, 2009, 2011, 2012, and 2013. By 2010, 5,000 foreign companies had operations in TEDA, including Motorola, Samsung, Panasonic, FAW Toyota, GlaxoSmithKline, Novo Nordisk, Bunge, Nestlé, Coca-Cola, Vestas, Kyocera, Otis, SEW, John Deere, and Cabot Corporation. By 2014, TEDA had attracted some 5,439 foreign projects and USD 45.8 billion in investment to Tianjin (author's interviews). The Tianjin Free Trade Zone was founded in 1991. By 2010, 7,500 companies had been registered in the Zone, including 72 of the Global 500 Companies. Companies like Airbus, Toyota Tsusho, Sumitomo, 3M, Lufthansa, SK, NYK, Metro, Heidelberg, SM Group (Philippines), IBM, Citibank, Mylin Holding Group, Morgan Stanley, and Sequoia Capital had offices or operations in the Zone. Tianjin High-Tech Park was approved by State Council in 1991. By 2015, it had attracted a cumulative USD 12.6 billion in FDI. By the end of 2015, more than 500 companies from 26 countries had invested in the Park, including LG (Korea), Gaoqiu Liune (Japan), Knauf (Germany), and Chen Shin (Taiwan) (China Daily, 2015b; HKTDC, 2015b; Tianjin, 2005).

In 1994, the Tianjin Government proposed the idea to construct Binhai New Area, a large area covering the east coastal part of Tianjin including TEDA and the Tianjin Free Trade Zone. Unlike the development of Pudong New Area in Shanghai, which had been a state-level strategy from the very beginning, the construction of Binhai New Area had been a local initiative of the Tianjin Government until the end of 2005, when the development of Binhai New Area was written into the national Twelfth Five-Year Program and became a state-level strategy. In May 2006, the State Council approved the designation of the Tianjin Binhai New Area as a Pilot Zone of National Comprehensive Reform. The Binhai New Area was authorized to experiment with reform in various areas such as financial innovation, land management, opening policy, corporate structure, urban and rural planning, and social development.

Experimental reform in the financial area was considered as a key mission of the Binhai New Area. A series of documents were issued at the state level to facilitate the experimental reform in financial enterprises, financial business, financial market, and financial opening in the Binhai New Area, including *The State Council's Opinion on the Facilitation of the Development and Opening of Tianjin Binhai New Area* issued in June 2006, and the *Opinions on Facilitating the Experimental Reform of Insurance in Tianjin Binhai New Area* issued in November 2007. Foreign investors responded quickly to the government moves. HSBC, The Bank of Tokyo-Mitsubishi UFJ, Shinhan Bank, and

Citibank all set up branches in the Binhai New Area at the end of 2006. The global accounting service centre of Motorola and the China operation centre of Standard Chartered Bank were also opened in the Binhai New Area.

Early investments and industries

Tianjin's history of inward investment was shaped by the policies and priorities of China's Government, as well as market evolution, and the strategy of major multinational companies. Tianjin became a preferred location in Northern China for many manufacturing and logistics companies given its location in one of China's three dynamic coastal regions, the Bohai Rim (the other two being the Yangtze River Delta in East-Central China, and the Pearl River Delta in Southern China). One of the first important investments was China Tianjin Otis Elevator Company (CTOEC), a joint venture between US-based Otis Elevator and Tianjin Elevator Company (one of China's most sophisticated elevator companies at the time) set up in 1984. Other early investors included Remy Martin of France and Wella AG of Germany. By the end of 1984, there were 55 Sino-foreign joint ventures in Tianjin with foreign investment of only USD 24 million. In 1985, another 88 joint venture agreements were signed with companies from Hong Kong (39), Japan (21), the United States (15), Singapore (3), the United Kingdom (2), and one each from France, Thailand, Australia, Canada, Malaysia, Germany, Denmark, and the Philippines (Hendrischke, 1999). Despite these investments, Tianjin was specifically questioned by Deng Xiaoping in 1986 for its slow progress in reforming its economy and attracting investment. This criticism was echoed in a 1993 article that faulted the city for not attracting more inward investment (Hendrischke, 1999).

Despite the aforementioned questioning, foreign investment in Tianjin began to pick up in the early 1990s. In 1992, Motorola entered Tianjin by setting up factories in TEDA, producing pagers and mobile phones. Tianjin eventually became Motorola's largest production base in the world. Motorola's Tianjin branch, one of the first wholly foreign-owned enterprises in China, set a record for a single investment value at the time at USD 120 million and eventually grew to over USD 3 billion in investment. Many of Motorola's suppliers set up in Tianjin to serve the new facilities. Samsung entered Tianjin in 1993 by setting up a joint venture in TEDA with Tianjin Communication and Broadcasting Group, producing a wide range of electronic products and components. By 2014, its investments in Tianjin reached USD 1.3 billion. These companies provided the base for what became a sizable electronics and telecommunications equipment industry in Tianjin, which eventually included Honeywell, General Instrument, Canon, Panasonic, Sanyo, Fujitsu, and LG.

Coca-Cola opened in Tianjin in 1989 and set up a factory in TEDA in 1992. Ting Hsin, the Taiwanese company best known as a producer of instant noodles, opened in Tianjin in 1992, and eventually became one of the largest food companies in China. Nestlé set up a joint venture in 1994. Eventually, Tianjin's food sector would also include Kraft, Heinz, Pepsi, Yakult, and several other leading international companies.

Novo-Nordisk, which opened a USD 250 million Tianjin subsidiary in 1994, was among the first foreign pharmaceutical companies to set up in Tianjin. Tianjin became Novo's largest facility outside its home country of Denmark. It subsequently also located a sizable enzyme facility in Tianjin. Smithkline Beecham (which merged with Glaxo Wellcome to form GlaxoSmithKline in 2000) opened a USD 338 million operation in 1996. These companies provided the initial impetus for the bio-pharmaceutical sector in Tianjin. FAW Toyota set up in Tianjin in 2000. Honda, Yamaha, Volkswagen, John Deere, AW Transmission, and numerous other automotive and machinery suppliers eventually followed. Other significant early investors included Yazaki, BOC, President (Taiwan), Huanmei (Singapore), and Chiz Tai (Thailand).

By 1995, foreign invested enterprises accounted for nearly 36 percent of gross industrial output in Tianjin, compared to 13 percent nationally, and roughly 23 percent of the city's fixed asset investment (Tianjin, 1996). By 2004, foreign companies accounted for an estimated 20 percent of Tianjin's GDP (China Economic Review, 2005). Since around 2005, Tianjin also has seen a shift of foreign investment focus from manufacturing industries to tertiary industries. Before 2005, over 60 percent of the FDI into Tianjin went into manufacturing industries, but from 2006 to 2013, this percentage decreased to around 45 percent. Although Tianjin is still considered as an industrial city in its positioning compared to Beijing, tertiary industries, especially production-oriented services, have grown along with secondary industries.

New challenges and directions

The upgrading of the Binhai New Area to a state-level zone provided a strong stimulus to Tianjin's economic development and to its attractiveness to foreign investment. Several high-profile investments were made upon the new designation of the Binhai New Area. In October 2006, Airbus signed an agreement to set up a joint venture, Airbus (Tianjin) Final Assembly Company, in the Tianjin Airport Economic Zone, mainly for production of the Airbus A320 series, and the facility started operation in 2008. In November 2007, the Ministry of Construction of China and the Ministry of National Development of Singapore signed an agreement to build the Sino-Singapore Tianjin Eco-City (SSTEC) in the Binhai New Area. This was another high-profile project between China and Singapore after the China–Singapore Suzhou Industrial Park, and was reported to be the first eco-city co-developed by two countries in the world. The eco-city has a land area of 31.23 square kilometres, and a planned total population of 350,000. In 2010, China National Petroleum Corporation and Rosneft, the Russian oil firm, set up a joint venture in the Binhai New Area, with a total investment of USD 5 billion (author's interviews and Cheng, 2010).

By the end of 2010, some 285 Global 500 companies had set up in the Binhai New Area. By 2014, the Binhai New Area accounted for 55.7 percent of Tianjin's GDP, 61.6 percent of its gross industrial output, 49.6 percent of its fixed asset investment, 62.5 percent of its exports, and 65.1 percent of its utilized foreign investment (Tianjin,

2015). Binhai's GDP growth had averaged 20.5 percent from 2005 to 2014 (Liu, 2015). It was reported that in 2014 there were 320 newly registered foreign companies in the Binhai New Area, with total registered capital of USD 4.75 billion, and tertiary industries accounted for 94 percent in terms of the number of newly registered foreign companies and 97 percent in terms of total registered capital in 2014. The top five FDI recipient industries in the Binhai New Area in 2014 were Leasing and Business Services (USD 4.78 billion); Finance (USD 2.28 billion); Scientific Research and Technological Services (USD 0.21 billion); Manufacturing (USD 0.19 billion); and Information Transmission, Computer Services, and Software (USD 0.14 billion) (Bohai Morning Post, 2015).

In early 2013, when the application for the Shanghai Free Trade Zone was submitted to the State Council, the application for the Tianjin Free Trade Zone was also submitted by the Ministry of Commerce of China, but only the Shanghai proposal was approved at that time. After another two years' effort, at the end of 2014 the Tianjin Free Trade Zone got approved and was officially launched in the Binhai New Area in April 2015. The FTZ covered a land area of 120 square kilometres, including three separate zones, i.e. the Tianjin Port area (30 square kilometres), the Tianjin Airport area (43 square kilometres), and the Central Business area in Binhai New Area (47 square kilometres). On the same day as the opening, 26 financial institutions set up branches in the FTZ. Ping'an Bank also set up its factoring business centre and cross-border trade settlement centre in the FTZ. The Tianjin FTZ enjoys similar preferential policies as those in the Shanghai FTZ, and is expected to be a new engine of Tianjin's economic opening and institutional reform (Tianjin Daily, 2015). Again, further opening to foreign companies is seen as a major step to enhance Tianjin's development and prosperity.

Overview of FDI and FIEs in Tianjin

Although Tianjin was formally opened to international investment in 1984, the annual utilized investment amounts remained under USD 100 million until 1992, when utilized FDI reached USD 231 million (Table 5.4). The figure rose to over USD 1,000 million in 1994 and over USD 2,000 million in 1996. The annual utilized investment values remained more or less between USD 2,000 million and USD 4,000 million until 2006, when they started to rise rapidly. By the end of 2013, the cumulative contracted value of FDI was USD 176,251 million and the cumulative utilized value was USD 111,940 million.

Hong Kong has been the most important source of FDI into Tianjin, accounting for 44 percent of total FDI from 1991 to 2013, followed by Japan and Korea, accounting for 9 percent and 7 percent of FDI respectively. Other major investors include the United States, the British Virgin Islands, and Singapore, with each accounting for 6 to 7 percent of total FDI during the period. Around 51 percent of the FDI during the period went into manufacturing industries, although the importance of manufacturing

Table 5.4 Inward FDI into Tianjin

Year	Number of Contracts		Contracted Value (USD mn)		Utilized Value (USD mn)	
	Annual	*Cumulative*	*Annual*	*Cumulative*	*Annual*	*Cumulative*
1979–1984		52		80		21
1985	79	131	55	134	44	65
1986	47	178	66	200	43	108
1987	49	227	14	214	55	163
1988	92	319	89	304	24	187
1989	96	415	85	388	81	268
1990	129	544	164	552	83	352
1991	354	898	197	748	94	445
1992	1,702	2,600	1,219	1,968	231	677
1993	3,538	6,138	2,256	4,223	541	1,218
1994	1,890	8,028	3,502	7,726	1,015	2,233
1995	1,389	9,417	3,851	11,576	1,521	3,754
1996	1,087	10,504	3,924	15,501	2,006	5,759
1997	1,056	11,560	3,851	19,351	2,511	8,271
1998	859	12,419	3,637	22,989	2,518	10,789
1999	575	12,994	3,620	26,609	2,532	13,321
2000	626	13,620	4,600	31,209	2,560	15,881
2001	618	14,238	4,630	35,839	3,220	19,101
2002	816	15,054	5,812	41,651	3,806	22,907
2003	941	15,995	3,513	45,164	1,633	24,540
2004	1,102	17,097	5,589	50,753	2,472	27,012
2005	575	17,672	7,323	58,075	3,329	30,341
2006	1,050	18,722	8,112	66,187	4,131	34,472
2007	906	19,628	11,519	77,706	5,278	39,750
2008	691	20,319	13,256	90,962	7,420	47,170
2009	596	20,915	13,838	104,800	9,020	56,189
2010	592	21,507	15,296	120,096	10,849	67,038
2011	634	22,141	16,837	136,933	13,056	80,094
2012	632	22,773	18,585	155,518	15,016	95,111
2013	564	23,337	20,733	176,251	16,829	111,940

Source: *Tianjin Statistical Yearbooks* (various years).

has seen a downward trend over the years, from over 60 percent until 2006 and in the mid-40 percent range since then. Real estate has been the second largest recipient of FDI, accounting for 13 percent of total inward FDI into Tianjin in the period (Tianjin, various years).

The importance of FDI and FIEs

Foreign investment represented a small part of Tianjin's gross capital formation and fixed asset investment until around 1993 (Figure 5.3). FDI as a percent of gross capital

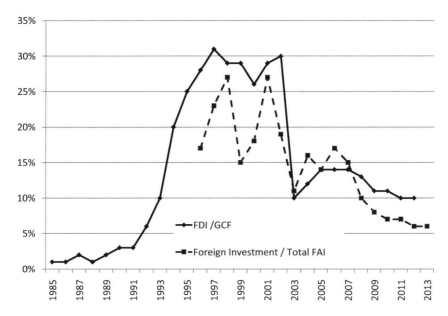

Figure 5.3 Foreign investment versus total investment in Tianjin
Source: *Tianjin Statistical Yearbooks* (various years).

formation peaked at 31 percent in 1997 before starting to decline as a percent in 2003 to low double digits. The foreign share of fixed asset investment peaked at 27 percent in 1998 before falling below 10 percent in 2009 and onward to 6 percent by 2013. In terms of specific industries, in 2013, FIEs accounted for more than 60 percent of industry revenues in the Manufacture of Communications Equipment, Computers, and Other Electronic Equipment and Manufacture of Beverage industries; over 50 percent in the Manufacture of Transport Equipment, and Manufacture of General Purpose Machinery industries; and over 40 percent in several others (Table 5.5).

Foreign invested enterprises have played a dominant role in Tianjin's export and import trade (Figure 5.4). In the late 1990s and early 2000s, over 80 percent of Tianjin's trade was done by FIEs, and in recent years, FIEs continued to contribute over 60 percent of the city's trade. In many years, FIEs in Tianjin registered a trade deficit, importing more than they exported. This trend is becoming more prominent in recent years. In 2013, FIEs in Tianjin reported an export value of USD 32,280 million and an import value of USD 47,325 million, indicating a trade deficit of USD 14,505 million or around 6 percent of GDP. As a result, the net export contribution to Tianjin's GDP in most years has been negative. The main reason is that even though FIEs account for the bulk of Tianjin's exports, on average the industries populated by FIEs in Tianjin are more oriented to serve the local market. The equipment, inputs, and finished goods they import to do so tip the balance.

Table 5.5 Foreign invested industrial enterprises by industry in Tianjin, 2011

	Revenue (RMB mn)	% Tianjin Total	Profits (RMB mn)	% Tianjin Total	FIE Profits/ Revenue (%)
Manufacturing	700,137	31	39,346	26	5.6
Manufacture of Communications Equipment, Computers, and Other Electronic Equipment	185,975	61	6,743	34	3.6
Manufacture of Transport Equipment	143,875	57	10,716	48	7.4
Manufacture of General Purpose Machinery	56,265	56	7,649	94	13.6
Manufacture of Electric Machinery and Equipment	44,822	46	2,336	42	5.2
Manufacture of Chemical Raw Materials and Chemical Products	30,228	22	1,704	38	5.6
Manufacture of Special Machinery	17,079	16	752	12	4.4
Manufacture of Non-metallic Mineral Products	15,344	45	381	21	2.5
Manufacture of Textile, Wearing Apparel, Footwear, and Caps	14,449	46	1,240	29	8.6
Manufacture of Medicines	14,440	28	864	14	6.0
Smelting and Pressing of Ferrous Metals	13,965	3	139	1	1.0
Manufacture of Food	12,836	12	1,076	6	8.4
Manufacture of Beverage	11,867	63	397	N/A	3.3
Manufacture of Plastic	9,462	21	255	8	2.7
Manufacture of Textile	1,432	14	−45	N/A	−3.1

	Revenue (RMB mn)	% Tianjin Total	Profits (RMB mn)	% Tianjin Total	FIE Profits/ Revenue (%)
Production and Supply of Electricity, Gas, and Water	6,968	8	131	4	1.9

Note: Total assets data is not available.

Source: *Tianjin Statistical Yearbooks* (various years).

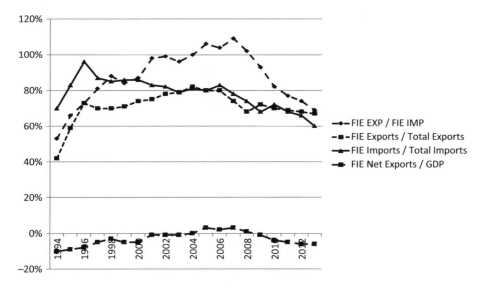

Figure 5.4 Trade performance of foreign invested enterprises in Tianjin

Note: The FIE trade figures are extracted from *China Statistical Yearbooks* while the Tianjin trade figures are extracted from *Tianjin Statistical Yearbooks*, which might have some discrepancy in statistical scope.

Sources: *Tianjin Statistical Yearbooks* (various years); *China Statistical Yearbooks* (various years).

Economic impact of FDI and FIEs on Tianjin

In this section, we apply the tools of economic impact analysis described above to estimate the economic impact that FIEs have had on output, value added (GDP), and employment in Tianjin. Statistics were available for FIE sales and employment in Tianjin in 21 industry categories (Tianjin, 2012). Tianjin has its own input–output tables that were used to generate multipliers specific to the city. The industries covered in the analysis accounted for approximately 51 percent of the inward FDI in Tianjin in the years 1991 to 2013. The analysis was carried out for 2011, the latest year in which data on the operation of FIEs in Tianjin was available.

The estimated impact for the investment phase for investments made in 2011 was USD 20,555 million in output, USD 6,411 million in value added, and 314,909 persons in employment. The total impact of the capital investment associated with FDI accounted for 3.7 percent of Tianjin's GDP and 3.7 percent of Tianjin's total employment in 2011. In 2011, FIEs were responsible for 34 percent of the total revenue generated in Tianjin. The estimated economic impact based on the operations of FIEs in the Mining, Manufacturing, and Utilities sectors in 2011 was USD 138,667 million in total output, USD 32,051 million in value added, and 927,437 persons in employment. This was equivalent to 18 percent of Tianjin's GDP and 11 percent of Tianjin's total employment from all sources in 2011. Again, these impacts are the result of operations of FIEs in industries that accounted for 51 percent of the total FDI into Tianjin over the period 1991 to 2013. If the service sectors could be included, the estimated impacts would be even higher. The estimated combined economic impact of the investment phase associated with all foreign direct investment in Tianjin and the sales of FIEs in the Mining, Manufacturing, and Utilities sectors in Tianjin in 2011 was USD 159,232 million in output, USD 38,461 million in value added, and 1,242,346 persons in employment. The combined impacts were equivalent to 22 percent of Tianjin's GDP and 15 percent of Tianjin's total employment from all sources in 2011.

Again, we note that the impacts from operations are just for the Mining, Manufacturing, and Utilities industries for which the sales data for FIEs is available. The impacts do not include the impact of the operation of FIEs in the service sector. We note that since the multipliers are derived from Tianjin input–output tables, the estimates do not include wider spillovers into China's economy beyond Tianjin. Thus they understate the economic contribution of FDI and FIEs in Tianjin to China's total economy.

Table 5.6 shows the estimated economic impact of the operations of FIEs in each industry for which we have data in 2011. The operations of FIEs in the Computers, Communication, and Other Electronic Equipment industry (direct revenue RMB 185,975 million) generated a total impact of USD 34,146 million in output, USD 7,415 million in value added, and 222,538 jobs. The operations of FIEs in the Transport Equipment industry (direct revenue RMB 143,875 million) generated a total impact of USD 28,307 million in output, USD 5,643 million in value added, and 135,980 jobs. The operations of FIEs in General Purpose Machinery (direct revenue RMB 56,265 million) generated a total impact of USD 10,787 million in output, USD 2,815 million in value added, and 71,690 jobs in 2011.

Tianjin conclusions

Tianjin saw a slow increase in inward FDI in the years immediately after its opening, but by the mid-1990s was receiving sizable amounts of investment. The trend in recent years, particularly since the establishment of the Binhai New Area, has been extremely positive. FIEs are major contributors in several important industries, and have dominated Tianjin's international trade.

Table 5.6 Total impact of the operations of FIEs, Mining, Manufacturing, and Utilities Sectors in Tianjin by industry, 2011

Industry	Output (USD mn)	Value Added (USD mn)	Employment (persons)
Manufacture of Computers, Communication, and Other Electronic Equipment	34,146	7,415	222,538
Manufacture of Transport Equipment	28,307	5,643	135,980
Manufacture of General Purpose Machinery	10,787	2,815	71,690
Manufacture of Electrical Machinery and Apparatus	8,697	2,005	52,222
Manufacture of Raw Chemical Materials and Chemical Products	5,720	1,466	30,362
Manufacture of Special Purpose Machinery	3,274	854	27,527
Smelting and Pressing of Ferrous Metals	2,895	671	12,273
Manufacture of Non-metallic Mineral Products	2,869	662	18,065
Manufacture of Medicines	2,733	700	20,912
Manufacture of Textile, Wearing Apparel, and Accessories	2,609	671	73,655
Manufacture of Food	2,454	670	27,852
Manufacture of Liquor, Beverages, and Refined Tea	2,269	619	22,498
Manufacture of Rubber Products	1,791	459	23,302
Manufacture of Textile	269	69	4,734
Other Manufacturing	24,693	5,830	166,858
Mining	3,761	1,149	7,913
Production and Supply of Electric Power, Gas, and Water	1,404	352	9,056

Source: Enright, Scott & Associates analysis.

While the economic impacts of FDI and FIEs in Tianjin are not as great as in Shenzhen, this is to be expected. After all, Shenzhen is immediately adjacent to Hong Kong, and Shenzhen basically did not exist in anything like its present form before the economic opening and the entry of foreign companies. The fact that FDI and FIEs are still extremely important is all the more impressive when we recognize that they do not include the impact of the sales of FIEs in the service sector (which accounted for 49 percent of the inward FDI in the period 1991 to 2013) and do not include any catalytic benefits such as spillovers into the local economy, the impact on productivity in indigenous firms, the impact on technological and managerial capabilities in Tianjin, the social contributions by FIEs, or other impacts.

The results suggest that even a traditional manufacturing centre like Tianjin has benefitted tremendously from foreign investment and the presence of foreign companies. We also note that the city's leading initiatives to reach the next stage of development involve attracting more foreign investment and foreign invested enterprises. Since Tianjin, along with Beijing, is a leader in the development of the Bohai Rim, one of China's main economic regions, the importance of FDI and FIEs in Tianjin again goes well beyond the impact on the city itself.

Shanghai

Shanghai has received more foreign direct investment and is home to more foreign companies than any other city in China by a wide margin. From 1996 to 2013 for example, Shanghai received USD 139 billion in foreign investment, much higher than second place Tianjin's USD 108 billion. By the end of 2014, Shanghai had attracted a total of 76,300 foreign-invested projects. These projects had contracted foreign capital valued at USD 274.1 billion, of which USD 169.16 billion had been paid in. According to Shanghai officials, this accounted for over 10 percent of the utilized foreign direct investment in China. Shanghai had also attracted 490 regional headquarters of multinational companies, 381 foreign-funded research and development centres, and 216 foreign-invested financial institutions. The Shanghai Foreign Investment Development Board estimated that two-thirds of exports, imports, and industrial output came from foreign invested enterprises in 2014. FIEs also accounted for one-third of tax revenue and employment in the municipality in 2014 (Invest Shanghai, 2015). By April of 2015, the number of foreign-invested regional headquarters in Shanghai was 506 and the number of foreign invested R&D centres was 384 according to the Shanghai Association of Enterprises with Foreign Investment.

The evolution of FDI and FIEs in Shanghai

Foreign investment has shaped Shanghai's economy in its past. In the first part of the 20th century, Shanghai was the leading business and commercial centre in Asia. A combination of local and Western influences made Shanghai the 'Paris of the Orient' and China's leading manufacturing centre, port, and financial centre. After 1949, Shanghai was eclipsed by other centres in Asia in terms of economic size and importance. At the beginning of China's opening and reform period in 1979, the main focus of attention was the coastal area in Southern China, and during that time Shanghai received only a small amount of foreign investment. The first Sino-foreign joint venture post-reforms in Shanghai was Shanghai United Woollen Company, a joint venture between Shanghai Industrial Holdings (a Shanghai Government company) and Hong Kong interests set up in 1981 (Shanghai Industrial, 2003). Despite this early start, there were few foreign entrants until China's next round of opening in 1984.

Shanghai's opening

Shanghai was one of the 14 cities designated for greater openness by the Chinese Government in 1984. The Shanghai Government set up departments to attract foreign investment and set up several development zones including the Minhang Economic Development Zone, the Hongqiao Economic Development Zone, and the Caohejing Technological Development Zone. A number of major FDI projects were set up around that time. Alcatel's Shanghai joint venture, the first true high technology joint venture (a telecommunications equipment joint venture) in China, was founded in 1984 (Alcatel-Lucent Shanghai Bell, 2014). In 2000, Alcatel was the first major Western multinational to place its Asia-Pacific regional headquarters in Shanghai (China Telecom, 2000). One of the first joint ventures in China's automotive sector, between Volkswagen and Shanghai's SAIC Motor, was also formed in 1984. The venture's initial registered capital of RMB 0.16 billion had grown to RMB 11.5 billion by 2013 (CECIC, 2013). When the American chemical company W.R. Grace was granted the first approval for a wholly foreign-owned enterprise in China, it set up its first Chinese factory in the Minhang Economic Development Zone in Shanghai in 1987 (Hui, 2010).

China's State Council had initially called for the opening of the Pudong area of Shanghai in 1985. In 1990, the opening of Pudong was finally approved as a key step in Shanghai's development. Pudong's strategic priorities were identified as finance, trade, infrastructure, and high technology industries. Four functional zones, the Waigaoqiao Bonded Zone and Port, the Lujiazui Finance and Trade Zone, the Jinqiao Export Processing Zone, and the Zhangjiang Hi-tech Park received a range of supporting policies to attract foreign investment, including tax and tariff breaks, lower barriers to entry, more flexible land use rights, and authorization of foreign investment approval.

The opening of Pudong heralded a refocusing of China's development efforts to Shanghai and the Yangtze River Delta. Having learned from the experiences in Shenzhen and the Pearl River Delta, China's leaders felt it was time to open and develop what had historically been China's leading economic city and leading economic region. Deng Xiaoping gave Shanghai a further boost during his Shanghai stopover as part of his 'Southern Tour' in February 1992, indicating that the city should be a new growth centre for China. He stated:

> Shanghai now entirely has the conditions [to develop] a bit more quickly. In the areas of talented personnel, technology, and administration, Shanghai has obvious superiority, which radiates over a wide area.
>
> (Jacobs and Hong, 1994, p. 224)

President and Communist Party Chairman Jiang Zemin indicated that Pudong would play an important part in this development. In a speech at the 14th National Party Congress in October 1992, he stated:

> We must take the development and opening of Pudong in Shanghai as the dragon head, advance another step to open cities on the banks of the Yangtze River and establish Shanghai as an international economic, financial, and trading center, as soon as possible, in order to induce a new economic leap in the Yangtze River Delta and the entire Yangtze River Valley.
>
> (Jacobs and Hong, 1994, p. 225)

Deng was also reported to have said that the mistake he had made several years earlier was not including Shanghai in the first set of cities to be opened. Shanghai was to receive substantial support for its ambitions from the nation's President Jiang Zemin and Premier Zhu Rongji, each of whom had been Mayor and Communist Party Secretary of Shanghai. Pudong's development became a national priority. Provincial governments and state companies from other parts of China were encouraged to make investments in Pudong.

Foreign investment in Shanghai grew dramatically, rising from USD 279 million in 1991 to USD 1,860 million in 1992. Pudong became a driving force in Shanghai's economy, attracting USD 1,353 million in contracted FDI in 1992 (up from USD 101 million in the previous year) accounting for 73 percent of total contracted FDI in Shanghai in 1992. Pudong got a further boost from the opening of the Pudong International Airport (in 1999), the Shanghai New International Expo Center (a German managed Sino-German joint venture opened in 2001), and Yangshan Port (the first phase of which opened in 2004). The Lujiazui Zone became the home to Shanghai's Stock Exchange, China's largest, as well as several of the world's tallest buildings. From virtual emptiness, Lujiazui would eventually be transformed into one of the world's leading city centres. Yangshan Port, along with the earlier Waigaoqiao, would eventually make Shanghai the world's leading port city in terms of both tonnage and containers handled.

The economic development zones that had been set up previously (i.e. Minhang, Hongqiao, and Caohejing) also received substantial additional investments. Foreign enterprises in these and the new development zones still enjoyed preferential policies (such as low tax rates and tax holidays) and support services (including specialized infrastructure provided in the zones) from the government. By the end of 1998, the Minhang Development Zone had attracted 142 foreign projects, with total FDI of USD 1,786 million; the Hongqiao Development Zone had attracted 105 foreign projects; and the Caohejing Development Zone had attracted 234 foreign projects, with total FDI of USD 1,350 million (Shanghai Government, 2015).

Diversifying the economy

From 1993 to 2002, around 56 percent of total FDI in Shanghai was invested in secondary industries, including the electronics, automobile, bio-medicine, petro-chemical, equipment manufacturing, and steel industries. General Motors' joint venture with SAIC, which was approved in 1997, would go on to become one of China's leading auto producers. By 2015, SAIC-VW and SAIC-GM had an estimated 23.4 percent share of the Chinese sedan market (Securities Times, 2015). BASF set up several Shanghai joint ventures starting in 1988 and would set up its first wholly owned facility in China in Shanghai in 2005 (BASF, 2014). Other industrial giants such as 3M, Intel, NEC, Honeywell, Cisco, IBM, Coca-Cola, Johnson & Johnson, DuPont, Michelin, Mitsubishi, Sony, Citibank, Philips, Sumitomo, ABB, OMRON, Fujifilm, Unilever, Pfizer, and others all had significant investments in Shanghai by the early 2000s.

Roughly half of the 44 percent of total FDI that went into tertiary industries in Shanghai during the 1993 to 2002 period went into the real estate industry. China began to open the real estate sector to foreign investment in the late 1980s. The first large-scale project completed by a foreign developer in Shanghai was the Shanghai America Center (also known as the Portman complex after its US-based developer) on Nanjing Road completed in 1990. This project included a hotel, serviced apartments, residences, offices, retail, a supermarket with imported goods, and exhibition space. This complex in a stroke made Shanghai much more accessible to international business people and companies coming to Shanghai. Even into the late 1990s, this single complex was home to a large portion of the offices of foreign companies and foreign consulates in Shanghai.[3]

Hong Kong developers became major players in the Shanghai real estate sector. A whole stretch of Huai Hai Road, one of Shanghai's two most important commercial streets (the other being Nanjing Road), saw developments by Wharf Holdings, Sun Hung Kai Properties, New World Development, and others. The centrepiece of the Huai Hai Road area, however, is Shui On's Xintiandi/Taipingqiao development, a 52-hectare site that houses restaurants, galleries, and shops in reconstructed historical buildings as well as modern office and residential complexes. Shui On has also developed several other complexes in other parts of Shanghai. Other Hong Kong developers, such as Hang Lung and Kerry Group, put up iconic developments along Nanjing Road, and Sun Hung Kai's International Financial Centre is one of the landmarks in Pudong's Lujiazui financial district. Other landmarks such as the Shanghai World Financial Center (Mori from Japan) were also developed by foreign companies. Although indigenous companies have become larger than the foreign developers in Shanghai, the foreign developers still play a crucial role in the cutting-edge developments in the city, such as Shui On's Hongqiao Transportation Hub project in western Shanghai, which opened in 2015.

The retail sector also received considerable foreign investment. The first foreign-invested retail complex approved in China was a USD 100 million complex invested by Japan's Yaohan in Pudong. By 1999, companies from Hong Kong, Taiwan, France, the United States, Japan, and Europe had set up more than 40 chain store outlets in Shanghai, and these stores accounted for 6 to 7 percent of the city's entire retail sales (Gamble, 2003). Foreign 'big box' retailers soon followed. The foreign retailers introduced foreign brands, new formats, new merchandising, new distribution systems, and new business models. They became trend setters that local competitors soon emulated. While more foreign retailers entered and some existing ones grew, eventually as competition became tougher and local competitors more capable, several of the foreign retailers were forced to exit. By 2015, notable retail complexes included Xintiandi (Shui On), Plaza 66 (Hang Lung), Kerry Center (Kerry Group), IFC (Sun Hung Kai), and many others.

The sector whose opening in Shanghai received more attention globally than any other in the early 1990s was the financial sector. In 1990 the *Shanghai Regulatory Measures relating to Foreign Financial Institutions and Joint Chinese-Foreign Financial Institutions* were issued. Soon 30 foreign banks applied for licenses, and six banks (two from the United States, two from Japan, and two from France) received approvals in early 1991.[4] AIG, the first foreign insurance company to receive permission, opened a Shanghai office in 1992. Thirty foreign financial institutions, including many world leaders, had set up branches in Shanghai by the end of 1994 (Fu, 2000). According to the Shanghai Banking Regulatory Bureau, at the end of 2014, more than half of the foreign-funded banks and branches of foreign banks operating in China were registered in Shanghai and Shanghai accounted for 47.3 percent of the total assets of all foreign banks in China. Foreign banks were also said to have 11.7 percent of the banking assets in Shanghai, compared to 1.7 percent nationally (China Daily, 2015a). In some cases, the entry of foreign financial institutions represented a return home. AIG had been founded in Shanghai, while HSBC had been founded in both Hong Kong and Shanghai. AIA, an AIG subsidiary, even returned to the building that it had occupied along the Bund on the banks of the Huangpu River in the 1920s and 1930s.

China's accession to the World Trade Organization had a substantial impact on the country and in particular on Shanghai. The WTO accession agreement called for China to open many sectors of its economy, particularly the service sectors, to foreign companies and many of these companies targeted Shanghai as the city with the largest market in China, but also the city with one of the most advanced economies and workforces in the Chinese Mainland, as well as one of the cities with the most experience in dealing with foreigners and foreign investment. The Shanghai Government issued a series of documents concerning foreign investment in the service industries. In the *Industrial Directions on Foreign Investment in Shanghai* published in 2003, eight service industries including finance, logistics, trade and commerce, social services (education, cultural, sports), scientific research and technological services, real estate, tourism, and information services were included as key industries encouraged for foreign investment. By 2013, the share of tertiary industry in FDI into Shanghai had risen to 81 percent. The share of tertiary industry in Shanghai's GDP also rose to 62 percent in 2013 from 46 percent in 2002 (Shanghai, 2014). Leading tertiary sectors receiving foreign investment included real estate, leasing and business services, transport and warehousing, information and computer services, and finance.

High-value activities

Shanghai also began to focus its efforts on attracting higher value activities of foreign companies. Specific policies included the *Opinions on Encouraging Foreign Investment to Set up R&D Centers in Shanghai* and the *Regulations on Encouraging Multinational Companies to Set up Regional Headquarters in Shanghai*. The idea was that these activities were more knowledge-intensive than others, would train and employ local knowledge workers, would provide sophisticated demand for more advanced support services, and would provide spillovers and examples for local firms (author's interviews). By April 2015, there were 506 foreign-invested regional headquarters and 384 foreign-invested R&D centres in Shanghai according to the Shanghai Association of Enterprises with Foreign Investment (Wang, 2015). Fifty-eight multinationals, including Delphi Packard Electric Systems Co Ltd, American Bureau of Shipping (China) Ltd, Asahi Breweries (China) Co Ltd, Meidensha (Shanghai) Corporate Management Co Ltd, and Burger King (China) Co Ltd received their regional headquarters certificates on a single day in December 2014 (Wang, 2014).

Some foreign companies moved global business units or business headquarters to Shanghai, thus embedding Shanghai in global management structures. In 2006, ABB opened a global headquarters for its Robotics Business (and one of ABB's five key businesses) in Shanghai (ABB, 2006). IBM established its global 'Growth Markets' headquarters in Shanghai in 2008, responsible for the Asia-Pacific (excluding Japan), Latin America and Russia, Eastern Europe, the Middle East, and Africa (IBM, 2013; Shanghai Daily, 2008). In 2011, Bayer Materials Sciences transferred the global polycarbonates headquarters from Germany to Shanghai (Bayer, 2012, pp. 5, 32). Also in 2011, Roche China announced Shanghai would become its third strategic operations centre in the world, after Basel and San Francisco (Wang, 2011).

New challenges and directions

In 2010, the National Development and Reform Commission began planning for a large-scale Free Trade Zone in Shanghai. The China (Shanghai) Pilot Free Trade Zone was officially launched in September 2013. The Free Trade Zone initially included the Waigaoqiao Bonded Zone, the Yangshan Bonded Port Zone, and Pudong Airport Bonded Zone, with a total area of 29 sq. km. In March 2015, the Lujiazui Finance and Trade Zone, the Jinqiao Development Zone, and the Zhangjiang Hi-tech Park were incorporated into the China (Shanghai) Free Trade Zone, expanding its area to 121 sq. km. The Free Trade Zone was touted as a laboratory for economic reform, a testing ground for financial opening, and an accelerator for Shanghai's establishment as an international financial centre. Overseas firms were expected to thrive under its zero tariffs and international-standard protection of intellectual property rights. It was also to foster economic and regulatory transparency, with no subsidies for state-owned enterprises, and liberalized financial services to pave the way for currency convertibility.

However, the Free Trade Zone was plagued by uncertainty about what would and would not be allowed and as of 2016 had not had much of an impact. The establishment of the Zone, and the limited additional freedoms that it afforded reaffirmed both China's (and Shanghai's) recognition that the path to greater prosperity involved allowing foreign investment and foreign enterprises to make more of a contribution, and a reluctance to open further to allow this to happen. Many analysts expected that foreign firms would gradually be allowed to carry out more and more activities in the Shanghai Free Trade Zone, and that the Zone would ultimately create a new growth dynamic for Shanghai, again with significant foreign firm involvement.

Overview of FDI and FIEs in Shanghai

Foreign investment into Shanghai took off in the early 1990s, with the refocusing on Shanghai and the opening of the Pudong New Area and then took another leap in the early 2000s around China's accession into the WTO (Table 5.7). FDI into Shanghai increased from USD 175 million in utilized value in 1991, to USD 1,259 million in 1992, to USD 3,160 million in 2000, to USD 16,780 million in 2013. By the end of 2013, the cumulative contracted value of FDI was USD 242,198 million and the cumulative utilized value of FDI was USD 150,981 million, indicating that investment would continue at high levels for the foreseeable future.

Hong Kong has been the leading source of FDI into Shanghai, accounting for 36 percent of total inward FDI from 1991 to 2013, followed by Macau (11 percent) and Taiwan (8 percent). Together they accounted for 55 percent of total FDI into Shanghai. Other important sources of investment include Japan (6 percent), Korea (4 percent), and Singapore (3 percent). Although Shanghai does not give a very detailed breakdown of FDI by recipient industry, one prominent feature in the available data is the mix of sectors that received FDI. From 1991 to 2013, the tertiary (service) sector received 64 percent of Shanghai's inward investment in the period, and the industrial sector (including mining, manufacturing, and utilities) received only 35 percent. This is almost the reverse of the proportions in most other places in China and for China as a whole. From 2011 to 2013, only 17 percent of the inward FDI into Shanghai went into industrial sectors, while 82 percent went into tertiary industries.

The importance of FDI and FIEs in Shanghai

Foreign investment became significant in total investment in Shanghai in the 1990s, with FDI accounting for more than 10 percent of gross capital formation from 1992 through at least 2012 and foreign investment in fixed assets exceeding 10 percent of the Shanghai total every year since 1996. Although the percentages peaked at 24 percent of gross capital formation in 1994 and 28 percent of fixed asset investment in 2004, both have remained solidly in double digit territory since (Figure 5.5). In the industrial sector, in 2013, foreign invested industrial enterprises reported total revenues of RMB

Table 5.7 Inward FDI into Shanghai

Year	Number of Contracts		Contracted Value (USD mn)		Utilized Value (USD mn)	
	Annual	Cumulative	Annual	Cumulative	Annual	Cumulative
1980	100	100	3	3	–	–
1981	300	400	6	9	3	3
1982	700	1,100	17	26	3	6
1983	600	1,700	47	73	11	17
1984	4,100	5,800	195	268	28	45
1985	9,400	15,200	305	573	62	107
1986	6,200	21,400	95	668	98	205
1987	7,600	29,000	129	797	212	417
1988	21,900	50,900	166	963	364	781
1989	19,900	70,800	177	1,140	422	1,203
1990	20,300	91,100	214	1,354	177	1,380
1991	36,500	127,600	279	1,633	175	1,555
1992	201,200	328,800	1,860	3,493	1,259	2,814
1993	365,000	693,800	3,757	7,250	2,318	5,132
1994	380,200	1,074,000	5,347	12,597	3,231	8,363
1995	284,500	1,358,500	5,360	17,957	3,250	11,613
1996	210,600	1,569,100	5,808	23,765	4,716	16,329
1997	180,200	1,749,300	5,320	29,085	4,808	21,137
1998	149,000	1,898,300	5,848	34,933	3,638	24,775
1999	147,200	2,045,500	4,104	39,037	3,048	27,823
2000	181,400	2,226,900	6,390	45,427	3,160	30,983
2001	245,800	2,472,700	7,373	52,800	4,391	35,374
2002	301,200	2,773,900	10,576	63,376	5,030	40,404
2003	432,100	3,206,000	11,064	74,440	5,850	46,254
2004	433,400	3,639,400	11,691	86,131	6,541	52,795
2005	409,100	4,048,500	13,833	99,964	6,850	59,645
2006	406,100	4,454,600	14,574	114,538	7,107	66,752
2007	420,600	4,875,200	14,869	129,407	7,920	74,672
2008	374,800	5,250,000	17,112	146,519	10,084	84,756
2009	309,000	5,559,000	13,301	159,820	10,538	95,294
2010	390,600	5,949,600	15,307	175,127	11,121	106,415
2011	432,900	6,382,500	20,103	195,230	12,601	119,016
2012	404,300	6,786,800	22,338	217,568	15,185	134,201
2013	384,200	7,171,000	24,630	242,198	16,780	150,981

Source: *Shanghai Statistical Yearbooks* (various years).

2,147 billion, total assets of RMB 1,662 billion, and total profits of RMB 146 billion, accounting for 62 percent, 50 percent, and 61 percent of the respective Shanghai totals. This is quite striking given that the bulk of inward investment has actually gone into Shanghai's service sectors.

FIEs in Shanghai accounted for 60 to 70 percent of Shanghai's export and import trade, and in most years generated a trade deficit (Figure 5.6). This would in part be due to FIEs importing equipment, machinery, and inputs, and in part to FIEs importing finished goods to sell into the local market. In 2013, FIEs in Shanghai reported an export

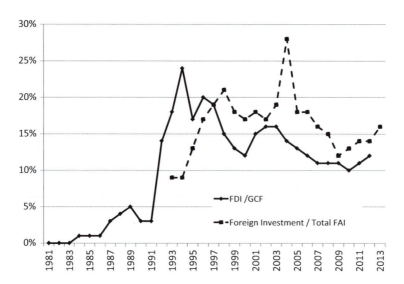

Figure 5.5 Foreign investment versus total investment in Shanghai

Source: *Shanghai Statistical Yearbooks* (various years).

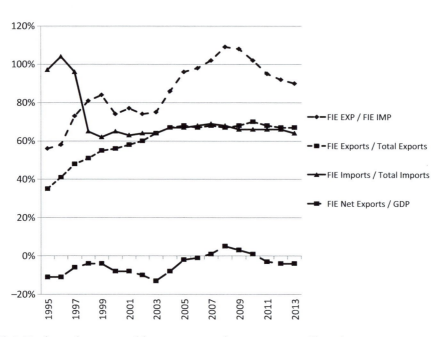

Figure 5.6 Trade performance of foreign invested enterprises in Shanghai

Note: The FIE trade figures are extracted from *China Statistical Yearbooks* while the Shanghai trade figures are extracted from *Shanghai Statistical Yearbooks*, which might have some discrepancy in statistical scope, potentially explaining the very high percentages in 1995 through 1997.

Sources: *Shanghai Statistical Yearbooks* (various years); *China Statistical Yearbooks* (various years).

value of USD 136,740 million and an import value of USD 151,821 million, indicating a trade deficit of USD 15,081 million, an amount equivalent to 4 percent of Shanghai's GDP.

The economic impact of FDI and FIEs on Shanghai

Due to lack of available data, it is not possible to do the same type of economic impact analysis for FDI and FIEs in Shanghai as was carried out for Shenzhen, Tianjin, and Chongqing. As indicated above, the Shanghai Foreign Investment Development Board estimated that two-thirds of exports, imports, and industrial output came from foreign invested enterprises in 2014. FIEs also accounted for one-third of tax revenue and employment in the municipality in 2014. When combined with the impact of the physical investments themselves, as well as supply chains, and investments in the service sector, it is safe to conclude that foreign investment and foreign companies account directly or indirectly for a quite large portion of Shanghai's economy.

It is interesting to note, however, that foreign companies remain crucial to Shanghai's success and its plans for the future, particularly in technology, tourism, finance, and headquarters. As of 2013, foreign firms, for example, accounted for 89.6 percent of Shanghai's high technology output, a higher portion than ten years earlier (Shanghai, 2014). A new Disney theme park is a key part of Shanghai's tourism plans. In the banking sector, according to statements of the Shanghai Banking Regulatory Bureau in 2015, foreign banks were playing an important role in Shanghai. According to the Bureau:

> Foreign banks settling in Shanghai contribute to consolidating Shanghai's position as an international financial center. They strive to develop cross-border businesses and support Chinese and foreign enterprises to expand businesses overseas.
>
> (China Daily, 2015a)

Zhu Wenbin, vice chairman of the Shanghai Association of Enterprises with Foreign Investment, in August 2015 described the importance of foreign firms to Shanghai's ambitions to be a global innovation centre, as reported by the *Shanghai Daily*:

> Foreign companies are a leading force in Shanghai's drive to become a global science and innovation center . . . Shanghai has a tradition of being the home to many quality foreign companies in China . . . We should treasure such a tradition, and make the best use of it to push ahead Shanghai's growth.

Zhu said a lot of foreign companies based in Shanghai are very strong in research and development, which makes them a leading force in Shanghai's build-up of innovation capability.

> Foreign investment is indeed a main engine of Shanghai's growth . . . Chinese companies, both state-owned and private, should be humble in learning from the good practice by foreign firms to enhance their ability in innovation.
>
> (Wang, 2015)

Shanghai conclusions

Shanghai became Asia's leading economic city in the early 20th century in part due to foreign investment and foreign invested enterprises. In the reform period, Shanghai has become the leading location for FDI and FIEs in China. The breadth and depth of foreign investment in China is unparalleled by any other Chinese city. Shanghai has shown the full range of influences of foreign investment, whether it has been developing the manufacturing sector, creating modern service industries, building the world-class buildings, helping Shanghai become the world's leading shipping centre, participating in Shanghai's rise as an international headquarters location, aiding in Shanghai's rise as a financial centre, investing in research and development, or working to link Shanghai to the rest of the world. In return, foreign companies have benefitted from Shanghai's emergence as a leading centre to make and manage investments all over China, a leading market, a leading source of talent, and a major hub in their own global networks.

It is striking how much FDI and FIEs influence Shanghai's development more than 30 years after the city was first opened. FIEs still account for nearly 90 percent of the high-technology output in Shanghai and are major participants in other important industries. In addition, Shanghai's most important initiatives to improve its economy also involve the attraction of FDI and FIEs. If this is true of what in many ways is China's most advanced business city, then it should be clear that foreign investment and foreign invested enterprises should continue to have a major role in China's development going forward.

Chongqing

Chongqing, the only municipality in western China with provincial-level status, has come on as a destination for foreign investment since the start of the 21st century. From 1996 to 2013, Chongqing received USD 27.38 billion in foreign investment, which ranked it ninth among Chinese cities (Chongqing, 2014; CEIC, 2015).[5] Foreign invested enterprises are especially important in the chemical, automotive, electronics, and real estate industries, which account for substantial portions of Chongqing's economy. Foreign investment has also been notable in the retail, financial service, and hospitality industries. By 2008, 93 companies from the Global 500 had activities in Chongqing, and by 2013, this figure was 225 (Netherlands Consulate, 2014b). By the end of 2014, 243 of the top Global 500 companies had set up operations in Chongqing (HKTDC, 2015a). Chongqing is an example of a late-mover in terms of China's development and has developed a distinctive pattern of foreign investment and economic growth.

The evolution of FDI and FIEs in Chongqing

Before 1992, foreign investment in Chongqing was negligible. Chongqing was not one of the cities opened in the first wave of China's reform process in 1980. Nor was it among the 14 cities opened in 1984. In August 1992, based on Deng Xiaoping's direction of 'opening along the coast, along the river, and provincial capital cities', China's State Council authorized the opening of another 16 Chinese cities, including Chongqing. The impact of the opening on investment into Chongqing was immediate. The contracted FDI value into Chongqing grew almost nine times from USD 43 million in 1991 to USD 379 million in 1992 (Chongqing, 2014).

In March 1997, Chongqing was designated as the fourth municipality under the direct administration of the Central Government. This gave Chongqing the same status as China's provinces in the governmental hierarchy, and it allowed for more direct Central Government interaction and monitoring of the Three Gorges Dam project as well as the massive resettlements required by the project (author's interviews). Before that, Chongqing had been part of Sichuan Province, whose capital is Chengdu. In 2000, the Central Government initiated its Great Western Development Strategy (GWDS), an effort to mitigate the economic gaps between coastal areas and western inland China, and improve the living standards of the more than 360 million Chinese who lived far from more prosperous coastal China. The designation, along with active Central Government policies to channel investment into Chongqing, and substantial infrastructure investment, resulted in a substantial increase in investment in the municipality.

Industrial development

Chongqing set up several industrial parks to attract foreign investment starting in the 1990s. These included the Chongqing Economic and Technological Zone established in 1993, the Chongqing Hi-Tech Development Zone, established in 1991, and the Changshou Chemical Industrial Park, established in 2001. The Chongqing Economic and Technological Zone was the first state-level development zone in western China. By 2006, it had attracted 447 investors from 22 countries, including companies like Ford, Ericsson, Metro, Honda, and Fiat. The Chongqing Hi-Tech Development Zone was approved as a state-level industrial zone in 1991. By 2006, the Zone had attracted 4,000 companies, 300 of which came from Japan, the United States, Germany, France, Hong Kong, and Taiwan (Gao, 2013). The Changshou Chemical Industrial Park was founded to leverage nearby supplies of natural gas and minerals, and became the home of facilities of BP, BASF, Linde, Degussa, Mitsubishi, and several other foreign and domestic firms.

Some foreign investors were attracted to Chongqing by the municipality's natural resources, which include natural gas and more than 40 different minerals. British Petroleum (BP) invested USD 200 million in a joint venture with Sinopec to set up acetic acid facilities in Chongqing that opened in 1998 and was later expanded to reach an annual production capacity of 350,000 tonnes. In 2008, BP signed an agreement with SINOPEC to invest in another facility with an annual production capacity of 650,000 tonnes, making Chongqing the biggest production location for acetic acid in China. In 2007, BASF formed a joint venture to build a 400,000 tonne methyl diphenyl di-isocyanate facility in Chongqing. In 2009, Linde formed a joint venture to supply industrial gases for Sinopec in Chongqing. In 2011, Linde agreed to build a joint venture facility for hydrogen and synthesis gas in the municipality. In 2014, the US Natural Resource Group set up a joint venture with Chongqing Energy Group, together investing RMB 1.7 billon in the exploration and extraction of shale gas in Chongqing. By 2012, the chemical industry accounted for approximately 8 percent of Chongqing's industrial output (Chongqing Government, private communication).

Other foreign companies were attracted by Chongqing's existing industrial base and Chinese industrial policy. Chongqing's auto industry had its roots in military trucks and motorcycles. In 1984, after the Central Government began to place greater emphasis on civilian production, Chongqing Chang'an Group, which was founded as a military truck supplier, started seeking cooperation with external partners. In May 1993, Chang'an Suzuki Automobile Co., Ltd was set up as a joint venture between Chang'an, Suzuki, and Nissho Iwai, using designs and production technology from Suzuki for 'mini-cars'. In 2001, Ford Motors and Chang'an entered into a joint venture, Chang'an Ford, which began producing larger passenger cars for the Chinese market in 2003. At the time, Ford was directed to Chongqing by the Central Government as a condition for entering the Chinese market (author's interviews). In 2002, General Motors formed a Chongqing joint venture with SAIC Motor (based in Shanghai) and Wuling Auto (based in Guangxi Province). In 2006, Chang'an Ford Mazda Automobile Co. Ltd, was formed after Mazda Motor joined Chang'an Ford. In 2007, the joint venture between IVECO, the Italian industrial vehicle manufacturer, and SAIC Motor, formed a cooperative arrangement with Chongqing Heavy Vehicle Group (another auto manufacturer with military roots), to produce commercial vehicles in Chongqing.

By the mid-2010s, the automotive sector in Chongqing covered the whole supply chain from raw materials, components, and spare parts to advanced R&D facilities and the production of finished vehicles. Chongqing had become the largest automotive producer in Western China, and in 2012, Chongqing ranked third in China for number of units produced. The automotive industry became extremely important to Chongqing, and contributed around 22 percent of the city's gross industrial output in the mid-2010s. By 2012, foreign brands accounted for 38.5 percent of Chongqing's auto output (Netherlands Consulate, 2014a). The vast majority of the products were for the domestic market. Chongqing also contributed one-third of the total number of motorcycles produced in China, with leaders such as Yamaha, Suzuki, Honda, and BMW all outsourcing a substantial portion of their production to local partners in Chongqing.

Building up Chongqing

Chongqing's opening, designation as the only directly-administered municipality in Western China, and policies to channel investment into Chongqing resulted in substantial investment into the hospitality and real estate sectors. In 2001, the real estate sector attracted 31 percent of total FDI (utilized value) into Chongqing. This figure reached 61 percent in 2005 and 62 percent in 2008 (Chongqing, various years). This is a much higher portion than in most other cities in China and reflects the fact that Chongqing has required a great deal of modernization of its office, industrial, and residential stock and has had limited local capital to do so (author's interviews).

The starting point for the luxury hotel market in Chongqing was the opening of the Harbour Plaza Hotel, the first international five-star hotel in Chongqing, by Hong Kong-based Hutchison-Whampoa in 1998 (Savills, 2013). As late as 2008, however, there were only three five-star hotels in Chongqing (CNTA, 2009). By 2012, after a major construction boom, there were approximately 20 (Chongqing Currents, 2012). International brands in the hotel sector in Chongqing include Marriott, Hilton, Sofitel, Intercontinental, Radisson, Le Meridien, Westin, Hyatt, Sheraton, and many others. In addition to traditional hotel investors, Chongqing has also attracted investment into the hotel sector from foreign-owned equity funds. Atkis (Chongqing), for example, one of the first foreign-owned equity investment funds in China, started investing in Chongqing hotels in 2006 (Chen, 2011).

In 1986, there were only 19 real estate developers registered in Chongqing. By 1999, this number had risen to 1,339 developers, of which 150 were foreign companies or Sino-foreign joint ventures (Chongqing, 1999). Hutchison developed several commercial and residential projects in Chongqing in the years after it opened the Harbour Plaza Hotel. Its Metropolitan Plaza, developed in 1997, the leading Grade A office building in Chongqing for many years, facilitated the entry of other foreign companies that located in the building. Hutchison also developed the first large-scale residential project in Chongqing as well as the city's first high-end villa project (Jones Lang LaSalle, 2007). In 2003, Hong Kong developer Shui On Land signed an agreement with the Chongqing Government to re-develop the old town Hualong Bridge area into a modern district with commercial, office, and residential space with an expected total investment over RMB 10 billion. Other foreign companies including Yanlord (Singapore), Hang Lung Properties (Hong Kong), Wharf (Hong Kong), Hong Kong Land (Hong Kong), Henderson (Hong Kong), and New World Development (Hong Kong) all developed projects in Chongqing.

In 2011, the Singaporean developer CapitaLand partnered with other investors to purchase a land parcel in the city centre at a total price of RMB 6.5 billion, planning to develop it into a mixed-use landmark in Chongqing (National Business Daily, 2015). This represented the largest single investment by a Singaporean enterprise in China. The foreign developers had improved the physical image of the city, provided high calibre physical environments for businesses in Chongqing, raised the standard for residential construction, and developed numerous retail centres to serve the local population. This in turn also made Chongqing far more accessible and therefore attractive to other foreign investors in a virtuous cycle.

Foreign investment has also figured in the utilities sector in Chongqing. Chongqing granted a 25-year concession to Sino-French Water Company, a Suez Environment–New World (Hong Kong) joint venture, to operate three water treatment plants in 2002. The company is also responsible for water production, sale of potable water, construction of new water treatment and support facilities, and construction and operation of water pipelines in several areas of Chongqing. The arrangement also involved the foreign group obtaining a 60 percent equity stake in the Chongqing Jiangbei Tap Water Company. According to industry analysts, by 2005, the company had developed a vastly improved customer service system, an updated and expanded pipeline system with lower leakage, improved technology and monitoring, improved water quality, and greatly expanded management training and development (Fu et al., 2008; Sino-French Water, 2011).

Service and technology development

Chongqing took advantage of hosting the 2005 Asia Pacific Cities Summit to project itself to the outside world and to accelerate inward investment. In that year, the tertiary sector accounted for 69 percent of total FDI into Chongqing, and since then tertiary industries have continued to attract more FDI in Chongqing than secondary industries. In addition to real estate, the top service industries in terms of foreign investment have been Leasing and Business Services, Finance, and Wholesale and Retail. In May 2006, Ericsson established its fourth global purchasing centre in Chongqing. In December 2006, Honeywell invested USD 300 million in Chongqing to develop special software for Chinese and global industrial enterprises. In October 2005, Liberty Mutual Insurance decided to locate its China headquarters in Chongqing, the first China headquarters of a Fortune 500 company in the city. ABN Amro opened its Chongqing branch in January 2007 and Standard Chartered opened its Chongqing branch in June 2007. As of the end of 2014, there were 17 foreign banks operating branches in Chongqing (Cq People, 2015). Wal-Mart, B&Q, Metro, Carrefour, New World (Hong Kong), Maison Mode, Far Eastern Department Store (Taiwan), and other foreign retailers had also set up in the city.

Chongqing has become one of the world's leading locations for personal computer manufacturing, a phenomenon driven almost entirely by foreign investment. In 2008, Hewlett-Packard decided to open a plant in Chongqing, its second in China, to focus on producing notebook and desktop computers for sale in China. The plant started operation in 2010, with an annual capacity of 24 million units. Since then, numerous foreign computer and electronics companies set up in Chongqing, including Inventec Corp. (Taiwan), Quanta (Taiwan), Acer (Taiwan), Foxconn (Taiwan), and numerous component suppliers (Want China Times, 2012). In 2015, AT&S announced that it would increase its investment in Chongqing from € 350 million (USD 388 million) to € 480 million by mid-2017, building one of the first high-end Integrated Circuit (IC) substrate factories in China (Ma, 2015). In 2013, the Chongqing produced 55 million laptop computers, 29.5 percent more than in 2012, with a value of RMB 157 billion. In that year, PCs accounted for 10 percent of the city's industrial output, up from zero in 2008 (do Rosário, 2015). In 2014, Chongqing produced 64 million computers, the vast majority for export, including 40 percent of the world's notebook computers and one-third of all computers produced worldwide (Chongqing News, 2015).[6]

This wave of foreign investment growth in Chongqing driven by PC manufactures has been the largest in Chongqing's FDI history. Before 2006, the annual contracted FDI value had never exceeded USD 1,000 million. In 2007, the contracted FDI value in Chongqing was USD 4,405 million, and in 2011 it reached USD 6,246 million. Gross industrial output in Communication, Computers, and Other Electronic Equipment in 2013 was RMB 212,833 million, roughly 58 times the RMB 3,701 million value in 2006, and 88 percent of the output in 2013 was from foreign invested enterprises (Chongqing, 2014).

New challenges and directions

Much of the new investment into Chongqing has been going into the Liangjiang New Area. The Liangjiang New Area became only the third sub-provincial 'new area' in China (after Pudong in Shanghai and Binhai in Tianjin) in 2010. The New Area covers 1,200 sq. km., with 550 sq. km. available for development, and is designed to become a centre for advanced manufacturing, trade, commerce, transport, and logistics. It contains China's first bonded inland zone, and has transport links westward via rail to Europe; as well as to the south via road and rail; and to the east via road, rail, and waterways. Attracting investment from foreign companies is at the heart of the New Area's strategy. The New Area received USD 4.49 billion in foreign investment in 2014, up more than 40 percent from the previous year, and equal to roughly one-third of the total foreign investment into Chongqing in that year. By early 2015, more than 200 Global 500 companies had set up in Liangjiang. Prominent companies investing in the New Area have included Ford, GM, Hyundai, Kawasaki, ABB, and AT&S, as well as many prominent Chinese companies. Hyundai, for example, started construction of a new USD 1.2 billion facility to produce 300,000 motor vehicles per year in the New Area in June 2015 (Zhuan, 2015).

The Liangjiang New Area has been planned, not just to be a leader for Chongqing's development, but a leader for all of western China. As such, it has taken on national and international importance as a gateway to western China and a jumping off point for the 'One Belt, One Road' initiative to link China to Central Asia, the Middle East, South and Southeast Asia, and Europe. It benefits from similar policies as the Pudong and Binhai New Areas, as well as special policies and programs to support China's western development and urban–rural integration. Corporate income taxes in the Area will be levied at the rate of 15 percent through 2020, which can be reduced to 10 percent with a tax holiday for the first three years of profitability for firms designated as 'high-technology' companies. The Chongqing Government also has committed RMB 10 billion for infrastructure for the Area (Chongqing Government, 2014; author's interviews). The New Area is the single most important economic development initiative in Chongqing.

Overview of FDI and FIEs in Chongqing

The flow of FDI into Chongqing before the 2000s was quite small. Annual utilized FDI reached USD 100 million for the first time in 1992 and USD 500 million for the first time in 2005 (Table 5.8). In fact, FDI began to really take off only around 2007. Inward FDI grew from USD 696 million in 2006 to USD 5,826 million in 2011, before easing to USD 3,524 million in 2012 and USD 4,144 million in 2013. This reflects the 'lumpiness' of inward investment as well as the opening of the Liangjiang New Area, a flood of investment in the real estate sector, and the wholesale movement of personal computer makers and their suppliers to Chongqing.

Hong Kong has been the largest source of FDI into Chongqing, accounting for 63.1 percent of the total in the 1991 to 2013 period. Its importance was particularly

Table 5.8 Inward FDI into Chongqing

Year	Number of Contracts		Contracted Value (USD mn)		Utilized Value (USD mn)	
	Annual	Cumulative	Annual	Cumulative	Annual	Cumulative
1985	–	–	–	–	4	4
1986	6	6	15	15	8	12
1987	10	16	8	23	19	31
1988	18	34	19	42	21	52
1989	15	49	71	114	8	60
1990	55	104	62	176	3	63
1991	80	184	43	219	10	73
1992	443	627	379	598	102	175
1993	681	1,308	729	1,327	259	434
1994	364	1,672	479	1,806	450	884
1995	280	1,952	746	2,552	379	1,263
1996	160	2,112	242	2,794	219	1,482
1997	229	2,341	460	3,254	385	1,867
1998	222	2,563	476	3,730	431	2,298
1999	169	2,732	507	4,237	239	2,537
2000	190	2,922	357	4,594	244	2,781
2001	172	3,094	443	5,037	256	3,037
2002	148	3,242	502	5,539	281	3,318
2003	187	3,429	553	6,092	311	3,629
2004	258	3,687	663	6,755	405	4,035
2005	208	3,895	802	7,557	516	4,550
2006	223	4,118	1,116	8,673	696	5,246
2007	240	4,358	4,405	13,078	1,029	6,275
2008	135	4,493	2,088	15,165	2,452	8,727
2009	161	4,654	2,443	17,608	3,376	12,103
2010	232	4,886	4,028	21,636	3,043	15,145
2011	326	5,212	6,246	27,882	5,826	20,971
2012	248	5,460	5,057	32,939	3,524	24,495
2013	192	5,652	3,825	36,764	4,144	28,639

Source: *Chongqing Statistical Yearbooks* (various years).

prominent after 2005, when FDI into Chongqing began to take off. Singapore was the second largest source of FDI into Chongqing, accounting for 8.5 percent for the 1991 to 2013 period, followed by Japan (3.5 percent), the United States (2.5 percent), and Taiwan (2.0 percent). Unlike the situation in many other places in China, where manufacturing has been the leading recipient sector for FDI, the real estate industry has been the leading recipient of FDI in Chongqing, accounting for 37.5 percent of the total for the period 1991 to 2013. Industrial sectors (i.e. Mining, Manufacturing, and Utilities) accounted for 34 percent of the total during the period. Other important industries included Leasing and Business Services (7.7 percent), Financial Intermediation (7.4 percent), and Wholesale and Retail Trades (4.9 percent).

Importance of FDI and FIEs in Chongqing

Foreign investment has been less prominent as a source of capital in Chongqing than in the other cities profiled in this chapter. Over the last 20-plus years inward FDI has been equivalent to 2 to 7 percent of gross capital formation and foreign investment has accounted for around 1 to 9 percent of total fixed asset investment (Figure 5.7). Chongqing is a relative newcomer when it comes to foreign investment, and since it has not been as advanced economically as many coastal cities, it has not been as attractive to foreign investors as other locations. In addition, the relatively high percentages of FDI in gross capital formation and fixed asset investment in places like Shenzhen, Tianjin, and Shanghai occurred at times when China as a whole was lacking sufficient domestic investment capital. By the time Chongqing was opened and became attractive to foreign investors, China had already developed the ability to deploy large amounts

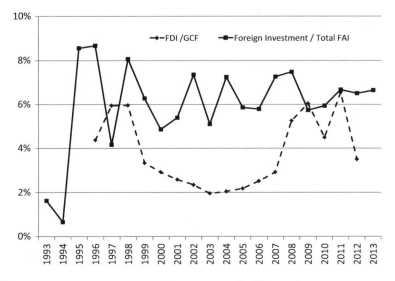

Figure 5.7 Foreign investment versus total investment in Chongqing

Source: *Chongqing Statistical Yearbooks* (various years).

of domestic capital, so that FDI never attained the importance as a percentage of gross capital formation or fixed investment in Chongqing as in some other cities.

Overall, foreign invested industrial enterprises accounted for 28 percent of total revenue, 24 percent of total assets, and 22 percent of total profits of all industrial enterprises in Chongqing in 2013 (Table 5.9). Manufacture of Computers, Communication, and Other Electronic Equipment (2013 revenue RMB 184,885 million) and Manufacture of Motor Vehicles (2013 revenue RMB 121,179 million) together accounted for 71 percent of the total revenue of FIEs in all industrial sectors in Chongqing in 2013. Industries where FIEs have played a particularly important role include Manufacture of Computers, Communication, and Other Electronic Equipment (where FIEs accounted for 88 percent of industry revenue), Manufacture of Motor Vehicles (41 percent), Manufacture of Paper and Paper Products (54 percent), Liquor, Beverage, and Refined Tea (32 percent), and Manufacture of Furniture (37 percent).

FIEs play a critical role in Chongqing's trade (Figure 5.8). FIEs accounted for over 60 percent of the city's imports from 2005 to 2012, and 54 percent in 2013. The FIE share in Chongqing's exports was less than 10 percent from 2001 to 2003, and less than 20 percent by 2010, before increasing dramatically to around 55 percent in 2013. In the earlier period, FIEs imported goods to sell in local markets and capital equipment that was used for facilities producing for the domestic market. It was not until the emergence of the FIE-invested, export-oriented computer industry that Chongqing's FIEs began to export in significant volumes and exports began to exceed imports by a wide margin. It should be noted that the net exports of FIEs alone, again driven by the computer industry, contributed 7 percent of the city's GDP in 2013.

Economic impact of FDI and FIEs on Chongqing

In this section, we apply the tools of economic impact analysis described above to estimate the economic impact that FIEs have had on output, value added (GDP), and employment in Chongqing. Data were available for FIE sales, value added, and employment in Chongqing in 33 industry categories (Chongqing, 2014). Chongqing's own input–output tables were used to generate multipliers specific to the city. The industries covered in the analysis of FIE operations accounted for approximately 34 percent of the inward FDI in Chongqing in the years 1991 to 2013. The analysis was carried out for 2013, the latest year in which data on the operation of FIEs in Chongqing was available.

The estimated impact for the investment phase for investments made in 2013 was USD 8,076 million in output, USD 2,857 million in value added, and 173,647 in employment. The total impact of the capital investment associated with FDI was estimated to equal 1.4 percent of Chongqing's GDP and 1.0 percent of Chongqing's total employment. The estimated economic impact based on the operations of the FIEs in the Mining, Manufacturing, and Utilities sectors in Chongqing in 2013 was USD 96,445 million in total output, USD 30,077 million in value added, and 957,925 persons in employment. This was equivalent to 15 percent of Chongqing's GDP and 5.7 percent

Table 5.9 Foreign invested industrial enterprises by industry, Chongqing, 2013

Industry	Revenue (RMB mn)	% of Chongqing	Assets (RMB mn)	% of Chongqing	Profits (RMB mn)	% of Chongqing	Revenue/ Assets (%)	Profit/ Revenue (%)	Profit/ Assets (%)
All Industrial Sectors	431,797	28	327,686	24	19,680	22	132	4.6	6.0
Manufacture of Communication Equipment, Computers, and Other Electronic Equipment	184,885	88	86,412	85	884	31	214	0.5	1.0
Manufacture of Motor Vehicles	121,179	41	76,570	32	12,521	50	158	10.3	16.4
Smelting and Pressing of Ferrous Metals	18,147	25	47,713	70	-2,452	-229	38	-13.5	-5.1
Manufacture of Paper and Paper Products	10,843	54	15,882	76	1,076	60	68	9.9	6.8
Manufacture of Non-metallic Mineral Products	10,192	13	20,355	22	272	5	50	2.7	1.3
Manufacture of Rubber and Plastics	9,504	25	9,183	41	565	20	103	5.9	6.2
Manufacture of General Purpose Machinery	8,746	18	6,205	13	1,053	26	141	12.0	17.0

(Continued)

Table 5.9 (Continued)

Industry	Revenue (RMB mn)	% of Chongqing	Assets (RMB mn)	% of Chongqing	Profits (RMB mn)	% of Chongqing	Revenue/ Assets (%)	Profit/ Revenue (%)	Profit/ Assets (%)
Manufacture of Railway, Ship, Aviation, and Other Transporting Equipment	7,985	6	4,009	4	372	5	199	4.7	9.3
Manufacture of Raw Chemical Materials and Chemical Products	7,540	10	11,006	13	178	22	69	2.4	1.6
Processing of Food from Agricultural Products	7,226	11	3,343	13	165	4	216	2.3	4.9
Smelting and Pressing of Non-ferrous Metals	6,680	12	4,602	10	639	45	145	9.6	13.9
Manufacture of Electrical Machinery and Equipment	6,182	8	5,691	11	665	11	109	10.8	11.7
Production and Supply of Electric Power and Heat Power	5,315	8	6,349	4	834	33	84	15.7	13.1
Liquor, Beverage, and Refined Tea	5,033	32	5,577	43	431	27	90	8.6	7.7
Manufacture of Furniture	3,116	37	2,679	48	394	49	116	12.6	14.7

Manufacture of Special Purpose Machinery	3,048	11	2,526	12	267	9	121	8.8	10.6
Production and Supply of Gas	2,852	26	6,271	45	346	31	45	12.1	5.5
Manufacture of Measuring Instruments and Machinery for Cultural Activity and Office Work	2,606	19	1,606	11	257	24	162	9.9	16.0
Manufacture of Foods	2,018	12	2,181	18	249	18	93	12.3	11.4
Manufacture of Textile Wearing Apparel, Footwear, and Caps	1,990	21	1,401	30	124	13	142	6.2	8.9
Manufacture of Textile	1,599	9	348	4	100	8	459	6.3	28.7
Printing, Reproduction of Recording Media	1,498	14	1,338	19	140	17	112	9.3	10.5
Manufacture of Medicines	1,295	4	1,720	4	288	9	75	22.2	16.7
Manufacture of Metal Products	934	3	860	3	37	1	109	4.0	4.3

(Continued)

Table 5.9 (Continued)

Industry	Revenue (RMB mn)	% of Chongqing	Assets (RMB mn)	% of Chongqing	Profits (RMB mn)	% of Chongqing	Revenue/ Assets (%)	Profit/ Revenue (%)	Profit/ Assets (%)
Manufacture of Culture, Education, Handicraft, Fine Arts, Sports and Entertainment Articles	589	11	1,100	27	220	25	54	37.4	20.0
Production and Supply of Water	541	23	2,571	18	44	11	21	8.1	1.7
Mining and Washing of Coal	127	0	46	0	4	0	276	3.1	8.7
Processing of Timber, Manufacture of Wood, Bamboo, Rattan, Palm, and Straw Products	89	3	27	1	12	5	330	13.5	44.4
Mining and Processing of Non-metal Ores	20	0	103	2	−9	−1	19	−45.0	−8.7
Manufacture of Leather, Fur, Feather, and Related Products	19	0	11	0	1	0	173	5.3	9.1
Comprehensive Utilization of Waste Resources	–	–	–	–	–	–	–	–	–

Extraction of Petroleum and Natural Gas	—	—	—	—	—	—	—	—	—	—
Manufacture of Chemical Fibers	—	—	—	—	—	—	—	—	—	—
Manufacture of Tobacco	—	—	—	—	—	—	—	—	—	—
Mining and Processing of Ferrous Metal Ores	—	—	—	—	—	—	—	—	—	—
Mining and Processing of Non-Ferrous Metal Ores	—	—	—	—	—	—	—	—	—	—
Mining of Other Ores	—	—	—	—	—	—	—	—	—	—
Mining Support Activities	—	—	—	—	—	—	—	—	—	—
Other Manufacture	—	—	—	—	—	—	—	—	—	—
Processing of Petroleum, Coking, Processing of Nuclear Fuel	—	—	—	—	—	—	—	—	—	—
Repair of Metal Products, Machinery and Equipment	—	—	—	—	—	—	—	—	—	—

Source: *Chongqing Statistical Yearbook 2014*.

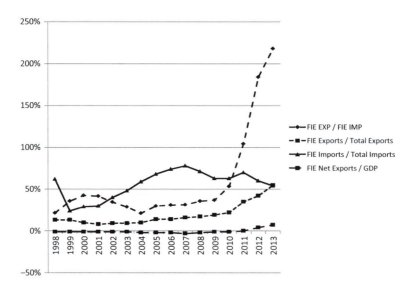

Figure 5.8 Trade performance of foreign invested enterprises in Chongqing

Note: The FIE trade figures are extracted from *China Statistical Yearbooks* while the Chongqing trade figures are extracted from *Chongqing Statistical Yearbooks*, which might have some discrepancy in statistical scope.

Sources: *Chongqing Statistical Yearbooks* (various years); *China Statistical Yearbooks* (various years).

of Chongqing's total employment from all sources in 2013. The estimated combined economic impact of the investment phase associated with all foreign direct investment in Chongqing and the sales of FIEs in the Mining, Manufacturing, and Utilities sectors in Chongqing in 2013 was USD 104,521 million in output, USD 32,934 million in value added, and 1,131,572 in employment. The impacts were equivalent to 16 percent of Chongqing's GDP and 6.7 percent of Chongqing's total employment from all sources in 2013. Again, we note that these impacts are just for the Mining, Manufacturing, and Utilities industries for which the sales data for FIEs is available. The impacts do not include the impact of foreign investment in the service sector. Thus these impacts are the result of 34 percent of the total FDI into Chongqing over the period 1991 to 2013. If the impacts of the other 66 percent of FDI into Chongqing were taken into account, the GDP and employment impact would be much higher than 16 percent and 6.7 percent.

Table 5.10 shows the economic impact of the operations of FIEs by industry for the year 2013. The operations of FIEs in Computers, Communication, and Other Electronic Equipment (direct revenue RMB 184,885 million) generated a total impact of USD 37,823 million in output, USD 12,606 million in value added, and 337,042 jobs. FIEs in Transport Equipment (direct revenue RMB 129,164 million) generated a total impact of USD 30,779 million in output, USD 8,119 million in value added, and 250,456 jobs. FIEs in the Smelting and Pressing of Ferrous and Non-ferrous Metals (direct revenue RMB 24,828 million) generated a total impact of USD 5,299 million in output, USD 1,416 million in value added, and 40,313 jobs.

Table 5.10 Impact of the operations of FIEs, Mining, Manufacturing, and Utilities Sectors in Chongqing by industry, 2013

	Output (USD mn)	Value Added (USD mn)	Employment (persons)
Manufacture of Computers, Communication, and Other Electronic Equipment	37,823	12,606	337,042
Manufacture of Transport Equipment	30,779	8,199	250,456
Smelting and Pressing of Ferrous and Non-ferrous Metals	5,299	1,416	40,313
Manufacture of Paper and Paper Products; Printing, Reproduction of Recording Media; Manufacture of Articles For Culture, Education and Sport Activities	2,799	843	31,690
Manufacture of Non-metallic Mineral Products	2,417	795	31,305
Manufacture of Rubber, Plastic, and Chemical Fiber Products	2,252	760	30,168
Production and Supply of Electric Power, Gas, and Water	2,204	978	28,524
Manufacture of General Purpose Machinery	2,080	636	22,464
Processing of Food from Agricultural Products	1,969	841	43,770
Manufacture of Raw Chemical Materials and Chemical Products	1,787	603	18,715
Manufacture of Electrical Machinery and Apparatus	1,473	419	16,018
Manufacture of Liquor, Beverages, and Refined Tea	1,372	586	35,799
Wood processing and Furniture manufacturing	805	246	12,108

(Continued)

Table 5.10 (Continued)

	Output (USD mn)	Value Added (USD mn)	Employment (persons)
Manufacture of Special Purpose Machinery	725	222	8,475
Manufacture of Food	550	235	13,686
Manufacture of Measuring Instruments and Machinery for Cultural Activity and Office Work	533	178	5,837
Manufacture of Textile, Wearing Apparel, and Accessories	520	152	10,954
Manufacture of Textile	491	172	12,579
Manufacture of Medicines	307	104	3,775
Manufacture of Metal Products	228	72	3,660
Mining	34	16	588

Source: Enright, Scott & Associates analysis.

Chongqing conclusions

Chongqing was a late mover in terms of attracting foreign direct investment. However, the combination of the spread of economic development to China's West, large-scale infrastructure investment, and policies that funnelled investment toward Chongqing allowed it to become an important destination for foreign direct investment. At the same time, foreign direct investment has been crucial to Chongqing's growth. Several of its main industries, including the chemical, automotive, computer, and real estate industries, are dominated or have substantial contributions from foreign enterprises. Foreign investment in these industries, and others, has been vital to Chongqing's emergence as an economic power.

While the economic impacts of FDI and FIEs in Chongqing are not as great as in Shenzhen and Tianjin, this is to be expected. Shenzhen and Tianjin were opened to foreign investment well before Chongqing. Shenzhen and Tianjin benefit from their coastal locations and easier access to international trade. There are also distinct features of Chongqing's inward investment. One is the large share of foreign investment into the Real Estate sector. Foreign investment is literally developing the city. Another is the rapid rise of the computer sector, which is due almost exclusively to the investment of foreign firms, and which has resulted in the FIE net export contribution to Chongqing's economy to go from negative to positive 7 percent in just a few years. It is also informative that the main initiative to further develop Chongqing's economy, the creation of the Liangjiang New Area, also depends heavily on the ability to attract foreign investment. This shows that foreign investment remains crucial for this later developing municipality, and is suggestive for other later developing municipalities in China.

Conclusions

The municipal case studies provide a number of insights into China's development, and the role of foreign investment and foreign invested enterprises in this development. One insight is on the sequential nature of China's opening to foreign investment in terms of locations, organizational forms, and industries. Shenzhen was an early mover in terms of opening to inward investment followed by Tianjin and Shanghai, and then by Chongqing. The notion of geographic asymmetry still pervades China's approach toward investment promotion and development, with 'Special Economic Zones' and 'New Areas' as major focal points for development.

In terms of industry mix, export-oriented industries were opened first in Shenzhen. In Shanghai and Tianjin, production for the domestic market was more important in the early days of their opening. Ultimately, foreign investment and foreign invested enterprises were sought to develop critical industries, technology-based industries, and the service sector. In the meantime, foreign investment in infrastructure, real estate, retail, and other sectors helped create a modern economic and business base. In many cases, key industries would not exist in the cities without the presence of foreign investment. The relative importance of foreign investment and foreign enterprises is also seen to differ with the stage of development of China, as well as the increasing experience of foreign companies in China, but in each case, the tendency has been toward greater investment and greater involvement over time.

In each case, the impact of FDI and FIEs on the municipal economies has been large, even when the impact estimates are based on only a modest portion of the total inward investment in the cities. For the most recent year available, in Shenzhen we estimated that foreign investment and the operations of foreign invested enterprises in industries that account for 66 percent of cumulative investment accounted for 41 percent of GDP and 43 percent of employment. For Tianjin when the operations in industries that account for 51 percent of cumulative FDI are taken into account, the impact of FDI and FIEs was 22 percent of GDP and 21 percent of employment. In Chongqing, when the operations in industries that account for 34 percent of FDI are taken into account, the impact of FDI and FIEs was 16 percent of GDP and 7 percent of employment. If FDI and FIEs in other industries where the impacts cannot be traced at present have anything like the impacts in the other sectors, then the total impact of FDI and FIEs in these cities could range from 35 to 60 plus percent of GDP. And in Shanghai, where data was not available to carry out this type of analysis, official sources have indicated that FIEs directly account for two-thirds of exports, imports, and industrial output; one-third of tax and employment; and 90 percent of high technology output.

Finally, the case studies show that attracting and retaining foreign investment, and providing more freedom of action for foreign firms is still a major component of the new initiatives that are hoped will push the cities to the next stage in development. Since the four cities profiled, Shenzhen, Tianjin, Shanghai, and Chongqing, are each supposed to be leaders within their respective regions, we can only expect that other Chinese cities will seek to gain the benefits of inward investment.

Notes

1 Supporting work for this chapter was carried out by Ella Dong and David Sanderson of Enright, Scott & Associates.
2 Note that Mainland Chinese statistical sources often combine investment from Hong Kong and Macau into a single category.
3 In a 1999 research project on foreign firms active in Shanghai the author was able to carry out over 90 percent of the relevant interviews in only three buildings or complexes: the Shanghai America Center, Shui On Plaza (developed by Hong Kong's Shui On Group), and a German invested complex near Hongqiao Airport.
4 Citigroup, Bank of America, Industrial Bank of Japan, Sanwam, Banque Indosuez, and Credit Lyonnais.
5 The cumulative utilized FDI number is from Chongqing (2014) and the ranking is from CEIC (2015). The FDI figure for Chongqing in the CEIC database is larger than that in the city yearbook.
6 Note that other sources indicated a slightly lower figure. For example, Chongqing's share of global laptop computer production was cited as 25 percent in 2013 in Netherlands Consulate (2014b).

References

ABB, 2006, 'ABB Global Robotics Business Headquarters Opens in Shanghai', *ABB Press Release*, 4 April.
Alcatel-Lucent Shanghai Bell, 2014, *Company Presentation*, January.
BASF, 2014, *BASF in Greater China*.
Bayer, 2012, *Annual Report 2011*.
Binhai New Area, 2015, *Binhai New Area Briefing*.
Bohai Morning Post, 2015, '[Strong Momentum in Foreign Investment in Binhai New Area Last Year]', *Bohai Morning Post*, 23 January, (in Chinese).
CECIC, 2013, '[First Mover Advantages in Emerging Markets-Volkswagen's Business in China and Its Implications]', *China Export and Credit Insurance Corporation*, 9 June, (in Chinese).
CEIC, 2015, *CEIC Database*, accessed October 2015.
Chen, K., 2011, 'Foreign Equity Investment Fund Establishment in Chongqing – First Investment Amount of 5 Billion in Chongqing Tourism', *Chongqing Economic Times*, 22 June.
Chen, X. and T. de'Medici, 2009, *The Instant City Coming of Age: China's Shenzhen Special Economic Zone in Thirty Years*, Trinity College Working Paper, no. 2.
Cheng, G., 2010, 'Hat Trick Pulled Off in Tianjin', *China Daily*, 22 September.

China Briefing Media, 2004, *Business Guide to the Greater Pearl River Delta*, Hong Kong, China Briefing Media.

China Daily, 2015a, 'Foreign Banks Eye Shanghai to Open Branches', *China Daily*, 6 August.

China Daily, 2015b, 'Industrial Parks in Tianjin', *China Daily*, October 21.

China Economic Review, 2005, 'Tianjin', in *China Business Guide 2005*, Beijing, China Economic Review.

China Telecom, 2000, 'Alcatel to Establish Headquarters in Shanghai', *China Telecom Monthly Newsletter*, February, p. 10.

Chongqing, various years, *Chongqing Statistical Yearbooks*.

Chongqing, 1999, *Chongqing Urban Development Yearbook 1999*, Chongqing Urban Development Office.

Chongqing, 2014, *Chongqing Statistical Yearbook 2014*.

Chongqing Currents, 2012, 'Chongqing Currents Talks to Raymond Bragg, General Manager of Kempinski Chongqing', *Chongqing Currents*, March–April, p. 4.

Chongqing Government, 2014, *Introduction of Liangjiang New Area*.

Chongqing News, 2015, 'Chongqing Made Computers Take up 1/3 of World Output', *Chongqing News*, 9 January.

CNTA, 2009, *The Yearbook of China Tourism Statistics, 2008*, Beijing, China National Tourism Administration.

Cq People, 2015, '[Chongqing has 17 Foreign Funded Banks, Ranked First in Midwest]', *Cq People*, 23 January, (in Chinese).

do Rosário, L., 2015, 'Carriage of Trade – Railway from Chongqing Opens New Silk Road to Europe', *Macau Hub*, 6 March.

Fu, J., 2000, *Institutions and Investments: Foreign Direct Investment in China during an Era of Reforms*, Ann Arbor, University of Michigan Press.

Fu, T., M. Chang, and L. Zhong, 2008, *Reform of China's Urban Water Sector*, London, IWA Publishing, 2008.

Gamble, J., 2003, *Shanghai in Transition: Changing Perspectives and Social Contours of a Chinese Metropolis*, London, Routledge.

Gao, R., 2013, *Regional China: A Business and Economic Handbook*, London, Palgrave Macmillan.

Gu, G.Z., 2006, *China and the New World Order*, Palo Alto, Fultus Books.

Hendrischke, H., 1999, 'Tianjin- Quiet Achiever?', in H. Hendrischke and F. Chongyi, eds, *The Political Economy of China's Provinces*, London, Routledge, pp. 183–206.

HKTDC, 2015a, *Chongqing Market Profile*, Hong Kong Trade Development Council.

HKTDC, 2015b, *Tianjin Beichen High-tech Industrial Park*, Hong Kong Trade Development Council.

Hui, Z., 2010, 'Trailblazer-Tracing the First Wholly Foreign-owned Company in China', *China Today*, December.

IBM, 2013, *IBM in the Growth Markets*.

Invest Shanghai, 2015, *About Shanghai*.

Jacobs, J. B. and L. Hong, 1994, 'Shanghai and the Lower Yangzi Valley', in D.S.G. Good and G. Segal, eds, *China Deconstructs: Politics, Trade and Regionalism*, London, Routledge, pp. 224–52.

Jones Lang LaSalle, 2007, *Emerging City Winners Profiles: Chongqing*, April.

JPRD, 1983, 'Wage System in Shenzhen Special Economic Zone', *Journal of the Pearl River Delta*, 82822, 8 February.

Leong, A. and S. Pratap, 2011, *China's Capitalist Development and Its Implications for Labour with Special Reference to the Shenzhen SEZ*, Hong Kong, AMRC.

Liu, Y., 2015, 'Tianjin Binhai New Area's GDP Leaps in the Past Decade', *China Daily*, 10 March.

Ma, Z., 2015, 'AT&S Expands Chongqing Site for Next-generation PCB', *China Daily*, 6 May.

MOFCOM, 2015, [*The Current Situation of Foreign Investment in Shenzhen, Characteristics and Main Issues*], (in Chinese).

National Business Daily, 2015, '[Capital Land Invest RMB 6.5 Billion in Chongqing Land Market]', *National Business Daily*, 7 April, (in Chinese).

Netherlands Consulate, 2014a, *Automotive Industry in Chongqing, Sichuan, and Hubei*, Consulate General of the Kingdom of the Netherlands in Chongqing.

Netherlands Consulate, 2014b, *Chongqing Municipality Profile*, Consulate General of the Kingdom of the Netherlands in Chongqing.

Savills, 2013, *Chongqing Hospitality*, 2H 2013.

Securities Times, 2015, '[Sales Slump From Five Out of the Top 10 Auto Companies], *Securities Times*, 16 July, (in Chinese).

Shanghai, 2014, *Shanghai Statistical Yearbook*.

Shanghai Daily, 2008, 'IBM Locates New Unit HQ in Shanghai', *Shanghai Daily*, 25 April.

Shanghai Government, 2015, 'The Second Economic Development: Introduction of Foreign Capital', *Shanghai Government Blog*.

Shanghai Industrial, 2003, 'Shanghai Industrial to Acquire A-Share Company SI United Holdings' Control Interest for HK$817m', *Shanghai Industrial Press Release*, 22 May.

Shenzhen, various years, *Shenzhen Statistical Yearbooks*.

Shenzhen, 2000, *To Commemorate the 20th Anniversary of the Establishment of the Shenzhen Special Economic Zone*, Shenzhen Government.

Shenzhen, 2014, *Shenzhen Statistical Yearbook 2014*.

Shenzhen ETO, 2013, 'Shenzhen Economic Statistics Review', *Shenzhen Economic and Trade Office Sydney: Newsletter*, May.

Sino-French Water, 2011, *Committed to China's Sustainable Development*.

Tianjin, various years, *Tianjin Statistical Yearbooks*.

Tianjin, 1996, *Tianjin Statistical Yearbook 1996*.

Tianjin, 2005, *Doing Business in Tianjin- 2005*, Tianjin Government.

Tianjin, 2012, *Tianjin Statistical Yearbook 2012*.

Tianjin, 2015, *Tianjin Statistical Gazette 2015*.

Tianjin Daily, 1994, *Tianjin Daily*, 8 August, (in Chinese), quoted in Hendrischke (1999).

Tianjin Daily, 2015, '[First 26 Financial Institutions Awarded Licenses in the Tianjin Free Trade Zone]', *Tianjin Daily*, 22 April, (in Chinese).

Wang, H., 2011, 'Roche Sees New Shanghai Center One of its Hubs', *China Daily*, 15 April.

Wang, Y., 2014, 'Another 58 Multinational Companies Locate Headquarters in Shanghai', *Shanghai Daily*, 10 December.

Wang, Y., 2015, 'Foreign Firms Leading Force in Shanghai's Innovation Center Drive', *Shanghai Daily*, 11 August.

Want China Times, 2012, 'Quanta to Move Almost All Production to Chongqing', *Want China Times*, 18 August.

Wilson, S., 2009, *Remade in China: Foreign Investors and Institutional Change in China*, Oxford, Oxford University Press.

The World Bank, 2013, *Urbanization beyond Municipal Boundaries*, Washington, DC, The World Bank.

Wu, W., 1997, 'Proximity and Complementarity in Hong Kong – Shenzhen Industrialization', *Asian Survey*, August.

Xie, Z., G. Zhong, H. Yu, N. Tian, and Y. Wang, 2013, *Research on Shenzhen's Role in Facilitating the Transformation of Chinese Migrant Workers*, Shenzhen, Survey Office of the National Bureau of Statistics in Shenzhen.

Zhu, J., 1999, *The Transformation of China's Urban Development: From Plan-controlled to Market-led*, Westport, CT, Praeger.

Zhuan, T., 2015, 'Liangjiang New Area at Core of China's Growth', *China Daily*, 13 August.

6

Corporate case studies

Introduction

The preceding chapters have focused on the range of contributions that foreign investment and foreign invested enterprises have made to China's development. In this chapter, we highlight the specific contributions of pioneering Hong Kong investors, the US-based consumer products company P&G, the Danish shipping and logistics company Maersk, and the Korean electronics company Samsung. Each firm or group of firms has charted a different path in China has made its own specific contributions to China's development. Their stories show a finer grained picture of foreign contributions.

Hong Kong companies were pioneers among investors in China. Hong Kong's proximity to the Shenzhen Special Economic Zone, cultural similarity, family ties, history in light manufacturing, and global business and financial links allowed Hong Kong investors to take the risks to make the business connections that others hesitated to take. Hong Kong's ability to link Chinese land, labour, and resources to global markets, and to link global finance, skills, and capabilities to China's needs allowed Hong Kong pioneers to become major investors in China's manufacturing, infrastructure, utilities, property, hospitality, and service sectors. In many industries and many locations in China, it was Hong Kong companies that were the first to enter, and while this pioneering function is less pronounced today than it once was, Hong Kong investors are critical contributors in a wide range of industries and geographies in China.

P&G was an early entrant into China among major western multinational companies. P&G showed commitment to the China market early on, advertising its brands three years before it was even allowed to sell in the Chinese Mainland. P&G introduced entire new product categories that had been unknown in China previously. It invested to develop suppliers that it eventually incorporated into its global supply chain, and helped create distribution systems in much of China. P&G, and similar companies, also introduced modern marketing and advertising practice to China. P&G committed to developing its local staff, eventually becoming a net exporter of managerial talent from its China operations. Its extensive CSR activities in China have included investments in public health, hygiene awareness, education, and international expositions. The impact of its investments and operations on China's economy has been several times its investment and sales totals.

Maersk's interaction with China has been multifaceted. It has been a major customer for China's shipyards, in fact it helped some Chinese shipyards to develop world-class capabilities. Through its investments in ports and its shipping operations, Maersk has been a leader in connecting China to the rest of the world, and in facilitating China's emergence as the world's leading trading nation. It also has been a leader in introducing efficient port practices to China, reducing costs and improving environmental practices in the process. Maersk's logistics arm has helped reduce the costs of moving goods within China and between China and overseas markets. The company has also participated through a variety of CSR activities in support of China.

Samsung has been one of the largest foreign investors in China. It has built a China structure that rivals that found in its home country of Korea. Samsung has invested extensively in production facilities, research and development, and marketing and sales in China. It has supported China in telecommunication standards development and indirectly supported the emergence of Chinese electronics companies by championing open standards internationally. Samsung has attracted numerous foreign suppliers to set up in China, and has fostered the development of Chinese suppliers as well. As costs and competition have heated up in China, however, Samsung has diversified its production activities. In particular, it is investing in Vietnam operations that will rival its China operations in size. This is perhaps a cautionary tale that major multinationals can find other places if China becomes too expensive, or not as hospitable to foreign companies as other countries.

Hong Kong pioneers[1]

Hong Kong has been the largest single source of foreign investment into the Chinese Mainland since the onset of the reform period. While the amounts of investment are impressive, so too are the contributions that Hong Kong and Hong Kong companies have made to China's economic development. Hong Kong companies were among the first non-Mainland companies to invest in export-oriented production in China. They helped develop the supply chains and production systems that made China in general (and South China in particular) one of the world's leading manufacturing and export locations. Many of the systems that were developed in China for dealing with foreign investment, including the legal regime, property rights, export processing rules, customs systems, labour regulations, and land use rules, were first worked out in the context of Hong Kong investment and investors.

Hong Kong companies were also early investors in the infrastructure that helped link China to the global economy. This included investments in ports and roads in China's major manufacturing and exporting regions. Hong Kong developers were among the first to create mixed-use developments that made Chinese cities 'user-friendly' to international companies and foreign residents. Hong Kong investors were also instrumental in the transfer of technology, management capabilities, and knowledge of world markets from the rest of the world to China, at least in the early days of China's reform program. While the relative importance of Hong Kong investors has diminished over the years, they still make vital contributions to China, and it is hard to imagine that

China would have emerged so quickly as a world-leading economy without the investment and other linkages to Hong Kong.

Investment and employment

Hong Kong has been by far the largest foreign investor into the Chinese Mainland. From 1985 to 2014, the Chinese National Statistical Bureau reported that Hong Kong was the source of USD 744.8 billion in foreign direct investment, or 47 percent of all of the FDI into the Chinese Mainland.[2] While some of that investment is likely to have been 'round tripped' investment from the Chinese Mainland, and some is likely to have been brought into Hong Kong by foreign companies and then redeployed into the Mainland, the fact remains that Hong Kong and Hong Kong companies have been huge investors into the Chinese Mainland. This is particularly true in neighbouring Guangdong Province, but Hong Kong companies have been prominent if not leading investors in Shanghai and many other major cities and provinces in China.

Hong Kong investors paved the way for other foreign investors into China. China began opening to outside investors for the first time in decades in 1979. At the time, there was considerable uncertainty about the rules governing such investment and how China's economy would evolve. In the early years, much of the investment from Hong Kong into China relied on family ties as Hong Kong business people invested in their ancestral hometowns (Leung, 1993). One reason for this focus was a sense of contributing to the development of the ancestral hometown. A less prosaic reason was that many Hong Kong entrepreneurs still had family or friends in these towns that could help reduce the uncertainty and risk associated with investment. In any case, it was Hong Kong entrepreneurs who were willing to take the risks to work out how to do business in China at a time when China was still working out its approach toward foreign investment, its legal regime was unclear, and enforcement of agreements uncertain.

The bulk of the early Hong Kong investment went into manufacturing. In the years 1979 to 1984, 69 percent of the Hong Kong investment into Guangdong Province was in the secondary sector, 28 percent in the tertiary sector, and only 2.4 percent the primary sector (Zhongshan University, 2002, pp. 7–8). Most Hong Kong investment into China in this period involved labour-intensive export processing attracted by very low land and labour costs (Wang, 1994, p. 169). Much of the investment was in industries in which Hong Kong companies had developed strong competitive positions, but for which Hong Kong was becoming too expensive. Thus Hong Kong companies fed their existing sales and distribution networks with China-sourced production. The investments were concentrated in the Shenzhen Special Economic Zone and areas along the Guangzhou–Shenzhen railway line, especially in Dongguan. This minimized the travel times from Hong Kong at a time when travelling to adjacent cities in China could take hours or more (Li et al., 2002, p. 38; Zhongshan University, 2002, p. 7). Early successes attracted new investors and development of several infrastructure projects allowed for easier transportation from Hong Kong to the eastern portion of the Pearl River Delta region. Investment from Hong Kong into China increased rapidly, spreading beyond areas neighbouring Hong Kong further into the Pearl River Delta region and beyond.

After Deng Xiaoping's South China tour in 1992, China launched a second round of reform and economic opening, and received another round of investment from Hong Kong, with the stock of Hong Kong investment in China rising by nearly a factor of ten from 1992 to 2002. Again much of this investment was in traditional industries in the Pearl River Delta region of Guangdong Province (Hong Kong Commercial Daily, 2002; Ta Kung Pao, 2002a, 2002b). By 2000, some 70 percent of the Hong Kong-invested enterprises in the Pearl River Delta region were engaged in production of textiles, garments, electronics, toys, metal products, plastics, and other labour-intensive light industrial products. Some 80 to 90 percent of Hong Kong's plastic industry, roughly 85 percent of its electronic industry, and 90 percent of its watch and toy industries had moved to the Pearl River Delta region. The vast majority of these facilities were engaged in export activities in export processing OEM or ODM arrangements (Zhongshan University, 2002, p. 10). The Hong Kong Chinese Manufacturers' Association estimated that 86.1 percent of its members had set up factories in the Chinese Mainland by October 2001 and that the total number of Hong Kong-invested entities in the Chinese Mainland was 198,188, most of these in manufacturing and most of those in Guangdong Province (Ta Kung Pao, 2002a). In general, the Hong Kong companies kept their pre-production and post-production activities, including design, development, marketing, sales, and logistics in Hong Kong, along with senior management and finance, while decentralizing production and activities closely related to production (author's interviews).

Deng's tour and subsequent developments heralded greater opening in the service sector in China and established the Yangtze River Delta as a second engine of economic growth and destination for foreign investment. Hong Kong investment also became more diversified, with Hong Kong firms investing in finance, insurance, real estate, building materials, and a range of services. Although the geographic focus remained in the Pearl River Delta region, investments also started to be made elsewhere in Guangdong. Many Hong Kong entrepreneurs with family ties to Shanghai, for example, began to explore opportunities in the Yangtze River Delta. For many years, Hong Kong accounted for more than 50 percent of the external investment into Shanghai. Hong Kong began to be viewed as a partner for Shanghai's development (HKTDC, 2001).

While many of the Hong Kong manufacturing companies that invested in the Chinese Mainland were small companies, a number leveraged their China production facilities to become internationally prominent, such as Johnson Electric (mini-motors), VTech (electronics and toys), Gold Peak (batteries and electronics), Techtronic (tools), TAL (garments), Esquel (garments), and many others. In addition to the manufacturers and traders, Hong Kong-based property developers, infrastructure companies, retailers, banks, logistics companies, and others joined in on investing in the Chinese Mainland, their path eased somewhat by several rounds of CEPA (Closer Economic Partnership Arrangements) between Hong Kong and the Chinese Mainland (which provided easier access to the Mainland market for Hong Kong firms), the first round of which was agreed in 2003. In the meanwhile, conditions for smaller Hong Kong companies began to change in the 2000s as Mainland competitors emerged, costs began to rise in the Pearl River Delta, and some of the leading localities for Hong Kong investment began placing greater emphasis on sustainable development, favouring investments involving cleaner manufacturing processes, and targeting investments with higher levels of technology content. In any case, the stock of foreign investment in the Chinese Mainland from Hong Kong roughly tripled in the years 2003 to 2013.

Hong Kong investment also generated employment in the Chinese Mainland, particularly on the Pearl River Delta region of Guangdong Province. In 1981, Hong Kong manufacturing firms employed roughly 870,000 manufacturing workers in Hong Kong and few elsewhere. By 2001, they employed only around 230,000 manufacturing workers in Hong Kong (HKCSD, 2002). By our estimates, by 2002, Hong Kong firms employed up to 10 million to 11 million (directly or indirectly) in the Pearl River Delta region and between 500,000 and 1 million elsewhere in Asia.[3] While we are not aware of any subsequent study of the employment of Hong Kong companies in the Chinese Mainland, we note that the stock of Hong Kong sourced foreign direct investment into China roughly tripled in the years 2003 to 2014, and that the 11 million figure for 2003 represented employment in just one province, albeit the province that had received the largest portion of Hong Kong investment.

Connecting China to the world

Hong Kong and Hong Kong firms have long played a role in connecting China to the rest of the world. Examples include Hong Kong's role in physically connecting China through the port and airport in Hong Kong; connecting China commercially through trading, trade fairs, and B2B communication; and connecting China to global capital markets. For the first two decades of China's reform period, the port of Hong Kong provided the connections for the seaborne exports of South China to the rest of the world. Hong Kong's share of South China direct export container traffic was around 95 percent as late as 1996. With massive investments in capacity and increased efficiency in the ports in Guangdong Province, this figure began to fall. Hong Kong's share of South China direct export container traffic fell to 76 percent in 2001 to 47 percent in 2006 and to 40 percent in 2011 (HKTHB, 2008, 2014). Thus while Hong Kong's importance has diminished, it is clear that Hong Kong provided the port access from South China to the rest of the world for the first two decades of China's reform period, a time within which South China became established as a world leading export location.

Hong Kong has been the dominant supplier of air cargo services that link China with the rest of the world. Hong Kong International Airport accounted for around 70 percent of the total air cargo of the Greater Pearl River Delta (GPRD) region and 90 percent of the international air cargo for the region in 2004 (Lam, 2005). In 2014,

HKIA accounted for on the order of 65 percent of the total air cargo traffic in the GPRD, and a larger share of international air cargo.[4]

Hong Kong has emerged as a leading location for trading, trade fairs, and international B2B communication. The import–export trading sector in Hong Kong employed 516,700 people in 2013 (HKCSD, 2014),[5] the vast majority of whom were involved in China trade. Large trading companies, like Hong Kong's Li & Fung competed alongside tens of thousands of small companies in this sector. Trade fairs organized in Hong Kong and by Hong Kong-based trade fair operators such as Global Sources and the Hong Kong Trade Development Council attract millions of buyers each year to more than 100 events a year. Most of these events are dominated by Chinese manufactured goods. Hong Kong has also emerged as a leading B2B media hub, again largely, though not exclusively, connecting China-based buyers and suppliers to the rest of the world, with Global Sources again a major player.

Hong Kong has also been a principal avenue for companies from the Chinese Mainland to access international sources of capital. The first 'Red Chip' companies from the Chinese Mainland were listed on the Hong Kong Stock Exchange in 1973.[6] In 1993, Tsingtao Brewery became the first 'H Share' company from the Chinese Mainland to list on the Hong Kong Stock Exchange.[7] By the end of September 2015, a total of 212 H share companies, 144 Red Chip companies, and 564 non-H share private enterprises from the Chinese Mainland were listed on the Hong Kong Stock Exchange. These companies had a total market capitalization of HKD 14.3 trillion (or around USD 1,850 trillion), or around 62 percent of the total capitalization of the Hong Kong Stock Exchange (Hong Kong Stock Exchange, 2015). While international and Chinese joint venture investment banks have managed the lion's share of Chinese IPOs in Hong Kong in recent years, in the early days, Hong Kong-based Peregrine (which failed during the Asian Financial Crisis of 1997–99) was the leader in taking Chinese companies to international capital markets.

Hong Kong has been the location of several other 'firsts' when it comes to the internationalization of China's financial sector. Hong Kong became the first offshore centre to launch RMB business in 2004 and has become the main global centre for RMB trade settlement, financing, and asset management. The Shanghai-Hong Kong Stock Connect, launched in 2014, offered the first channel for foreign investors to access the Shanghai stock market, China's largest. These examples show that Hong Kong plays an important role as a laboratory for the internationalization of China's financial markets.

Creating infrastructure and utilities in China

Hong Kong companies have been pioneers in investing in infrastructure in China, particularly in the Pearl River Delta region of Guangdong Province. This has been true in land transportation, sea transportation, utilities, and energy. In the early days of China's reforms, most foreign investors shied away from investing in infrastructure in China. Without a clear legal framework and track record in place, many potential foreign investors feared that their investments in China would be subject to changes in rules or regulations that would affect the viability of their investments. Hong Kong companies, on the other hand, were willing to take the risks and find solutions to these issues with their Chinese counterparts.

Hong Kong enterprises made early investments in land transportation in China, particularly in the Pearl River Delta region (author's interviews; Yeung, 1994, pp. 149–50). Hong Kong companies Hopewell Holdings, New World Infrastructure, Cheung Kong, Tai He Group, and Hui Ji Group helped build the roads and bridges that opened up much of Guangdong Province to investment. Hong Kong investment in roads in China has brought not only capital, but also new concepts, such as toll highways. While Hong Kong infrastructure investment has benefitted several parts of China, it had a particularly important influence on the Pearl River Delta region (PRD). Infrastructure investment from Hong Kong in the 1990s allowed the PRD to become the leader in the Chinese Mainland in terms of density of expressways, a feature that was instrumental in linking the Pearl River Delta factories to the ports of Hong Kong and Shenzhen, and therefore the rest of the world.

Hong Kong firms have played a key role in the development of ports in China (Comtois and Slack, 2000, p. 16). The port of Yantian in Shenzhen was jointly developed by Shenzhen Dongpeng Holdings and Hong Kong-based Hutchison Port Holdings (HPH). HPH, the world's leading port investor and operator, has been a major investor and operator in the ports of Shanghai, Ningbo, Huizhou, Xiamen, Zhuhai, Foshan, and Jiangmen. Modern Terminals, once part of the Hong Kong-based Swire Group and now a subsidiary of Hong Kong-based Wharf Holdings, invested in port facilities in Da Chan Bay, Shekou, and Chiwan in Guangdong, as well as Taicang (Jiangsu Province). New World Infrastructure invested in container terminals at the ports in Xiamen and Tianjin. In addition to investment, Hong Kong firms provide management and expertise in several of the most important ports in China, and worked with Chinese Customs and other agencies to streamline procedures and paperwork. This combination allowed the Chinese ports to operate at world standards well before they would have been able to do so otherwise (author's interviews). The fact that Hong Kong companies are still major investors and operators in several of China's most important ports shows that they still are making substantial contributions.

Hong Kong companies have pioneered other infrastructure investments in China as well. Hong Kong's MTR Corporation, the first non-Mainland company to invest in and operate a metro line in China is active in Beijing, Shenzhen, and Hangzhou (MTR Corporation, 2014). The Airport Authority of Hong Kong (AAHK), the first non-Mainland entity to invest in an airport in the Chinese Mainland acquired a 35 percent stake in Hangzhou's Xioashan International Airport in 2006, and set up joint ventures to manage the airport in Zhuhai (in 2006) and terminal and retail operations at Shanghai's Hongqiao Airport (in 2009) (AAHK, 2014). The MTR and AAHK investments, the first of their kind in China, set the tone for subsequent investments by other foreign entities in these sectors.

Hong Kong companies have also invested in public utilities and energy in the Chinese Mainland. New World Infrastructure has investments in power plants in Guangdong and Sichuan, as well as in water plants and/or treatment facilities in Zhongshan, Siping (Jilin Province), Baoding (Hebei), Zhangzhou (Henan), Panjin, (Liaoning), Changdu (Liaoning), Dalian (Lioaning), Shanghai, Sanya (Hainan), Chongqing, Tianjin, Wuhan, and Chengdu (NWS Holdings, 2015). Cheung Kong Infrastructure has invested in power plants in Zhuhai, water facilities in Hunan, and gas fields in the South China Sea (Cheung Kong Infrastructure, 2015). Hopewell is a major investor in power plants in Guangdong Province (Hopewell Holdings, 2015). China Light and Power has invested in coal power facilities in Guangxi, Beijing, Tianjin, and Shandong; nuclear power in Guangdong Province; wind power in Lioaning, Yunnan, Sichuan, Shandong, Shanghai, Guizhou, Hebei, Inner Mongolia, Heilongjiang, Xinjiang, Gansu, Jilin, and Guangdong; hydroelectric facilities in Sichuan, Yunnan, and Guangdong; and solar power facilities in Gansu, Jiangsu, and Yunnan (CLP, 2015). In many cases, Hong Kong companies found solutions in an ambiguous environment that allowed them to be early investors in utilities in China, often working with Chinese officials to develop the rules and regulations governing investment into the sector and paving the way for other foreign investors to enter as well.

Developing China's cities

Hong Kong developers have been pioneers in development in several of China's leading cities. In the 1990s, developments like Shui On Plaza in Shanghai and Kerry's China World Center in Beijing helped make Chinese cities user-friendly for international companies and business. Shui On's Xintiandi and Taipingqiao developments in Shanghai helped set the standard for city centre development in China. Other Hong Kong developers like Sun Hung Kai Properties, Hutchison, Wharf, Hang Lung, and Henderson have been leaders among foreign developers in China. As of October 2015, the Kerry Group had completed projects or had projects underway in more than 20 Mainland cities, the Wharf Group in 15 cities, Henderson Land 16 cities, and Hang Lung in eight cities. Shui On became known for historically sensitive city-centre development; Hang Lung for retail complexes; Kerry for mixed-use city-centre developments; and Sun Hung Kai for large-scale office and retail complexes; etc. Hong Kong developers have been particularly prominent in Shanghai, where the busiest part of Huai Hai Road, one of Shanghai's leading commercial streets, is called 'Hong Kong Street' after the investments by Hong Kong developers.

Hong Kong companies have also been active in developing hotels in the Chinese Mainland, including the first international calibre hotel in many Chinese cities. Hong Kong joint ventures developed the White Swan Hotel, which opened in 1983, and the China Hotel, which opened in 1984, which were for many years the leading hotels for foreign business people in Guangzhou. The China World and nearby Traders Hotels (developed by Hong Kong-based Kerry Group), have been leading hotels for foreign business people visiting Beijing for many years. The early investments by Hong Kong developers have facilitated other companies investing in China. By late 2015, the Kerry Group had invested in 54 hotels across the Chinese Mainland under the Shangri-La, Traders, and other brands. Other Hong Kong hotel groups with substantial Mainland activities include Langham (12 hotels in China as of October 2015), New World (nine hotels), the Wharf Group (eight hotels), Regal (eight hotels), and Marco Polo (seven hotels). Other groups like the Mandarin Oriental Group (a Jardine company), Swire Hotels, and Hong Kong and Shanghai Hotels (Peninsula Brand) had fewer but high-profile properties in China.

Hong Kong companies were early foreign investors into the property and hotel sectors in China. In several cases, they introduced new quality standards and international best practice into China, features that several Chinese developers quickly emulated. They worked with local officials to create a regime that would make foreign investment in these sectors feasible. They also paved the way for developers from other countries to invest in China, magnifying their overall impact. Thus while by 2015 the Hong Kong developers active in the Chinese Mainland were small compared to the leading Mainland developers, they still occupied prominent positions in many cities around China.

Technology and management transfer

In the early days of China's reforms, Hong Kong was instrumental in the transfer of technology and management capabilities to the Pearl River Delta region and other parts of China. This transfer came about largely through the direct transfer accompanying investments by Hong Kong firms, the copying of Hong Kong sourced technology and management practices by facilities in the Chinese Mainland, and by Hong Kong acting as a technology and management intermediary between China and the rest of the world.

A substantial amount of technology and management transfer has been coupled with the investments of Hong Kong firms (Wang, 1994, pp. 172–3). After 30 years of a closed economy, China had limited capacity to create or absorb needed technologies or management expertise. Foreign technology and management capabilities were needed if China were to start to meet domestic demand, as well as to produce for export markets. In the early years of the reform process, much of the technology that was transferred was embodied in capital equipment imported by Hong Kong investors, while management capabilities were embodied in Hong Kong managers. The Hong Kong companies brought modern product design, production equipment, production management, quality control, packaging expertise, and marketing knowledge (author's interviews; Cheng and Zheng, 2001; Wong, 2003). Local companies soon copied the Hong Kong company practices. This form of transfer continued into the late 1990s, by which time many companies in China had developed their own capabilities and the ability to absorb or copy foreign technology.

Since the mid-1990s, the role of Hong Kong in technology and management transfer to China has changed. In technology, Hong Kong companies have become intermediaries, sourcing technology globally and introducing it into China. The role in management has changed as well. Better education and greater experience in the Mainland has improved local management capabilities, leading to a situation in Hong Kong-invested enterprises in which Hong Kong people fill senior management, marketing, finance, and international roles and Mainland managers fill operational roles. The same pattern can also be seen in many major multinational firms, with Hong Kong people often in senior and international roles for China activities. It should also be noted that many of the Mainland managers developed by Hong Kong firms subsequently became entrepreneurs that have helped develop the private economy in China (author's interviews).

Hong Kong's contribution

The contribution of Hong Kong and Hong Kong companies to the development of the economy of the Chinese Mainland is difficult to overestimate. According to Chinese statistics, Hong Kong has been the dominant source of foreign direct investment into China. Even if some of the capital claimed to have come from Hong Kong originated elsewhere, this still shows Hong Kong's role of linking the Chinese Mainland to the rest of the world. In industry after industry and in policy area after policy area Hong Kong companies or Hong Kong models were extremely influential in China's development.

One simple example of the value of Hong Kong to China's development involves the comparison of two pairs of cities in the Pearl River Delta region, Shenzhen and Dongguan on the one hand, and Zhongshan and Zhuhai on the other. Shenzhen, which is just north of Hong Kong on the east side of the Pearl River Delta was home of one of China's first Special Economic Zones in 1980. Zhuhai, which is just north of Macau on the west side of the Pearl River Delta was also home of one of the first SEZs. In 1980, the combined GDPs of Shenzhen and Dongguan, the municipality just north of Shenzhen (USD 650 million), was significantly less than the combined GDPs of Zhuhai and Zhongshan, the municipality just north of Zhuhai (USD 760 million). By 1990, the combined GDP of Shenzhen and Dongguan was USD 4.2 billion, compared to USD 1.8 billion of Zhuhai and Zhongshan. By 2002, the numbers were USD 35.4 billion (SZ + DG) and USD 9.9 billion (ZH + ZH); by 2008 USD 165.4 billion and USD 34.3 billion; and by 2013, the GDP of Shenzhen + Dongguan was USD 322.6 billion while that of Zhuhai + Zhongshan was USD 69.4 billion, a difference of over USD 250 billion.

The main reason for the GDP difference was the export performance of the Shenzhen + Dongguan combination, which in turn was due mostly to the difference in foreign investment between the two city pairs, which in turn was due largely to the fact that the vast majority of foreign investment into the Pearl River Delta went into locations that were a quick car ride from Hong Kong. It turns out that the Hong Kong company owners and managers, many managers of multinational companies with a Hong Kong base, service providers from Hong Kong, and international buyers who fly into Hong Kong and want to see the factories in which the goods they purchase are produced take the car, not the ferry, and therefore prefer the eastern part of the delta to the western side. Thus in a very real way the present and past advantages of easier land access to Hong Kong resulted in a USD 253.2 billion difference in GDP between two cities with easy land access to Hong Kong versus two cities less than two hours from Hong Kong by ferry.[8]

What is clear is that Hong Kong companies have been pioneers in many aspects of China's development and particularly its interaction with the rest of the world. This has been true in the manufacturing, trading, transportation, infrastructure, real estate, hospitality, and service sectors. While the Hong Kong influence is far less today than it was in the early days of China's opening, recent events show that Hong Kong is still a pioneer when it comes to China's opening.

P&G

Procter & Gamble (P&G) is one of the world's great consumer goods companies. P&G began exploring the potential of China's market shortly after China announced its economic opening. However, in the early 1980s, foreign companies still could not sell into China. P&G began market studies in Beijing and Shanghai in 1985. It began to advertise in China in the same year to build up recognition for the company, even though it was not allowed to sell any products in China until three years later (Dyer et al., 2004, p. 387). P&G formally entered China in a joint venture with the Hong Kong-based company Hutchison Whampoa in 1988. P&G increased its initial 69 percent stake in the venture to 80 percent in 1997 and 100 percent in 2004.

P&G introduced its first product in China, Head & Shoulders shampoo, in 1988. It was introduced in a variety of product sizes, down to single-use sachets costing RMB 0.5 to allow poorer Chinese to buy packaged shampoo for special occasions.[9] P&G later introduced Oil of Ulan (elsewhere Oil of Olay) skin care products (1989), Rejoice shampoo (1989), Pantene shampoo (1991), Safeguard soap (1991), Crest toothpaste (1997), and Pampers disposable diapers (1997). By 2015, P&G had also introduced the Clairol, Vidal Sassoon, Zest, Whisper, Ariel, Tide, SK2, Sebastian, Braun, Gillette, Oceana, and Duracell brands into China (P&G, 2015a). According to retail consultants Kantar Media, P&G sold at least one product to 98 percent of Chinese households in 2009, while Unilever reached 85 percent of households (Kantar, 2010).

P&G opened its first Chinese facilities in Guangzhou and Shanghai. By 2005, it had factories and subsidiaries in Guangzhou, Shanghai, Beijing, Chengdu (the capital of Sichuan in Western China), and Tianjin. By 2015, P&G had operations in Guangzhou, Beijing, Shanghai, Chengdu, Tianjin, Dongguan, and Nanping as well as its China headquarters in Guangzhou and a technical centre in Beijing. The Tianjin plant was the company's largest in the world, while the Guangzhou distribution centre was the company's second largest globally.

Creating product categories in China

P&G has introduced product categories into China that have improved the offerings to local consumers. In parts of China, for example, shampoo had not been a packaged product. People either used normal soap or were supplied from bulk containers at local stores. P&G was among the first to introduce shampoo as a separately packaged product in China, and the first to introduce anti-dandruff formulated shampoos and shampoos with conditioners added. While there were Chinese toothpaste factories dating to the early 20th century, P&G was among the first to introduce silica-based and special cavity-fighting toothpastes into China along with modern mechanized production techniques. P&G also advertised heavily to bring modern dental hygiene to parts of China where daily tooth brushing was not the norm (Young, 2006).

Disposable diapers did not exist as a product category in China before P&G introduced Pampers in China in 1997 (Grant, 2005). By 2011, disposable diapers had achieved a 39 percent market share, with P&G the market leader (Lockett, 2014). By 2014 sales of disposable diapers in China were estimated to exceed those in the United States (Neff, 2015). P&G also introduced the first whitening skin care products to China under the Olay brand in the early 1990s. The introduction was based on perceived needs in the China market, as Olay had not previously included whitening products. By 2014 AC Nielson data indicated that Olay ranked first in whitening/sunscreen products sold through retail channels in China, accounting for 20.1 percent of the market (Cosmetic Observer, 2015).

Leveraging consumer research in China

In 2000, P&G embarked on a program to dramatically expand its position in developing markets (Penhirin, 2004). China became a major focal point for this strategy. P&G began to study the Chinese customer in detail and to develop products specifically for the needs and price points affordable for these customers. Thousands of P&G personnel were sent to live with and observe consumers or potential consumers around China, and special product-testing programs were initiated. P&G discovered that in some parts of China shampoos were used with only a few cups of water because of water shortages, that soaps were often lathered and wiped off due to privacy concerns in homes without bathrooms, that salt was considered good for tooth cleaning, that tea was considered a remedy for bad breadth, that hand washing of clothes required different detergents than machine washing, and so on. Several lines of Tide detergent were developed to suit differences in water and water quality around China. The Crest 7 Effect toothpaste was developed based on the preference for multi-functional toothpaste among Chinese consumers (Finance Ifeng, 2012).

China's rapid development also created income disparities and different price segments in consumer markets. By the mid-2000s, P&G estimated that of its China sales, 15 percent of its unit volume and 30 percent of value were in premium segments, 30 percent of volume and 40 percent of value were in middle segments, and 55 percent of volume and 30 percent of value were in low-end segments. In addition, an individual or a single household might purchase premium skin care products, mid-tier toothpastes, and low-end detergents. Thus P&G had to figure out how to serve the same customer in different segments for different products (Penhirin, 2004).

Addressing multi-tiered markets in China required a different type of product development. P&G began developing products for particular price points, such as a disposable diaper that would cost USD 0.10. According to one P&G executive, 'We changed our standard of innovation so we can serve more of the world's consumers. So it's a better brand experience for the target consumer and a lower product cost structure than the competition can deliver' (Grant, 2005). The research carried out in China has been used to inform P&G activities worldwide. In April 2015, P&G hosted an event in Beijing that displayed innovative products developed for China in just the past year, including a Bluetooth intelligent tooth brush (the first of its kind globally) and ten other cutting-edge products (Xinhuanet, 2015).

Building supply chains and distribution capabilities in China

P&G has invested heavily to build supply and distribution capabilities in China. While P&G China imported equipment and inputs in its early days in the country, the company worked extensively with local and foreign suppliers in China to develop the quality and consistency of inputs that were required for world-class operations (Young, 2006). To reduce the cost of equipment, it developed a network of low-cost component suppliers in Asia and Latin America, plus an assembly facility in Shanghai. The system allowed P&G to reduce the cost of production lines by up to 30 percent and has been so successful that P&G began exporting equipment back to the United States and Europe from China, thus leveraging China not only as a market and a production location for end products, but as a supplier of sophisticated production equipment (Grant, 2005). In the process, P&G has helped to internationalize its Chinese suppliers of inputs and equipment.

P&G has been a leader in building distribution and retail capabilities in China. When P&G entered China, there was limited national distribution for consumer goods. Most retail purchases were made in small local shops that were supplied by state-owned distributors. Most brands were local, logistics expertise was limited and distribution was often on a transaction basis rather than through relationships. By 2010, P&G had nearly 150 distribution centres of its own in China. The company's Guangzhou Center, opened in 2010, is P&G's largest in Asia and second largest worldwide. P&G has equipped its China distribution centres with the latest in mobile technologies to ensure smooth operation. In 2012, P&G invested RMB 250 million (USD 40 million) in Kunming, Yunnan Province, to construct a distribution centre covering a land area of 16 acres (Yunnan, 2012). In 2014, P&G set up a 9,000 square meter warehouse and a 1,300 square metre secondary packaging facility in Shenzhen for cross-border supply to the Hong Kong market (Dyer et al., 2004, p. 391).

P&G also helped develop a wide range of third-party distributors around China, teaching them the techniques of modern distribution and inventory management (Dyer et al., 2004, p. 391). P&G even set up shadow management structures for major distributors, supervising daily activities and training them in distribution management.

The approach helped create what became some of China's most effective consumer goods distributors (Hexter and Woetzel, 2007, p. 140). P&G also helped develop retail networks covering over 500,000 stores in urban and rural areas in China. P&G, for example, trained people in 10,000 Chinese villages in retailing in an arrangement with China's Commerce Ministry. The idea was to bring more consumer goods to China's villages and rural areas to improve local quality of life (Roberts, 2007). In 2009, P&G required its 100 distributors in China to set up branches covering 30,000 counties and towns in China (NetEase Finance, 2010). With the growth of e-commerce in China's consumer market, P&G was also expanding its online distribution. Since 2009, P&G has allowed its distributors to set up online outlets on Taobao (National Business Daily, 2009), and in 2013 P&G launched its online experience centre on Taobao, which was the first of its kind in China (P&G, 2013).

Bringing green standards to China

P&G has brought its most advanced plant designs and concepts to China. Its Tianjin plant is the company's largest in the world. Its Taicang (Jiangsu Province) plant, which opened in 2012, was P&G's first plant globally to be registered under the US Green Building Council's Leadership in Energy and Environmental Design standards. This entailed minimizing water consumption and maximizing water reuse, cutting energy consumption and using renewable sources such as onsite solar cells, and maximizing recycling to generate zero waste for landfills. The plant was the first in a global plan to use only renewable energy, only renewable or recyclable packaging materials, and no landfill space, and to design products to minimize their environmental impact (GreenerBuildings, 2011). The facility achieved the LEED Gold certification for administrative buildings and Silver for manufacturing buildings (P&G, 2015c). The plant uses 100 percent wind energy, saving 5,000 tonnes of CO_2 emission each year (P&G, 2014d). In November 2013, P&G opened a LEED certified plant in Luogang, Guangzhou, that has 100 percent of its production waste recycled (P&G, 2014d).

P&G has repeatedly been praised for its environmental performance in China. It received the 'Green Gold' Platinum Award from Sohu and A.T. Kearney in 2010 (P&G, 2010b). P&G was named as one of the 'China Green Companies Top 100' at the Annual China Green Companies Summit in 2010, where it ranked fourth among foreign companies in China and first in the fast-moving consumer goods category (P&G, 2011a). In December 2012, P&G won the World Green Design Contribution Award from the International Design Federation (P&G, 2012). In July 2014, P&G was recognized as a Green Shipper by the China Green Freight initiatives hosted by China Road Transportation Association (P&G, 2014c). In the same year, P&G was listed among the China Top 100 Green Companies for the fourth time (P&G, 2014a).

P&G has also worked to improve the sustainability of its suppliers in China as part of a world-wide program. By 2011, over 600 suppliers globally joined the plan, including 24 Chinese suppliers from seven industries. In the first year of implementation,

63 percent of the suppliers reduced their energy consumption, 64 percent reduced emission of greenhouse gases, and 62 percent improved the efficiency of water usage. The improvement by suppliers in China was reportedly even greater than the global average (P&G, 2010c). In 2015, P&G initiated the 'Pioneer Plan' to sponsor environmental protection projects for selected student groups at Chinese universities in an attempt to cultivate future leaders in environmental protection in China (P&G, 2015d).

Building marketing capabilities in China

P&G is one of a handful of leading international consumer goods companies credited with bringing modern advertising and brand building to China. According to one academic, 'Modern advertising returned to the People's Republic of China in 1979' (Wang, 2003, p. 247). In fact, corporate advertising had been banned during the Cultural Revolution. P&G started advertising years before it actually sold any products in China. Subsequently, the introduction of new product categories was usually preceded by an extensive advertising campaign. P&G became the largest advertiser in China. As of 2012, according to a Deutsche Bank analyst, 'P&G is so entrenched in China. They made the investments early and their brands have great cachet now' (quoted in Beattie, 2012). P&G reportedly works with numerous leading advertising agencies in China, including Saatchi & Saatchi, Grey Group, Wieden & Kennedy, Leo Burnett, BBDO, and Publicis (Beattie, 2012). Most of the major international ad agencies followed their clients, like P&G, to China.

Advertising Age estimated that P&G spent USD 1.1 billion on advertising in China in 2009 and USD 1.8 billion in 2013 (well above L'Oreal's USD 1 billion and Unilever's USD 842 million) (Wentz, 2009; Madden, 2014). While television received the lion's share of P&G's China advertising budget, P&G has also made extensive use of print and other forms of media in China, including online media such as Tencent Weibo, and created a flagship store on Taobao Mall, China's largest online marketplace. P&G has also used Weibo to promote its Hope Schools projects in China (Sina Finance, 2015).

In October 2015, P&G won five awards at the Effie Awards (Greater China) ceremony with its marketing projects for Olay, Pantene, and Safeguard (P&G, 2015g). In the same month at the ROI Festival in Shanghai, P&G received 17 awards for its creative advertising and marketing projects, covering P&G's marketing activities in social media, Internet, outdoor, public service, and other marketing channels. P&G was also named 'best brand of the year' at the festival (P&G, 2015f). In the 2015 Brand Power Index released by Chnbrand under the direction of the Ministry of Industry and Information Technology of China, several of P&G's brands, such as Safeguard, Olay, Head & Shoulders, Tide, Pampers, and Whisper, were ranked at the top in their categories (P&G, 2015b).

Setting up global research in China

P&G has developed global scale research and development in China. P&G opened a USD 10 million R&D facility in Beijing in 1998. Approximately 80 percent of the 200 scientists employed initially at the centre were from China. The centre is located adjacent to Tsinghua University in Beijing, one of China's leading centres for scientific research. The initial mandate of the centre was to ensure that global products were meeting the needs of Chinese customers, to gain access to China's scientific and technological resources, and to work toward improving products for global markets. The lab developed many formulations tailored for the China market and became a global enter of excellence within P&G for detergents and toothpastes (Walfish, 2001). In 2010, P&G opened a new USD 80 million R&D centre in Beijing, its largest such centre anywhere. The new centre, which employed more than 500 scientists from 16 countries, was expected to become a major centre in P&G's worldwide network of R&D centres, with global responsibilities, and the only centre worldwide that would work on all of P&G's product categories.

P&G also engaged in research cooperation with Chinese institutions. For example, in 2011, P&G signed a strategic cooperation memorandum of understanding with the Chinese Academy of Sciences, to cooperate in research and development in fields including recyclable bio-materials, substitutes for petroleum, surface technology, and consumer psychology (P&G, 2011c). In December 2014, P&G set up a laboratory in Guangzhou for cooperation with Research Institute of Microbiology of Guangdong Province (GIM, 2014).

Developing human resources in China

From its initial entry into China, P&G focused on building up a local employment base and was among the earliest foreign firms to actively recruit at major Chinese universities. It also developed extensive training programs for its China staff. P&G followed a similar pattern in China as in the United States and elsewhere of hiring local people at an entry level and then promoting from within. While foreigners were sent to fill key positions in P&G's early days in China, as time went on locals increasingly occupied senior positions. By 2015, only around 2 percent of P&G China's employees were non-Chinese, and the percentage of Chinese in senior management had increased to 65 percent from 30 percent ten years earlier (Guangzhou Daily, 2015). P&G China had become a net exporter of managerial talent, that is, more Chinese from P&G China were in P&G management in other countries than there were foreigners in management inside of China.

P&G has been known as one of the more desirable employers in China. In 2008, 51Job, a leading human resources company in China, gave P&G its top prize for 'best campus recruiter', second place for 'best new-hand trainer', and a place within the '2008 Top 100 HR Companies in China' (P&G, 2008). In May 2011, P&G was listed among 'the most desirable employers in China' based on a survey by Universum of 46,000 university students. P&G was ranked as the second most desirable employer among students majoring in business, first among students majoring in natural sciences, and seventh among students majoring in engineering (P&G, 2011b). In September 2014, P&G was ranked seventh among 'Ideal Employers in China' in the Universum survey (P&G, 2014b).

Economic impact on China

By 2014, sales of P&G goods in China by retailers (including distribution and retail mark-ups) were estimated at USD 10 billion, some 63.3 percent higher than in 2009 (Coolidge, 2014). P&G's sales to retailers and distributors in Greater China (the vast majority of which would be to the Chinese Mainland) were around USD 6.44 billion.[10] If we assume that 85 percent of these sales were to the Chinese Mainland, the Mainland sales figure would be USD 5.47 billion. This would indicate that P&G's distributors and retailers realized mark-ups on the order of USD 4.53 billion selling P&G goods in Greater China. During a 2010 visit to China, CEO Robert McDonald indicated that P&G had invested USD 1.5 billion in China since 1988 and planned to invest an additional USD 1 billion in China by 2015 (Reingold, 2011).

From this information, we have made rough estimates of the economic impact of P&G on China's output, value added, and employment. In order to do so, we took the estimates of P&G's China's investments and sales, and the downstream sales of distributors and retailers, and applied economic impact multipliers generated from China's input–output tables (China Statistics Press, 2009). This process allows us to estimate the impact of P&G's activities, plus those of its supply and distribution chains, but not any other spillovers into China's economy.

Assuming that one-third of the USD 2.5 billion capital investment went into land and construction, one-third into supporting services, and one-third into machinery and equipment (and further assuming that one-half of the machinery and equipment was imported and therefore had limited China impact), we estimate that the total cumulative impact of P&G's capital investments was USD 7.00 billion in output, USD 2.15 billion in value added (which is essentially the GDP contribution), and 247,863 full time equivalents in job-years (one job for one year). We note that these are cumulative not annual effects. Averaging the cumulative employment impact over 30 years, for example, would give an average impact of over 8,262 jobs per year just in terms of the impact of the physical developments associated with capital investment.

Taking the estimates of P&G's Chinese Mainland sales of USD 5.47 billion and distributor and retail margins on P&G products of USD 4.53 billion in 2014 and applying the same method as above, the total impact of P&G's own revenues in 2014 was on the order of USD 20.25 billion in output, USD 6.53 billion in value added, and over 355,523 in employment. The impact of the revenues of P&G's distributors and retailers was estimated at USD 8.93 billion in output, USD 4.75 billion in value added, and 246,499 in employment. Thus impact from what might be called the 'P&G system' can be estimated to have reached on the order of USD 11.28 billion in value added, and over 612,000 in employment in 2014 alone. We recognize that these are speculative estimates and employ numerous assumptions and that the multiplier method used may tend to overstate economic impacts. However, the estimates do suggest the magnitude of the impact a major foreign company can have on China.

Corporate social responsibility in China

P&G pays close attention to corporate social responsibility in China. P&G has worked with the central and local governments in areas such as education, public health, and rural development, and participated in other programs and projects of importance to China's leaders. In 2010, P&G was named a member of China-based Hurun Institute's 'Corporate Responsibility Top 50' for the fourth consecutive year and ranked ninth in terms of the 'Most Respected CSR Projects' among foreign companies. P&G was one of two consumer packaged goods companies in the top 50 (P&G, 2010a). In the same year, *Southern Weekend* magazine named P&G one of the 'Top 500 Company Contributors in China'. P&G was ranked first in the fast-moving consumer goods sector for the fourth consecutive year, eighth overall, and second in 'Corporate Philanthropy'. P&G was honoured for its contribution to society, including work on education, health, and sustainability.

By June 2013, P&G had built 200 Hope Schools in 28 provinces in China, more than any other foreign company, and representing donations of RMB 76 million (USD 12 million). Over 200,000 children were studying in or had graduated from P&G Hope Schools (P&G, 2015e). P&G initiated a school health program in 1997 and had donated RMB 300 million to the program by 2007. P&G donated a portion of its sales in China to charitable programs and expected to spend RMB 200 million between 2008 and 2012 in support of health, dental, sanitation, and adolescent health matters. By 2010, P&G estimated that more than 160 million students in over 600 cities in 31 provinces in China had been helped by the school health program. By 2010, P&G was also collaborating with Chinese officials on the '10,000 Villages Project', which was 'designed to create distribution networks for household products in rural areas in China' (P&G, 2010e). P&G donated over RMB 8 million (USD 1.2 million) in relief funds after the 2013 earthquake in Sichuan Province. Within two weeks after the earthquake, P&G had set up a Hope School in Longmen County with 20 classrooms (P&G, 2014d).

P&G also participated in high-profile events and forums. China's leaders viewed the 2010 Shanghai World Expo as an important world stage for the country. P&G signed on to be an Official Premier Sponsor of the USA Pavilion, exclusive in the

Wellness, Beauty, and Household Care categories. According to Chris Hassall, P&G Global External Relations Officer:

> This sponsorship represents a perfect fit with our corporate purpose of touching and improving more consumer lives in more parts, in more parts of the world, more completely. We accomplish this through our quality products and our involvement in the social responsibility causes in the communities where we work and live. . . . And with our partnership with the USA Pavilion, we are gratified by the thought that we are making a humble contribution to bringing Chinese and American people even a little closer.
>
> (P&G, 2009)

Making an overall contribution to China

P&G's contribution to China has gone well beyond that generated by its capital investments and sales. It has developed new product categories for the Chinese consumer, advanced supply and distribution networks that did not exist before in the country, as well as world-class research and development in China, advertising and marketing expertise new to China, and Chinese managers that it sends to P&G's international operations. P&G has contributed substantially to public health, education, and rural development.

Chinese officials have voiced praise for P&G's contribution to China on numerous occasions. In meetings with P&G senior officials in 2014, the Vice Secretary General of the Shanghai Municipal Government noted P&G's contribution to the local economy and expressed the Shanghai Government's willingness to support P&G in its operation and talent policies (Pudong Times, 2014). The Party Secretary of the Guangzhou Municipal Government, Vice Governor of Fujian Province, and Party Secretary of the Suzhou Municipal Government have also expressed their recognition of P&G's contribution to local economies.

Perhaps the appreciation was best expressed by Vice Minster Wang Chao of the Ministry of Commerce at the opening of P&G's R&D centre in Beijing in August 2010 when he stated:

> P&G is an excellent example of Sino-US economic cooperation. I am very optimistic about P&G's future in China. Foreign companies are an important part of China's national economy. Advanced technology, management expertise and philosophy have had a profound impact on every aspect of China's economic and social life. They have positively facilitated the development of China's high tech, labor intensive and service industries, furthering China's economic development and China's integration into globalization. China will adopt a more open approach in conducting economic cooperation internationally and create a better environment for companies investing in China.
>
> (P&G, 2010d)

Maersk

Maersk, the shipping and logistics conglomerate, is represented in more than 130 countries. In 2014 Maersk generated USD 47.6 billion in revenue and employment of 89,200. Maersk businesses include Maersk Line (shipping), APM Terminals (container terminals and port operations), Maersk Oil, Maersk Drilling and Services, DAMCO (logistics), and other shipping and services businesses.

The first Maersk ship to call on a Chinese port arrived in Shanghai in 1924. By 2014, Maersk had approximately 26,000 employees in China and registered USD 11 billion in China-related revenues. The Group estimates that its direct investment and procurement of ships and other items in China exceeded USD 15 billion from 1996 to 2014 (Maersk, 2014c). Procurement in China was USD 2.24 billion in 2013 alone and USD 2.6 billion in 2014 (Maersk, 2015a). As of 2014, its shipping arm, Maersk China Limited, had branches in 28 Chinese cities and its logistics arm had branches in 17 cities. Maersk has been a significant player in port operations in China, with its activities in 2015 in Qingdao, Dalian, Guangzhou, Shanghai, and Tianjin, as well as Hong Kong.

The impact of Maersk on China, however, has gone well beyond its employment and investment amounts. It has been an earlier investor in Chinese ports, a major customer providing substantial technology transfer to Chinese shipyards, a force for improving logistics in China, and a major enabler of China's development into a leading trading nation.

Connecting China to the world

Maersk Line made its first call on a Chinese port in 1924 and opened its first office in the Chinese Mainland in 1984. From 2000 to 2012, the company increased its China port calls by 310 percent and is container movements by 270 percent. In 2012, Maersk loaded and discharged 13.3 percent of all containerized goods in China, was responsible for 16.2 percent of all calls to Chinese ports, and transported 14.5 percent of all containerized goods between China and its main trading partners (Maersk, 2014b, p. 21).

Maersk has had a significant impact in its ability to connect China to the rest of the world. According to a report commissioned by Maersk, better container ship connectivity has contributed significantly to China's growth in trade. Better connectivity lowers trade costs, which in turn increases trade, and improves economic growth. According to the report:

> The direct impact of maritime transport costs accrues from lower trade costs and better access to markets. The results show that a 10 percent improvement in maritime container transport has been associated with a 3 percent decrease in Chinese trade costs, a 6 percent increase in Chinese manufactured imports and a 9 percent increase in Chinese manufactured exports.

Since 2004, this means that improvements in liner shipping connectivity have been associated with a 30 percent increase in Chinese manufactured imports and a 40 percent increase in exports. This constitutes approximately a fourth of accumulated year-on-year growth over the period. Converted to trade value, this year-on-year growth has resulted in additional imports and exports worth USD 686 billion corresponding to 35 percent of total trade growth since 2004. . . .

Given its market share, the results show that a 10 percent improvement in Maersk Line's services and capacity alone has been associated with a 0.8 percent increase in Chinese imports and a 1.1 percent increase in Chinese exports.

(Maersk, 2014b, p. 5)

From 2004 to 2012, Maersk increased its port calls in China by 107 percent and its container movements by 115 percent. From these figures and the results presented in the cited report, we have estimated that the impact of the increase in Maersk China-related capacity from 2004 to 2012 resulted in a total increase of China's exports by between USD 120 billion and USD 135 billion per year.[11] In addition, if we take the Maersk share of China's seaborne exports in 2012 as 14.5 percent, and the share of China's export value carried by sea as 69.5 percent (China Customs, 2012), then Maersk carried approximately USD 206 billion in China's exports in 2012.[12] Clearly, Maersk's shipping operations have been instrumental in helping Chinese companies and facilities increase their exports. While Maersk was the largest foreign shipping company servicing China's trade, it was not the only one. According to a State Council report in 2014, Chinese shipping companies carried only around 25 percent of the country's seaborne trade, leaving 75 percent in the hands of foreign companies (Nicholson, 2014).

In addition, Maersk Group companies have helped Chinese companies globalize their production systems and thereby expand their international reach. Maersk's Damco logistics company, for example, has supported the internationalization of numerous Chinese companies. Damco has helped pioneer the use of rail links from China to Europe for many Chinese companies, saving time and cost in the process, while offering a full portfolio of land, sea, and air linkages (Shao, 2014). Damco has provided logistics solutions to Shandong Kerui Holding Group that has allowed the oilfield products and services company to serve clients in 40 countries (Damco, 2014). Damco has also provided auto maker Geely and home appliance maker Haier with the logistics solutions necessary to export parts and knocked-down kits to assembly plants elsewhere, allowing the Chinese companies to expand their manufacturing footprints and international reach (Yang, 2015; Maersk, 2014c). Damco has also supported Chinese companies undertaking hydroelectric projects, oil and gas exploration and production, infrastructure construction, and telecommunications projects (Guan, 2015) by providing the global logistics capabilities that Chinese companies are not yet able to provide, thus greatly facilitating the internationalization of Chinese companies in these areas.

Working with Chinese suppliers

Maersk has worked extensively with Chinese shipyards, placing orders as early as 1996, at a time when China accounted for around 4 percent of global ship deliveries. By 2014, China accounted for roughly 40 percent of global ship output. Between 1996 and 2014, Maersk ordered more than 117 ships of various kinds from Chinese shipyards with a cumulative value in excess of USD 3.5 billion. Its total procurement and direct investment in China reached USD 15 billion (Maersk, 2014b, p. 5). In total, by 2015, Maersk had ordered 118 ships from China (Maersk, 2015a).

Maersk worked extensively with Chinese shipyards, especially the Guangzhou Shipyard, bringing engineers to China for months or even years to transfer expertise and knowledge related to producing world-class ships. Maersk had a particularly strong role in the development of product and chemical tankers, accounting for nearly half of the orders of Chinese shipyards (by weight) from 1998 to 2001. Maersk worked with Chinese shipyards to develop product and chemical tankers that could be operated by only 14 people, compared to the previous 30 to 40 people. In the process, Maersk helped establish Chinese shipyards as leaders in their field. Chinese shipyards used the experience developed while working with Maersk to build capabilities to allow them to sell to customers world-wide. Maersk orders went from nearly half the orders of Chinese shipyards in product and chemical tankers in 1998 to 2001 to under 3 percent between 2008 and 2013 (Maersk, 2014b, p. 5). By that time, Maersk represented only a small portion of China's ship deliveries. Maersk's container operations have also influenced suppliers. Maersk has been the largest customer for ZPMC, the crane manufacturer, and has worked with ZPMC to improve designs and capabilities too, but not to the same extent as with the shipyards.

Maersk has an extensive supplier compliance program to help improve the social and environmental performance of its supply chain. Its procurement program incorporates international anti-corruption, social, and environmental standards into Maersk's own procurement process as well as the procurement processes of its suppliers. In 2014, Maersk audited suppliers in China, Cameroon, Korea, Singapore, and Turkey, and found health and safety, working hours and compensation, and environmental performance as areas for improvement. Maersk's Responsible Procurement Team also travelled to the Ivory Coast, Myanmar, Angola, Cameroon, and China to hold supplier development workshops that emphasized Maersk procurement standards in an effort to raise the social and environmental performance of the suppliers (Maersk, 2014d). Damco and other Maersk Group companies have also brought their Responsible Procurement practices to China and have worked with suppliers to improve standards.

Improving efficiency in ports and logistics in China

Maersk has been working to improve port and logistics efficiency in China for decades. It was one of the initial investors in Yantian Port (in Shenzhen) in partnership with Hong Kong-based Hutchison Whampoa in 1994 (this interest was sold off in 2010).

Maersk was also an investor in Phase 4 of the Waigaoqiao Container Port and in Phase 2 of the Yangshan Port, both in Shanghai. By 2014, it had investments in ports in Dalian, Guangzhou, Tianjin, Xiamen, Qingdao, and Shanghai, a set that included four of the ten most efficient ports in the world (in terms of container movements per hour) in Qingdao, Dalian, Shanghai, and Tianjin (JOC Group, 2013). Maersk had sold out of a fifth member of the top ten (Yantian), in 2010.

Maersk has worked extensively with Chinese ports to improve operational efficiency. The company has arranged and facilitated study trips and fact-finding visits for representatives from Chinese ports, terminals, and government agencies to leading facilities around the world. Maersk has also worked with terminal operators to reduce the process time for vessel calls in Chinese ports, using techniques that the terminal operators then use with other customers. Maersk's Terminal Partnering Project is a cooperative project between Maersk Line terminal operators to reduce port stays to improve efficiency and reduce emissions. This project identified potential port stay reductions of 27 percent to 40 percent in Chinese ports, and had realized 12 to 18 percent of the gains by 2014. Should a 30 percent reduction be achieved, this could reduce total port hours for Maersk Line ships in these ports by 11,436 hours per year (Maersk, 2014b, p. 41). Should the terminals use a similar planning process for the vessels of other lines, the benefits could be a factor of 10 or 11 greater. Economists have estimated that a 10 percent increase in efficiency in container ports can increase trade by on the order of 3.2 percent, indicating substantial benefits from reducing port berthing time.

China has long faced challenges in its logistics sector. Logistics costs have been estimated at on the order of 18 percent of GDP in China in 2012 compared to 9 percent in North America and Europe. Logistics costs have been estimated at 30 to 40 percent of production costs in China (Maersk, 2014a). Economists commissioned by Maersk estimated that a 6 percent improvement in logistics in China from 2007 to 2012 resulted in a 19 percent decrease in trade costs, which in turn led to a 27 percent increase in China's manufactured exports and a gain of USD 213 billion in trade value (exports plus imports) (Maersk, 2014b, pp. 43–4).

Maersk's Damco logistics arm has been working to improve the efficiency of the supply chains of its customers in China using a combination of process flow optimization, network optimization, and inventory optimization. Process flow optimization uses consolidation and packaging to streamline flows. Network optimization uses the best transport and warehousing solutions to improve efficiency. Logistics cost reductions of 10 to 20 percent have been achieved in a number of projects through these means. If we take Damco's estimated handling share of China's exports to the Americas and to Europe, estimates of export margins, estimates of logistics costs for exports from China, and an estimated savings of 15 percent of the logistics costs, we estimate that Damco could well have saved Chinese exporters over USD 1.3 billion in logistics costs in 2014.[13]

Improving environmental performance in China

Environmental sustainability has become a key imperative for the Chinese Government and for foreign companies operating in China as well. From 2007 to 2014, Maersk Line reduced its CO_2 output by 34 percent per container and planned to reach 40 percent by 2020. Maersk was also the first shipping line to adopt the 'Fair Winds Charter', a voluntary arrangement to adopt low sulphur fuels that had resulted in an 80 percent reduction in Maersk's sulphur emissions. Since Maersk is the leading shipping line for the international shipping of goods from China and China is Maersk's largest market, the impact of these reductions has been felt most in China.

Maersk Line's Terminal Partnering Project also has an environmental benefit. An hour of berthing at a Chinese port results in fuel consumption and pollution emission. Should a 30 percent reduction be achieved for Maersk Line calls at Xiamen, Yantian, Shanghai, and Hong Kong, Maersk projects that this could save over 10,000 tonnes of fuel and 552 tonnes of SO_2 emissions per year across these four ports just for the port calls of Maersk ships. Should the terminals use a similar planning process for other vessels, as they have every incentive to do, the total reduction could be over 110,000 tonnes of fuel and 6,450 tonnes of SO_2 per year across these four ports (Maersk, 2014b, p. 41).

Maersk has also provided technical advice and has accepted below market prices for obsolete ships in China to ensure that they are disposed of in an environmentally sound way (Galley, 2014, p. 206). Maersk even set up an internal group to manage ship disposal and has undertaken disposals for other ship owners. Maersk set the standard for working with Chinese yards to ensure that ship disposal minimized the impact on local workers and the local environment. China has gone on to set up some of the most advanced ship-breaking facilities in the world. In fact, in a February 2016 statement, Maersk indicated that only a limited number of yards in China and Turkey could recycle ships responsibly (MarEx, 2016). While committed to using designated shipyards in China that could recycle ships responsibly, Maersk was criticized in 2016 for disposing of some ships in other countries with lower standards. In return, Maersk indicated that it was committed to helping yards in other countries raise standards (Zawadzki and Bartunek, 2016).

Maersk's Damco logistics arm has been working to cut CO_2 emissions through the supply chain within China and has carried out projects that show that on the order of 11 percent of CO_2 can be taken out of many supply chains and up to 27 percent in some cases. It has introduced a five-step process for mapping existing supply chains, calculating carbon emissions, reporting carbon hotspots, evaluating the potential to reduce cost and emissions, and implementing solutions (Maersk, 2014b, pp. 43–4). Damco has also performed audits of its own activities for energy efficiency and reduced emissions.

Developing human resources in China

Maersk has been committed to building its local staff in China. As of 2015, the vast majority of Maersk's 26,000 employees in China, including most management staff, were Chinese. Maersk has also invested heavily in training in China, not just for operational positions, and has brought its naval, sales, and world-leading[14] CARE PRO customer service training systems to China, as well as state-of-the-art safety training, in each case helping to raise the standards of the transport and logistics sectors in China. Damco also reported extensive training activities, for example, 800 employees in China had been trained on its advanced Kewill global forwarding platform by the first quarter of 2014. Damco has also brought its International Graduate, IMPACT, and Global Talent training programs to China to enhance workforce capabilities (Damco, 2013, pp. 19, 27).

Maersk has also invested in developing local management capabilities. This has involved formal training as well as ongoing mentoring and the ability to switch jobs within the company on occasion (Maersk, 2015b). One initiative created a program to train roughly 400 middle-level managers a year for Maersk's China operations. This program included classroom instruction, hands-on training, and the involvement of the participants' supervisors, and was tailored to the particular challenges of developing leadership capabilities in China (Neal, 2007). Another initiative sought to develop director-level leaders and then put them through a four-year program to build management capabilities. The program followed up with promotions for high achievers during the program. At the end of four years, the program participant group had registered zero turnover (Huang, 2013). The various programs have helped Maersk bring local employees into important management roles. As of November 2015, for example, the new head of Maersk's North China operations was someone who started as a graduate trainee in 1993 and had gradually worked his way up the organization (IS Maritime 360, 2015). Similarly, the head of Maersk's East and Central China operations named in May 2015 had started with the company as a sales representative in 1994 (Lakshmi, 2015).

Maersk Group companies have taken steps to improve worker retention in China as well. Damco instituted a pioneering program of flexible hours and resource sharing, including assembling a pool of nannies, to help mothers stay in the workforce. The program resulted in a sharp increase in women returning to work after having a child, thus increasing family incomes and reducing the costs associated with turnover. Introduced first in Shenzhen, the 'Baby Care Project' has since been spread to other offices in China (Maersk, 2013).

The human resource situation for Maersk in China, however, has remained a challenge as it has for many large companies. Strikes and disturbances at Maersk's Dongguan container facility in 2008 led to a temporary shutdown, meetings with worker representatives, NGO complaints, an independent third-party audit of working conditions, and the engagement of an employee rights consultancy. Accusations of illegal firings, nepotism among mid-level staff, and poor working conditions precipitated several changes in employment, promotion, and safety policies (Maersk, 2009, pp. 8, 68). For the company as a whole, lay-offs in China during the economic downturn in 2008 and 2009 hurt Maersk's reputation as an employer, which in turn caused the company to review its human resource strategy for China and to introduce changes in compensation structures, benefits, and employee communications to better attract and retain critical personnel (Knowledge@Wharton, 2010).

Economic impact of procurement and investment

We can get a rough estimate of the economic impact on China of Maersk's direct investment and procurement using multipliers derived from China's input–output tables, and assumptions about the distribution of expenditures. If we assume that roughly half of the USD 15 billion in 'direct investment and procurement' of Maersk in China was in procurement and half in direct investment, and if we further assume that one-third of the direct investment was spent on land and construction, one-third on supporting services, and one-third on equipment (with half of the equipment imported); and if we assume that the bulk of the procurement was for ships and marine equipment and inputs of one type or another, we can come up with an estimate of the impact of this spending on China's economy.

When we make the assumptions indicated, we estimate that the total cumulative impact of the direct investment (including the direct, indirect, and induced impacts) was on the order of USD 21.5 billion in output, USD 6.7 billion in value added, and over 991,000 in full-time equivalents in job-years (one job for one year, or an average of nearly 50,000 jobs each year over the period). The impact of the procurement is estimated at USD 25.8 billion in output, 7.9 billion in value added, and 1.125 million in full-time equivalents in job-years (or an average of over 56,000 jobs each year over the period).[15]

Corporate social responsibility in China

Since its establishment in mainland China in 1994, Maersk China has been actively contributing to and participating in local communities where it operates. Maersk and its subsidiaries reportedly engage in over 100 local CSR activities each year. These include activities focused on rural education, community development, and the environment (Maersk, 2014c). Maersk and its subsidiaries have funded construction for more than 20 Hope Schools, supplied poor children in Sichuan with winter clothing, contributed to the responses to natural disasters (earthquakes and floods for example) with financial contributions and blood drives, and provided other charitable contributions around the country (Damco, 2013). Maersk in fact won a special award from the Sichuan Government for its response to the May 2008 earthquake in that province, in particular its use of containers to replace a destroyed school (Shipping Online CN, 2009).

Maersk has also set up education programs for the shipping and logistics sectors around China. For many years, it has also hosted senior Chinese business leaders participating in the Chinese Executive Leadership Program in Copenhagen and London. The Program is organized by the National Development and Reform Commission for top government and state-owned enterprise leaders to study at the Judge Cambridge

Business School at Cambridge. Maersk has added programs in Copenhagen and London focusing on the 'Nordic model' of economic development and on the creation and management of successful conglomerates (private communication).

Maersk has also participated in several advisory bodies in China, including the International Advisory Councils in Guangdong Province and in Chongqing. Maersk is an active member of the EU and Danish Chambers of Commerce in China, and has participated in numerous Chamber of Commerce and industry forums designed to help China improve its overall economy as well as its shipping sector. The company also has regular dialogues with Chinese Customs and has encouraged standardization, simplification, and automation of Customs processes, using its experience in Europe and the United States as models.

Making an overall contribution to China

Maersk's overall contribution to China has been recognized many times. The company took awards in the 'Best 10 Comprehensive Service Carrier', 'Best 3 Container Lines in Asia-Europe Trade', and 'Best 3 Container Lines in the Asia-South America Trade' categories at the tenth China Freight Industry Awards ceremony in June 2013 (World Maritime News, 2013). Maersk Line was also named 'Shipping Line of the Year' at the Supply Chain Asia Logistics Awards 2011 held in Shanghai (World Maritime News, 2011). Damco had won several contracts to support the international logistical needs of internationalizing Chinese companies, thus contributing to China's 'Go Global' goal. APM Terminals has also won numerous awards, including five at the Chinese Ports Association Awards in 2009, including 'Best Contributor to the Development of China's Terminal Industry' (APM Terminals, 2009). Maersk has also received praise from a range of Chinese officials. In March 2015, Shanghai Party Secretary Han Zheng thanked the Maersk Group for the contribution that it has made to Shanghai's goal of becoming an international shipping centre (Shanghai Daily, 2015).

The overall contribution that Maersk has made to China, however, is largely behind the scenes, at least to most people. In providing cost-effective connectivity, Maersk has facilitated China's emergence as the world's leading trading nation. As an early customer and technology partner, it has contributed to China's emergence as the world's leading shipbuilding nation. As a world-leading shipping company, it has worked extensively to improve port operations in China, as well as streamline customs activities. As a provider of logistics services, it has helped reduce one of the major inefficiencies in China's economy. Thus once again, the company's contribution to China has gone well beyond its own investments, employment, and purchases.

Samsung

Samsung Electronics, the flagship subsidiary of the Samsung Group, is a world leader in consumer electronics, IT and mobile communications, and device solutions. Samsung

Electronics was one of the first of the major Korean companies to enter China in the early 1990s. Its initial China strategy was to use low-cost labour to produce low-to-medium priced products mostly for export. In the second half of the 1990s, Samsung as a company shifted to higher value-added and more technologically advanced products, and began to use China as a launching ground for this new strategy. By the early 2000s, Samsung recognized that China was central to its future, and began to rebuild its global strategy around Korea and China (Choi, 2003). In 2014, Samsung Electronics had revenues of 206 trillion Korean Won (USD 201 billion), with China accounting for 33 billion Korean Won (USD 32 billion), or 16 percent of worldwide sales (Samsung, 2015a). China was the location of two of Samsung's 15 Regional Headquarters, 13 out of its 38 Global Production bases, two out of its 54 Global Sales Bases, seven out of its 36 R&D Centers, and one out of its six Global Design Centers (Samsung, 2015d). Samsung's subsidiaries were all over China with seven in Jiangsu, six in Tianjin, three in Shanghai, three in Beijing, two in Shaanxi, one in Shandong, and one in Hainan.

Committing to China

Samsung committed to development in China early on. One sign of this commitment is the sheer value of Samsung's China investments. In 1994, Samsung established an integrated production complex in Tianjin with an investment of nearly USD 1 billion, bringing together several Samsung units into one complex for electronics and electronic parts. Following on from the Tianjin complex, Samsung developed another integrated production complex in Suzhou for home appliances (Lee, 2006). In 2014, Samsung Electronics completed a USD 3 billion liquid crystal display facility in Suzhou. At the time, it was the largest ever single foreign investment in China by a Korean company. It also announced a joint effort with Xi'an Hi-Tech Group to build a production base for electronic car batteries, to be the biggest in China, with a combined investment of USD 600 million and projected revenues in excess of USD 1 billion by 2020.

In 2015, Samsung Electronics opened the USD 2.3 billion first phase of a NAND flash memory chip fabrication complex in Xi'an. With a total planned investment across multiple phases of USD 7 billion, this would be the single largest investment by Samsung in China, and Samsung claimed it would be the single largest foreign direct investment in China to date (Samsung, 2012a). The complex, Samsung's first semiconductor production complex in China, is expected to generate annual sales of USD 5 billion. With the official opening of the project, Samsung had created a global semiconductor production system with three major production bases, one each in South Korea (systems and storage semiconductors), China (storage semiconductors), and the United States (systems semiconductors).

The Samsung Group opened its first China headquarters in 1995 (Samsung, 2015c). This headquarters supervised 21 manufacturing companies, including Samsung Electronics, Samsung SDI, and Samsung Corning. The Group created a second China headquarters in the early 2000s to control the recruitment and deployment of personnel as well as sales channels in China. It has also been responsible for establishing Samsung's long-term vision for the China market, conducting market surveys covering all business fields, and drawing up marketing strategies. The goal was to consolidate strategic planning to maximize the group's synergies. The China head was promoted from President to Vice Chairman of Samsung globally (Choi, 2003). By 2011, 23 of the Samsung Group's 30 companies had invested in China and Samsung was estimated to have become the largest foreign investor in China, with 155 subsidiaries and a total investment of USD 12.7 billion (Chen et al., 2015).

Ho-moon Kang, Vice Chairman and head of Samsung China in 2011 stated that 'Our goal is creating a whole new Samsung for China. In China, where opportunities and risks co-exist, the key to success is "strategic imagination" that helps you look beyond what is happening right now around us and envisage what will happen' (Samsung, 2011). Analysts described this approach to the Samsung China Headquarters as creating an independent and localized 'Second Samsung' in China that would enjoy the respect of the Chinese society (Lee, 2006). In essence, Samsung had done what virtually no other foreign company had done, elevated the China operations and headquarters to a status virtually on par with the global corporate headquarters.

Building supply chains in China

Unlike many other electronics companies, Samsung did not outsource most of the products sold under its name, nor did it simply carry out low-value added assembly in China. Instead, it committed to building an entire electronics ecosystem in China, including key components, major subassemblies, and finished products. This approach contributes more to a local economy that just doing electronics assembly as the key components often involve higher levels of technology, higher value added, and more potential for technological spillovers than simple assembly. In particular, Samsung not only manufactures mobile phones, communications equipment, computers, home electronics, and appliances in China, it also manufactures LCDs, LEDs, screens and monitors, semiconductors, opto-electronic components, and other key components in China. In most cases, Samsung has brought its global best technology and practices, rather than older generations as many other foreign companies have.

In some cases these investments have created their own dynamic. Samsung's USD 7 billion memory chip complex in Xi'an's High-tech Industrial Development Zone was expected to create 2,000 jobs directly and to generate another 11,000 jobs indirectly among local 'affiliates' (Lu and Ma, 2015). The facility was expected to attract more than 100 parts and components producers to create a semiconductor manufacturing cluster with a production value of more than USD 16 billion per year. On a smaller scale, the opening of Samsung Electronics' liquid crystal display production line in Suzhou in 2013 quickly fostered a local concentration of producers involved in every step of the LCD industrial chain, from raw materials, parts and components, to production and logistics (Want China Times, 2015).

Samsung Electronics initially located in parts of China with existing electronic and electrical manufacturing capabilities such as Tianjin, Suzhou, and Guangdong, where it could take advantage of existing supplier networks. Even so, it had to import a number of components from Korea, as the local offerings were not of sufficient quality. Samsung worked extensively to develop local suppliers in China. It began to run several programs through which potential suppliers are offered opportunities to become Samsung partners (Samsung, 2014a). According to Samsung, 'As partners, we will work together towards a win-win scenario of co-prosperity and the ultimate goal of any business: to be the world's best.' In order to achieve this goal, Samsung operates a policy of 'Mutual Growth' whereby it offers support in the form of training, technology, and funding to its first-tier suppliers along with strengthening communication between them and Samsung. This program is being expanded to their second- and third-tier suppliers as well (Samsung, 2012b).

Samsung has also helped its Chinese suppliers develop their supply chain management systems. Samsung's LCD headquarters established a Supply Chain Management (SCM) system to ensure the quality of component parts suppliers and raw material suppliers encompassing its Enterprise Resource Planning (ERP), Manufacturing Execution System (MES), Transportation Management System (TMS), and Warehouse Management System (WMS). Samsung also introduced a new SCM system (SLJ-Network) connecting first- and second-tier suppliers to reduce inventory levels and improve supply chain network efficiency (Park and Hong, 2011).

Samsung also helped develop other members of the 'Samsung China ecosystem' by providing free training workshops to software developers. Samsung runs workshops in major Chinese cities disseminating information about Samsung's platforms to developers, bringing together hundreds of developers including existing Samsung partners, start-up companies, individual developers, and university students (Samsung, 2013a). Samsung has also run global Smart App Challenges for the GALAXY Note. In 2012 entries from 70 countries were received with 80 apps chosen as the final winners. The country with the largest number of winners was China followed by South Korea and Poland (Samsung, 2012c; Samsung, 2013b).

Building distribution relationships in China

Samsung Electronics also developed strong links to distributors in China. It has worked with national electronics retailers, offering high margins and cutting off retailers that hurt the brand image by cutting prices (Moon, 2002). While national retailers provided good access to the developed markets along the China eastern seaboard, Samsung's access to inland cities was held back initially by the limitations of the networks of existing national retailers. To gain better access, Samsung Electronics established its own stores to specifically introduce its products to these cities. By having its own stores, Samsung was able to get more direct feedback from customers, allowing it to become more attuned to the differences that exist not just between Chinese and Western consumers, but also between different regions in China (Kwong and Song, 2012). By 2015, Samsung had three times the number of retail stores in China as Apple, and has been more aggressive in courting consumers and creating partnerships with phone operators, former company executives, analysts, and industry sources say (Lee and Kim, 2013).

Setting up global research in China

Samsung is one of the world's largest spenders on research and development. Its global network of research and development spans Korea, North America, Europe, and Asia. Samsung moved significant R&D into China shortly after China's entry into the WTO (Fujitsu, 2010). When other companies were concerned about the impact of IP theft, Samsung made a decision to move to China, understanding that in order to both develop new products for the world as a whole it also had to develop products specifically for China. In the 2000s, Samsung aimed to shift from a 'Made in China' model to a 'Created in China' model. According to Ho-moon Kang, Vice Chairman of Samsung Electronics and head of Samsung China in 2011, 'Through the "Created in China" idea, we will create products and business models designed to serve the Chinese market first, and eventually export them to the rest of the world' (Samsung, 2011).

As of 2015, three of Samsung Electronics' global R&D centres were in China, and China was the home of seven Samsung Electronics' R&D centres in total. The roughly 7,000 R&D staff in China as of 2015 accounted for around 11 percent of the company's global R&D staff (Samsung, 2011). The company expected China spending on R&D to reach USD 300 million annually by 2015, up from USD 180 million in 2010 (Samsung, 2011). Samsung Electronics developed its TD-SCDMA hand phones at its Beijing Technology Center together with the Chinese hand phone maker Datang Mobile (Kwong and Song, 2012). Its chip-making division worked with China Mobile to develop China's 7D-SCDMA standard for 3G hand phones. At its new manufacturing complex in Xi'an, Samsung is including a research centre that will consolidate expertise from other locations in China and cooperate with local education institutions on state-of-the-art NAND flash memory chip technology.

Developing human resources in China

Samsung Electronics employed a total 319,000 employees globally in 2014 (Jung, 2015). China was responsible for 25 percent of Samsung Electronics total workforce, 60,000 individuals, with the average employee numbers having grown 14 percent per annum since 2010 (Samsung, 2014c). Samsung chose new sites based in significant part on the availability of workers and researchers. Samsung said that it chose Xi'an for its semiconductor complex because of the city's excellent investment environment, its fast-developing electronics industry, a deep pool of researchers, and a well-trained labour force from more than 100 research institutes and universities. By May 2014,

Samsung had hired approximately 1,300 local university graduates for its Xi'an project (Lu and Ma, 2014).

Samsung China has had a strong focus on developing and promoting Chinese talent not just on the factory floor but in management as well. By 2006, at one of Samsung's subsidiaries, Samsung SDI, about 95 percent of upper management was Chinese (Li, 2006). In 2010, the then CEO of Samsung China spearheaded a localization drive for higher-level managers to make the company 'more like a Chinese company than a Korean' one. In 2010, 20 percent of the department heads at Samsung's China operations were Chinese, but by 2012, the figure was 70 percent (Kwong and Song, 2012). Wang Tong, a Chinese national, who rose to executive vice president of Samsung (China) Investment Co. Ltd, said, 'The highest level of localization is shown in the talent and decision-making structure, Chinese are in charge of the business in China, including the R&D, production and sale for real localization and faster development' (Lunwenwang, 2014).

In terms of the workforce, each Samsung China worksite operates a labour council to promote workers' benefits and rights. Labour councils have worked to facilitate a culture in which management and employees discuss matters regarding working conditions and work environment. By 2013, Samsung China's 16 labour councils had 165 employee representatives elected through direct and anonymous voting (Samsung, 2015a). Samsung China operates various employee counselling centres including a Life Coaching Center, which offers counselling services for employees with difficulties in marriage, child-rearing, office life, and other areas. The centres also provide specialized psychological services including personality tests and stress management education. The counselling staff at the Life Coaching Center consists of licensed professionals who have received systematic education and intensive training. All counselling information remains confidential so that employees can comfortably use the counselling centres (Samsung, 2015a).

Since 2014, Samsung Electronics has participated in the 'Women in Factories in China' project, which was launched by Business for Social Responsibility (BSR), a specialized CSR organization. The program provides tailored education opportunities for newly hired female employees and for female managers. For new hires, the program is designed to provide work and life skills training as a part of orientation. For female managers, the program provides technical and leadership training. Samsung also works with BSR to develop customized life skills training for female employees, focusing on stress and health management (Samsung, 2015d).

Samsung has come under criticism for allegations of child employment at some of its suppliers. In response, Samsung Electronics announced a Child Labour Prohibition Policy in June 2014 developed in collaboration with the Center for Child Rights and Corporate Social Responsibility (CCR CSR) based in China. The policy called for a zero tolerance policy on underage labour and claimed to hold the company and its supplier companies to the highest labour standards (CCR CSR, 2014).

Supporting Chinese standards and open systems

China's leadership has been concerned that foreign standards would dominate mobile telecommunications and that this would disadvantage Chinese consumers and Chinese firms, and create national security issues. As a result, China has pushed to develop its own standards. Samsung has demonstrated consistent commitment to helping the development of Chinese telecommunication standards, developing the technology needed to realize those standards, and promoting them to a wider audience beyond China. This enabled Samsung to bring compatible products to the China market sooner than their international competitors, while providing Chinese consumers with improved performance and choice.

Samsung was one of the first foreign-owned companies to release a phone compatible with China's home-grown 3G network standard (TD-SCDMA), releasing a compatible phone in 2007, just a year after the standard was activated (Middleton, 2007; Wei, 2009). Apple by comparison did not support TD-SCDMA until the iPhone 5 was released in 2013. The 3G TD-SCDMA standard gained little international reach, but China took the lead in developing the 4G TD-LTE standard, which has been supported by global firms in dual use TD/FD LTE devices (Jakobs, 2015). Samsung was an early member of the TD-LTE consortium along with Chinese companies like China Mobile and Huawei. When China Mobile switched on its TD-LTE 4G network in December 2013, and Apple had no phone capable of handling the standard, Samsung was ready with its S4 (Millward, 2013). The TD-LTE standard has become popular in Asia, particularly India and China, and China Mobile expected to hit 80 million TD-LTE subscribers by the end of 2014 (Wu, 2014).

Samsung's support of open systems has facilitated, though perhaps inadvertently, the rise of Chinese smartphone producers. The first smart phones introduced by companies like Apple, Nokia, Blackberry, and Motorola used closed proprietary technology. Samsung, on the other hand, developed products for the open source Android platform developed by Google, legitimizing the Android operating system in the process. Samsung's success in smartphones attracted the interest of Chinese electronics and phone manufacturers. The Android operating system championed by Samsung enabled companies like Xiaomi, Huawei, ZTE, and numerous other Chinese companies to focus their R&D on hardware and China-specific applications, without the need to develop and gain acceptance for an operating system of their own. Without Samsung's support for the Android system, Chinese smartphone makers would not be nearly as prominent as they have become (author's interviews).

Bringing green standards to China

Energy efficiency and a cleaner environment have become high priorities within China in recent years. Samsung China has contributed to these priorities in several ways. The company has brought the global Green Management program it founded in 1992 to China. Through the operation of G-EHS (Global Environment, Health & Safety System), Samsung integrates management of environment-related information such as reduction of greenhouse gas emissions, response to regulations on product environment, and performance management in environmental and safety hazard prevention (Samsung, 2015d).

Samsung's Green Management System in China encompasses Greening of Management (Strategy, Procedures, and Systems), Greening of Factories (Energy Saving, Green House Gas Reduction, and Pollution Reduction), Greening of Products (R&D), and Greening of Communities. For example, Samsung China operates an eco-partner certification process whereby raw material suppliers, parts suppliers, and Samsung Electronics materials and processes undergo environmental certification. Since 2005, Samsung China has setup collection bins and put up guidelines in over 400 repair service centres to collect obsolete cell phones and accessories. Samsung commissions qualified companies to undertake non-hazardous treatment of the waste and to take advantage of recycling resources (Chen et al., 2015).

Samsung Electronics has repeatedly been praised for its environmental performance in China. It received the 'Top Green Company Award' from the Daonong Center for Enterprise in 2014 and 2012; the 'Energy Saving Contribution Award' from the China Energy Saving Association in 2013, 2012, 2011, and 2010; the 'Green Medal Award' in recognition of its use of advanced technology in green products from the *China Business News* in 2012; the 'Sustainable Development Award' in recognition of its excellent eco-friendly products from *The Economic Observer* in 2012; the 'Energy Efficiency Star Award' for high efficiency products from the China Ministry of Industry and Information Technology in 2012; and was selected as the greenest company among the top 100 foreign companies in China in the 'Green company assessment', by the China Europe International Business School (CEIBS) in 2011 (Samsung, 2015b).

Corporate social responsibility in China

Samsung also has an advanced global corporate social responsibility program that it has brought to China. In China Samsung was ranked first among foreign companies and thirteenth among all companies (foreign and domestic) for corporate social responsibility initiatives in China in 2014 (Samsung, 2014b).

Samsung hopes to develop more technical talents to meet the industrial needs in China, making contributions to vocational education in China while enhancing the social recognition of blue-collar workers. In 2002, Samsung set up a university scholarship program and as of 2013 it had partnered with 26 key Chinese universities and offered more than 5,000 scholarships (Invest Guangzhou, 2013). The company launched its 'Tech Institute' program with the Ministry of Human Resources and Social Security in 2014 to provide technical education to vocational school students in China. The program has run major training bases in Tianjin, Suzhou, Chengdu, Shenyang, and Xi'an involving over 300 trainees with vocational education. Samsung planned to establish five more training bases by the end of 2015 (Sun, 2014).

Samsung Electronics' corporate social responsibility efforts in China include the Samsung Dream Class to bring summer school classes to children in remote rural areas. Other Samsung CSR projects in China include summer camp for children with autism; a foundation to assist cataract patients; anti-pollution campaigns by its staff; and disaster relief (Yang, 2013). Samsung donates RMB 10 million annually to the China Foundation for Disabled Persons. In 2012, the company organized a total of 834 public welfare events that involved as many as 43,000 people. Samsung adheres to its business philosophy of 'shared management'. It donated a total of RMB 60 million to earthquake-hit areas in Ya'an in 2013, RMB 30 million for the emergency response to the 2008 Sichuan earthquake, and RMB 10 million for relief efforts for Qinghai's Yushu earthquake relief efforts in 2010. Samsung Electronics supports a variety of healthcare programs with its advanced medical equipment technology, products, and services. It operates a mobile medical centre for areas that lack convenient medical facilities and provides medical training for local medical associations (Samsung, 2015a).

Making an overall contribution to China

Samsung Electronics' overall contribution to China has been multifaceted. It has made massive investments that make it one of the largest foreign direct investors in the country. It provides employment directly for 60,000 people in China, and many more through its supply chain. It has contributed to the development of China's electronic manufacturing base by engaging not just in electronics assembly in China, but also in advanced componentry, extensive research and development in China, and bringing much of its most advanced technology to China. By championing the Android operating system, it inadvertently helped pave the way for many Chinese companies to enter the smartphone business. It has contributed greatly to the development and utilization of advanced capabilities in the electronics industry in China.

Samsung has also invested extensively to build capabilities in its own Chinese workforce and has localized the vast majority of key management and research positions in China. Samsung has engaged in extensive activities to promote China's energy efficiency and environmental goals. Through its CSR programs it has participated in helping promote education, disaster relief, and programs for the disabled within China. In the process it has focused on becoming a part of Chinese society, rather than a firm just interested in profiting from the China market.

Samsung's contribution to China has been noted on many occasions over the years. In 2005, Samsung was ranked as 'the best foreign investor in China' and in 2006, Samsung was selected as the 'best contributor' among foreign enterprises in China (Zheng and Pearce, 2012, p. 77). In 2006 and 2007, Samsung was awarded a Public Welfare Prize for its outstanding contribution to Chinese society (Lee, 2013). In 2013 and again in 2014, Samsung was ranked first among foreign companies for corporate social responsibility, as awarded by the Chinese Academy of Social Sciences (Samsung, 2014b). In 2015, Samsung China was among ten companies named 'The most respected enterprises in China', by *The Economic Observer*, a business publication. This was the tenth year that Samsung was on the list (China News, 2015).

China's senior leaders have also expressed their gratitude to Samsung. The importance of the partnership between Samsung and China was underscored by a meeting in 2013 between the Chinese Vice Premier Liu Yandong and Vice Chairman of Samsung Group Lee Yae-yong, in which the Vice Premier lauded Samsung's contributions to economic cooperation between China and the Republic of Korea (ROK) (Xinhua, 2013). During a Korea–China business forum held by the Korean Chamber of Commerce in 2014, China's President Xi Jinping was given a personal tour of an exhibition of Samsung's products by Samsung Electronics' Vice Chairman Jay Y. Lee, in addition to holding private talks (Lee, 2014; Seo et al., 2014). The degree of involvement at the highest levels clearly underscores the mutual importance of the relationship between China and Samsung.

Moving beyond China

Samsung has made major investments and major commitments in China. However, there are signs that Samsung is moving beyond China, due to cost increases, and incentives to invest. In particular, Samsung Electronics has made major investments in Vietnam. The company opened its first facility in Vietnam in 2010. By 2015, Samsung had invested USD 2.5 billion in factories in Bac Ninh Province, USD 5 billion in an assembly plant in Thai Nguyen Province, and USD 1.4 billion in another facility in Ho Chi Minh City. Estimates of the total investment in Vietnam by the end of 2015 were USD 14.2 billion, making Samsung Vietnam's largest foreign investor by a substantial margin. Vietnamese officials claimed that Vietnam had become Samsung Electronics' largest overseas production location. Roughly one-third of Samsung's smart phones were reportedly being made in Vietnam (Vietnam News, 2015). The company's exports from Vietnam reached USD 26.3 billion in 2014, equal to 17.5 percent of Vietnam's total exports, and its Vietnam factories employed over 110,000 (Bich, 2015), or roughly one-third of Samsung Electronics' global employment, and well above its China employment. In June 2015, the company announced it was targeting sales growth of 40 percent from its Vietnam facilities in 2015 (The Chosunilbo, 2015).

Samsung was not just assembling electronics in Vietnam; it was placing complete production systems and research support into the country. Samsung opened a research and software centre in Vietnam in 2012 and by 2015, the centre was supplying around 10 percent of the software used in Samsung phones. Only five of the centre's 1,500 employees were foreign and Samsung planned to expand employment to 2,600 by 2018 (Vietnam News, 2015). It was also tooling up its Vietnamese factories for more precision manufacturing, reportedly shipping 20,000 machines to Vietnam to match the milling performed on Apple iPhones (Vincent, 2015). Several Samsung subsidiaries had set up facilities to supply the Vietnam plants. Samsung also had pushed other suppliers to set up in the country and was actively developing local suppliers and working with government to improve Vietnam's electronics sector (Nhan Dan, 2015). By 2015, approximately 90 partner and supplier companies, mostly from Korea, had followed Samsung to Vietnam (Kang, 2015).

The main reason for investments in Vietnam, as opposed to China, was labour costs roughly one-third of what was available in China after several rounds of government-imposed wage increases in China. Samsung was also offered tax exemptions for the first four years of operation of its Vietnam facilities, a 5 percent tax rate for the next 12 years, and a 10 percent tax rate for the next 34. Samsung was also offered exemptions on import tariffs and VAT, as well as help with land development, training, and customs. A young population, worker availability, and prospective membership in the Transpacific Partnership (TPP) were also reasons to prefer Vietnam to China for new investment (Kang, 2015).

Samsung's impact on Vietnam has been profound. Just two years after Samsung opened its first facility in the country, Vietnam exported more than it imported for the first time in 20 years. Samsung was also investing aggressively in developing the Vietnamese workforce, making arrangements with local universities, providing study materials, sponsoring libraries, and digitizing content to make it available on Samsung smartphones (Tibken, 2015). In 2015, Samsung was exploring investing in the insurance and energy sectors, and was seeking out promising local entrepreneurial companies to fund (Goh, 2015). Samsung had led the way for other Korean companies, some of which opened facilities in Vietnam to supply Samsung, and others that benefitted from Samsung paving the way in terms of negotiations with government, infrastructure, and business systems. By 2015, Korean firms had invested a total of USD 39.2 billion, making Korea the leading foreign investor in Vietnam. Samsung reportedly did not want to be known as Vietnam's largest exporter or foreign investor, but as 'Vietnam's national enterprise' (Ngoc, 2015).

Samsung's investments in Vietnam represent something of a cautionary tale for China. Samsung had become one of the largest foreign investors in China. As costs increased in China, local governments pushed up wages, Chinese competitors emerged, and the Chinese Government began to favour Chinese technology companies over foreign companies more overtly, Samsung wound up investing about as much in Vietnam in six years as it had in China in 20. While in the short run, most of the jobs and production that were located in Vietnam, instead perhaps of China, involved relatively simple assembly, Samsung was moving to put higher value-added production and jobs into Vietnam as rapidly as possible, and it was pulling other companies into Vietnam to do the same. While Vietnam will never come close to China's scale as a manufacturer or as a market (its population of 91 million is less than one-tenth that of China), the Samsung example shows that there are other alternatives for foreign companies and China cannot assume that it will automatically continue to attract some forms of investment.

Conclusions

The corporate case studies provide a range of insights into the roles played by foreign companies in China. Hong Kong companies have been pioneers in many if not most aspects of China's economic opening. At each stage of development and across a wide range of industries and activities, new opening in China has meant new opportunities, but these opportunities have never been without risk. For a range of reasons, including proximity, family ties, ability to form relationships, cultural ties, and specific business experience, Hong Kong companies have been willing to make investments and take risks in advance of other 'foreign' companies. Whether in light manufacturing, infrastructure, transportation, or real estate, Hong Kong companies have been able to serve and leverage the Chinese economy earlier than firms from other economies. This has benefitted China and has allowed Hong Kong companies a much broader reach and scope than if they had stayed at home. The result has been an economic integration that has helped modernize and internationalize China's economy.

In P&G, we have a story of how comprehensive a major company's impact can be on a foreign host economy. P&G has been at the forefront in China in developing suppliers, teaching and training distributors, training the workforce, introducing modern advertising and marketing techniques, building up local research and development capabilities, introducing advanced human resource and management systems, and internationalizing its Chinese management staff. In addition, P&G has been a corporate leader in green production standards, public health education, and sustainability reporting to China. Finally, through its various product developments and introductions it has changed the way millions of people in China live. P&G has had an impact on China in almost every aspect where companies interact within larger societies.

The Maersk story is a somewhat different one. While Maersk's involvement in China has many of the attributes of the involvements of other foreign companies, Maersk stands out in terms of its impact on improving connectivity within China through its logistics arm and between China and the rest of the world through its shipping and logistics activities. Companies that produce and sell in China, like P&G and Samsung, tend to be better known than the companies that provide the vital connections that have allowed China to become a global economic and trade power. Without the experience and international networks of multinational companies like Maersk, making the right connections and leveraging China's advantages into international markets would be far more difficult. The Maersk case shows how valuable it has been for China to connect to world markets and how extensive the resulting impact of the foreign companies that facilitate this process can be.

Samsung went from producing in China for export to producing in China for China as well as the rest of the world. Samsung recognized China's importance, not just as a production location, but as the location for a wide range of corporate activities, including research and development and senior management. In the process, the company almost created a 'second Samsung' in China and places some of its most senior managers in the country. However, the Samsung case also shows that major multinationals have other countries in which they can invest. As China becomes more expensive, the market tougher, and perhaps not as hospitable to foreign firms as it might be, foreign firms can look to other countries for their investment. In addition, there are companies large enough to make investments in new countries and pull in suppliers, partners, and others sufficient to make the investments successful. What is more, major multinationals can undertake the same sorts of investment, supplier development, workforce development, technology development, educational, CSR, and related activities in other countries, thereby making them more competitive, as they have in China.

Thus the corporate case studies show the extent to which foreign companies have had an impact on China's development, but they also raise some questions about how China's economy will fare if for whatever reason foreign companies choose to lessen or reduce investment in the country.

Notes

1 This section draws upon Enright et al., (1997), Enright et al. (2005), Enright et al. (2003), Enright, Scott & Associates (2010); and numerous interviews by the author.
2 See Chapter 2.
3 Research sponsored by the Federation of Hong Kong Industries has reached a similar estimate (Wong, 2003).
4 Based on statistics from Airports Council International.
5 Hong Kong Census and Statistics Department.
6 A 'Red Chip' company is a Chinese company incorporated outside of the Chinese Mainland, listed on a foreign stock exchange (usually Hong Kong), and controlled by Mainland Government entities.
7 An 'H share' company is incorporated in the Chinese Mainland, listed on a foreign stock exchange (usually Hong Kong), and controlled by Mainland Government entities or individuals.
8 For earlier versions of this argument see Enright et al. (2003, 2005).
9 The average official exchange rate was RMB 3.7221 to 1 US dollar in 1988.
10 Calculated from USD 80,510 million in global sales and 8 percent of global sales in Greater China from the P&G 2015 *Annual Report*.
11 China's exports were USD 593 billion in 2004 and USD 2,049 billion in 2012 according to World Trade Organization statistics.
12 Enright, Scott & Associates estimates.
13 Using market share and logistics costs estimates found in Maersk (2014b); WTO trade statistics; and Enright, Scott & Associates estimates of export margins from China.
14 As assessed by Corporate Executive Board (CEB), a company that focuses on talent management and works with 90 percent of the Fortune 500.
15 Enright, Scott & Associates estimates.

References

AAHK, 2014, *Annual Report 2014*, Airport Authority of Hong Kong.

APM Terminals, 2009, *Awards*.

Beattie, A.C., 2012, 'Early Foothold in China Pays Off', *Advertising Age*, 29 October.

Bich, T., 2015, 'Samsung Plots Energy and Insurance Sector Expansion', *Vietnam Investment Review*, 30 September.

CCR CSR, 2014, 'Samsung Electronics Announces Child Labor Prohibition Policy in China', *CCR CSR*, 8 July.

Chen, J., Q. Huang, H. Peng, and H. Zhong, 2015, 'China Samsung: To Foster a Favorite Brand for Chinese People and Contribute to Chinese Society', in J. Chen, Q. Huang, H. Peng, and H. Zhong, eds, *Research Report on Corporate Social Responsibility of China*, Berlin, Springer, pp. 263–82.

Cheng, J.Y.S. and P. Zheng, 2001, 'Hi-Tech Industries in Hong Kong and the Pearl River Delta: Development Trends in Industrial Cooperation', *Asian Survey*, 41(4), pp. 584–610.

Cheung Kong Infrastructure, 2015, *Our Business*.

China Customs, 2012, *China Customs Statistical Yearbook 2012*.

China News, 2015, '[Samsung China Won the 'Most Respected Enterprises' Award for the Tenth Time]', *China News*, 31 July, (in Chinese).

China Statistics Press, 2009, *The Basic Matrix, Input-Output Tables of China 2007*, Beijing, China Statistics Press.

Choi, C.H., 2003, 'The China Strategies of Korea's Winning Companies', *Nomura Research Institute Paper No. 67*, 1 August, pp. 2–4.

The Chosunilbo, 2015, 'Samsung's Vietnam Plants Set Ambitious Sales Target', *The Chosunilbo*, 3 June.

CLP, 2015, *Our Operations: Power Generation*.

Comtois, C. and B. Slack, 2000, 'Hong Kong: Adding Value to China – Transport Hub and Urban Super-Region', *China Perspectives*, 29, May-June.

Coolidge, A., 2014, 'Procter & Gamble's Global Reach Changing', *USA Today*, 7 September.

Cosmetic Observer, 2015, '[Distribution Strategy of Brands 2014 – Olay]', *Cosmetic Observer*, 26 July, (in Chinese).

Damco, 2013, *Sustainability Progress Report 2013*.

Damco, 2014, 'Damco Supports Chinese Company Kerui to Go Global', *Damco Press Release*.

Dyer, D., F. Dalzell, and R. Olegario, 2004, *Rising Tide: Lessons from 165 Years of Brand Building at Procter & Gamble*, Boston: Harvard Business School Press.

Enright, M.J., E.E. Scott, and K.M. Chang, 2005, *Regional Powerhouse: The Greater Pearl River Delta and the Rise of China*, Singapore, Wiley.

Enright, M.J., E.E. Scott, K.M. Chang, and W. Zhu, 2003, *Hong Kong and the Pearl River Delta: The Economic Interaction*, Hong Kong, 2022 Foundation.

Enright, M.J., E.E. Scott, and D. Dodwell, 1997, *The Hong Kong Advantage*, Hong Kong, Oxford University Press.

Enright, Scott and Associates, 2010, *Hong Kong Manufacturing SMEs: Preparing For the Future*, Hong Kong, Federation of Hong Kong Industries.

Finance Ifeng, 2012, '[P&G Localization in China]', *finance.ifeng.com*, 10 February, (in Chinese).

Fujitsu, 2010, *Foreign Companies Accelerating R&D Activity in China*, Fujitsu Research Institute, 13 May.

Galley, M., 2014, *Shipbreaking: Hazards and Liabilities*, Cham, Springer.

GIM, 2014, 'P&G Launched a Laboratory Cooperated with Guangdong Institute of Microbiology', *Guangdong Institute of Microbiology Press Release*, 16 December.

Goh, G., 2015, 'Samsung and Leo Burnett to Kickstart Entrepreneurs in Vietnam', *Campaign Asia-Pacific*, 26 November.

Grant, J., 2005, 'Switch to the Low-Income Customer', *Financial Times*, 14 November.

GreenerBuildings, 2011. 'P&G Commits to LEED for Factory in China and All New Facilities', *GreenerBuildings*, 25 February.

Guan, G., 2015, 'Chinese Companies in Central Africa Overcome Logistics Challenges', *Damco Blog*, 16 June.

Guangzhou Daily, 2015, '[Guangzhou as the Starting Point for P&G]', *Guangzhou Daily*, 3 January, (in Chinese).

Hexter, J. and J. Woetzel, 2007, *Operation China: From Strategy to Execution*, Boston, Harvard Business School Press.

HKCSD, 2002, Hong Kong Special Administrative Region Government, Census and Statistics Department.

HKCSD, 2014, *Employment by Industry*, Hong Kong Census and Statistics Department.

HKTDC, 2001, *The Two Cities – Shanghai and Hong Kong*, Hong Kong Trade Development Council, March.

HKTHB, various years, *Port and Cargo Statistics*, Hong Kong Transport and Housing Bureau.

Hong Kong Commercial Daily, 2002, 'Lu Ruihua Expects Guangdong's Exports to Increase 10% this Year', *Hong Kong Commercial Daily*, 6 June.

Hong Kong Stock Exchange, 2015, *HKEx Monthly Market Highlights*, 30 September.

Hopewell Holdings, 2015, *Corporate Profile*.

Huang, J., 2013, 'Developing Local Talent for Future Leadership', *China Business Review*, 1 January.

Invest Guangzhou, 2013, 'Samsung Guangzhou Mobile R&D Center: Localization leads to Growth', *Invest Guangzhou*, 12 September.

IS Maritime 360, 2015, 'Former trainee to lead Maersk Line for North China', *IHS Maritime 360*, September.

Jakobs, K., 2015, *Modern Trends Surrounding Information Technology Standards and Standardization within Organizations*, Hershey, PA, IGI Global.

JOC Group, 2013, *Key Findings on Terminal Productivity Performance Across Ports, Countries and Regions*, July.

Jung, Y.J., 2015, 'Exponential Growth, Number of Samsung Employees Exceeds 300,000', *Business Korea*, 24 April.

Kang, H., 2015, *Global Cooperation and Corporate Internationalization Strategy – Samsung Electronics' Manufacturing Complex in Vietnam*, Samsung Economic Research Institute.

Kantar, 2010, *Who Are Winning the Chinese Consumers?*

Knowledge@Wharton, 2010, 'Rethinking the Power of Money: How Has the Financial Crisis Affected HR Management in China?', *Knowledge@Wharton*, 5 October.

Kwong, R. and J.A. Song, 2012, 'Samsung's China Strategy Pays Off', *Financial Times*, 20 May.

Lakshmi, A., 2015, 'Maersk Line Gets New Head in China', *MarineLink.com*, 22 May.

Lam, E., 2005, 'Moving Forward with You', *HACTL*, 13 April.

Lee, C.S.E., 2013, 'The Role of Corporate Social Responsibility in China's Sustainable Development', in B. Wu, S. Yao, and J. Chen, eds, *China's Development and Harmonization:*

Towards a Balance with Nature, Society and the International Community, London: Routledge, pp. 207–17.

Lee, D., 2006, *Samsung Electronics: The Global Inc*, YSM.

Lee, M.J., 2014, 'Samsung, LG Gun for China President Xi's Attention', *The Wall Street Journal*, 4 July.

Lee, M.J. and M. Kim, 2013, 'How Samsung is Beating Apple in China', *Reuters*, 26 July.

Leung, C.K. 1993, 'Personal Contacts, Subcontracting Linkages and Development in the Hong Kong – Zhujiang Delta Region', *Annals of the Association of American Geographers*, 83(2), pp. 272–302.

Li, J., 2006, 'On Display', *China Daily*, 26 June.

Li, J., X. Yan, and C. Zhou, 2002, '[An Investigation into the Current Situations and Development Trends of MNC Investment in the Pearl River Delta]', *Guangdong Development Magazine*, 1, (in Chinese).

Lockett, H., 2014, 'How Marketing and Market Forces Created a China Boom for Formula and Disposable Diapers', *China Economic Review*, 20 October.

Lu, H. and L. Ma, 2014, 'Samsung Chip Facility Opens in Xi'an', *China Daily*, 11 May.

Lu, H. and L. Ma, 2015, 'Samsung Production Line put into Operation in Xi'an', *China Daily*, 20 April.

Lunwenwang, 2014, '[China to Have a More Localized Samsung]', *Lunwenwang*, 16 May, (in Chinese).

Madden, N., 2014, 'P&G's Take on Targeting China's Fast-Changing Consumers', *Advertising Age*, 20 August.

Maersk, 2009, *Sustainability Report 2009*.

Maersk, 2013, 'Damco Retains Woman Talent in China', *Maersk Stories*, 29 October.

Maersk, 2014a, *A Leading Trade Nation*.

Maersk, 2014b, *A Leading Trade Nation: Technical Report*.

Maersk, 2014c, *Exploring Maersk in China*.

Maersk, 2014d, 'Zooming in on Critical Suppliers', *Sustainability Report*.

Maersk, 2015a, 'Maersk to move China office from HK to Beijing', *Maersk Press Release*, 7 May.

Maersk, 2015b, 'Switching Jobs, Staying Aboard', *Maersk Post*, August.

MarEx, 2016, 'Maersk to Help Ship Breakers', *The Maritime Executive*, 11 February.

Middleton, J., 2007, 'Samsung Intros TD-SCDMA/HSDPA Multimode Handset', *Telecoms*, 12 November.

Millward, S., 2013, 'China Mobile Turns on Nation's First 4G Network, but Still no Sign of iPhone Deal', *Tech In Asia*, 18 December.

Moon, I., 2002, 'How Samsung Plugged into China', *Bloomberg Business*, 3 March.

MTR Corporation, 2014, *Annual Report 2014*.

National Business Daily, 2009, '[P&G Distributer Opened Online Shops]', *National Business Daily*, 5 June, (in Chinese).

Neal, A., 2007, 'Maersk in China Builds Talent Pipeline to Meet Challenge of Rapid Growth', *Human Resource Management International Digest*, 15(7), pp. 5–10.

Neff, J., 2015, 'P&G Recovers U.S. Diaper Lead, But Kimberly-Clark Gains in China', *Advertising Age*, 25 March.

NetEase Finance, 2010, '[Shiseido and P&G Targeting at Second and Third Tier Cities]', *NetEase Finance*, 25 May, (in Chinese).

Ngoc, N.T.B., 2015, 'Samsung Keen on Bigger Play in Vietnam, Mulls Investments in Energy & Insurance Sectors', *Deal Street Asia*, 9 September.

Nhan Dan, 2015, 'Samsung Devises Measures to Boost Vietnam's Electronics Industry', *Nhan Dan*, 15 July.

Nicholson, L., 2014, 'China Outlines Plan to Modernise Shipping Industry, Shares Jump', *Reuters Business News*, 3 September.

NWS Holdings, 2015, *Business: Infrastructure*.

P&G, 2008, 'P&G China was crowned the "2008 Best HR of China"', *P&G Press Release*, 23 October.

P&G, 2009, 'P&G Joins as Official Premier Sponsor of the USA Pavilion at the Shanghai World Expo', *P&G Press Release*, 15 November.

P&G, 2010a, 'P&G Again Ranks in 2010 Hurun CSR Top 50', *P&G Press Release*, 5 August.

P&G, 2010b, 'P&G China Wins Platinum Award for Sustainability', *P&G Press Release*, 15 November.

P&G, 2010c, 'P&G Facilitates Energy Saving and Emission Reduction in Supply Chain', *P&G Press Release*, 10 June 2010.

P&G, 2010d, 'P&G Makes New Stride in Innovation in China Ministry of Commerce Highly Commends P&G's Contribution to China', *P&G Press Release*, 23 August.

P&G, 2010e, 'P&G Promises 'Full Court Press' in China', *P&G Business Daily Update*, 19 August.

P&G, 2011a, 'P&G China honored as Top 100 China Green Company in 2011', *P&G Press Release*, 29 April.

P&G, 2011b, 'P&G Listed among Best Employers in China by Universum', *P&G Press Release*, 7 June.

P&G, 2011c, 'P&G Signed MOU with Chinese Science Academy on Cooperation', *P&G Press Release*, 10 October.

P&G, 2012, 'P&G China Won 2012 International Green Design Award', *P&G Press Release*, 19 December.

P&G, 2013, 'P&G Opened Experience Center on Taobao', *P&G Press Release*, 30 July.

P&G, 2014a, 'P&G Included in the China Top 100 Green Companies 2014', *P&G Press Release*, 19 May.

P&G, 2014b, 'P&G Listed among Best Employers in China by Universum again in 2014', *P&G Press Release*, 8 October.

P&G, 2014c, 'P&G Recognized as a Green Shipper by the China Green Freight Initiatives', *P&G Press Release*, 17 July.

P&G, 2014d, *P&G Sustainability Report 2013*.

P&G, 2015a, *Brand List*.

P&G, 2015b, 'Brands under P&G Included in China Brand List by MIIT', *P&G Press Release*, 16 April.

P&G, 2015c, *Building a Sustainable Future*.

P&G, 2015d, 'P&G China Pilot Program Cultivates Environmental Protection Leader', *P&G Press Release*, 5 June.

P&G, 2015e, *P&G China, Public Service*.

P&G, 2015f, 'P&G Win in Internet Marketing by Creation', *P&G Press Release*, 23 October.

P&G, 2015g, 'P&G won 5 Awards at the Effie Awards (Greater China)', *P&G Press Release*, 2 November.

Park, Y.W. and P. Hong, 2011, *Building Network Capabilities in Turbulent Competitive Environments: Practices of global Firms from Korea and Japan*, New York, CRC Press.

Penhirin, J., 2004, 'Understanding the Chinese Consumer', *McKinsey Quarterly*, July, p. 46–57.

Pudong Times, 2014, '[Vice Secretary General of Shanghai Meets President of P&G China]', *Pudong Times*, 12 December, (in Chinese).

Reingold, J., 2011, 'Can P&G Make Money in Places Where People Earn $2 a Day?', *CNN Money*, 6 January.

Roberts, D., 2007, 'Scrambling to Bring Crest to the Masses in China', *BusinessWeek*, 24 June.

Samsung, 2011, 'Samsung's China Dream: From "Made in China" to "Created in China"', *Samsung Village*, 19 May.

Samsung, 2012a, 'Samsung Breaks Ground for Memory Manufacturing Complex in China', *Samsung Press Release*, 12 September.

Samsung, 2012b, *Sustainability Report 2012*, Samsung Electronics.

Samsung, 2012c, 'Winners of Samsung Smart App Challenge 2012 Unveiled', *Samsung Developers*, 15 November.

Samsung, 2013a, 'Samsung Electronics China hosts Samsung Developers Training', *Samsung Developers*, 8 August.

Samsung, 2013b, 'Samsung Electronics China Hosts the Second Round Samsung Developers Training Beijing', *Samsung Developers*, 4 November.

Samsung, 2014a, *Global Harmony, Sustainability Report 2014*, Samsung Electronics.

Samsung, 2014b, 'Samsung Ranks No. 1 for CSR in China for Two Years in a Row', *Samsung Village*, 25 November.

Samsung, 2014c, *Talent Management Facts and Figures*, Samsung Electronics.

Samsung, 2015a, *Annual Report 2014*, Samsung Electronics.

Samsung, 2015b, *Awards and Recognitions*, Samsung Electronics.

Samsung, 2015c, *China History*.

Samsung, 2015d, *Global Harmony, Sustainability Report 2015*, Samsung Electronics.

Seo, J.Y., H.K. Park, and J.Y. Lee, 2014, 'Korean Conglomerates to Woo Chinese Delegation', *The Korea Herald*, 3 July.

Shanghai Daily, 2015, 'Han Zheng Meets with Maersk Group CEO', *Shanghai Daily*, 1 April.

Shao, F., 2014, 'A Fast and Economic Rail Solution Between China and Europe', *Damco Blog*, 7 October.

Shipping Online CN, 2009, 'Maersk Wins Social Responsibility Award for Sichuan Quake Role', *Shipping Online.CN*, 25 August.

Sina Finance, 2015, '[P&G Cut 40% Its Advertising Agency Moving to Internet Marketing]', *Sina Finance*, 11 August, (in Chinese).

Sun, X., 2014, 'Samsung Supports Vocational Skills Competition', *China Daily*, 14 August.

Ta Kung Pao, 2002a, '[Hong Kong Businesses Prepare Domestic Sales]', *Ta Kung Pao*, 22 January, (in Chinese).

Ta Kung Pao, 2002b, '[Trade Between Hong Kong and Guangdong Reaches USD 38.7 Billion]', *Ta Kung Pao*, 10 April, (in Chinese).

Tibken, S., 2015, 'Schooling Vietnam: How Tech Companies are Training the Next Wave of Workers', *Cnet*, 22 July.

Vietnam News, 2015, 'Samsung R&D Centre Hitting Stride', *Vietnam News*, 3 December.

Vincent, J., 2015, 'Samsung Shipped 20,000 Milling Machines to Vietnam to Match the iPhone's Metal', *The Verge*, 12 May.

Walfish, D., 2001, 'P&G China Lab Has Global Role', *Research-Technology Management*, 44(5), pp. 4–5.

Wang, J., 1994, 'Expansion of the Southern China Growth Triangle', in M. Thant, M. Tang, and H. Kakazu, eds, *Growth Triangles in Asia: A New Approach to Regional Cooperation*, Hong Kong, Oxford University Press, pp. 151–75.

Wang, J., 2003, 'Framing Chinese Advertising: Some Industry Perspectives on the Production of Culture', *Journal of Media and Cultural Studies*, 17(3), pp. 247–70.

Want China Times, 2015, 'Samsung Strengthens Grip on China's Industrial Chain', *Want China Times*, 21 February.

Wei, M., 2009, 'China Issues 3G Licenses to Main Carriers', *Reuters*, 7 January.

Wentz, L., 2009, 'Top 100 Global Advertisers Heap Their Spending Abroad', *Advertising Age*, 30 November.

Wong, R., 2003, *Made in PRD: The Changing Face of HK Manufacturers*, Federation of Hong Kong Industries.

World Maritime News, 2011, 'Maersk Line Receives Shipping Line of the Year Award in Shanghai, China', *World Maritime News*, December.

World Maritime News, 2013, 'Maersk Line Wins China Freight Industry Awards', *World Maritime News*, June.

Wu, B., 2014, 'China Mobile to have 80 Million TD-LTE Users at End of 2014', *Digitimes*, 29 December.

Xinhua, 2013, 'Chinese Vice Premier Meets Samsung Vice Chairman', *Xinhua*, 21 June.

Xinhuanet, 2015, '[P&G Moving Its Eye to High-end Market]', *xinhuanet.com*, 30 April, (in Chinese).

Yang, C., 2013, 'Samsung Gives Back through Social Responsibility Initiatives', *China Daily*, 28 June.

Yang, C., 2015, 'From China to Belarus: Damco is a Vital Link in Carmaker Geely's Supply Chain', *Damco Blog*, 29 September.

Yeung Y., 1994, 'Infrastructure Development in the Southern China Growth Triangle', in M. Thant, M. Tang, and H. Kakazu, eds, *Growth Triangles in Asia: A New Approach to Regional Development*, Oxford, Oxford University Press, pp. 114–50.

Young, S., 2006, 'Market Dynamics of Toothpaste in China', *Personal Care*, January.

Yunnan, 2012, '57 Projects in Kunming Breaking Ground with Total Investment 16.3 billion Yuan', www.yunnan.cn, 5 November, (in Chinese).

Zawadzki, S. and R.J. Bartunek, 2016, 'Maersk to Scrap Ships at Certain Alang Sites, NGO Dismayed', *Reuters*, 12 February.

Zheng, F. and R. Pearce, 2012, 'The Growth and Strategic Orientation of Multinationals' R&D in China', in R. Pearce, ed, *China and the Multinationals: International Business and the Entry of China into the Global Economy*, Cheltenham, UK, Edward Elgar.

Zhongshan University, 2002, *A Study of the Economic Relationship Between Hong Kong and the Pearl River Delta*, The Centre for Urban and Regional Studies, Zhongshan University, (in Chinese).

7

Econometric analysis of foreign investment in China[1]

Introduction

There is an extensive econometric literature on the impact of foreign investment on China's economy. This literature is important in that it tends to shape much of the discussion and debate about foreign investment that goes on in policy circles in China and elsewhere. Since this literature is technical in nature, and much of it is in Chinese, it is largely inaccessible to the general international audience. Even so, it is necessary for anyone interested in the impact of foreign investment in China, or in discussions that can influence policy toward foreign investment behind the scenes in China, to understand this literature. In this chapter, we will introduce this literature and report our own econometric analysis of the impact of foreign investment and foreign invested enterprises on China's economy. We do so because this type of analysis provides additional insights on the role of foreign investment on China's economy that are not available through other means.

The econometric literature on foreign direct investment in China addresses a wide range of questions, including the impact of foreign investment on overall economic performance, productivity, industrial structure, innovation, trade, domestic investment, employment and wages, inequality, and the environment. A particularly large literature focuses on the impact of foreign investment on the development and performance of indigenous firms, which is not surprising given the emphasis that China's leaders have always placed on foreign investment as a stimulus to improve the performance of Chinese firms. Researchers have also investigated whether the impact of foreign investment depends on the source countries, mode of entry (joint-venture versus wholly foreign-owned enterprises), industry, geography, or type of local firm (state-owned enterprises versus privately owned enterprises). The literature also examines different features of local economies in China that may affect the ability to benefit from foreign investment, such as local institutional strength, skill levels, infrastructure, and technological capabilities. The literature on social issues, such as regional inequalities, income disparities, and the environment, addresses the question of whether foreign investment works to help or hinder China in its efforts to address these issues.

In surveying the literature, we have tended to include works that are widely cited, that have been published in reputable publications, that cover issues of particular importance, and that provide a balance between works that have appeared in English and

Chinese. We also report results from our own analysis, where we have included issues of general interest, issues where we could check existing results (sometimes over extended time periods, using different variables, or using different statistical techniques), and where data was available to us.[2] The result is coverage of a broad range of impacts of foreign investment and foreign invested enterprises on China's development. The full results of our analysis are available separately.[3]

The literature in general provides support for a positive impact of foreign investment on China's economic growth, productivity, innovative capacity, trade, wages, and environmental performance (the latter when compared to indigenous enterprises). On the other hand, there is conflicting evidence regarding the impact of foreign investment on domestic investment, employment, and capacity in Chinese firms. Some works, for example, claim that foreign investment may 'crowd-out' domestic investment in some cases, and that there can be negative impacts in some regions within China where domestic firms compete with foreign firms or where the locations lack the ability to absorb the benefits of foreign investment. Our own results, covering extended time frames and using up-to-date statistical techniques, shows even stronger support for a positive impact of foreign investment, where even some of the 'negatives' associated with foreign investment (a negative impact on employment in some regions, for example) are due as much to a 'positive' impact of FDI (higher productivity that results in fewer workers required for similar levels of output) as to a negative. The overall results suggest a wide range of impacts of foreign investment supported by large amounts of historical data.

The vast majority of literature on the impact of foreign investment on the Chinese economy has actually been published in Chinese. This literature has focused on the impact of foreign investment on economic growth, productivity, innovation, industrial structure, domestic investment, employment and wages, inequality, trade, the environment, the financial sector, and others. What is particularly interesting is the topics that get substantial attention, including the impact of foreign investment on the productivity, innovation performance, export propensity, and efficiency of local Chinese firms; whether foreign investment promotes or hinders domestic investment; whether foreign investment increases or reduces regional disparities; and whether foreign investment is a positive or negative influence on the environment. On the other hand, there appears to be little research on the impact of foreign investment on consumer welfare or on foreign investment's potential to improve domestic institutions.

Background

Econometric analyses attempt to draw conclusions about the historical impact of one set of variables (representing foreign investment, for example) on another set of variables (economic performance, for example) using a variety of statistical techniques. This type of analysis can generate statistically defensible results in a way that is not possible to do through case studies and anecdotes. However, this type of analysis is limited by the availability of data and the tools with which to analyse the data. The basic idea is that there is some dependent variable whose value is hypothesized to be a function of a series of independent explanatory variables. The explanatory variables are often separated into 'control variables' (those that are either considered obvious or have been established by prior work) and 'variables of interest' (those that are the main subject of the specific study).

Many of the relations studied are of the following form:

Dependent Variable = f (Control Variables) + g (Variables of Interest) + an error term

Where f and g represent functions of the relevant variables. While we have used an 'additive' formulation for demonstration, in reality a wide range of functional forms can be employed depending on the specific relationship that is being tested. A variety of econometric and statistical techniques are used to estimate the key relationships between dependent and explanatory variables depending on the variable forms; functional forms; whether the data is longitudinal (the same variables over time), cross-section (the same variables across a range of cases at the same time, like provinces or cities or industries), or panel (both longitudinal and cross-section); and whether the relationships investigated are represented by a single equation or multiple equations.

Care must be used in interpreting the results of the econometric investigations. The models used are always simplifications of real life. In addition, researchers are often forced to use proxies to represent variables for which an actual measure does not exist. Econometric tests do not provide 'proof' of a relationship, instead they provide statistical evidence that either supports or does not support a proposition. The relationship between a dependent variable and an explanatory variable is termed 'statistically significant' if it can be shown that the relationship is positive (or negative) with a given probability, usually 95 percent. An effect can be 'statistically significant' and still be very small. Failure to find a 'statistically significant' relationship does not mean that the relationship does not exist; it means that given the data and analytical techniques available, the analysis does not provide support for the existence of the relationship.

Particular care must be used when attempting to examine the impact of foreign investment on economic performance. Foreign investment may have impacts that only show up in the longer run. Using current year FDI as an explanatory variable might only capture the impact of constructing a new facility, rather than the impact of the operation of that facility in later years. There can be a number of mediating features that influence the impact of foreign investment. The interpretation of coefficients on variables that represent absolute values (amount of FDI in a given year) is different from the interpretation of coefficients on variables that represent ratios (FDI / GDP or FDI / Total Investment). Furthermore, the impact of foreign investment on economic variables might shift over time, and might be sensitive to the precise specification of a given model.

Economic growth

Several works have found a positive impact of foreign investment on national economic growth or per capita economic growth for China, but a number of works have found a limited contribution or even a negative contribution. Other papers have compared economic growth across China's provinces as a function of foreign investment and have generally found a positive contribution to provincial level growth. However, some researchers have found a negative impact of certain types of foreign investment and of foreign investment in certain regions. This suggests the potential for complex relationships between foreign investment and economic growth that are linked not just to the activities of the foreign firms, but whether they displace the activities of local firms.

English literature

Whalley and Xin (2010) concluded that foreign invested enterprises (FIEs) in China might have contributed over 40 percent of China's economic growth in 2003 and 2004, and without foreign investment, China's overall GDP growth rate could have been 3.4 percentage points lower. Zhao (2013) concluded that an increase of 1 percent in the ratio of FDI to fixed asset investment was associated with an increase of 0.14 percent in GDP in China for the 1978 to 2008 period. Chaudhry et al. (2013) and Nica (2013) also found a strong positive relationship between foreign investment and GDP growth and GDP per capita growth. On the other hand, Liu et al. (2014) found that the impact of FDI on national real GDP growth was ambiguous, with FDI in a given year having a positive effect on real GDP growth in the next year, but a negative effect the year after. Yalta (2013) failed to find a statistically significant relationship between FDI and GDP growth for the 1982 to 2008 period and claimed this finding could be due to FDI having different and offsetting effects at the regional level. Wei (2010) found an ambiguous or slightly negative impact of FDI on GDP growth for the period from 1970 to 2006, possibly because China was growing from such a small base in the 1980s before the large influx of FDI.

Other papers have looked at the impact of foreign investment in China at the regional and provincial levels. Jiang (2015a) concluded that per worker FDI stock had a statistically significant positive impact on total factor productivity growth and output growth in China's regions from 1996 to 2011. Zhang (2006) concluded that FDI promoted growth in China's provinces from 1992 to 2004; the positive effect grew over time, and was stronger in the coastal than inland provinces. Chartas (2013) found a positive and statistically significant impact of FDI on economic growth across China's provinces in the 1985 to 2010 period. The impact was stronger from 1999 to 2010 than in the earlier period, and stronger in coastal provinces than in inland provinces. Yao and Wei (2007), in a study of output growth across China's provinces from 1979 to 2003, concluded that technological progress contributed 3.5 percent to 4.3 percent of aggregate annual economic growth and that FDI contributed up to 30 percent of total technological progress in that period.

Chinese literature

Zhong (2010) found that FDI stock had a positive effect on economic output in the same province as the investment (1986 to 2008) and a positive effect on economic output in other provinces too (1993 to 2008). Wei (2002) found a positive impact of FDI on GDP growth in the eastern part of China and a positive but not statistically significant impact on economic growth in the western part from 1985 to 1999. Guo and Luo (2009) found that both foreign investment and domestic investment contributed to economic growth in China's provinces from 1999 to 2006, but the marginal contribution of foreign investment to GDP growth was larger. Gao and Kang (2006) found that a 1 percent increase in FDI resulted in a 0.02 percent increase in GDP from 1997 to 2004. While this impact was statistically significant, it was small. Ma (2006) found that a 1 percent increase in the FDI to GDP ratio increased per capita GDP growth by 0.65 percent in single year analysis (2001), 0.671 percent in time series analysis for 1983 to 2003, and 0.367 percent in panel data analysis across 28 provinces from 1991 to 2002.

Jin and Fu (2011) found that FDI had a statistically significant positive relationship with GDP and that Chinese provinces with higher absorptive capacity benefited more from FDI in terms of GDP growth. Cheng and Liu (2010) found that FDI had a positive impact on GDP growth in Guangdong in the short run, but a negative impact in the long run, while the impact of FDI on Jiangsu's GDP growth was negative in the short run, but positive in the long run from 1985 to 2008. The Guangdong result is surprising given the continued importance of foreign investment in Guangdong's economy and Guangdong's rapid growth throughout the reform period.

Literature results

Much of this literature indicates a significant positive impact of foreign investment on economic growth and performance in China, with some notable exceptions. The impact depends on the state of development in the host economy, as well as the type, industry, and source of the foreign investment. It should be noted that capturing the impact of foreign investment on economic performance at the national level is complicated by the small sample size. Investigations at the provincial level tend to wind up assessing the relative contributions of foreign investment across provinces rather than absolute contributions. One must also take care in analyzing results that use different variables to represent the presence of foreign investment. The interpretation of the results for relative variables (FDI / GDP or FDI / Total Investment) can be different than for absolute value variables (amount of FDI received in a given year). Care must also be taken in that the impact of foreign investment on economic performance can have uncertain time lags.

Project results

Wang, Zhang, and An (2002) (WZA) published one of the more influential studies of the impact of FDI on economic growth in China. They used provincial level data from

1990 to 1998 and considered GDP growth to be dependent on the growth of domestic investment, the growth FDI, the growth of employment, and the level of human capital. They included control variables reflecting the marketization, export growth, and import growth in the local economy, and added terms reflecting the interaction of FDI with human capital, marketization, and domestic investment to see if these factors influenced the benefits from FDI. Their results indicated that FDI growth was positively related with GDP growth at the provincial level. Moreover, FDI had a large positive effect on GDP growth in the eastern region, a mild positive effect in the central region, and a minor positive effect in the western region. In their results, human capital did not have an accelerating impact on FDI, but a higher marketization rate (greater presence of the private sector) did.

We replicated the WZA tests using provincial panel data from 1986 to 2013, including 27 provinces, excluding Hainan, Chongqing, Tibet, and Qinghai due to data limitations. Similar to WZA, our results indicated that, in a longer period from 1986 to 2013, FDI growth was positively and statistically significantly related to the growth of GDP. Our results, like those of WZA, showed no statistically significant crowding-in or crowding-out of domestic investment. Our results also indicated that higher levels of marketization enhanced the positive impact of FDI on GDP growth, in agreement with WZA. Our results indicated that higher levels of human capital enhanced the positive contribution of FDI to GDP growth, which is different from WZA. We also found a strong positive impact of FDI on GDP growth in Eastern China, but a much weaker positive result for Central and Western China.

We further examined the impact of FDI on GDP growth in specific time periods (1985 to 1991, 1992 to 2001, 2002 to 2008, and 2009 to 2013) to capture the impact of foreign investment on China under the changed policy, environmental, and absorptive capacity circumstances. Depending on the formulation, the results indicated that the strongest relationship between FDI growth and GDP growth was in the last period (2009 to 2013), which is interesting given the fact that FDI has been diminishing as a percentage of capital formation and fixed investment in China. While conventional wisdom is that the impact of FDI on China's economy is diminishing, our results indicate that the impact of FDI on GDP had been more direct in recent years than previously.

Productivity

Researchers have examined the impact of FDI on the productivity of China, Chinese regions, Chinese industries, and Chinese firms directly or indirectly through its impact on innovation, technological capabilities, or human capital. Productivity is usually measured by total factor productivity (TFP) or labour productivity. Measurements of FDI include annual inflow of FDI and its lagged terms, the ratio of FDI to GDP, industrial output, or industrial value added, or the accumulated FDI stock. The main conclusion is that the impact of FDI on the productivity or innovation of Chinese regions and firms is generally positive, but not universally so. Some researchers found a positive relationship, some no significant relationship, and some a negative relationship. In addition, the effect can vary with the absorptive capacity of regions, the type of industry, and the origin and strategy of investing companies.

English literature

Hong and Sun (2011) found a statistically significant positive impact of FDI spill overs on TFP within and across China's regions for the 1980 to 2005 period. The authors found that a 10 percent increase in the ratio of FDI to total fixed asset investment would lead to more than 1 percent growth in the level of TFP and per capita income. The authors concluded that FDI can make important contributions to economic growth, and that the contribution from productivity enhancement was greater than through capital accumulation. Zhao and Niu (2013) found that FDI contributed by adding capital and by improving China's total factor productivity from 1990 to 2009 through the greater productivity of foreign firms, however that this impact was small.

Zhang et al. (2014) found that FDI provided significant impetus to higher technical efficiency across China's provinces from 1998 to 2012, but the effects varied by source country and local features (degree of marketization and level of human capital, for example). Du et al. (2011) found that investment from OECD countries enhanced the technical efficiency of domestic firms in the same industry, but investments from Hong Kong, Macau, and Taiwan had a negative effect or no impact. Tian et al. (2015) found that positive FDI technology spillovers were more likely to take place in joint ventures than in wholly foreign-owned enterprises, with wholly foreign-owned enterprises more likely to generate a market and skill stealing effect. Zhang (2014) found that FDI had large positive effects on China's industrial performance and that such effects were much greater on low-tech industries than on medium- and high-tech industries, and the contribution was enhanced by the interaction of foreign investment with local capabilities. Zhao and Niu (2013) found that FDI inflows had statistically significant positive direct effects and spillover effects on growth of capital-intensive industries, resource-intensive industries, and labour-intensive industries in China, and that the capital-intensive industries benefitted the most.

Liu et al. (2014) found that FDI had a positive effect on total factor productivity (TFP) growth in the east/coastal region, an insignificant impact in the central region, a negative impact in the western regions, and a negative impact at the national level from 1978 to 2011. Huang et al. (2012) found that there was a statistically significant positive relationship between FDI, regional innovation, and productivity spillovers from FDI across Chinese provinces from 1985 to 2008, but that FDI in a region generated positive spillovers only when the level of regional innovation reached a minimum threshold, and that the spillovers would increase substantially when a second higher threshold was reached. Fu (2008) found that FDI had a significant positive impact on regional innovation capacity across China's provinces from 1998 to 2004. FDI intensity was also positively associated with innovation efficiency in the host province, though the strength of this positive effect depended on the absorptive capacity and innovation-complementary assets in the province.

Several researchers have investigated whether foreign investment results in positive spillovers through horizontal linkages (spillovers within the same industry), backward linkages (spillovers to upstream supply chains), and forward linkages (spillovers to downstream firms). Jeon et al. (2013) found negative horizontal linkages (driven apparently by competition effects and most prominent in low-technology industries) and positive backward and forward spillovers. Long and Miura (2010) found a mixture of positive and negative horizontal spillovers, but generally positive vertical spillovers. Zhang (2005) found significant positive backward spillovers and agglomeration effects on TFP from foreign investment, but limited forward spillovers (perhaps due to the substantial portion of foreign investment in export-oriented firms where there would be no forward linkages in China). Du et al. (2011) found positive backward spillovers of FDI on local firms. FDI from OECD nations was also found to have positive horizontal spillovers, while that from Hong Kong, Taiwan, and Macau was not. The authors found that FDI had particularly large positive backward spillovers for state-owned enterprises, but only positive horizontal spillovers for non-SOEs. This means that SOEs benefitted as suppliers, but not when they were in direct competition with foreign firms.

Chinese literature

Sun et al. (2012) found that R&D investments by foreign firms had a significant positive impact on total factor productivity in 15 manufacturing industries in China from 2000 to 2009. Chen and Sheng (2008) found that local R&D stock and FDI both had positive effects on productivity in China's provinces from 1992 to 2006, with the impact more pronounced in the eastern part of China than in other regions. Qin and Zhang (2011) found that FDI generated positive horizontal and backward spillovers, but negative forward spillovers, to domestic firms from 2000 to 2007. FDI increased TFP and technical efficiency in domestic firms in the same industry through demonstration-imitation and competition effects, and in upstream firms through technology sharing and the setting of specifications. The negative forward spillovers meant that market power and lack of local linkages overcame any positive impacts for downstream industries. Wang et al. (2009) found that positive horizontal spillovers from FDI appeared only for higher productivity Chinese firms among firms covered in the 2004 national economic census. The impact of backward and forward spillovers tended to be negative for middle-to-high productivity firms and low-to-middle productivity firms, indicating that a threshold of development was needed for private firms to absorb horizontal and backward spillovers from FDI. Yang and Chen (2015) found that FDI resulted in positive horizontal spillovers to Chinese industrial enterprises from 2000 to 2006 and that the positive effects came mainly from indirect influences (foreign investment resulting in positive spillovers to upstream firms who then had positive spillovers to their other downstream customers). Moreover, they found that the spillover effects of FDI from

HMT (Hong Kong, Macau, and Taiwan) were much lower than those of FDI from non-HMT economies.

Lu (2008) found that foreign investment had positive spillover effects on private-domestic firms within the same city and industry of the investment from 1998 to 2005 and this effect was larger for firms that had better absorptive capabilities and those that could attract employees from foreign-owned firms. The impact on SOEs in the same industry and city was negative. Lu also found that national level FDI had negative spillover effects within the industry of the investment and the negative effect was stronger if the product similarity and competition between foreign-owned and domestic firms were higher and more direct. The demonstration/imitation effect apparently dominated within a city, but competitive effects dominated at the national level. Wang (2009) found a negative impact of foreign investment on technological progress of local firms in high-technology industries and an insignificant impact on lower technology industries from 2005 to 2006. The impact on technological progress in local firms in labour-intensive industries was insignificant and the impact on capital-intensive industries was negative. The results suggested that technology gaps between foreign and local firms in high-technology industries were too large for local firms to bridge so the latter lost out due to competitive effects, and that state-owned enterprises prominent in capital-intensive industries might have internal barriers to improvement.

The literature also indicated that absorptive capacity as reflected by human capital, infrastructure, and openness levels influenced the ability of Chinese provinces to benefit from technology spillovers from foreign investment (Lai et al. 2005; Li 2007). Xie and Wu (2014) found that FDI significantly improved TFP in China from 1992 to 2012, but this effect only manifests itself when the level of economic development, infrastructure, and human capital in the local environment exceeds a threshold level. He et al. (2014) found a double threshold effect, with moderate benefits for China's provinces from 2003 to 2007 that had reached a first threshold in economic development, human capital, and infrastructure, and greater benefits for those that had reached a second threshold.

Qin and Zhang (2011) found that the impact of FDI on TFP in firms in China from 2000 to 2007 depended on the nature of the industries investigated, with positive horizontal effects in 18 of the 23 industries studied, positive backward spillovers for TFP in 16 industries, and a negative forward spillover effect for TFP on downstream industries. FDI had a positive horizontal spillover effect on the technological progress of local firms in 11 industries (mostly labour-intensive industries) and a negative impact in nine industries (mostly machinery and equipment industries). FDI had a positive impact on the technological development of firms in 10 upstream industries and a negative impact on 11 upstream industries. FDI had a positive impact on technological development of local firms in 11 downstream industries and a negative impact in 12 downstream industries. The results clearly indicated that FDI spillovers can vary substantially by industry and by type of spillover (horizontal, forward, or backward).

Literature results

The research on the impacts of foreign investment on productivity in China indicates that foreign investment has increased productivity in China in part because foreign firms have been more productive than their Chinese counterparts. The impact of foreign investment on the productivity of domestic firms in China shows some strong positives and negatives. There is strong evidence that there are positive spillovers through horizontal and backward linkages, and these tend to dominate, but either no impact or a negative impact through forward spillovers. This could be due to industry mix, market focus (foreign companies focusing on international markets and domestic consumer markets rather than domestic industrial markets, for example), and business linkages. The impact of foreign investment varies by industry and by region, with regions with higher absorptive capacity benefitting the most from foreign investment (with some threshold effects). In addition, the impact could vary with the geographic distance between the foreign investment and the local companies. Private domestic companies appear to have benefited more than state-owned enterprises. However, the impacts vary by firm ownership, firm size, spillover channels, the foreign investor's entry mode, and the source economies of foreign investment. One reason for results that indicate insignificant or even negative impacts of foreign investment is that foreign firms compete with local firms. If foreign firms take market share away from local firms, then the impact of foreign investment on productivity can be negative. It is worth noting that there is a difference in goals between foreign invested enterprises, which generally wish to protect their technological and other advantages, and Chinese policy, which explicitly seeks to maximize the spillovers (or leakage) from foreign invested enterprises.

Project results

Productivity growth generally has three components: labour productivity, capital productivity, and total factor productivity. Labour productivity is usually measured by GDP per hour worked or GDP per employee. Capital productivity is usually measured in terms of output per unit of capital deployed. Multifactor productivity (MFP), or total factor productivity (TFP), is a residual that accounts for output growth beyond that explained by the rate of change in the services of labour, capital, and intermediate outputs, and is often interpreted as the contribution to economic growth made by factors such as technical and organizational innovation, but can include other factors, such as exports, human capital, FDI, and institutions as well. Our analysis focused on TFP and labour productivity.

TFP analysis

There are two ways to incorporate total factor productivity into the analysis. One way is to first calculate total factor productivity values from capital stock and labour input data and then perform the analysis with total factor productivity as the dependent variable in a second step. Another way is to incorporate capital stock and labour input data into a production function as independent variables in a regression in which GDP growth is the dependent variable and in which the FDI variable is designed to capture the influence of FDI on total factor productivity (Hong and Sun 2011; Yao and Wei 2007).

Yao and Wei (2007) (YW) were among the first to use the integrated, one-step method. Using provincial panel data for the period 1979 to 2003, the authors built a model that related GDP to capital stock, total labour force, measures of human capital, FDI, exports, the exchange rate, and transportation infrastructure. The analysis tested two types of impacts of foreign investment, improved efficiency within the existing production frontier and a shifting of the production frontier. Yao and Wei found that, at the national level, FDI/total investment and its cross term with time trend had significant and positive effects on output. Their results suggested that technological progress contributed 3.5 percent to 4.3 percent to aggregate economic growth on an annual basis and foreign investment contributed up to 30 percent of total technological progress. Given that FDI accounted for about 5 percent of total investment, the contribution to technological progress lends powerful support to the proposition that FDI is a shifter of China's production frontier over time.

Following YW, we built a similar model and extended the time period to 1985 to 2013. Provincial level data for 27 provinces was examined. The results for the longer time period were similar to those of YW, though of smaller magnitude, indicating that the frontier shifting role of FDI may have been lesser over the longer time period. Replacing the capital stock estimated using a single national depreciation rate with one estimated using province-specific depreciation rates (which should be a better estimate) and replacing a trade variable based solely on exports with one based on imports plus exports did not change the results.

In the two-step method, total factor productivity (TFP) is first estimated and then it is used as the dependent variable in regressions that include a foreign investment variable and control variables. Zhao and Niu (2013) used the two-step method, generating TFP estimates and then testing a simple three variable model for the direct effect of productivity advantages of foreign-funded enterprises over domestic firms and the indirect technology spillover effects from FIEs into the local economy using provincial data from 1990 to 2009. The authors found that foreign investment had a positive impact on technological improvement in China across the entire economy and within each of the primary, secondary, and tertiary sectors. However, the authors also claimed that the coefficients were small, the gap between the productivity of Chinese enterprises and foreign-funded enterprises was falling, and the overall quality of the FDI inflow was not high (as evidenced by relatively small spillovers).

We replicated this work by generating TFP estimates and examining FDI spillovers across China's provinces over an extended time period of 1985 to 2013. Preliminary analysis indicated that different statistical techniques from Zhao and Niu (2013) were necessary for the extended dataset.[4] The results indicate that the foreign invested sector not only had higher production efficiency than the domestic sector, but also had positive spillovers to the domestic sector that benefited China's economy. We then expanded the model to include additional control variables capturing the impacts of capital stock, R&D spending, government expenditures, marketization of the local economy, infrastructure, openness to trade, and human capital, which should allow a clearer separation of the impact of FDI on TFP. Our results indicated a strong positive relationship between FDI and TFP across several different formulations of the FDI variable. When we tested across regions, FDI had a strong positive impact on TFP in the eastern and western regions, with the impact larger on the eastern region, and a weak slightly negative impact on TFP in the central region.

Labour productivity

Foreign investment can also improve labour productivity in local companies and the local economy through demonstration effects, competition effects, and through the mobility of workers from foreign invested to local firms. We developed a model that included capital stock, FDI, education levels, openness, government spending, marketization, and infrastructure to test the impact of foreign investment on labour productivity in China. Analysis was carried out for China as a whole and for the three major regions. The results suggest that, after controlling for other variables, the higher the proportion of FDI in capital stock in a region, the higher the labour productivity in that region.

Innovation

Researchers have also investigated whether foreign investment improves the innovation performance of indigenous Chinese firms. Conventional wisdom would be that foreign investment would bring technological capabilities and competitive pressures that would stimulate innovation in a developing economy like China. On the other hand, there has been suspicion in China that foreign companies do not bring their best technology, that a great deal of foreign investment is in relatively low-technology industries or activities, and foreign companies do their best to protect their technology and therefore limit spillovers to local firms.

English literature

Cheung and Lin (2004) used provincial-level data for the period 1995 to 2000 and found that FDI had positive spillovers on the innovation activities of Chinese firms. Teixeira and Shu (2012) examined the relationship between FDI, human capital, and innovation at the corporate level using a survey of large and innovative firms (local and foreign invested) from 2005 to 2007. They found that the direct impact of foreign investment on the level of human capital in firms was negative (foreign-invested firms tended to perform human capital-intensive tasks abroad with less need to improve human capital in China than local firms). On the other hand, FDI had a positive indirect impact on human capital through investment in research and development activities, and through an overall impact on general human capital (i.e. formal education).

Chinese literature

Liu and Zhao (2009) examined the impact of foreign investment on local innovation capacity in China's provinces from 2000 to 2006 and found that foreign investment had a significant positive impact on design patenting by Chinese firms, a lesser but still positive influence on invention patenting, and a negative impact on utility patenting by local firms. The impact on all types of patenting was positive in the eastern region, positive but less so in the central region, and negative in the western region. Li and Zhang (2008) found a positive impact of foreign investment on innovation (measured by technology licensing and patenting) by indigenous companies in data spanning 29 regions in China from 2002 to 2006. The positive impact was stronger in the eastern region, smaller in the central region, and statistically insignificant in the western region. In addition, it appeared that foreign companies hiring talent away from local companies could result in lower innovation levels in the local companies. Hou and Guan (2006) reached similar main results to Liu and Zhao (2009) and Li and Zhang (2008), finding that foreign investment was positively associated with local firm patenting activity, with the biggest benefit in China's most innovative regions, and the smallest benefit in the least innovative regions.

On the other hand, Zhang (2008a) found that while factor endowments and technological opportunities had a positive impact on innovation capacity in Chinese firms, that the impact of FDI was not significant. Xian and Bo (2005) found that foreign investment was associated with an increase in innovative activity in domestic firms when the FDI was focused on serving the Chinese market and where technology gaps were small, but there was no effect when technology gaps were large or the FDI was export oriented. Jiang and Xia (2005) analysed the influence of foreign investment on the innovation capacity of local industries from 1998 to 2002 and found a negative impact due to competition effects as foreign firms outcompeted local firms resulting in some exit and overall reduced capacity in the local firms.

Literature results

The literature suggests a positive impact of foreign investment on innovation and innovation capacity in China, but again the results are mixed. Foreign investment is seen as increasing the patenting activity of local firms, with the biggest impact in the more advanced regions in China. On the other hand, there are limits to the benefits. If the technology gaps are too big between foreign and local firms, or the region does not have sufficient innovative capacity, or the local firms have other barriers to innovation, then foreign investment could have no effect, or even a negative effect on local innovation capacity. This perhaps explains the reluctance of China to open up some of its high-technology sectors to foreign firms and its attempts to force foreign firms to carry out more of their innovative activities in China and to share technology and results of innovative activities with Chinese enterprises.

Project results

Foreign investment, especially from industrialized countries to developing countries, is often believed to have a positive effect on innovation in the host country. Innovation, of course, can take place in any aspect of a business, including new technologies, new production and management processes, or new business practices. However, most investigations of the impact of foreign investment on innovation focus on technological innovation as measured by patenting. This is an extremely imperfect measure of innovation, as many scientific innovations are not patented or patentable, a simple count of patents says nothing about their importance, and patents fail to capture the huge range of potential innovations in business systems, strategies, management, government relations, and other areas. However, that is the measure that is often used.

In an influential paper on the impact of foreign investment on innovation in China, Liu and Zhao (2009) estimated the effect of FDI on innovation capabilities by analyzing R&D inputs, FDI spillovers, per capita income, and relative policy and environmental factors. The idea is that the innovation process is influenced by the inputs to research and development, the level of economic development (which is used as a proxy for the ability of a region to effectively use R&D inputs), and the educational background in the region (again used as a proxy for absorptive capacity). Using data on 31 provinces in China from 2000 to 2006, the authors found that FDI had a significant positive influence on China's overall innovation ability.

We replicated the tests of Liu and Zhao (2009) using provincial panel data for the period 1999 to 2013. Tibet and Qinghai were eliminated from consideration because of missing data in some years, leaving 29 provinces. Initial analysis indicated that different statistical methods than used in the original paper were appropriate.[5] Even so, the result that FDI has had a positive impact on patenting in China was confirmed. We also carried out investigations that used lagged variables (on the assumption that R&D inputs and FDI might influence patenting with a lag), eliminated a redundant variable, and added a variable for technology imports. The positive relationship between FDI and patenting was confirmed in an analysis that covered 28 provinces for the years 2001 to 2013.

In order to deal with the shortcomings of the patent measure, we also analysed the impact of foreign investment on technology transaction (outflow) value (TTV). Technology transaction outflow traces technology sales through licenses, leases, or other forms of contractual technology transfer. Although the information is gathered by

Chinese statistical authorities, we are not aware of any other research that uses TTV in analysis of the impacts of FDI on China's economy. Since the innovation inputs and FDI may take more than one year to have an impact on technological outputs, we used FDI and R&D expenditure and personnel variables lagged by two years, and included a technology imports variable (TECIMP) in the analysis. Interestingly, the FDI variables had a negative effect on TTV across China's provinces, indicating that while FDI has had a positive impact on patenting in China's provinces, that FDI apparently had a negative influence on the value of technology sold by the provinces. This might indicate that foreign companies have less incentive to sell locally developed technology beyond the regions in question, or that the technology generated by FDI or FDI spillovers was not particularly valuable on the open market.

Trade

One reason for China's opening to foreign investment was so China could build an export economy, initially through the exports of foreign firms and then through the exports of indigenous Chinese firms. Researchers have tended to focus on foreign investment's impact on overall exports, on exports by local firms, and on the overall export structure of China's economy. They have also examined the impacts of FDI from different source countries, through different spillover mechanisms, and on indigenous firms with different ownership structures. Again, the usual question is as much or more about whether foreign investment has improved the performance and sophistication of Chinese firms, as opposed to China's economy. The research has consistently shown that foreign investment has been an important driver of China's exports throughout the reform period, and that foreign investment has generated a positive impact on the export intensity and export participation of Chinese firms.

English literature

Zhang (2015) found that foreign investment was a key driver of China's exports from 2005 to 2011. However, foreign investment contributed more to export capacity than to export upgrading, which was viewed as consistent with the view that foreign companies used China for labour-intensive exports, and higher technology FDI was more related to the domestic market. Sun (2010) found that the presence of FDI significantly affected the probability of a firm becoming an exporter, but the impact depended positively on firm size and negatively on firm age, capital-intensity, and average wages across Chinese manufacturing industries from 2000 to 2003. Foreign investment also had significant impacts on the export intensity of domestic firms, with domestic firms that were bigger, older, more capital-intensive, and with higher average wages being less positively affected by the presence of FDI. These firms were viewed as more similar to the foreign-invested firms and, therefore, had less to learn from FIEs.

Chen et al. (2013) found that FDI had a positive impact on the export performance of indigenous firms in the same and in upstream industries in China from 2000 to 2003, but a negative impact on the export performance of indigenous firms in downstream industries. The positive horizontal spillovers were seen to come from technology spillovers (including imitation through reverse engineering and workers moving from foreign to domestic enterprises) and from export-related information spillovers (including leakage or spillover of export market intelligence, international marketing know-how, and other information from the export operations of FIEs). The positive spillovers from FIEs to domestic firms in the upstream industries were seen as coming from FIEs transferring technology to local suppliers, thus improving the domestic firms' productivity, competitiveness, and export performance. The negative effect of FIEs on the export performance of domestic firms in downstream industries was attributed to FIEs supplying each other more so than indigenous firms due to the differences in product quality standards, technology levels, and costs of doing business.

Wang et al. (2014) examined the impact of FDI on the exports and domestic sales of the indigenous firms in China and found that the presence of foreign firms as a whole was likely to have a negative impact on indigenous firms' domestic sales but a positive impact on their exports. The authors found that investment from Hong Kong, Macau, and Taiwan was more likely to generate this pattern of impact than firms from other countries. Buck et al. (2007) found that the presence of foreign firms in China resulted in market competition, information externalities, market access, and labour market spillovers that contributed to the incentives and abilities of Chinese firms to export. Fu (2011) found that export processing FDI generated less of a spillover effect on indigenous firm exports than other FDI from 2000 to 2007 due to the limited interaction of export processing entities with local firms.

Li et al. (2007) investigated the seeming paradox of foreign investment being associated with higher levels of trade, but deteriorating terms of trade in China. The authors concluded that foreign investment was attracted into labour-intensive, low value-added, highly competitive sectors in China to take advantage of the abundant labour supply. At the same time, FIEs often imported capital goods and advanced components that were less subject to price pressures and more subject to quality improvements and price increases. What the authors seem to have missed is that the FDI stimulated a large increase in China's net exports as well as exports over the period and that as a result China could purchase larger amounts of imports based on these exports even if the terms of trade (unit value of exports versus imports) fell. Thus the authors were focusing on a largely non-existent problem.

Chinese literature

Song (2013) found a positive impact of FDI on Chinese company exports across an industry-level panel database covering 2001 to 2009. This effect was largest for firms that had developed their own innovation capabilities, which were better able to absorb spillovers from the foreign firms. Wang and Guo (2007) found that foreign investment and foreign invested enterprises had a positive impact on China's imports and exports in the years 1980 to 2004 and that the impact had increased from 1996 to 2004. Wang and Feng (2006) reached similar results, finding a positive impact on imports and exports from 1992 to 2003 at the national level. At the regional level, only the positive results for the eastern region were statistically significant. Yang and Chen (2005) reached similar results in data covering 1979 to 2003. Yao (2007) found a positive relationship between foreign investment and exports in the three major regions of China from 1994 to 2004, with the largest impact on the eastern region.

A number of researchers have focused on the impact of foreign investment on China's overall export structure. Zhou (2014) found that FDI had a significant positive impact on the portion of exports in capital-intensive goods (the measure of structural improvement of exports adopted in the paper) from 1990 to 2011. Hu et al. (2013) also found a positive relationship between FDI and capital-intensive exports in China. Ding and Fu (2012) found a positive relationship between foreign investment and exports in China, with the biggest impact on low-technology exports, followed by high-technology exports, and then mid-tech exports. They concluded that foreign investment had diversified China's export profile, but had limited impact on upgrading China's export structure, in part because high-tech exports were mostly through export processing. FDI from Japan, Macau, Hong Kong, Taiwan, Korea, and Singapore had a larger influence on exports than investment from elsewhere due to the export-oriented investment from those economies.

Literature results

The literature indicates that FDI has been found to have a positive impact on the export performance of indigenous firms in the same industry as the foreign invested enterprises (through horizontal linkages) and in upstream industries (through backward linkages). These effects have been seen as the result of imitation, labour market effects, information spillovers, and in some cases direct technology sharing. The positive horizontal impacts tend to overcome the negative effects of competition from foreign firms. On the other hand, forward linkages from FIEs are seen as having no impact or a negative impact on the export performance of indigenous firms due to indirect competitive effects, a lack of local linkages, and/or the substantial portion of foreign investment in export processing, which by definition had little or no forward linkages in China. The impact of foreign investment on indigenous firm exports depends on the size, age, capital intensity, average wage, ownership structure, and geographical location of the indigenous companies. While the Chinese literature tends to find that FDI did not result in an 'upgrading' of China's export structure, the measures of industrial upgrading are coarse and not necessarily that informative. Export of 'capital-intensive' goods might reflect an upgrade, or not, versus other types of goods. Export of 'high-technology' goods might reflect an upgrade, or not, depending on whether they involve technology development in China, or just assembly of imported components. These measurement challenges make drawing conclusions on 'upgrading' from this literature problematic.

Project results

Wang and Feng (2006) used provincial data from 1992 to 2003 and found that FDI had a statistically significant export creation effect in China as a whole and in the eastern region, but that the impact of FDI on China's exports from the central and western regions was not statistically significant. We used a similar model to Wang and Feng and extended the time frame to cover provincial data from 1985 to 2013 and found that current year FDI had a statistically significant positive impact on trade, but FDI lagged by two years did not have a statistically significant impact. We investigated a more complex model that incorporated GDP, employment, wages, human capital, marketization, infrastructure, and the real exchange rate, and examined the impact of the explanatory variables on both exports and total trade. The coefficients on the FDI variables are positive and statistically significant in both models, indicating that FDI is a contributor to both exports and total trade in China, i.e. provinces with higher levels of FDI also had higher levels of trade, which is not surprising given the importance of foreign invested enterprises in China's trade reported in an earlier chapter.

Domestic investment

Another stream of literature investigates the impact of foreign investment on domestic investment in China. Researchers have studied whether foreign investment tends to stimulate more indigenous investment than would be the case otherwise (either in the same sector, vertically related sectors, or horizontally related sectors), which would be a 'crowding-in' effect, or whether foreign investment would act to reduce the indigenous investment that would otherwise take place, which would be a 'crowding-out' effect. While on the surface, this might seem a secondary issue compared to the overall impact on China's economy, the reality is that China's leaders have looked for foreign investment to strengthen the indigenous economy, not for foreign investment to displace indigenous investment. This helps explain the large amount of attention that Chinese researchers in particular have paid to this issue.

English literature

In a study that focused on 300 cities in three regions of China from 1991 to 2008, Zhang (2011) found that FDI had a negative long-term impact (crowding-out) on domestic investment in the eastern region. In the central region, FDI was found to have a significantly positive (crowding-in) effect on domestic investment. There was no explicit effect of FDI on domestic investment in Western China. The author argued that the findings were in line with the view that FDI was more likely to displace domestic investment in economically advanced areas, where the industrial structure was more mature and production approached its full capacity, and that there was too little investment in Western China to have an impact. It turned out that the above results were mostly due to impacts in the pre-2001 period, and in the latter period the impact on foreign investment was less negative in the eastern region, still positive in the central region, and still had no impact on the western region. Liu et al. (2014) found similar results to Zhang (2011) for the period 1978 to 2011 and concluded that the crowding-out effect of FDI on domestic investment at the national level, and in the eastern region significantly weakened the expected positive effect of FDI on output growth. He (2012) concluded that foreign investment had tended to crowd-out domestic investment in China and that financial deregulation had increased the crowding-out effect. The author viewed financial deregulation as providing preferential policies to foreign firms that put domestic firms in an inferior position.

In contrast, Wu et al. (2012) concluded that foreign investment had a long-term crowding-in effect in the Yangtze River Delta region. The authors claimed that an increase of one unit of FDI was associated with an increase of 2.42 units of domestic investment. At the national level, some papers indicated that FDI accelerated capital formation, complemented domestic investment, and thus stimulated stronger economic growth and a stronger indigenous economy (Nica, 2013; Wei, 2010; Tang 2007).

Chinese literature

Yang and Shen (2002) analysed national level FDI data from 1983 to 1999 and concluded that foreign investment had a significant crowding-out effect on domestic investment. They reasoned that this could be due to foreign investment concentrating in highly competitive industries and foreign companies not having the same linkages with local suppliers as local firms. However, this paper used 'ratio' variables to indicate both the domestic and foreign direct investments, so it not surprising that if the FDI/GDP ratio goes up that the Domestic Investment/GDP ratio goes down, leaving the 'crowding-out' conclusion questionable. Gao and Kang (2006) found a crowding-out effect of FDI from 1997 to 1999 and a crowding-in effect from 2000 to 2004, claiming that preferential policies gave foreign companies advantages over domestic companies in the early years, but that policies changed, China's firms eventually improved, more foreign-invested firms entered, and foreign firms generated new backward and forward linkages that stimulated domestic investment. Wang, Xiong, and Yang (2015) found almost the opposite, a statistically significant positive effect of foreign investment on domestic investment from 1990 to 2001 and a statistically significant negative impact from 2002 to 2011. Both papers suggest that the impact was time dependent, which was perhaps not surprising given the vast changes in China over the years.

Xian and Ou (2008) found support for the crowding-in hypothesis from 2003 to 2006, concluding that FDI inflows had a positive impact on domestic investment overall, with a significant positive impact on industries with low entry barriers and a negative but statistically insignificant impact on industries with high entry barriers. Xu (2006) found that foreign investment resulted in crowding-in at the national level. At the regional level, 14 provinces exhibited a significant crowding-in effect while eight exhibited a significant crowding-out effect and seven exhibited no significant effects. Notably, eight of the 11 coastal provinces in the sample exhibited a crowding-in effect, but three of the largest recipients of FDI, Guangdong, Tianjin, and Jiangsu, exhibited crowding-out.

Wang and Li (2004) cautioned that papers that used relative variables (FDI in a ratio to GDP or total investment) rather than absolute variables (amounts of FDI) to investigate the crowding-in and crowding-out effects could be subject to misinterpretation, as the coefficients on the relative variables could be negative if the impact of the numerator was positive, but that of the denominator more positive. In their own work, the authors found a statistically significant crowding-out effect of FDI on domestic investment at the national level, a statistically significant crowding-out effect for the eastern part of China, but a statistically significant crowding-in effect for the central part of China. There were no statistically significant results for the western part of China.

Literature results

The focus on whether foreign investment 'crowds-in' or 'crowds-out' domestic investment is an interesting one, and one where the results need to be interpreted with care. On the one hand, foreign investment can help generate new supply chains, create business, and create linkages with foreign markets. On the other hand, it can result in losses of market share by domestic firms. The literature on the impact of foreign investment on domestic investment in China is mixed. However, there are issues with some of this literature. For example, most scholars have used investment rates, ratios of total investment, foreign investment and domestic investment to GDP as indicators to test the crowding-in versus crowding-out phenomenons. The trouble with such terms is that the analysis cannot distinguish between situations in which foreign investment truly crowds out domestic investment versus situations in which it crowds in domestic investment, but to a lesser extent that other domestic investment (domestic investment induces more domestic investment than is induced by foreign investment). Thus care must be taken in interpreting the results of studies of crowding-out and crowding-in.

One feature lacking from this literature is a sense of whether there has been an overall displacement of local investment, particularly in industries or in locations where local companies had not developed extensively before the inflow of foreign investment. Guangdong Province, for example, had a history of economic underperformance before China's economic opening, and much of the province's economy has relied on foreign investment. Another question is whether domestic capital 'crowded-out' by foreign investment has simply been allocated to other economic activities, perhaps in other provinces, not captured in the various analyses. If, for example, foreign investment in coastal regions resulted in domestic capital being deployed into the central and western parts of China, then some of the tests in the papers of this section could have shown a 'crowding-out' effect on a regional basis even if there was no impact or even a positive effect on China as a whole. The results on 'crowding-in' versus 'crowding out' appear to be very sensitive to the particular model specification, time period, and region investigated. Some researchers have claimed that crowding-out results from earlier periods may have been due to foreign firms competing with domestic firms in highly competitive sectors and in more advanced regions that were opened first. Subsequently, the nature of foreign investment evolved as did the capabilities and ability to compete of Chinese firms, potentially shifting the balance.

Project results

Wang and Li (2004) explicitly questioned the results on crowding-in and crowding-out from models that used relative FDI and investment variables. They tested a relatively simple model using FDI, investment, and GDP variables in relative and absolute terms in a panel dataset covering 30 provinces in China from 1987 to 2001. They found that FDI had a statistically significant negative effect (crowding-out) on domestic investment at the national level. In the regional analysis, they found a significant crowding-out effect of FDI on domestic investment in eastern provinces, a significant crowding-in effect in the central provinces, and no statistically significant results in the western provinces. This result indicated that, in the eastern region, the high economic development level and the high capability of local firms made the domestic firms and foreign firms most likely to target the same market segments, but that local firms were still not competitive enough to compete with foreign firms. The authors claimed that an unfair environment created by favourable tax policies for foreign firms aggravated the disadvantages of domestic firms.

We replicated the Wang and Li (2004) analysis using panel data for 27 provinces from 1985 to 2013. Initial tests indicated that statistical techniques different than those used by Wang and Li were appropriate for the data.[6] Our results, using appropriate statistical techniques and a longer time frame, indicate that the inflow of FDI has a crowding-in effect on domestic investment at the national level, in direct contradiction to the Wang and Li results. We note that our analysis contradicts perhaps the most important 'negative' results associated with FDI in the literature, that some of the literature claims that FDI crowds-out domestic investment at the national level.

Given the simplicity of the Wang and Li model, we subsequently developed a model that incorporates additional control variables (based on Luo 2006; Wang and Li 2004; Wang, Xiong, and Yang 2015). As suggested by Wang and Li (2004), we used absolute values (rather than ratios) for domestic investment, FDI, and GDP. Control variables included government expenditure, openness, marketization, condition of loans by financial institutions, and transportation infrastructure. Using panel data for 27 provinces for the period 1985 and 2013 we found that FDI had a positive effect on domestic investment within the same region and nationally, again contradicting Wang and Li's original national result.

We then tested for cross-region effects. The logic is that even if FDI displaces or crowds out investment in one province or region, the capital freed up may well be redeployed in other provinces or regions in China, thus generating benefits in these provinces or regions that would not be captured by the usual approach. This test has not to our knowledge been reported previously and could be an important contribution to this literature. In particular, we tested for impacts of FDI in the eastern region on domestic investment in the central and western regions. We found that current year FDI into the eastern region had a positive and statistically significant impact on domestic investment in the central and western regions, but prior year FDI had a negative and statistically significant impact on domestic investment in the central and western regions. Since the magnitude of the positive impact outweighed the negative, the overall effect was positive. The explanation could be that foreign investment in the eastern region freed up domestic capital for investment in the central and western regions in the current year, but the creation of competitive production in the eastern region could have a negative impact on domestic investment in the other regions in the future. Again, the overall impact was positive and we believe this cross-regional result may be the first of its kind reported in the literature.

Employment and wages

Various researchers have argued that foreign investment is a two-edged sword for employment in China. On the one hand, foreign investment creates demand for labour by building and staffing new facilities, and creates indirect labour demand through upstream and downstream linkages in the local economy. On the other hand, foreign investment can reduce employment when the establishment of foreign firms increases labour productivity to the point where less labour is needed, crowds-out local firms, or forces local firms to improve their efficiency and thus reduce the demand for labour. The challenge is how to accurately model, measure, and test for the potentially contradictory effects in order to draw clear conclusions. The results in this literature vary, with a higher employment growth rate in foreign-invested firms than domestic firms, and a positive impact of FDI share in an industry on the employment growth of private Chinese firms, but a limited impact of foreign investment on the overall employment level in China.

The general presumption is that increases in foreign investment will increase wages in the host economy. However, the way wage rates get measured can influence the results. In China, for example, foreign investment in labour-intensive industries attracted tens of millions of people from the countryside into the urban workforce. If these people were employed at wages lower than the previously prevailing urban average wage, then foreign direct investment would appear to reduce the average measured (urban) wage even though the new urban workers would see a substantial rise in their own incomes from their previous (usually unmeasured) rate.

English literature

Karlsson et al. (2009) examined the effect of FDI on employment in China based on firm-level information during the periods 1998 to 2001 and 2001 to 2004. The authors found that foreign and private domestic firms had comparable growth in employment, while employment in non-private domestic firms decreased. Only when they controlled for firm survival rates did they find higher employment growth in foreign firms than in private domestic firms. The conclusion was that employment growth was higher in foreign firms than in the reference group due to a higher survival rate in foreign firms. The authors found a positive indirect impact of FDI on employment growth of privately owned domestic firms, presumably because spillovers and learning or demonstration effects were more important than the effect of competition. Liu et al. (2015) examined the employment effects of foreign acquisitions and found that acquisition by foreign firms increased the employment level of the acquired firms, but had no impact on their employment growth, indicating that the employment effects of foreign acquisition were one-off.

Hale and Long (2011) found that foreign-invested firms paid higher average wages to skilled and unskilled labour. However, the wage differential between foreign-invested companies and local companies was much smaller for ordinary workers than for skilled workers. Another interesting finding was that the presence of foreign investment in a city had a strong positive impact on the wages and quality of skilled workers in domestic private firms, but that the impact was far less on workers in SOEs. The authors claimed this could be due to SOEs having protected markets, soft budget constraints, or rigid internal systems compared to other Chinese firms. Zhao (2001) concluded that foreign invested enterprises (FIEs) had to pay much higher wages to employ skilled labour, but did not have to do so for unskilled labour, due to the relative abundance of unskilled labour and the privileged position of skilled labour in state enterprises in which most skilled labour had been employed. Liu et al. (2015) found that foreign acquisitions of domestic firms had significant positive effects on the levels of wages of target firms, but an insignificant impact on wage growth (i.e. the impact was apparently one-off).

Chinese literature

Wang (2015) found a positive impact of foreign investment on employment in China in the years 1989 to 2010, though this impact decreased after 2005. The author claimed the latter result could have been due to foreign investment focusing on less labour-intensive industries and activities in the latter period. Li et al. (2014) found a positive impact of foreign investment on employment in China's provinces from 1998 to 2010, with the largest effect on eastern provinces, and the smallest on western provinces. Wen and Tan (2010) found that foreign investment positively influenced employment at the national level from 1985 to 2008, but the effect diminished after China's WTO entry. In the eastern region, the effect was positive in the pre-WTO period, but insignificant afterwards. For the central and western regions, the impact of foreign investment was positive, but only significant after WTO entry.

Wang and Zhang (2005) found a positive direct effect and a negative indirect effect (through crowding-out and competition) of FDI on employment in China from 1983 to 2002, with the positive direct effect outweighing the negative, resulting in the creation of 4.7 million jobs from 1994 to 2002. Yan and Guo (2012) found a statistically insignificant direct impact of FDI on employment in Chinese provinces from 1998 to 2012, but a statistically significant positive indirect employment impact, with the latter outweighing the former to yield an overall positive result. The different results in the two papers can be due to different time frames, different variables used to measure the impact of foreign investment, and difficulty in isolating direct and indirect employment effects.

Mao (2009) found a negative impact of FDI on employment in labour-intensive industries, possibly due to limited spillovers and foreign companies outcompeting or crowding-out local firms, thus reducing employment. In capital-intensive industries, the short-term impact was negative and the longer-term impact positive. Luo and Chen (2014) found that in Chinese provinces with limited human capital that FDI had a positive effect on low-skilled employment and a negative effect on high-skilled employment, and that in provinces with higher levels of human capital that foreign investment had a positive impact on high-skilled employment and a negative impact on low-skilled employment in the years 2002 to 2012. The first set of results was apparently due to foreign companies only placing low-level activities in interior provinces and higher level activities in coastal provinces.

Researchers have also investigated the impact of foreign investment on wages in China. Xu (2015) found that foreign investment had a negative impact on the wage to revenue ratio in China from 1995 to 2007. On the other hand, Wang, Li, and Liu (2015) found that foreign enterprises had a higher labour share in income than domestic firms in the service sector in China and the entry of foreign firms resulted in local firms increasing the labour share of income. This result was not necessarily conflicting with Xu (2015) as Wang, Li, and Liu only addressed the service sector. Qiao et al. (2015) found that foreign investment had a positive impact on labour's share of income across China's provinces from 1978 to 1994. In a regional breakdown, the impact was negative in eastern provinces, but positive in China's other regions. Liang (2010) found that foreign investment had a positive impact on wage rates in Chinese firms from 2000 to 2003. Shao and Bao (2010) concluded that foreign investment had a positive impact on local wages across 36 industries in China from 1999 to 2006, with the positive impact resulting from a strong positive impact on wages for unskilled labour and an insignificant impact on wages for higher skilled labour. Xu et al. (2009) analysed data from the annual survey of industrial firms for 1999 to 2001 and found that foreign companies paid higher wages than local firms, that local firms adjusted by paying higher wages themselves, and the effect varied by region. Chen and Zhou (2009) reached similar conclusions. Yang and Yang (2004) also found a positive effect of FDI on local wages, though they claimed this effect only emerged after 1997.

Literature results

The literature indicates that foreign investment overall has been a positive for employment and for wages in China. This means that foreign investment has, through the employment that it has generated directly and indirectly, more than compensated for any reduction in employment due to competition effects and greater efficiency. The impact on wages has also been positive, though overall economic growth is likely to have been a larger factor than foreign investment itself. The impact has varied over time and it will be interesting to see the extent to which foreign investment continues to have these effects as China's economy further develops and as China moves from labour surpluses to labour shortages. One issue in interpreting the results on the impact of foreign investment on employment and wages is the fact that there are relatively few works in the international literature that address these issues. In addition, the results may be affected by the specific environment in China, in which state-owned enterprises, which once dominated the Chinese economy and undertook a huge social employment burden, underwent a process of reform that resulted in massive layoffs. Another issue is that labour has become much scarcer in China in recent years due to population policies and China's economic growth, which means that the impact of foreign investment on employment and wages could be very different going forward from what it was in the past.

Project results

Li et al. (2014) (LWS) used a simple model to examine the impact of FDI on employment and average wages in China using provincial level panel data from 1998 to 2010. They found that FDI had a positive impact on employment in China's provinces, though the contribution was smaller than that of domestic investment. The contribution of FDI to employment was largest in the eastern region, second largest in the central region, and smallest in the western region. The authors further found that the inflow of FDI appeared to result in an increase in the average wage level in China at the national level and in the eastern region of China, but in a decrease in the average wage level in the central and western regions. The latter result could have been due to foreign investment bringing more people into the formal or urban work force, but at wages (on average) below that of the previous average. Thus the result does not suggest so much that FDI depressed wages, but rather FDI expanded the formal or urban workforce.

We extended the LWS analysis using provincial panel data from 1985 to 2013 and found that FDI was associated with a positive impact on employment at the national level and in the central and western regions, but a negative impact on employment for the eastern region, indicating that FDI may have contributed to a reduction in employment, perhaps through greater efficiency and competitive effects in that region in the extended period. Domestic investment had a large and statistically significant impact on employment nationally and in all three major regions. FDI had a strong positive impact on average wages nationally and in the eastern region, and a positive, but not statistically significant, impact on average wages in the central and western regions. When we matched the period of the LWS results, we found no statistically significant impact of FDI on employment, indicating some differences in statistical methods may have influenced the results. When we added in several additional control variables, including GDP, exports, imports, average wages, education levels, government spending, transportation infrastructure, and portion of employment in the private sector, the apparent impact of FDI on employment was negative. However, this result must be viewed carefully as FDI had been shown to positively influence some of these other variables, so part of its impact may have been absorbed by those variables in the analysis.

Wang and Zhang (2005) estimated the direct impact of FDI on employment and the indirect impact of FDI on employment through its impact on domestic investment and labour productivity using data from 1983 to 2002, and found a positive direct effect of FDI on employment and a negative indirect effect through crowding-out of domestic investment and increased labour productivity (which reduces the need for labour per unit of output). Taking reference to their work, we developed a model that related employment to domestic investment, foreign investment, average wages, and labour productivity to estimate the direct and indirect impact of FDI on employment and a second model that included a wider range of control variables, and ran the models from 1985 to 2013. Similar results were obtained, that is, FDI had a positive direct impact on employment, but a negative indirect impact by (small) crowding-out some domestic investment and by improving labour productivity, with the overall effect being positive.

Inequality

China has great disparities in per capita income, economic growth, and productivity between rural and urban regions, coastal and inland areas, and within the coastal region. Such disparities are shaped by many factors, such as the initial development state of the regions, location, natural resources, government policies, domestic investment, and cultural factors. There is also a view that foreign investment could be a source of inequality and a literature has emerged to address this question. An undercurrent in the Chinese literature is that in some senses foreign investment at times appears to be 'blamed' for being a cause of inequality or it is hoped that foreign investment will help reduce inequality. On the other hand, foreign investment has been restricted in China, often on a geographic basis, and presumably foreign investors will tend to gravitate toward markets and production locations where the workforces and infrastructure are suitable, just like local companies.

English literature

The empirical literature on the impact of foreign investment on regional disparities has shown mixed results. Liu et al. (2014) concluded that FDI resulted in higher total investment in the coastal region, but lower total investment in the interior region, and that FDI widened the growth gap between the east and west through physical capital accumulation. Dayal-Gulati and Husain (2000) showed that FDI flows contributed to greater inequality across provinces in the period of 1978 to 1997. Tang (2007) also found that FDI had a significant impact on regional income inequality in China by widening the difference in incomes across regions.

On the other hand, Yu et al. (2011) found that differences in stock of foreign direct investment accounted for just 2 percent of regional income inequality across China's provinces from 1990 to 2005. Differences in total investment, mostly due to domestic investment, accounted for over 50 percent of the income inequality across provinces. The other two important determinants of regional income inequality were province location and educational level. Yu et al. argued that FDI stock should not be viewed as the cause of China's regional income inequality, and that the Chinese Government should promote increases in domestic physical and human capital investment into the more backward provinces. Wei et al. (2009) and Yao and Wei (2007), in investigations covering 1979 to 2003, found that it was the uneven distribution of FDI, rather than FDI itself, that had been a cause of regional income inequality. As a result, in order to reduce regional inequality, they argued that FDI should be encouraged and directed toward the west and central regions through preferential policies, government intervention, and investments in capacity building to allow the inland regions to attract and absorb FDI.

Chinese literature

Yu and Lu (2014) studied provincial income distributions in China from 1995 to 2010 and concluded that foreign investment was associated with widening income inequality in China since foreign companies tended to focus on lower-technology production in China and performed high value activities elsewhere, thus limiting spillovers to local firms. Peng (2013) found that foreign investment was associated with an increase in urban–rural income gaps since most of the investment was in cities and that rural workers, even those that moved to the cities, often had to take low-paid jobs while the urban residents took the higher paying jobs. Sheng and Wei (2012) found that foreign investment tended to reduce urban–rural income disparities from 1998 to 2010, with the largest effect in the eastern region. The authors claimed that export processing, which attracted substantial numbers of rural workers to the cities, resulted in wages higher than the workers could earn in the rural sector. On the other hand, the rural workers tended to be in jobs with low wages and competitive labour markets, while urban workers were often in higher-skilled occupations where shortages of skills pushed up wages, thus increasing the income gap.

Chen et al. (2009) found that foreign investment tended to increase manufacturing wages in general and to reduce the gap between manufacturing workers in a province across 29 industries from 1998 to 2006. Since most foreign investment was into the eastern region, the result was also higher wage disparities across regions. Shen and Pan

(2008) found that foreign investment was associated with increased income disparities within Chinese provinces from 1987 to 2003 and that the biggest impact was in
the eastern region, followed by the western region, and then the central region. Zhou
(2006) found similar results across China's provinces from 1985 to 2003. Dai et al.
(2007) found that foreign investment was associated with increased income disparities
from 1979 to 2004, with the most significant effect on the urban disparities (within
a city), followed by national disparities (income distribution at the national level),
and followed by the urban–rural income ratio. On urban poverty, Zhang and Zhang
(2007) found that the inflow of FDI increased the income share of the poorest groups
(the lowest 5, 10, and 20 percent by income), which meant the inflow of FDI reduced
the income disparity in urban China as least for this quintile. Individuals at the lowest
10 percent of income, however, did not benefit as much as individuals in the 10 to
20 percent range.

Literature results

The literature suggests that foreign investment has contributed to income disparities
in China mostly through its positive impact on locations that have attracted foreign
investment, rather than negative impacts on other areas. This raises the question of
whether it is the responsibility of foreign investors to try to close income gaps across
regions that might be due to other forces or whether it is the responsibility of local and
national governments to make more places attractive to foreign companies and to give
more places the absorptive capacity necessary to maximize the benefits from foreign
investment. The reality is that the location of foreign investment has been influenced
by government policy, the state of markets, the state of the labour force, the state of
infrastructure, and the state of domestic investment across provinces. These all have
had much larger impacts on inequality than foreign investment. To the extent that
China wishes foreign investment to help in closing the gaps across provinces, these
underlying forces need to be addressed.

Project results

One approach to analyzing whether foreign investment produces more or less inequality in China is to examine the impact on the potential convergence of incomes across
China's provinces and see if foreign investment has contributed to a convergence or
divergence in incomes across regions in China. Wei et al. (2009) (WYL) used a panel
dataset covering all Chinese regions from 1979 to 2003 and found that the initially
poorer provinces did not have higher growth than the initially richer ones and thus
failed to catch up and that FDI contributed to the growing disparities between regions,
mostly because most FDI went into the more affluent eastern region.

We replicated the Wei et al. (2009) analysis using a panel of 27 provinces for the
period 1989 and 2013, and dividing the data into five non-overlapping intervals of

four years each (1989–1993, 1994–1998, 1999–2003, 2004–2008, and 2009–2013). Our results indicated that FDI contributed positively to growth in all regions, but that incomes in China's provinces did not converge but diverged. These results did not change when we included additional control variables for marketization and government expenditures, and substituted other indicators for several variables. So the result on convergence and divergence does not suggest that FDI was in any sense 'bad' for a province, but rather the fact that most FDI went into richer regions (which were also the regions opened first to foreign investment) tended to exacerbate existing inequalities.

Another question is whether foreign investment can be directly related to differences in income levels across provinces within regions in China. We generated another model to examine whether income differences between and within the eastern, central, and western regions are related to foreign investment. FDI was positively related to per capita GDP in China's provinces, so that higher levels of foreign investment in a province were associated with higher income levels in that province. This impact held across regions, again indicating that FDI was positive for host provinces and regions, but that FDI contributes to inequality by flowing preferentially into affluent regions.

The environment

In recent years, the impact of foreign investment on China's environment has become a key focus of FDI research. This has been due to the deterioration of China's environment that has occurred with economic growth and the increasing importance of sustainable development in Chinese policy. The results of this literature have been mixed. Some papers focusing on the early part of China's reform period found support for a 'pollution haven' hypothesis for investment from other parts of Asia in which foreign companies placed polluting activities in regions with less stringent environmental regulations. Some papers found that increasing foreign firm activity corresponded with increased pollution in some sectors, which is not surprising given that higher levels of economic activity are often associated with higher levels of pollution. Studies that have compared the environmental performance of foreign firms with domestic firms generally find that firms from OECD countries have the best environmental performance, followed by other foreign firms, followed by indigenous firms.

English literature

Di (2007) found that foreign firms in polluting industries in the years 1992 to 1995 tended to locate in provinces with lower abatement costs, 'dirtier' firms tended to locate in less developed provinces, firms in pollution-intensive industries were more sensitive to local regulation than firms in other industries, and firms in polluting industries tended to locate in provinces where they had more bargaining power with respect to local governments. Dean et al. (2009) found that Hong Kong, Taiwan, and

Macau firms in polluting industries shied away from provinces with stricter environmental regulations from 1993 to 1996, but that other foreign invested enterprises did not. Cole et al. (2011) found that increases in industrial output were associated with increases in industrial pollution from 2001 to 2004. Overseas investment was associated with statistically significant increases in pollution, but the magnitudes were less than for domestic investment with the exception of emissions of petroleum residues. The authors claimed that the latter result was due to disproportionate foreign investment into sectors that discharged petroleum waste. Zhang (2008b) found that economic growth was associated with environmental degradation in China, that domestic firm investment was the most polluting, HMT (Hong Kong, Macau, and Taiwan) investment was next, and that investment from other countries (mostly from the OECD) was the least polluting (with the exception of petroleum-related emissions). The author took the results to indicate that the 'other' firms had superior environmental practices, but that industry mix and local regulations could also affect emissions.

Wang and Chen (2014) found that FDI aggravated pollution, as measured by sulphur dioxide emissions relative to local investment across Chinese cities from 2000 to 2009. The authors claimed that weak and inconsistent environmental regulations and local government pursuit of economic growth combined to explain the negative environmental externalities brought about by FDI. He (2008) found a positive, but small impact of FDI on air pollution across Chinese cities from 1993 to 2001, and attributed the impacts mainly to scale effects (i.e. more economic activity meant more pollution). Jiang (2015b) found that FDI was associated with higher levels of SO_2 emission through the greater use of natural resources, impact on industrial mix (a relative increase in output in industries that polluted due to FDI), and impact on TFP (with an increase in TFP associated positively with economic development but also with more pollution) across Chinese provinces from 1997 to 2012. Song et al. (2015) also found a link between foreign investment, economic development, and environmental pollution and concluded that only a quarter of Chinese provinces had reached a development threshold where they could benefit from spillovers from foreign investment on innovation capacity without harming the environment.

Yang et al. (2013) compared the impact of foreign investment and domestic investment on pollution across Chinese provinces from 1992 to 2008 and separated the impacts into those due to economic scale, sectoral composition, and pollution intensity. The authors found that foreign investment was associated with lower levels of pollution compared to domestic investment for most, but not all, pollutants assessed. In the case of solid waste, foreign investment was associated with a 63 percent reduction compared to domestic investment of similar amounts, while for industrial dust emissions the reduction was 80 percent. The authors concluded that from an environmental standpoint, foreign investment should be encouraged.

Chinese literature

He and Wang (2012) investigated the impact of urbanization and foreign investment on pollution across China's provinces from 1997 to 2010 and found that FDI was associated with higher levels of waste water pollution (an economic activity effect), but there was no significant relationship with several other pollutants. Since the paper did not include domestic investment in the analysis, there was no way of telling whether foreign investment was more or less likely to result in pollution. Similarly, Su and Zhou (2010) found that a 1 percent increase in FDI was associated with a 0.035 percent increase in waste water emission on average. Sha and Shi (2006) looked at the impact of foreign investment on waste gas emission across China's provinces from 1999 to 2004 and found that a 1 percent increase in foreign-owned assets resulted in a 0.35 percent increase in waste gas emission. No comparison with domestic investment was provided. Lu et al.(2014) compared the environmental impact of foreign investment versus domestic investment on waste water and SO_2 emission. The authors found that while both FDI and domestic investment increased the waste water emission in a city, the impact of domestic investment on the environment was smaller than for foreign investment. The results for SO_2 emissions showed that foreign investment had less of an environmental impact than domestic investment.

Yang (2015) found that the impact of FDI on the environment depended on the amount and concentration of FDI across 227 cities from 2004 to 2012. Below a low threshold, foreign investment was associated with higher levels of pollution. Between two thresholds, FDI was associated with higher levels of pollution but with smaller impact. Above the second threshold, FDI was associated with lower levels of pollution. Yang and Lu (2014) analysed data from 247 Chinese cities from 2000 to 2011 and found that foreign investment was negatively associated with environmental pollution (greater concentration of foreign investment meant less pollution), and that the effect was higher in locations with higher per capita income levels for per capita waste water emissions. Guo et al. (2013) found that FDI had a negative impact on carbon emissions (i.e. lower emissions) in a dataset covering China's provinces from 1999 to 2010. The authors stressed that their finding was that there was an absolute decline in carbon emissions associated with foreign investment, not just a relative decline.

Xiao and Fang (2013) found that FDI was associated with lower pollution across several pollutants for 11 eastern provinces from 1995 to 2009. The impact varied by region, with FDI associated with lower per capita carbon emission in the Bohai Rim area, but higher per capita emissions in the Yangtze Delta area. The authors claimed that the last result could be because state-owned enterprises were more important in the Bohai area and that foreign companies continued to have superior environmental performance versus these firms. In the Yangtze Delta area, the authors claimed that local private-sector companies adapted more quickly, thereby reducing the gap in environmental performance and the apparent influence of FDI. Yao and Ni (2013) found that foreign investment was associated with a reduction in the carbon intensity (carbon emission/GDP) of China's development across its provinces from 1996 to 2008.

Sheng and Lv (2012) found that foreign investment was associated with higher levels of SO_2 pollution through scale (more economic activity) and structure (changing industrial structure) effects, but that the pollution reducing effect on technology (use of better technologies by foreign companies and by local companies that adjusted) was much larger. They concluded that a 1 percent increase in FDI intensity resulted in a 0.1 percent increase in SO_2 emission through the scale effect, a 0.17 percent increase due to the structure effect, and a 1.15 percent decrease in emission through the technology effect, leading to a net reduction of 0.87 percent in emissions. Guo and Han (2008) did a similar breakdown of effects (scale, structure, and technology) for nine different pollutants and found that FDI was associated with higher levels of pollution through the scale effect, but lower impact through the structure and technology effects resulting in a lower overall impact. Yu and Qi (2007) did a similar analysis for SO_2 emissions but found that FDI was associated with higher pollution levels through scale effects, higher levels through the structure effect, and lower levels through the technology effect, but this time the first two effects (more pollution) outweighed the latter.

Literature results

The language literature on the impact of foreign investment on the environment in China shows mixed results. Foreign investment is seen as contributing to emission of pollutants in China due to scale effects (more economic activity) and industry mix effects (some foreign companies have invested in industries that are more polluting than other industries). In addition, some foreign companies appear to have selected locations in China based in part on the stringency (or lack thereof) of environmental regulations. On the other hand, foreign companies have been shown to be less polluting than indigenous companies and to have brought higher environmental standards from their home countries. In addition, technological improvement, imitation, environmental standards, and know-how can actually result in less pollution in absolute terms than there would have been without the foreign investment. While such a result has a limited range of applicability (an infinite amount of FDI would not result in less pollution), it is the result over the range covered by the data in many of the studies. This result goes beyond a result that a foreign-invested facility might emit less pollution than a similar facility owned and operated by a local company and suggests that FIEs could play an important role in China's stated ambition to substantially improve its environmental performance.

Project results

We examined the impact of FDI on environment quality in China using models based on those found in the literature on panel data for 31 provinces for the period 2000 and

2013. We used per capita SO_2 and SO_2 per unit of GDP as dependent variables, as these were the variables for which the most complete data could be obtained. This single test was, of course, much narrower than the many tests found in the literature. Control variables representing total capital formation, per capita GDP, education levels, trade performance, government expenditures, infrastructure, and technical progress were also included. The results indicated that foreign investment had a negative impact on pollution (i.e. less pollution) whether we measured foreign investment using the share of FDI in total investment, FDI stock, or share of FDI stock in total capital stock. In each case, the results indicated a negative association between foreign investment and pollution and a positive association of domestic investment and pollution, indicating that foreign invested enterprises have had significantly better environmental performance than local firms. These findings duplicate those reported in the literature on the relative environmental performance of foreign firms versus domestic firm.

Conclusions

Several of the main conclusions of this literature are as one might expect. Most studies have found that inflows of foreign investment have made a substantial positive contribution to China's economic output and economic growth. This result holds throughout the different phases of China's opening and reforms. The impact of foreign investment on growth has differed by the host region within China, as well as characteristics of the investing companies. Some studies have found that foreign investment contributed more to economic growth than indigenous investment, though other studies (particularly in the Chinese literature) found the opposite.

There were a few surprising results, such as one Chinese paper that concluded that foreign investment had a negative long-run impact on the Guangdong economy. This is particularly surprising given that Guangdong was economically backward before China's economic opening and most industrial output from the province comes from foreign invested enterprises even today. Another Chinese paper found export-oriented investment and investment into high-technology industries had a negative impact on economic growth. The apparent reason was that export processing (including export processing in high-technology industries) had relatively low value added in China and as a result might use resources that could have had higher value added in other activities. These may be cases in which the actual variables used might not measure the desired concept.

The English language literature on the impacts of foreign investment on productivity in China indicates that foreign investment has increased productivity in China in part because foreign firms have been more productive than their Chinese counterparts and in part due to spill overs to local firms. Private domestic companies appear to have benefited more than state-owned enterprises from spill overs. However, the impacts of spill overs vary by firm ownership, firm size, spill over channels, the foreign investor's entry mode, and the source economies of foreign investment. One reason for results that indicate insignificant or even negative impacts of foreign investment is that foreign firms compete with local firms. If foreign firms take market share away from local firms, then the impact of foreign investment on productivity can be negative. In addition, some regions might not have the absorptive capacity to capture the benefits of spill overs from foreign investment.

In the Chinese literature, the results of the impact of FDI on productivity in China are largely positive. Foreign invested enterprises were generally more productive than domestic enterprises, so their presence represented a productivity gain for China as a whole. The impact of foreign investment on the productivity of domestic firms in China shows some positives and negatives. There is strong evidence that there are positive spill overs through horizontal and backward linkages, and these tend to dominate, but either no impact or a negative impact through forward spill overs. This could be due to industry mix, market focus (foreign companies focusing on international markets and domestic consumer markets rather than domestic industrial markets, for example), and business linkages. The impact of foreign investment varies by industry and by region, with regions with higher absorptive capacity benefitting the most from foreign investment (with some threshold effects). In addition, the impact could vary with the geographic distance between the foreign investment and the local companies. Again, the results indicate a positive impact of foreign investment on productivity in general, but not to all Chinese regions and firms.

With respect to innovation, the English literature reports a significant positive impact of foreign investment on innovation in China in general and as well as on Chinese firms through imitation, demonstration effects, and spill overs. The Chinese literature suggests a positive impact of foreign investment on innovation and innovation capacity in China, but with some mixed results. Foreign investment is seen as increasing the patenting activity of local firms. On the other hand, if the technology gaps are too big between foreign and local firms, or the region does not have sufficient innovative capacity, or the local firms have other barriers to innovation, then foreign investment could have no effect, or even a negative effect on local innovation capacity. This perhaps explains the reluctance of China to open up some of its high-technology sectors to foreign firms and its attempts to force foreign firms to carry out more of their innovative activities in China and to share technology and results of innovative activities with Chinese enterprises.

Both the English and Chinese literature indicate that foreign direct investment has also been an important driver of China's trade, with foreign companies adding substantially to China's exports, imports, and net export position, and also providing a strong stimulus to exports of indigenous companies. The literature indicates that FDI has been found to have a positive impact on the export performance of indigenous firms in the same industry as the foreign invested enterprises (through horizontal linkages) and in upstream industries (through backward linkages). On the other hand, forward linkages from FIEs are seen as having no impact or a negative impact on the export performance of indigenous firms due to indirect competitive effects, a lack of local linkages, and/or the substantial portion of foreign investment in export processing, which by definition had little or no forward linkages in China. The impact of foreign investment on indigenous firm exports depends on the size, age, capital intensity, average wage, ownership structure, and geographical location of the indigenous companies.

Much of the literature on the impact of foreign investment on investment in China has focused on whether foreign investment induces more or less domestic investment than might be the case otherwise. The results on the impact of foreign investment on domestic investment have been mixed. In the English literature, some studies have indicated that there have been 'crowding-out' effects overall and in the eastern part of China, especially in the early reform period, and that preferential policies for foreign investors might have contributed by putting domestic firms in an inferior position. Other papers found that foreign investment accelerated capital formation, complemented domestic investment, and thus stimulated stronger economic growth and a stronger indigenous economy. The Chinese literature also has shown mixed results. Some papers claimed a negative impact of foreign investment on local investment has been found for the early reform period, with a reversal after 1999. Other papers claimed the opposite. Both indicated that the impact has been dependent on time and policy mix. The impact has varied with the nature of entry barriers in the industry, and by region, with about half of China's provinces showing a positive impact, about a quarter showing a negative impact, and about a quarter no significant impact. The results appear to be sensitive to the particular model specification, time period, and region investigated, which means that the results of any particular analysis must be interpreted with care.

The English literature on the impact of foreign investment on employment and wages generally has found a higher employment growth rate in foreign-invested firms and a positive impact of FDI share in an industry on the employment growth of private Chinese firms, but a limited impact of foreign investment on the overall employment level in China. The Chinese literature indicates that foreign investment has been a positive for employment and for wages in China. This means that regardless of whether there has been a crowding-out impact on local companies, that foreign investment has, through the employment that it has generated directly and indirectly, more than compensated for any reduction in employment due to competition effects and greater efficiency. The impact on wages has also been positive, though overall economic growth is likely to have been a larger factor. The impact has varied over time and it will be interesting to see the extent to which foreign investment continues to have these effects as China's economy further develops and as China moves from labour surpluses to labour shortages.

Both the English and Chinese literature suggest that foreign investment has contributed to regional inequality in China, mostly through its positive impact on locations that have attracted foreign investment, rather than negative impacts on other areas. While the results might cast foreign investment in a negative light, the reality is that the location of foreign investment has been influenced by government policy, the state of markets, the labour force, infrastructure, and domestic investment across provinces. These all have had much larger impacts on inequality than foreign investment.

To the extent that China wishes foreign investment to help in closing the gaps across provinces, these underlying forces need to be addressed to make the less developed provinces more attractive to foreign investment.

The English and Chinese language literatures on the impact of foreign investment on the environment in China show mixed results. In some works, foreign investment is seen as contributing to emission of pollutants in China due to scale effects (more economic activity) and industry mix effects (some foreign companies have invested in industries that are more polluting than other industries). In addition, some foreign companies appear to have selected locations in China based in part on the stringency (or lack thereof) of environmental regulations. On the other hand, foreign companies have been shown to be less polluting than indigenous companies and to have brought higher environmental standards from their home countries. In some cases, researchers have found that through competition, displacement, and imitation effects that foreign investment has actually resulted in a net reduction of emissions. Some of the differences in results in this area reflect the wide variety of foreign invested enterprises in China, industry differences, and differences in provinces across China, including local environmental regulations and their enforcement.

Both the English and Chinese literatures found that the impact of foreign investment can differ by the source country of investment. Investment from Hong Kong, Macau, and Taiwan (HMT) has been found to provide smaller, or even negative, productivity spill overs into domestic firms, while the impact of investment from other locations has generally been positive and larger. Investment from HMT has had a negative impact on domestic sales of local firms, and was more likely to avoid provinces that had stricter environmental regulations and enforcement. Investment from Asian economies had a bigger impact on China's exports than investment from other countries. Investment from OECD countries was associated with greater positive productivity spill overs to Chinese firms in general in terms of efficiency, but negative impacts on technological capabilities through competition effects. Investment from OECD countries was also found to be less polluting than investment from other places or from local firms.

Both the English and Chinese literatures found that the impact of foreign investment can differ by the host province or region. In general, the eastern region, China's most advanced economically, has been seen as benefitting more from foreign investment in terms of economic growth, productivity, exports, innovation, and employment than other regions. On the other hand, the impact of foreign investment on investment by local companies in the eastern region was found to be negative, while it was positive in other parts of China. The various results could be explained by greater absorptive capability in the eastern region on the one hand, and the existence of a larger and deeper industrial base which could be hurt by foreign competition on the other hand.

Our own results provide strong support for the positive impact on foreign investment for the vast majority of economic performance indicators examined. Foreign investment is seen as having positive impacts on GDP, GDP growth, productivity, innovation (as measured by patenting), trade, domestic investment, wages, and the environment. A negative relationship between foreign investment and the value of outbound technology transaction value was found, perhaps indicating that through the time of investigation foreign-funded technology was not widely sold outside the area in which it was developed. Mixed results were found on employment, which on further breakdowns appears to be the case because foreign investment in some investigations has a positive direct impact on employment, but a negative indirect impact on employment due in part to increased labour productivity (which reduces the need for labour) on some regions in China. We also note that our results contradict the national level 'crowding-out' effect reported in some of the literature. In addition, we found evidence for a new effect, that is foreign investment in one region actually stimulating investment in other regions, either through a crowding-in effect, or by freeing up capital from one region that could be used in another.

We note that the econometric literature differs greatly from what appears in the international press on foreign investment and foreign companies in China. It differs substantially from the individual company stories, anecdotes, and case studies found in the business press. It also differs considerably from the surveys of foreign companies that focus on the opportunities and challenges faced by foreign firms operating in China. The econometric literature, particularly in the Chinese language, focuses much more on how policies to attract foreign investment placed local firms at a disadvantage, how the presence of foreign companies can have negative as well as positive impacts on Chinese companies, how foreign investment might help or hurt when it comes to certain social issues in China, and how policies are put in place to try to obtain the maximum benefit from foreign investment.

This disconnect reflects differences in goals between foreign invested enterprises and Chinese policy makers. The foreign companies wish to make profits, while the Chinese policy makers want to develop the Chinese economy, and in particular Chinese companies. The foreign companies generally want to protect their intellectual property, safeguard their know-how, and preserve their technological and other advantages. Chinese policy makers, on the other hand, want to maximize the spill over effects in order to strengthen indigenous firms. Seen in this light, policies that allow foreign companies to participate in some sectors only through joint venture, and policy initiatives designed to get foreign companies to share more of their intellectual property with local firms are perhaps more understandable to outside observers. Even so, the strong positive results for the impact of foreign investment on China's economy reported in this chapter, when combined with those of other chapters, indicate the strong benefits that China has received from openness to foreign investment.

Notes

1 Supporting work for this chapter was carried by Dr. Sophie Zhang of Enright, Scott & Associates.

2 Data sources included: *China Data Online*, CEIC data, *Statistical Yearbooks* for the 31 Provinces, *Educational Statistical Yearbooks*, *Labor Statistical Yearbooks*, *Science and Technology Statistical Yearbooks*, *Scientific Activity Statistical Yearbooks for Industrial Enterprises*, *Statistical*

Yearbooks of Investment in Fixed Assets, China Trade and External Economic Statistical Yearbooks, China FDI Statistics, and the Index of Marketization of China's Provinces Report (1997–2009).
3 See Enright, Scott & Associates (2016), The Impact of Foreign Investment on China: Phase 3: Econometric Tests, Hong Kong, The Hinrich Foundation.
4 We used system GMM (General Method of Moments) methods to perform the analysis.
5 We used system Generalized Method of Moments techniques instead of Liu and Zhao's Generalized Least Squares approach.
6 We used system GMM while Wang and Li used cross-section weighting to estimate the model with the national sample and Seemingly Unrelated Regression (SUR) for regional analysis.

References

Buck, T., X. Liu, Y. Wei, and X. Liu, 2007, 'The Trade Development Path and Export Spillovers in China: A Missing Link?', Management International Review, 47, pp. 683–706.

Chartas, V., 2013, The Impact of Foreign Direct Investment on Economic Growth in China, Master's Thesis, Erasmus School of Economics.

Chaudhry, N.I., A. Mehmood, and M.S. Mehmood, 2013, 'Empirical Relationship Between Foreign Direct Investment and Economic Growth: An ARDL Co-Integration Approach for China', China Finance Review International, 3(1), pp. 26–41.

Chen, C., Y. Sheng, and C. Findlay, 2013, 'Export Spillovers of FDI on China's Domestic Firms', Review of International Economics, 21(5), pp. 841–56.

Chen, J. and Y. Sheng, 2008, '[An Empirical Study on FDI International Knowledge Spillovers and Regional Economic Development in China]', Economic Research Journal, no. 12, (in Chinese).

Chen, Y. and S. Zhou, 2009, '[The Effect of FDI on Wages in Domestic-Funded Firms – An Empirical Study Based on China's Inter-provincial Panel Data]', Journal of Nanjing Agricultural University (Social Sciences Edition), no. 2, (in Chinese).

Chen, Y., S. Zhou, and H. Wang, 2009, '[The Effect of Foreign Direct Investment on the Income Gap: An Empirical Study Based on Wages GINI Coefficient of Manufacturing]', World Economy Study, no. 5, (in Chinese).

Cheng, P. and X. Liu, 2010, '[Differential Research on Foreign Direct Investment's Impact on the Sustainable Growth of Regional Economy – An Empirical Research Based on Guangdong and Jiangsu]', China Industrial Economics, no. 9, (in Chinese).

Cheung, K.Y and P. Lin, 2004, 'Spillover Effects of FDI on Innovation in China: Evidence from the Provincial Data', China Economic Review, 15, pp. 25–44.

Cole, M.A., R.J.R. Elliott, and J. Zhang, 2011, 'Growth, Foreign Direct Investment, and the Environment: Evidence from Chinese Cities', Journal of Regional Science, 51(1), pp. 121–38.

Dai, F., Y. Wang, and X. Jiang, 2007, '[Influences of FDI to Host Country's Income Distribution: Based on the Data of China]', Journal of International Trade, no. 9, (in Chinese).

Dayal-Gulati, A. and A.M. Husain, 2000, 'Centripetal Forces in China's Economic Take-off', IMF Working Paper.

Dean, J.M., M.E. Lovely, and H. Wang, 2009, 'Are Foreign Investors Attracted to Weak Environmental Regulations? Evaluating the Evidence from China', Journal of Development Economics, 90, pp. 1–13.

Di, W., 2007. 'Pollution Abatement Cost Savings and FDI Inflows to Polluting Sectors in China', *Environment and Development Economics*, 12, pp. 775–98.

Ding, Y. and Y. Fu, 2012, '[The Impact of FDI on China's Technical Export Structure: A Dynamic Panel Data Analysis]', *World Economy Study*, no. 10, (in Chinese).

Du, L., A. Harrison, and G. Jefferson, 2011, 'Do Institutions Matter for FDI Spillovers? Implication of China's Special Characteristics', *Policy Research Working Paper no. 5757*, World Bank Working Paper.

Enright, Scott and Associates, 2016, *The Impact of Foreign Investment on China: Phase 3: Econometric Tests*, Hong Kong, The Hinrich Foundation.

Fu, X., 2008, *Foreign Direct Investment, Absorptive Capacity and Regional Innovation Capabilities: Evidence from China*, OECD Global Forum on International Investment.

Fu, X., 2011, 'Processing Trade, FDI and the Exports of Indigenous Firms: Firm-level Evidence from Technology-intensive Industries in China', *Oxford Bulletin of Economics and Statistics*, 73, pp. 792–817.

Gao, T. and S. Kang, 2006, '[Dynamic Analysis of the Impacts of FDI on the Chinese Economy]', *The Journal of World Economy*, no. 4, (in Chinese).

Guo, H. and L. Han, 2008, '[Foreign Direct Investment, Environmental Regulation and Environmental Pollution]', *Journal of International Trade*, no. 8, (in Chinese).

Guo, P., G. Jiang, and S. Zhang, 2013, '[The Effect of Foreign Direct Investment on China's Carbon Emissions – An Empirical Study Based on Provincial Panel Data]', *Journal of Central University of Finance and Economics*, no. 1, (in Chinese).

Guo, X. and Z. Luo, 2009, '[The Impact of FDI Characteristics on Economic Growth in China: An Empirical Research]', *Economic Research Journal*, no. 5, (in Chinese).

Hale, G. and C. Long, 2011, 'Did Foreign Direct Investment Put an Upward Pressure on Wages in China?', *IMF Economic Review*, 59(3), pp. 404–30.

He, J., 2008. 'Foreign Direct Investment and Air Pollution in China: Evidence from Chinese Cities', *Région et Développement*, 28, pp. 132–50.

He, Q., 2012, 'Gradual Financial Liberalization, FDI, and Domestic Investment: Evidence from China's Panel Data', *Journal of Developing Areas*, 46(1), pp. 1–15.

He, X., Y. Ou, W. Shi, and Y. Liu, 2014, '[Technology Spillovers of FDI and the Absorptive Capability Threshold of China]', *The Journal of World Economy*, no. 10, (in Chinese).

He, Y. and L. Wang, 2012, '[Impact of Urbanization and FDI on Environment Pollution]', *Reform of Economic System*, no. 3, (in Chinese).

Hong, E. and L. Sun, 2011, 'Foreign Direct Investment and Total Factor Productivity in China: A Spatial Dynamic Panel Analysis', *Oxford Bulletin of Economics and Statistics*, 73(6), pp. 771–91.

Hou, R. and J. Guan, 2006, '[The Impact of FDI on China Regional Innovation Capacity]', *China Soft Science*, no.5, (in Chinese).

Hu, F., D. Lian, and Y. Xu, 2013, '[Foreign Direct Investment Effect on China's Export Trade Structure]', *International Business*, no. 1, (in Chinese).

Huang, L., X. Liu, and L. Xu, 2012, 'Regional Innovation and Spillover Effects of Foreign Direct Investment in China: A Threshold Approach', *Regional Studies*, 46(5), pp. 583–96.

Jeon, Y., B.I. Park, and P.N. Ghauri, 2013, 'Foreign Direct Investment Spillover Effects in China: Are they Different Across Industries with Different Technological Levels?', *China Economic Review*, 26, pp. 105–17.

Jiang, D. and L. Xia, 2005, '[The Empirical Study of the Function of FDI on Innovation in China's High-tech Industries]', *Journal of World Economy*, no. 8, (in Chinese).

Jiang, Y., 2015a, 'Potential Effects of Foreign Direct Investment on Development', in Y. Jiang, ed, *China: Trade, Foreign Direct Investment, and Development Strategies*, Oxford, Chandos, Chapter 5.

Jiang, Y., 2015b, 'Foreign Direct Investment, Pollution, and the Environmental Quality: A Model with Empirical Evidence from the Chinese Regions', *International Trade Journal*, 29(3), pp. 212–27.

Jin, N. and Q. Fu, 2011, '[Study of the Impacts of FDI Based on Technological Absorptive Capacity on Economic Growth – Evaluation on 28 Provinces in Mainland China using IVQR]', *R&D Management*, 23(2), (in Chinese).

Karlsson, S., N. Lundin, F. Sjöholm, and P. He, 2009, 'Foreign Firms and Chinese Employment', *World Economy*, 32(1), pp. 178–201.

Lai, M., Q. Bao, S. Peng, and X. Zhang, 2005, '[Foreign Direct Investment and Technology Spillover: A Theoretical Explanation of Absorptive Capability]', *Economic Research Journal*, no. 8, (in Chinese).

Li, H., P. Huang, and J. Li, 2007, 'China's FDI Net Inflow and Deterioration of Terms of Trade: Paradox and Explanation', *China & World Economy*, 15(1), pp. 87–95.

Li, X., 2007, '[Research on the Absorptive Capability of Technology Spillover From Foreign Direct Investment]', *Journal of International Trade*, no. 12, (in Chinese).

Li, X. and X. Zhang, 2008, '[Analysis of Different Regional Effect of FDI on Innovative Capacity in China]', *China Industrial Economics*, no. 9, (in Chinese).

Li, Y., K. Wang, and Y. Sun, 2014, '[The Employment Impact of FDI from the Host Country Stand Point]', *Macro Economy Study*, no. 12, (in Chinese).

Liang, Y., 2010, '[Econometric Analysis of the Impact of FDI Inflows on the Employment and Wages of Domestic Firms]', *Modern Finance & Economics*, no.5, (in Chinese).

Liu, Q., R. Lu, and C. Zhang, 2015, 'The Labour Market Effect of Foreign Acquisitions: Evidence from Chinese Manufacturing Firms', *China Economic Review*, 32, pp. 110–20.

Liu, X., Y. Luo, Z. Qiu, and R. Zhang, 2014, 'FDI and Economic Development: Evidence from China's Regional Growth', *Emerging Markets Finance & Trade*, 50 (Supplement 6), pp. 87–106.

Liu, X. and H. Zhao, 2009, '[Empirical Research on the Impact of FDI on China's Indigenous Innovation Capability]', *Management World*, no. 6, (in Chinese).

Long, C. and H. Miura, 2010, 'Where to Find Positive Productivity Spillovers from FDI in China: Disaggregated Analysis', *Hong Kong Institute for Monetary Research Working Paper*.

Lu, J., 2008, '[Does Foreign Direct Investment Benefit Chinese Indigenous Firms? Effects and Channels]', *Economic Research Journal*, no. 6, (in Chinese).

Lu, J., J. Yang, and H. Shao, 2014, '[FDI, Human Capital and Environmental Pollution in China: A Quantile Regression Analysis Based on Panel Data of 249 Cities]', *Journal of International Trade*, no. 4, (in Chinese).

Luo, C., 2006, '[The Impact of FDI on Private Capital in China]', *Journal of World Economy*, no.1, (in Chinese).

Luo, J. and J. Chen, 2014, '[FDI, Human Capital Threshold and Employment: An Analysis Based on Threshold Effect]', *World Economy Studies*, no. 7, (in Chinese).

Ma, Y., 2006, '[The Impact of Foreign Direct Investment on Economic Growth of China]', *Statistical Research*, no. 3, (in Chinese).

Mao, R., 2009, '[Export, FDI and Employment in Manufacturing Industries of China]', *Economic Research Journal*, no. 11, (in Chinese).

Nica, A., 2013, *Essays on the Impact of Foreign Direct Investment and Saving in China*, PhD Thesis, University of Iowa.

Peng, W., 2013, '[Empirical Study on the Foreign Direct Investment and the Income Gap between Urban and Rural in China]', *Journal of Central University of Finance & Economics*, no. 1, (in Chinese).

Qiao, M., G. Li, and S. Gao, 2015, '[Time and Spatial Impact of FDI on China's Labour Income to Revenue Ratio]', *International Economic Cooperation*, no. 2, (in Chinese).

Qin, Y. and S. Zhang, 2011, '[Spillover Mechanism of FDI on China's Industrial Enterprises' Productivities]', *China Industrial Economy*, no. 11, (in Chinese).

Sha, W. and T. Shi, 2006, '[The Environmental Impact of Foreign Direct Investment: Empirical Analysis Based on Provincial Panel Data]', *World Economy Studies*, no. 6, (in Chinese).

Shao, M. and Q. Bao, 2010, '[Impact of Foreign Investment on Domestic Wages: An Empirical Analysis Based on Industrial Panel Data]', *Journal of International Trade*, no. 11, (in Chinese).

Shen, Y. and S. Pan, 2008, '[An Empirical Analysis on the Relationship Between FDI and Regional Income Disparity]', *Journal of International Trade*, no. 2, (in Chinese).

Sheng, B. and Y. Lv, 2012, '[Impact of Foreign Direct Investment on China's Environment: An Empirical Study Based on Industrial Panel Data]', *Social Sciences in China*, no. 5, (in Chinese).

Sheng, B. and F. Wei, 2012, '[The Impact of Foreign Direct Investment on China's Urban-rural Income Gap: An Empirical Test Based on China's Provincial Panel Data]', *Contemporary Finance & Economics*, no. 5, (in Chinese).

Song, H., 2013, '[The Empirical Analysis of Effect FDI on Export Volume of Domestic Firms in China]', *Journal of Xi'an University of Finance and Economics*, no. 3, (in Chinese).

Song, M., J. Tao, and S. Wang, 2015, 'FDI, Technology Spillovers and Green Innovation in China: Analysis Based on Data Envelopment Analysis', *Annals of Operations Research*, 228, pp. 47–64.

Su, Z. and W. Zhou, 2010, '[Dynamic Effect of FDI on the Environment and the Regional Differential in China: Heterogeneity Analysis Based on the Panel Data by Province and Dynamic Panel Data Model]', *World Economy Study*, no. 6, (in Chinese).

Sun, S., 2010, 'Heterogeneity of FDI Export Spillovers and its Policy Implications: The Experience of China', *Asian Economic Journal*, 24(4), pp. 289–303.

Sun, X., J. Wang, and H. Zheng, 2012, '[The Influence of R&D Spillover on Total Factor Productivity of China Manufacturing Industry: The Empirical Test on Three Ways of R&D Spillover Through Inter-industry, International Trade and FDI]', *Nankai Economic Studies*, no. 5, (in Chinese).

Tang, S., 2007, *Foreign Direct Investment and its Impact in China: A Time Series Analysis*, PhD Thesis, Griffith University.

Teixeira, A.A.C and L. Shu, 2012, 'The Level of Human Capital in Innovative Firms Located in China. Is Foreign Capital Relevant?', *Journal of the Asia Pacific Economy*, 17(2), pp. 343–60.

Tian, X., V.I. Lo, and M. Song, 2015, 'FDI Technology Spillovers in China: Implications for Development Areas', *Proceedings of the Australasian Conference on Business and Social Sciences 2015*, Sydney.

Wang, C., J. Zhang, and H. An, 2002, '[Foreign Direct Investment, Regional Difference and China's Economic Growth]', *World Economy*, no. 4, (in Chinese).

Wang, D.T. and W.Y. Chen, 2014, 'Foreign Direct Investment, Institutional Development, and Environmental Externalities: Evidence from China', *Journal of Environmental Management*, 135, pp. 81–90.

Wang, H. and X. Guo, 2007, '[FDI's Influence on the Scale of Export and Import of China – Empirical Study Based on Virtual Variables, Co-integration and Granger Test]', *Journal of International Trade*, no. 3, (in Chinese).

Wang, J., Y. Wei, X. Liu, C. Wang, and H. Lin, 2014, 'Simultaneous Impact of the Presence of Foreign MNEs on Indigenous Firms' Exports and Domestic Sales', *Management International Review*, 54, pp. 195–223.

Wang, J. and H. Zhang, 2005, '[Empirical Test on the FDI Effect on Employment in China]', *World Economy Research*, no. 9, (in Chinese).

Wang, S. and F. Feng, 2006, '[Impact of FDI on the Trade Performance of China and the Regional Differentiation of the Impact: Analysis Based on a Dynamic Panel Data Model]', *Journal of World Economy*, no. 8, (in Chinese).

Wang, X., L. Li, and P. Liu, 2015, '[FDI Participation, Labour Income Share and Skill Wage Premium: An Empirical Analysis Based on the Census Data of Service Enterprises in 2008]', *Journal of Business Economics*, 280(2), (in Chinese).

Wang, Y, 2009, '[The Influence of FDI on the Technical Progress in China's Industry]', *World Economy Study*, no. 2, (in Chinese).

Wang, Y., F. Xiong, and Y. Yang, 2015, '[The Effect of FDI on Domestic Investment in Panel Data]', *Journal of Wuhan University of Technology*, 37(1), (in Chinese).

Wang, Z., 2015, '[How Did Foreign Direct Investment Affect China's Employment? – A Study Based on Prefectural Panel Data During 1989–2010]', *Review of Industrial Economy*, no. 1, (in Chinese).

Wang, Z. and Z. Li, 2004, '[Retesting the Crowd Out and Crowd In Effects of Foreign Direct Investments on Domestic Investments]', *Statistical Research*, no. 7, (in Chinese).

Wang, Z., L. Sun, and J. Shi, 2009, '[Heterogeneous Impacts of FDI Spillovers on the Productivity of Chinese Private Firms: Evidence From Census Data]', *China Economic Quarterly*, no. 1, (in Chinese).

Wei, H., 2002, '[Effects of Foreign Direct Investment on Regional Economic Growth in China]', *Economic Research Journal*, no. 4, (in Chinese).

Wei, H., 2010, *Foreign Direct Investment and Economic Development in China and East Asia*, PhD Thesis, University of Birmingham.

Wei, K., S. Yao, and A. Liu, 2009, 'Foreign Direct Investment and Regional Inequality in China', *Review of Development Economics*, 13(4), pp. 778–91.

Wen, H. and J. Tan, 2010, '[Impact of Trade, FDI on Employment in China: Based on Panel Data of Eastern, Middle, and Western Districts After or Before Access to WTO]', *Journal of International Trade*, no. 8, (in Chinese).

Whalley, J. and X. Xin, 2010, 'China's FDI and non-FDI Economies and the Sustainability of Future High Chinese Growth', *China Economic Review*, 21(1), pp. 123–35.

Wu, G., Y. Sun, and Z. Li, 2012, 'The Crowding-in and Crowding-out Effects of FDI on Domestic Investment in the Yangtze Delta Region', *China: An International Journal*, 10(2), pp. 119–33.

Xian, G. and W. Bo, 2005, '[The Impact of FDI on the Technology Innovation of Chinese Firms – Analysis at the Industry Level]', *Nankai Economic Studies*, no. 6, (in Chinese).

Xian, G. and Z. Ou, 2008, '[The Crowding-in and Crowding-out Effects of FDI on China's Domestic Investment and the Impact of Barriers to Entry on the Effects]', *World Economy Study*, no. 3, (in Chinese).

Xiao, M. and Y. Fang, 2013, '[The Impact of FDI on Carbon Emissions in the Eastern Region of China – An Empirical Analysis Based on STIRPAT Model]', *Journal of Central University of Finance and Economics*, no. 7, (in Chinese).

Xie, J. and G. Wu, 2014, '[The Threshold Effect of FDI Technique Spillover: An Empirical Study Based on 1992–2012 China's Provincial Panel Data]', *World Economy Study*, no. 11, (in Chinese).

Xu, H., P. Qi, and H. Li, 2009, '[Foreign Direct Investment, the Labour Market, and the Wage Spillover Effect]', *Management World*, no. 9, (in Chinese).

Xu, S., 2015, '[The Periodical and Regional Influence of FDI on Labour's Share]', *World Economy Study*, no. 3, (in Chinese).

Xu, Y., 2006, '[The Influence of FDI on Chinese domestic investment: Crowding in or out?]', *Journal of International Trade*, no. 8, (in Chinese).

Yalta, A.Y., 2013, 'Revisiting the FDI-Led Growth Hypothesis: The Case of China', *Economic Modelling*, 31, pp. 335–43.

Yan, M. and T. Guo, 2012, '[The Empirical Study of Effects of FDI on Chinese Employment: Based on Dynamic Analysis of Panel VAR]', *Statistics & Information Forum*, no. 7, (in Chinese).

Yang, B., S. Brosig, and J. Chen, 2013, 'Environmental Impact of Foreign vs. Domestic Capital Investment in China', *Journal of Agricultural Economics*, 64(1), pp. 245–71.

Yang, H. and Z. Chen, 2015, '[The Indirect Mechanism of the Horizontal Spillovers of FDI: A Research Based on the Upstream Suppliers]', *The Journal of World Economy*, no. 3, (in Chinese).

Yang, J. and J. Lu, 2014, '[The Threshold Effect of Foreign Direct Investment on Environmental Pollution: An Analysis Based on Panel Data Derived From 247 Cities of China]', *World Economy Studies*, no. 8, (in Chinese).

Yang, L. and G. Shen, 2002, '[The Squeeze-in and Squeeze-out Effects of Foreign Direct Investments on Domestic Investments]', *Statistical Research*, no. 3, (in Chinese).

Yang, Q. and P. Chen, 2005, '[Analysis on the Role of FDI on China's Exports]', *Management World*, no. 5, (in Chinese).

Yang, R., 2015, '[Industrial Agglomeration, Foreign Direct Investment and Environmental Pollution]', *Economic Management Journal*, no. 2, (in Chinese).

Yang, Z. and Q. Yang, 2004, '[The Impacts of FDI on China's Real Wage Level]', *Journal of World Economy*, no. 12, (in Chinese).

Yao, S. and K. Wei, 2007, 'Economic Growth in the Presence of FDI: The Perspective of Newly Industrializing Economies', *Journal of Comparative Economics*, 35(1), pp. 211–34.

Yao, Y., 2007, '[Regional Difference Analysis on the Effect of Foreign Direct Investment on the Import-Export Trade]', *Journal of International Trade*, no. 10, (in Chinese).

Yao, Y. and Q. Ni, 2013, '[The Impact of Foreign Direct Investment on Carbon Intensity – Empirical Study Based on Chinese Provincial Dynamic Panel Data]', *Journal of Applied Statistics and Management*, no. 1, (in Chinese).

Yu, F. and J. Lu, 2014, '[A Study on the Impact of Foreign Direct Investment on Chinese Provincial Income Distribution]', *Journal of Zhejiang Gongshang University*, no. 3, (in Chinese).

Yu, F. and J. Qi, 2007, '[Empirical Analysis on the Environmental Effect of Foreign Direct Investment in China]', *Journal of International Trade*, no. 8, (in Chinese).

Yu, K., X. Xin, P. Guo, and X. Liu, 2011, 'Foreign Direct Investment and China's Regional Income Inequality', *Economic Modelling*, 28, pp. 1348–53.

Zhang, C., B. Guo, and J. Wang, 2014, 'The Different Impacts of Home Countries Characteristics in FDI on Chinese Spillover Effects: Based on One-stage SFA', *Economic Modelling*, 38, pp. 572–80.

Zhang, H., 2008a, '[The Impact of FDI on the Independent Innovation Capacity of Chinese Home Manufacturing]', *Journal of International Trade*, no. 1, (in Chinese).

Zhang, J., 2008b, *Foreign Direct Investment, Governance, and the Environment in China: Regional Dimensions*, PhD Thesis, University of Birmingham.

Zhang, K.H., 2006, 'Foreign Direct Investment and Economic Growth in China: A Panel Data Study for 1992–2004', *Working Paper*.

Zhang, K.H., 2014, 'How Does Foreign Direct Investment Affect Industrial Competitiveness? Evidence from China', *China Economic Review*, 30, pp. 530–39.

Zhang, K.H., 2015, 'What Drives Export Competitiveness? The Role of FDI in Chinese Manufacturing', *Contemporary Economic Policy*, 33(3), pp. 499–512.

Zhang, N., 2011, *Foreign Direct Investment in China: Determinants and Impacts*, PhD Thesis, University of Exeter.

Zhang, Q. and J. Zhang, 2007, '[The Impact of FDI on Urban Poverty in China – Co-Integration Test Based on Household Survey Data from 1985 to 2005]', *Journal of International Trade*, no. 9, (in Chinese).

Zhang, Y., 2005, 'Do Domestic Firms Benefit from Foreign Direct Investment? The Case of China', Chapter 3, *Essays on Industrial Organization in China's Manufacturing Sector*, PhD Thesis, University of Pittsburgh.

Zhao, Q. and M. Niu, 2013, 'Influence Analysis of FDI on China's Industrial Structure Optimization', *Procedia Computer Science*, 17, pp. 1015–22.

Zhao, S., 2013, 'Privatization, FDI Inflow and Economic Growth: Evidence from China's Provinces, 1978–2008', *Applied Economics*, May, 45(13–15), pp. 2127–39.

Zhao, Y., 2001, 'Foreign Direct Investment and Relative Wages: The Case of China', *China Economic Review*, 12(1), pp. 40–57.

Zhong, C., 2010, '[Empirical Evidence on the Regional Spillover Effects of FDI in China]', *Economic Research Journal*, no. 1, (in Chinese).

Zhou, H., 2006, '[The Long-term Effects of Foreign Direct Investment on Host Country Income Distribution: By Data of China]', *Nankai Economic Studies*, no. 5, (in Chinese).

Zhou, Y., 2014, '[Foreign Direct Investment, Intellectual Property Protection and Industrial Restructure of Export – The Empirical Research Based on Simultaneous Equations and Vector Auto Regression Models]', *China Soft Science*, no. 11, (in Chinese).

8

Perspectives on foreign investment in China

Introduction

The chapters in this volume have provided several perspectives on the impact of foreign investment on China's economy and economic development. They have described the gradual approach that China has taken to inward foreign investment and the reasons for this approach. They have shown that although the raw investment numbers appear impressive, and there has been nearly USD 1.6 trillion in foreign direct investment since the onset of China's reform program, in recent years the FDI inflows are actually small compared to the total investment in China's economy. They have shown, through novel variations on economic impact assessment methods, that the actual impact of foreign investment and foreign invested enterprises is far greater than the raw investment figures would indicate. They have shown that there have been additional catalytic and spill over impacts that are difficult to quantify and that the leading initiatives to further economic development in four of China's leading cities all focus on attracting more foreign investment. They have also shown that the academic and think tank literature has tended to focus on the impact of foreign investment on Chinese companies rather than China's economy, and that some conclusions in this literature must be viewed with caution.

In this chapter, we highlight some of these findings and discuss what the future may hold for foreign investment in China. We then close with implications of the work for policy and government in China, for governments in other countries, and for foreign companies and their representatives.

China's approach to foreign investment

China's approach to foreign investment since the onset of its opening and reform program has been gradual. This is understandable given its experience with foreign investment in the 19th and early 20th centuries when foreign investment was associated with economic modernization, involving railways, port infrastructure, and modern manufacturing, but also with the forced opening to trade in opium, special privileges, extraterritoriality, and gunboat diplomacy. China's geopolitical experiences and diplomatic isolation of the 1950s, 60s, and 70s did little to dispel the idea that China had to view international engagement with caution if not suspicion. The gradual approach is also understandable in the context of a socialist economy which, at the time of the initial opening, lacked the legal and regulatory apparatus to administer an economy that included non-state enterprises. Given this combination, it is not surprising that the opening to foreign investment proceeded gradually in terms of geographies, industries, and corporate forms. It also is not surprising that China's initial approach to foreign investment focused on limits and controls and only gradually shifted from a system based on *ex ante* approvals toward one based on *ex post* regulation. Foreign companies and foreign governments need to understand this background if they are to understand how China views foreign investment, and is likely to do so in the future.

The legal and regulatory system governing foreign investment in China affected the types of firms that invested. In the early days, only companies from Hong Kong and Taiwan were willing, and in Hong Kong's case pressured by economic forces, to take the risks associated with investing in the Chinese Mainland. Companies that required more clarity and less risk did not begin to invest until the foreign investment regime, infrastructure, productive capability, and markets had changed enough to shift the risk/reward equation. Just as China only opened the economy to the extent it felt it could manage, foreign investors invested to the extent they felt they could reasonably take the risk. One of the ongoing pressures for China to open further and to adjust the regulatory and legal regime towards foreign investment has been the fact that it has had to in order to attract higher value activities and investments. This process of mutual discovery has continued to today and will continue to influence the foreign investment regime in China for the foreseeable future.

The impacts of foreign investment on China's economy

China's economic opening and reform program ushered in an era in which China's economy would grow to 28 times its previous size in real terms in a 35 year span. During that time, annual inward foreign direct investment has gone from essentially zero to on the order of USD 100 billion per year and cumulative FDI into China since the economic opening is on the order of USD 1.6 trillion. Even so, these are not big numbers when it comes to total investment of all forms in China.

While the foreign investment as a percentage of gross capital formation or fixed asset investment figures might lead one to conclude that the impact of foreign investment and foreign invested enterprises on China's development has been modest and diminishing in importance, the analysis in this volume suggests otherwise. Using variations on traditional economic impact analysis, we have shown that the impact of the establishment, operations, and supply chains of foreign invested enterprises in recent years has been on the order of 33 percent of GDP and 27 percent of employment in China. While some of the estimates are rough, their magnitude indicates a different starting point for the discussion on the impact of foreign invested enterprises on China's economy than is often the case.

These estimates do not include the catalytic impact of foreign investment and foreign invested enterprises in building supply chains that themselves can compete internationally, in building distribution channels and capabilities in China, in enhancing technological development in China, in fostering indigenous spinoffs, in introducing modern management education to China, in providing access to international capital markets to Chinese firms, in raising venture capital and private equity for emerging Chinese firms, in developing the logistics systems and infrastructure necessary to support China's growth as a trading nation, and in bringing modern environmental and CSR practices to China. Nor do the estimates include assessments of the value of foreign input and experience in helping China develop the legal and regulatory systems that have facilitated the emergence of China's own dynamic indigenous private sector. As the corporate case studies also show, foreign invested enterprises have been crucial in a wide range of sectors in China, have introduced new products and segments that have enhanced consumers' lives, have provided opportunities for Chinese employees, have linked Chinese businesses to global markets, and have contributed substantially to the enhancement of capabilities throughout Chinese business.

All of these developments have been facilitated and allowed by Chinese policy and have depended on the hard work of tens of millions of Chinese employees at all levels in their enterprises. However, they also have depended critically on the presence of the foreign invested enterprises. One contribution of the present volume is to give a sense of how large and far-reaching these developments and impacts have been. When we list the features that are not included in our quantitative estimates, it becomes clear that the quantitative estimates must be severe underestimates rather than overestimates.

Questions

The conclusions listed above lead to several questions. Does China need the money associated with inward foreign investment? Can't Chinese companies and indigenous investment play the roles that foreign companies have played? Don't foreign companies just displace Chinese companies? Has the value of Chinese partners in joint ventures been underestimated? China may have benefited from foreign investment when it had a relatively backward economy, but has China reached the point where it no longer needs foreign investment?

In the early days of China's opening, allowing foreign investment was a way to obtain more advanced technologies and improved productivity without having to purchase or license technology. However, the days in which China 'needed the money' associated with foreign direct investment are long gone. China itself is becoming a capital exporter and the low percentages of foreign investment in gross capital formation and fixed asset investment show that the raw amount of capital entering the country is not the major contribution of foreign investment to China and has not been for quite some time. So the value of foreign investment and foreign invested enterprises to China today and in the future must lie elsewhere.

While some might claim that if the foreign invested enterprises were not present that Chinese enterprises would pick up the slack, the most direct answer is that if Chinese enterprises could do so with the same productivity and effectiveness as FIEs they would already be doing so. The days of FIEs being favoured over domestic enterprises are long gone, and have been replaced with a regime that supports indigenous enterprises in major industries. The days of foreign enterprises willing to lose money for several years in order to get established in China are also gone, as FIEs that have not performed well in China have downsized operations or exited. Foreign invested enterprises that succeed in China do so because they have skills and capabilities that are not present in indigenous companies. Chinese companies have come a long way, but in a wide range of sectors they are still not quite as effective as the world's leading companies. And even many of China's indigenous success stories like Alibaba, Tencent, and others have relied on foreign venture capital, private equity, and capital markets. The best way for Chinese companies to attain world-class levels is through competition with and the example of foreign firms. Protection can allow companies to be followers, but it generally does not make them leaders.

So will China reach a point where it does not need foreign investment and foreign invested enterprises? China's economy and Chinese companies will doubtless continue to improve. However, even if Chinese companies and indigenous investment could provide everything that foreign companies and foreign capital can provide today, it would still make sense for China to be open to foreign companies and foreign investment. No single economy, no matter how large, can generate all of the ideas needed to drive economies forward. No single economy can produce companies that are world leaders in all industries. Historically, China went from an economic and technology leader to an economic and technology laggard in significant part because it closed itself off to foreign contact and foreign ideas. It would be a tremendous irony if China were to do so again.

The future of foreign investment in China

Despite these conclusions, the future of foreign investment and foreign invested enterprises in China is uncertain. Many foreign analysts and managers believe that China is targeting foreign companies with various legal actions in part to favour Chinese companies. This is in addition to the support that Chinese companies receive through the state banking sector, development and investment funds, and preferential treatment at home. It has become fashionable in certain intellectual and policy circles in China to claim that China really did not need foreign investment to reach its current level of development and foreign companies make limited positive contributions to China's economy today. Even some of those that admit that foreign investment played an important role in the past claim that they will not be necessary in the future. Others think that foreign companies stand in the way of success for Chinese firms or that foreign companies profit too much at the expense of Chinese companies and consumers. Attacks on foreign companies in the press often seem orchestrated to remind foreign companies that they operate as guests in the country.

Meanwhile, China's economic growth is slowing, there is overcapacity in many industries, China's economy is going through a series of difficult transitions, and Chinese companies are becoming tougher competitors. This means that the market basis for foreign investment in China is changing. Some high profile companies have decided to exit and many have cut back on planned investments. The days of 10 plus percent annual GDP growth and 20 plus percent annual growth in many individual industries are gone. A significant amount of the China hype that was factored into investment decisions has faded. All of these factors are causing companies to reassess their China investment programs.

On the other hand, the legal and regulatory regime governing foreign investment in China has evolved considerably towards what would be considered international norms. If the Draft Foreign Investment Law passes in its present form or something similar, then China's legal regime governing foreign investment and foreign invested enterprises will look very similar to that of many other nations. Foreign investment will be allowed without the need for prior approvals except for a negative list of industries or activities in which foreign investment will not be permitted or will require special approval. Foreign investments will be reviewed when it is believed that the investments may have national security implications. Foreign invested enterprises will otherwise be subject to the same Company Law, Anti-Monopolies Law, Labour Law, Environmental Law, and other laws as domestic enterprises, and each of these laws is similar to those found in many other countries. China's arbitration rules already look similar to that found elsewhere. In each of these areas, in fact, there has been a concerted effort in China to move towards 'international norms'.

However, there will continue to be differences between China's legal regime governing foreign investment and what one finds in advanced economies elsewhere. Should the present restricted and prohibited lists in the current catalogue for foreign investment become the negative list under the new Foreign Investment Law, then this list will be much larger than in most advanced economies. China's leaders tend to have a broader interpretation of what constitutes national security implications of foreign investment than leaders in advanced economies. The specific exemptions and overrides in China's Anti-Monopoly Law do not accord with those in advanced economies. In addition, there is a question of how the laws will ultimately be enforced in a country in which the legal processes and results are often difficult for outsiders to predict or understand.

Even so, the legal and regulatory regime governing foreign investment will be completely different, and much more familiar to international investors, from the time when China began its opening. One should not underestimate the importance in the shift from requiring all foreign investments to receive prior approval to one in which most foreign investments only need to be reported. One should also not be surprised that as China moves from a system of direct approval and control to one of monitoring and regulating through a legal process that focuses on the actual behaviour of firms that there will be an initial tendency to exercise the legal powers to send clear messages that while prior permission and approval of business plans is not required, that does not mean that foreign firms have a free hand in China. As always in China, one must view current events and positions as part of an evolutionary process.

Implications

There several implications of the present work. The first set of implications from the present analysis is for policy and government in China. China has probably benefitted more from foreign investment than any other country over the past 35 years. The positive impact must have been far beyond that imagined by Deng Xiaoping and the other architects of China's opening. At the same time, China has managed the process so that it is absolutely clear that China has not lost sovereignty or any significant amount of control to foreign companies. Thus it has managed to gain the benefits of foreign investment without what would normally be viewed as the major risks associated with foreign investment. The increasing capability of the Chinese state has allowed China to shift from a regime focused on *ex ante* approvals to one more based on *ex post* regulation. It is important that this shift allow more companies with new ideas and new ways to benefit China's development enter the country. No single country, even one as vast as China, can come up with all the ideas it needs, and just as many of the benefits that foreign investment and foreign invested enterprises brought to China in the past were unanticipated, it would be impossible for China to anticipate and plan for all the benefits that foreign investment and foreign invested enterprises might bring in the future.

The second set of implications is for other governments, particularly in developing nations. Foreign investment can contribute substantially to the development process on many dimensions, through the establishment of foreign invested enterprises, their operations, and their supply chains. There is also a vast range of catalytic impacts and spill overs that can be obtained from foreign invested enterprises, again in terms of the development of distribution channels, technology, management skills, connectivity to world markets, access to international financial networks, and policies related to business and economic development. On the one hand, these benefits seem so clear that it is often difficult to understand why some countries are not more open to foreign investment. On the other hand, many countries fear that foreign companies will exploit labour and resources without leaving lasting benefits behind, hurt local companies, degrade the environment, dominate local markets, abuse market positions, and be difficult to regulate. The Chinese experience shows that it is possible to obtain the benefits of foreign investment while managing these downsides.

Of course, China is an outlier in many ways. Its market is so large that foreign investors may be willing to put up with much greater restrictions and work harder to contribute to host country initiatives than in other countries. China also has stronger state-owned and now private sector companies than most other developing nations, so the potential for foreign companies to dominate is less than in other developing nations. China also has far greater administrative capacity than most other developing countries, and is thus better able to manage the presence of foreign as well as local private sector companies. The dominance of a single political party also means that there are potentially fewer opponents to foreign investment, or that that opposition can be overcome or overridden in China in the public interest. In any case, the Chinese experience with foreign investment could yield many lessons for other countries, particularly in terms of how to benefit from foreign investment without yielding sovereignty or suffering from foreign domination.

The third set of implications is for foreign companies, chambers of commerce, and governments with interests in foreign investments in China in particular and in foreign countries in general. There appears to be increasing pressure on foreign companies in many parts of the world. The nationalism caused by economic pressures in a slowing global economy, concerns about transfer pricing and tax arrangements, and issues about the behaviour of some foreign invested enterprises is causing many countries to scrutinize foreign investment and foreign companies more carefully than in the past. Many companies, and by extension the chambers of commerce and governments that represent them, simply do not have the tools necessary to 'make the case' for the contribution that they make to host economies. Few try to quantify the benefits beyond simple investment and employment statistics. Few attempt to put a value on their impact on supply chains, consumer welfare, distribution channels, technological capabilities, management skills, environmental focus, and CSR activities in host countries. The tools and information described in this book should allow many organizations to make a much better case for their positive impact on China and by extension to other host countries around the world. Their ability and willingness to make this case could have the largest impact of all in terms of shifting the discussion and assessment of the impact of foreign investment on host economies.

We hope that each of these groups will take on board the implications of this work to better understand the power of foreign investment to build economies and to help build better economies in China and in other countries around the world.

Index

3M 12, 114, 127

ABB 75, 83, 127, 129, 139
academic literature 5
advertising: Procter & Gamble (P&G)
  170
agriculture 11, 15, 19–20
Alcatel 74, 99, 125
Amway 73
Anti-Monopoly Law ('AML') 13, 86, 249
Apple 84, 86, 186, 188
Ashland 74–5
Astra-Zeneca 65, 74
auto industry 4, 60; Chongqing 136, 139;
  Ford Motors 67, 74, 83, 135–6, 139;
  General Motors (GM) 62–3, 66, 78, 80,
  82, 127, 136, 139; modernizing 60; Nissan
  62–3; research 67–8; Toyota 67, 82, 114,
  116; VW (Volkswagen) 62, 82, 86, 116,
  125, 127

Bank of America 71
banking sector: improving 70–2
BASF 66, 78, 81, 83, 127, 135
Bayer 66, 75, 129
Big Four 69, 70
Big Six 68–9, 70
Binhai New Area 95, 114–17, 122, 139
Boeing 73, 81
BP (British Petroleum) 78, 83, 135
Burger King 85, 129
Business for Social Responsibility (BSR)
  187
business practices: improving 68–70

Caohejing Technological Development Zone
  125–6
case studies 4, 96–7; Chongqing 134–51;
  Shanghai 124–34; Shenzhen 97–113;
  Tianjin 113–24
case studies, corporate 156–7, 193–4; Hong
  Kong companies 156, 157–66; Maersk
  156–7, 175–82; Procter & Gamble (P&G)
  156, 166–74; Samsung 156, 157, 182–92
catalytic impact: economic impact analysis 39
Center of Knowledge Interchange (CKI) 67
China: bringing R&D and technology
  development 64–6; corporate social
  responsibility (CSR) initiatives 59, 80–2;
  counterpoints 84–6; developing suppliers
  and distributors 61–4; environment and
  sustainability of 59, 78–80; foreign R&D,
  local linkages and spinoffs 66–8; future
  of foreign investment 248–50; improving
  business practices and standards 68–70;
  improving financial system 70–2; joint
  ventures 10–11; management training and
  education 72–4; modernizing industries
  and companies in 59–61; policy advice
  82–4; promoting legal and regulatory
  reform 75–7; regional and global
  management to China 74–5; regulation of
  foreign investment 11–20
China Banking Regulatory Commission
  (CBRC) 70
China Business Council for Sustainable
  Development (CBCSD) 78
China European International Business
  School (CEIBS) 72, 189

China European Management Institute (CEMI) 72

China International Economic Trade and Arbitration Commission (CIETAC) 77

China Mergers and Acquisitions Association (CMAA) 70

China Securities Regulatory Commission (CSRC) 70

China's provinces: foreign investment in 26–7

China Tianjin Otis Elevator Company (CTOEC) 115

Chinese Accounting Standards (CAS) 68

Chinese Communist Party 10–11, 126

Chinese Institute of Certified Public Accountants (CICPA) 68

Chinese literature: domestic investment 219–20; econometric analysis 233–7; economic growth 205; employment and wages 223–4; environment 231–2; inequality 227–8; innovation 213; productivity 208–9; trade 216–17

Chongqing 96; building up 136–8; case study 4, 134–51; economic city 4–5, 7; economic impact of FDI and FIEs on 142–51; evolution of FDI and FIEs in 134–9; FDI and FIEs in 140–1; FIEs by industry in 143–7; foreign investment *vs.* total investment in 141; importance of FDI and FIEs in 141–2; industrial development 135–6; inward FDI into 140; new challenges and directions 139; service and technology development 138–9; trade performance by FIEs in 148

Cisco 86, 127

Citibank 70, 71, 100, 114, 115, 127

cities: foreign investment in China's 151–2; Hong Kong investing in China's 163–4; *see also* Chongqing; Shanghai; Shenzhen; Tianjin

Closer Economic Partnership Arrangement (CEPA) 23, 100, 159

Coca-Cola 61–2, 80, 114–15, 127

companies: modernizing 59–61

Company Law of 1994 12–13, 249

computer manufacturing: Chongqing 138–9, 152n6

consumer research: Procter & Gamble (P&G) 167–8

Corning 78

corporate social responsibility (CSR) 4, 247, 251; foreign invested enterprises (FIEs) 4, 59, 80–2; Maersk 181–2; Procter & Gamble (P&G) 173–4; Samsung 187, 189–90

corruption 85–6

counterpoints 84–6

CP Group 61

crowding-in effect: domestic investment 206, 218–21, 237

crowding-out effect: domestic investment 202, 206, 218–21, 235, 237; employment 224, 226, 235, 237

Damco logistics: Maersk 175–82

Deloitte Touche Tohmatsu 17, 20, 68, 70, 79

Deng Xiaoping 11–12, 16, 82, 99, 101, 115, 125, 135, 159, 250

dependent variable 203, 211, 233

development zones: Shanghai 125–6; Shenzhen 97–9; Tianjin 114–15

direct impact: economic impact analysis 39

direct revenue: industrial FIEs 42–4

disaster relief: corporate social responsibility 81

distribution capabilities: Procter & Gamble (P&G) 168–9; Samsung 185–6

distributors: developing 61–4

domestic investment 218–22, 235; Chinese literature 219–20; crowding-in effect 206, 218–21, 237; crowding-out effect 202, 206, 218–21, 235, 237; English literature 218–19; literature results 220–1; project results 221–2

Dong, Ella 58n1, 152n1

econometric analysis: background 202–3; domestic investment 218–22, 235; economic growth 204–6; employment

and wages 222–6, 235; environment
229–33, 236; foreign direct investment in
China 201–2; inequality 226–9, 235–6;
innovation 212–15, 234; productivity
206–12, 233–4; trade 215–18, 234–5
Economic and Technological Development
Zones (ETDZs) 16–17, 19
economic growth 204–6, 233; China's future
248–50; Chinese literature 205; English
literature 204; project results 205–6
economic impact analysis (EIA) 31; catalytic
impact 39; deriving multipliers from
input-output tables 56–7; direct impact
39; indirect impact 39; induced impact 39;
introduction to 39–40; methodology 55–8
economy: Hong Kong investing in China
165–6; Maersk 175–6, 181; Procter &
Gamble (P&G) impact 172–3, 174;
Samsung contributions 190–1
ecosystem: corporate social responsibility
81–2
education: management 72–4
Eli Lilly 86
employment: combined impact of FDI and FIEs
53; crowding-out effect 224, 226, 235, 237;
economic impact analysis 39; FIEs in
Chongqing by industry 149–50; FIEs in
Shenzhen by industry 111–12; FIEs
in Tianjin by industry 121–2, 123; Hong
Kong companies 158–60; impact of FDI
in China 41; operations of FIEs in mining,
manufacturing and utilities sectors 45, 46–50
employment and wages 222–6, 235; Chinese
literature 223–4; English literature
223; labour productivity 222, 226, 237;
literature results 225; project results 225–6
Encouragement Provisions 11–12
English literature: domestic investment
218–19; econometric analysis 233–7;
economic growth 204; employment
and wages 223; environment 229–30;
inequality 226–7; innovation 212–13;
productivity 207–8; trade 215–16
Enright, Scott & Associates (ESA) 1–2, 6
Enterprise Income Tax Law 19–20

environment 229–33, 236; Chinese
literature 231–2; English literature
229–30; literature results 232; Maersk and
performance 179; project results 232–3;
rapid economic growth 85; sustainability
59, 78–80
Equity Joint Venture Income Tax Law 18
Ericsson 73, 83, 135, 138
Ernst & Young 68, 83
ExxonMobil 80

FDI see foreign direct investment (FDI)
FIEs see foreign invested enterprises (FIEs)
financial system: improving 70–2
Five-Year Programs 14–15, 65, 78, 114
food safety 85
food sector: Tianjin 115–16
Ford Motors 67, 74, 83, 135–6, 139
foreign companies: China opening to 87;
criticism of 86
foreign direct investment (FDI) 3, 31;
Chongqing 140; definition 28–9n6;
economic impact analysis 52, 54–5;
economic impact of capital investment
associated with 40–2; FDI flows into China
21; greenfield 21–2; impact of operations
of FIEs and 52, 53; importance for China's
total investment 32–3; Shanghai 131;
Shenzhen 102; Tianjin 118; see also
literature
Foreign Enterprise Income Tax Law
18, 19
foreign invested enterprises (FIEs) 3, 31;
Chinese enterprises 247–8; combined
impact of FDI and 52, 53; corporate
social responsibility (CSR) initiatives
59, 80–2; direct revenue and value added
of 42–4; economic impact analysis 31,
55–8; economic impact of operations
of industrial 42–51; English literature
204, 215–16, 223, 232, 234; impact of
operations in mining, manufacturing
and utilities sectors 45, 46–50; impact
of operations of service sector 51;
importance by industry 33–7; importance

in trade 37–9; by industry in Chongqing 143–7; by industry in Shenzhen 104–8; by industry in Tianjin 120–1; productivity 211

foreign investment 8–9; China's approach to 27–8, 245–6; in China's provinces/cities 26–7, 151–2; evolution in Chongqing 134–9; evolution in Shanghai 124–30; evolution in Shenzhen 97–101; evolution in Tianjin 113–17; future of, in China 248–50; history of China's 3, 9–10; Hong Kong companies 157–60; impact on China's economy 246–7; implications of 250–1; by industry 23–5; new China 10–11; number and value of projects 20–2; questions about China's 247–8; regulation of 11–20; sources of 22–3

Foreign Enterprise Income Tax Law 19

Four Modernizations 11

Foxconn 81, 82, 84, 101, 138

France 9, 22, 115, 127–8, 135

Free Trade Zones 17–18, 83, 114, 117, 129–30

Fujian Special Free Trade Zone (FTZ) 18

Fujitsu 67

General Electric (GE) 65

general equilibrium models: economic impact analysis 39–40, 55

General Motors (GM) 62–3, 66, 78, 80, 82, 127, 136, 139

Germany 9, 22, 66, 75, 114–15, 129, 135

GlaxoSmithKline (GSK) 85–6, 114, 116

Global Financial Crisis 71, 74, 101

global management: bringing to China 74–5

global research: Procter & Gamble (P&G) 171; Samsung 186

Global Sources 161

GMM (General Method of Moments) 238n4–6

Goldman Sachs 71

Google 86, 188

gradual approach: foreign investment 27–8, 245–6

greenfield foreign direct investment (FDI) 21–2

green standards: Procter & Gamble (P&G) 169–70; Samsung 188–9

gross domestic product (GDP) 2, 3, 5, 6, 31; Chongqing 148; Shenzhen 110, 111–12; Tianjin 121–2, 123

Guangdong Special Free Trade Zone 18

Hang Lung 127, 128, 137, 163

Hassall, Chris 174

health: corporate social responsibility 81

Henderson 137, 163

Hewlett Packard (HP) 68, 73, 83

Hinrich Foundation 1–2

Ho-moon Kang 184, 186

Honda 116, 135, 136

Hong Kong 4–5, 16, 18: business practices 68, 72–3; Chongqing 135, 137–8, 140; environment 85; investment from 22–3; labour 84; modernization 60; regulation 76–7; Shanghai 125, 127–8, 130; Shenzhen 98, 99–100, 102, 112; Tianjin 115, 117, 123; trade 37

Hong Kong, Macau, and Taiwan (HMT) 209, 230, 236

Hong Kong companies 7: case study 156, 157–66, 193; connecting China to world 160–1; contribution to China's economy 165–6; creating infrastructure and utilities 161–3; developing China's cities 163–4; employment 158–60; investment into China 157–60; technology and management transfer 164–5

Hong Kong Stock Exchange 23, 161

Hongqiao Economic Development Zone 125–6

Hope Schools project 80, 170, 173, 181

Hopewell 162, 163

H Share company 161, 194n7

HSBC 79, 83, 100, 114, 128

human resources: Maersk 179–81; Procter & Gamble (P&G) 171–2; Samsung 186–7

Hutchison Whampoa 100, 137, 166, 177

IBM 66–8, 73, 75, 86, 99, 114, 127, 129
IDG 71
import scale factor 57
indirect impact: economic impact analysis 39
induced impact: economic impact analysis 39
Industrial and Commercial Bank of China
    (ICBC) 71
Industrial and Commercial Tax Provisions
    18, 19
Industrial Directions on Foreign Investment
    in Shanghai 128
industrial enterprises 36, 58n2
industry 11; FIEs (foreign invested
    enterprises) in Chongqing by 143–7; FIEs
    in Shenzhen by 104–8; FIEs in Tianjin by
    120–1; foreign direct investment (FDI) 24;
    importance of FIEs 33–7; investment by
    23–5; modernizing 59–61
inequality 226–9, 235–6; Chinese literature
    227–8; English literature 226–7; literature
    results 228; project results 228–9
infrastructure: Hong Kong investing in China
    161–3
innovation 212–15, 234; Chinese literature
    213; English literature 212–13; literature
    results 213–14; project results 214–15
input-output tables: adjustments 57–8;
    China 172, 181; Chongqing 142; deriving
    economic multipliers from 56–7; matrix
    schematic 56; multiplier method 55–6;
    multipliers from 40–1; Shenzhen 110;
    Tianjin 121–2
Institute for Growth Policy Studies
    (ITPS) 66
Intel 67
Interim Provisions on Guiding Foreign
    Investment and the Catalogue for the
    Guidance of Foreign Investment Industries
    ('the Catalogue') 14, 15, 17
International Business Leaders' Advisory
    Council (IBLAC) 83
investment policies: geography-based 16–18;
    importance of FDI in 32–3; sector-based
    14–16; taxation of enterprises 18–20
'iron rice bowl' policy 77

Japan 9, 10, 13, 64, 85–6, 217: Chongqing
    135, 141; corporate social responsibility
    81; investment in China 22–3; research
    and development 64; Shanghai 127–30;
    Shenzhen 102; Tianjin 114–15, 117
Jiang Zemin 126
Jinqiao Export Processing Zone 17, 125
Johnson & Johnson 80, 127
joint ventures 10–11; Chongqing 135–7;
    Shanghai 124–7; Shenzhen 98–9; Tianjin
    113, 115–16

Kerry Group 100, 127, 128, 163, 164
Kodak 61
Korea 16, 22–3, 81, 217: LG 63–4, 114;
    Maersk 177; Republic of 191; Samsung
    156–7, 183, 185–7, 191–2; Shanghai 130;
    South Korea 16, 183, 185; Tianjin 117
KPMG 82
Kyoto Protocol 79

Labour Law 249
labour practices 84
labour productivity 206, 210, 212;
    employment 222, 226, 237
laissez-faire approach 98
Law of the People's Republic of China on
    Contractual Joint Ventures using Chinese
    and Foreign Investment ('Contractual JV
    Law') 11
Law of the People's Republic of China on
    Enterprises Operated Exclusively with
    Foreign Capital ('WFOE Law') 11–12
Law of the People's Republic of China on
    Joint Ventures Using Chinese and Foreign
    Investment ('Equity JV Law') 11–12
Leadership in Energy and Environmental
    Design (LEED) 79–80, 169
legal reform: promoting 75–7
LG 63–4, 80–1, 114, 115
Li & Fung 63, 161
Liangjiang New Area 139–40, 151
literature 201–2, 233–7; domestic
    investment 218–22; economic growth
    204–6; employment and wages 222–6;

environment 229–33; inequality 226–9; innovation 212–15; productivity 206–12; trade 215–18; *see also* econometric analysis
logistics efficiency: Maersk 177–8
Lujiazui 17, 125, 126, 127

McDonald's 73, 85
Maersk 5, 7; case study 156–7, 175–82, 193; connecting China to world 175–6; corporate social responsibility (CSR) 181–2; efficiency in ports and logistics 177–8; environmental performance in China 179; human resources 179–81; procurement and investment 181; working with Chinese suppliers 177
management: regional and global, to China 74–5; training and education 72–4
management transfer: Hong Kong investing in China 164–5
manufacturing sector *see* mining, manufacturing and utilities sectors
marketing capabilities: Procter & Gamble (P&G) 170
Metro 114, 135, 138
Microsoft 66, 67, 86
Minhang Economic Development Zone 125–6
mining, manufacturing and utilities sectors 54: economic impact of operations of FIEs 45, 46–50; operations of FIEs in Chongqing 149–50; operations of FIEs in Shenzhen 111–12; operations of FIEs in Tianjin 122, 123
Mitsubishi 114, 127, 135
most favored nation 9, 28n3
Motorola 67–8, 73, 114–15, 188
Multi-Fiber Agreement 25
multiplier models: economic impact analysis 39–40
municipal economies: impact of FDI and FIEs 96

national defense 11, 13
National Development and Reform Commission (NDRC) 15, 86, 100, 129, 181

Nestlé 81, 86, 114, 115
New Foreign Investment Law (FIL) 14, 249
New World 73, 127, 137, 138, 162, 163, 164
Nike 80, 84
Nissan 62–3
Nixon, Richard 11
Nokia 74, 80, 83, 188
Novartis 66, 73
Novo-Nordisk 114, 116

OECD *see* Organisation for Economic Cooperation and Development (OECD) countries
open systems: Samsung 188
Oracle 67, 86
Organisation for Economic Cooperation and Development (OECD) countries 85, 207–8, 229–30, 236
Otis Elevator 114, 115
output: economic impact analysis 39; FIEs in Chongqing by industry 149–50; FIEs in Shenzhen by industry 111–12; FIEs in Tianjin by industry 121–2, 123; impact of FDI in China 41; operations of FIEs in mining, manufacturing and utilities sectors 45, 46–50

Panasonic 79, 81, 83, 114, 115
partnerships: joint ventures 10–11
Pearl River Delta 16, 63, 99; Hong Kong investments 158–62, 165; investments 115, 125; technology and management 164
PepsiCo 66, 80
Philips 127
pillar industry 60–1
Policies and Measures for Western Development 2000
policy advice 82–4
port and logistics efficiency: Maersk 177–8
Procter & Gamble (P&G) 5, 7, 73; bringing green standards to China 169–70; case study 156, 166–74, 193; consumer research in China 167–8; contribution to China 174; corporate social responsibility (CSR) 173–4; creating product categories in

China 166–7; distribution capabilities
168–9; economic impact on China 172–3;
global research in China 171; human
resources 171–2; marketing capabilities in
China 170; supply chains 168–9
procurement and investment: Maersk 181
productivity 206–12, 233–4; Chinese
literature 208–9; English literature 207–8;
labour 206, 210, 212; multifactor 210;
project results 210–12
Provisions of the State Council of the
People's Republic of China for the
Encouragement of Foreign Investment
('Encouragement Provisions') 11–12
Provisions on Guiding the Orientation of
Foreign Investment 14
Provisions on Mergers and Acquisitions
of Domestic Enterprises by Foreign
Investors 13
Pudong: Shanghai 66, 95, 114, 125–7,
129–30, 139

Qianhai Shenzhen-Hong Kong Modern
Service Cooperation Zone 100, 101
Qualcomm 86

real estate: China 23–5, 150–1; Chongqing
95, 134, 136–8, 140–1; Hong Kong 159,
166, 193; Shanghai 127–8; Shenzhen 98,
100, 103; Tianjin 118
Red Chip company 161, 194n6
regional management: bringing to China
74–5
Regulations on Special Economic Zones in
Guangdong Province 11, 97
regulatory reform: promoting 75–7
regulatory regime 11–14
research & development: bringing to China
64–6; foreign 66–8
Rio Tinto 78, 85
Roche 65, 75, 129
Rule of Law program 76

SAIC General Motors Sales Co. 63, 66, 127
SAIC Motor 125, 127, 136

Samsung 5, 7, 81, 84, 99, 114–15; bringing
green standards to China 188–9; case study
157, 182–92, 193–4; Chinese standards
188; committing to China 183–4;
contribution to China 190–1; corporate
social responsibility (CSR) 189–90;
distribution relationships in China 185–6;
global research 186; human resources
186–7; investing in Vietnam 5, 157,
191–2; moving beyond China 191–2; open
systems 188; supply chains in China 184–5
Sanderson, David 58n1, 152n1
Sanofi-Aventis 66
science and technology 11
Scott, Edith 28n1, 88n1
service sector: Chongqing 138–9; operations
of FIEs 51, 54
SGS 61
Shanghai 95–6; case study 4, 124–34, 134;
diversifying the economy 126–8; economic
city 4–5, 7; economic impact of FDI and
FIEs on 133; economic opening of 125–6;
evolution of FDI and FIEs in 124–30;
FDI and FIEs in 130; foreign investment
vs. total investment in 132; high-value
activities 129; importance of FDI and
FIEs in 130–3; inward FDI into 131; new
challenges and directions 129–30; Pudong
66, 95, 114, 125–7, 129–30, 139; trade
performance of FIEs 132
Shanghai Pilot Free Trade Zone (FTZ) 17, 83,
117, 129–30
Shanghai New International Expo
Center 126
Shanghai Stock Exchange 70, 79, 126
Shell 78
Shenzhen 95; case study 4, 97–113;
development and diversification 99–100;
economic city 4–5, 7; economic impact of
FDI and FIEs 110–12; economic opening
of 97–9; evolution of foreign investment
in 97–101; FDI and FIEs in 101–3; FIEs
by industry 104–8; foreign investment
vs. total investment in 103; importance
of FDI and FIEs 103, 109; inward FDI

into 102; new challenges and directions
101; operations of FIEs in mining,
manufacturing and utilities sectors 111–12;
trade performance of FIEs 109
Shenzhen Special Economic Zones (SEZ) 16,
97–8, 101, 113
Shenzhen Stock Exchange 70, 79
Shui On 83, 127, 128, 137, 152n3, 163
Siemens 65–7, 73, 78, 81
Six Sigma 69
Smartdot 68
Sony 79, 127
sources: investment 22–3
Southern Tour 12, 101, 125
Soviet Union 10, 60
Special Economic Zones (SEZs) 16, 18–20,
97–9, 101, 113, 165
standards: improving 68–70; Samsung 188
Starbucks 85, 86
step-by-step approach: foreign investment 3,
9, 20, 27–8
Sun Hung Kai 127, 128, 163
suppliers: developing 61–4; Maersk 177
supply chains: Maersk 182; Procter &
Gamble (P&G) 168–9; Samsung 184–5
Swedish Institute for Growth Policy Studies
(ITPS) 66
Swire Group 162, 164

Taiwan 16, 18, 22–3, 25, 236; Chongqing
135, 138, 141; environment 85, 229–30;
investment from 76–7; labour 84; legal/
regulatory system 246; modernization 60;
productivity 207–9; Shanghai 127, 130;
Shenzhen 101; Tianjin 114–16; trade
216–17
taxation: foreign-invested enterprises 18–20
technology development: bringing to China
64–6; Chongqing 138–9; Hong Kong
investing in China 164–5; imports 214–15;
sharing in Shenzhen 99
10,000 Villages Project 169, 173
Tianjin 95; case study 4, 113–24;
development zones 114–15; early
investments and industries 115–16;

economic city 4–5, 7; economic impact
of FDI and FIEs in 121–2; evolution of
foreign investment in 113–17; FDI and
FIEs in 117–21; FIEs by industry in 120–1;
foreign investment vs. total investment
119; importance of FDI and FIEs 118–21;
inward FDI into 118; new challenges and
directions 116–17; trade performance of
FIEs in 121
Tianjin Economic and Technology
Development Zone (TEDA) 95, 114–15
Tianjin Pilot Free Trade Zone (FTZ) 18,
114, 117
total factor productivity (TFP) 206–12;
Chinese literature 208–9; English literature
207–8; project results 210–12
Toyota 67, 82, 114, 116
trade 234–5; Chinese literature 216–17;
English literature 215–16; importance of
foreign invested enterprises (FIEs) 37–9;
literature results 217–18; performance of
FIEs in Chongqing 148; performance of
FIEs in Shanghai 132; performance of FIEs
in Shenzhen 109; performance of FIEs in
Tianjin 121; project results 218
traffic safety: corporate social
responsibility 82
training: management 72–4
Transpacific Partnership (TPP) 192
Treaty of Nanking 9
Treaty of San Francisco 10
Treaty of Shimonoseki 9

UBS 100
Unilever 79, 127, 166, 170
unions: labour 82, 84
United Kingdom 9, 22, 68, 115
United Nations Development Program
(UNDP) 79
United States 9, 11: business practice
68; Chongqing 135, 141; Coca-Cola
62; investment 22–3; financial system
72; Maersk 182; management 72, 75;
Procter & Gamble (P&G) 167–8, 171;
research & development 64–6; Samsung

183; Shanghai 127–8; Shenzhen 102; Tianjin 115, 117
utilities: Hong Kong investing in China 161–3
utilities sector *see* mining, manufacturing and utilities sectors

value added: combined impact of FDI and FIEs 53; economic impact analysis 39; FIEs in Chongqing by industry 149–50; FIEs in Shenzhen by industry 110, 111–12; FIEs in Tianjin by industry 121–2, 123; impact of FDI in China 41; industrial FIEs 42–4; operations of FIEs in mining, manufacturing and utilities sectors 45, 46–50
venture capital (VC): foreign and domestic 71–2
Vietnam: Samsung investing 5, 157, 191–2
VW (Volkswagen) 62, 82, 86, 116, 125, 127

Wal-Mart 63, 84–6, 100, 138
Wang Chao 174
Wang Tong 187

Watson, Rob 79
Wharf Group 127, 137, 162, 163, 164
wholly foreign-owned enterprises (WFOEs) 12, 14, 76
World Business Council for Sustainable Development (WBCSD) 78
World Trade Organization (WTO) 8, 12; agreement 28n5; China's accession to 8, 12, 70, 76, 128, 186, 223; financial services 29n9

Xu Zongheng 101

Yangtze River Delta 16, 63; foreign investments 115, 125–6, 219; Hong Kong investments 159

Zhang, Sophie 237n1
Zhao Ziyang 60
Zhu Rongji 126
Zhu Wenbin 133
Zhu Xiaodan 83
Z-Park (Zhongguancun Science Park) 67–8